S0-BOH-587

THE CLASSICS
OF WESTERN
SPIRITUALITY

THE CLASSICS OF WESTERN SPIRITUALITY
A Library of the Great Spiritual Masters

Jean Leclercq—Professor of Spirituality, Institute of Spirituality and of Religious Psychology, Gregorian University, Rome, Italy.

George A. Maloney—Spiritual Writer and Lecturer, Seal Beach, Calif.

John Meyendorff—Professor of Church History, Fordham University, Bronx, N.Y., and Professor of Patristics and Church History, St. Vladimir's Seminary, Tuckahoe, N.Y.

Seyyed Hossein Nasr—Professor of Islamic Studies, George Washington University, Washington, D.C.

Heiko A. Oberman—Professor for Medieval, Renaissance and Reformation History, University of Arizona, Tucson, Ariz.

Raimundo Panikkar—Professor, Department of Religious Studies, University of California at Santa Barbara, Calif.

Jaroslav Pelikan—Sterling Professor of History and Religious Studies, Yale University, New Haven, Conn.

Annemarie B. Schimmel—Professor of Indo-Muslim Culture, Harvard University, Cambridge, Mass.

Sandra M. Schneiders—Associate Professor of New Testament Studies and Spirituality, Jesuit School of Theology, Berkeley, Calif.

Huston Smith—Thomas J. Watson Professor of Religion Emeritus, Syracuse University, Syracuse, N.Y.

John R. Sommerfeldt—Professor of History, University of Dallas, Irving, Tex.

David Steindl-Rast—Spiritual Author, Benedictine Grange, West Redding, Conn.

David Tracy—Greeley Professor of Roman Catholic Studies, Divinity School, University of Chicago, Chicago, Ill.

Rowan D. Williams—Lady Margaret Professor of Divinity and Dean of Christ Church, Oxford, England.

# Nizam Ad-Din Awliya

## MORALS FOR THE HEART

Conversations of Shaykh Nizam ad-din Awliya
recorded by Amir Hasan Sijzi

TRANSLATED AND ANNOTATED BY
**BRUCE B. LAWRENCE**

INTRODUCTION BY
**KHALIQ AHMAD NIZAMI**

PREFACE BY
**SIMON DIGBY**

PAULIST PRESS
NEW YORK • MAHWAH

Cover art: British Library Add.5601. 3f.5b. From the collected poems of Saᶜdi, a Persian miniature produced in Safavid Iran and then repainted in Mughal India. Ca. 1560–70. The Prophet Muhammad (veiled), escorted by angels, ascending the heavens on his steed, Buraq.





Library of Congress Cataloging-in-Publication Data

Nizāmuddīn Auliyā, 1236–1325.
[Fawa'id al-fu'ad. English]
Nizam ad-din Awliya: morals for the heart: conversations of Shaykh Nizam ad-din Awliya recorded by Amir Hasan Sijzi/introduction by Khaliq A. Nizami; translator's introduction, translation, and notes by Bruce B. Lawrence.
p. cm.—(Classics of Western spirituality; v. 74.)
Translation of: Fawa'id al-fu'ad.
Rypka attributes Fawa'id al-fu'ad to Amir Hasan Sijzi.
Includes bibliographical references and index.
ISBN 0-8091-0451-2 (cloth)—ISBN 0-8091-3280-X (pbk.):
1. Sufism—Early works to 1800. 2. Sufism—Prayer-books and devotions—Early works to 1800. 3. Chishtīyah—Prayer-books and devotions—Early works to 1800. 4. Nizāmuddīn Auliyā, d. 1236–1325. I. Lawrence, Bruce B. II. Hasan Dihlavī, 1253 or 4-ca. 1338. III. Title. IV. Series.
BP188.9.N58 1992
297'.4—dc20 91-36273
CIP

Published by Paulist Press
997 Macarthur Boulevard
Mahwah, New Jersey 07430

Printed and bound in the United States of America

# CONTENTS

Translator of this Volume

BRUCE B. LAWRENCE was born in Newton, NJ in 1941. He earned his A.B. at Princeton University, his M.Div. from Episcopal Divinity School (Cambridge), and his Ph.D. from Yale University. A specialist on Indo-Muslim culture who has studied both medieval Sufism and modern Islamic movements, he has been on the faculty of Duke University since 1971, becoming a full Professor in 1978.

He has received numerous academic awards and research fellowships. Between 1974–76 a Senior Faculty Research Fellowship from the American Institute of Indian Studies allowed him to reside in Aligarh and study with Professor Nizami. His work on Indo-Persian literature was assisted by a 1980 National Endowment of the Humanities Translation Fund grant. During 1990 he was awarded both a Harry Frank Guggenheim Fellowship and the American Academy of Religion prize for excellence in religious studies.

Professor Lawrence has published five books and over 120 articles, chapters and essays. Among his books the most relevant to the present work is *Notes from a Distant Flute: The Extant Literature of Pre-Mughal Indian Sufism.*

Author of the Introduction

KHALIQ A. NIZAMI was born in 1925 in Meerut, U.P., India. He was educated at Aligarh Muslim University, where in 1947 he joined the staff in the Department of History. He became reader, professor, then senior professor before serving as pro-vice-chancellor in 1972–73, then vice-chancellor in 1974.

In addition to these academic and administrative posts at Aligarh Muslim University, he has edited and translated numerous texts in medieval Indian history and culture, made substantial contributions to studies on Sir Syed Ahmad Khan and the Aligarh movement, and furthered both academic and popular perceptions of the Indian freedom movement and Muslim participation in it. Professor Nizami has published over 30 books in both Urdu and English as well as some 250 research articles, book chapters and encyclopedic surveys.

Distinguished in many scholarly pursuits, he is above all renowned for his work on Islamic mysticism. Two of his many books in this field are recommended for further reading, as is his exhaustive survey article in *The Encyclopaedia of Islam* (New Edition).

His diligence as an author is matched only by his patience as a teacher, and counting himself among his numerous students is the translator of this book.

## Author of the Preface

SIMON DIGBY is a former fellow of Wolfson College, Oxford and a former assistant keeper in the Department of Eastern Art, the Ashmolean Museum. He continues to serve as honorary Librarian of the Royal Asiatic Society of Great Britain and Ireland, a position he has held since 1971. The foremost British scholar of pre-Mughal India, he has written numerous foundational essays on Indo-Persian Sufism as well as contributing to *The Cambridge Economic History of India*, volume 1.

# PREFACE

Some thirty-five years ago, in one of the small Muslim bookshops close to the towering south wall of the great mosque of Old Delhi, I found an Urdu translation of Amîr Ḥasan's **Fawa'id al-Fu'ad.** I was then a postgraduate student, with a degree which had included the study of medieval European history and a reading knowledge of Persian and Urdu. I was not then familiar with the publications of Professor Khaliq Ahmad Nizami, who has contributed an introduction to this translation; and as I turned the pages of the little book in its scruffy blue cardboard binding I became aware of a class of record about the lives of Muslims in the early days of their ascendancy in medieval India that would flesh out the dry bones of narrative of the Indo-Persian chronicles. The **Fawa'id al-Fu'ad** contained an exactly dated record of the conversations of a great Indian Sufi Shaykh of the early fourteenth century.

I was indeed fortunate that I had stumbled on the earliest and the most attractive Indo-Persian work of this genre, in which a great poet has skillfully recorded the talk of one of the most lovable and charismatic of Indian Sufi Shaykhs, perhaps the most historically influential of them all.

Professor Nizami quotes the remarks of the contemporary historian, Barani, on the furor of piety which Shaykh Nizam ad-din inspired in the capital city of Delhi, incidentally mentioning the demand for copies of the **Fawa'id al-Fu'ad.** Since the early fourteenth century the **Fawa'id al-Fu'ad** has inspired imitations in the same genre. Some of these are genuine records of the conversations of Sufi Shaykhs, but in general they lack the charm, and one might say the genius, of this account. Other imitations are old but impudent fabrications, works of little edification or spiritual depth, though they are of some interest to the historian for the light they throw on medieval social conditions and attitudes. They are almost contemporary attempts to cash in on the boom of a "bestseller" among the Persian-reading population of the

Delhi Sultanate. But I was fortunate indeed, on that day thirty-five years ago in the Urdu Bazaar of Old Delhi, that it was not one of these works but the **Fawa'id al-Fu'ad** that I came across. In subsequent decades the direction of my own research turned toward the world to which the **Fawa'id al-Fu'ad** had introduced me.

In spite of the reputation that it has enjoyed through the centuries, copies of the **Fawa'id al-Fu'ad** have always been hard to obtain. There is a dearth of manuscripts of the work in public collections. It was some years before I managed to buy, from an antiquarian bookseller in London, a copy of one of the nineteenth-century lithographic printings of the original Persian text. This came from the library of Sir Richard Carnac Temple, the eminent folklorist and editor of *The Indian Antiquary*. In more recent times the 1966 Lahore edition, mentioned in the translator's introduction, remains virtually uncirculated.

In these circumstances I particularly welcome the publication of this translation by my old friend Professor Bruce Lawrence. It is the product of his many years of study of the text, and of an exceptional knowledge of nuances of emotion and sensibility of its Indian Sufi environment. It makes accessible to a wider English-reading public, in South Asia as well as in the West, a precious historical record which is also one of the most attractive monuments of Muslim piety that survive from medieval India.

# Introduction

Shaykh Nizam ad-din Awliya (1242–1325), whose conversations are recorded in **Fawa'id al-Fu'ad,** is one of the seminal personalities in the history of the Islamic mystical movement in South Asia. For about half a century he lived and worked in Delhi to save humankind from sin and suffering. His efforts to inculcate in people a respect for moral and spiritual values had a deep and far-reaching impact on medieval Indian society. His message of humanism, love, and benevolence still echoes through the corridors of time. In the Tughluq dynasty Sultan Firuz Shah (ruled A.D. 1351–1388) addressed him as **Sultan al-Masha'ikh** (King of the mystic teachers).[1] Ziya ad-din Barani, a renowned historian of the time, gives the following account of his popularity and influence:

> Shaykh Nizam ad-din admitted [all sorts of people into his discipline]—nobles and plebeians, rich and poor, learned and illiterate, citizens and villagers, soldiers and warriors, freemen and slaves. These people refrained from many improper things, because they considered themselves disciples of the Shaykh—[As a result of his teachings] the general public showed an inclination to religion and prayer. Men and women, young and old, shopkeepers and servants, children and slaves, all came [to the mosques] to say their prayers. . . . Many platforms with thatched roofs over them were constructed on the way from the city to Ghiyathpur;[2] wells were dug, water-vessels were kept, carpets were spread, and a servant and a reciter of the Qur'an (**hafiz**) was stationed at every platform so that the people going to the Shaykh may have no difficulty in saying their supererogatory prayers. Owing to regard for the Shaykh's discipleship all talk of sinful acts had disappeared from the people. . . . There was no quarter of the city in which a gathering of the pious was not held every month or after

every twenty days with mystic songs that moved them to tears. Owing to the influence of the Shaykh, most of the Muslims of this country took an inclination to mysticism, prayers and aloofness from the world, and came to have a faith in the Shaykh. This faith was shared by Sultan ʿAla ad-din and his family. The hearts of men having become virtuous by good deeds, the very name of wine, gambling and other forbidden things never came to nay one's lips. Sins and abominable vices appeared to people as bad as infidelity. Out of regard for one another Muslims refrained from open usury and hoarding (**ihtikar**) while the shopkeepers, from fear, gave up speaking lies, using false weights and deceiving the ignorant. In short, God had created the Shaykh as a peer of Shaykh Junaid and Shaykh Bayazid in these later days . . . the art of leading men found its fulfillment and final consummation in him:

Do not try to obtain eminence in this art,
For it has come to an end with Nizami.[3]

The conversations of a saint with such impact on contemporary life cannot fail to provide a glimpse into medieval society in all its light and shade. Amir Hasan Sijzi, who compiled these conversations, was a disciple of Shaykh Nizam ad-din Awliya and had direct access to him. His work came to be recognized as a manual of guidance[4] and a vade mecum for spiritual culture. It soon found a distinctive place in Muslim mystic literature. While mystics like Maulana ʿAla ad-din Nili kept themselves busy in reading it,[5] Amir Khusrau, the famous poet, offered to exchange all his works for it.[6] Men and women, young and old, all found spiritual solace in its study. Sir Syed Ahmad Khan, the nineteenth-century Indo-Muslim educator, informs us that in his day not only men but also women used to read it.[7] Muslims apart, even Hindus looked on these conversations with reverence. We find a Hindu landlord, Rao Umaro Singh of Kutchesar, ordering its transcription because he believed that whoever had it copied to fulfill some desire would achieve his objective before the transcript was completed.[8] For mystics of the Chishti order, those for whom it was primarily intended, it embodied a model to be emulated and an ideal to be pursued.

# INTRODUCTION

## The Malfuz and Its Ideological Content

It was on 3 Sha'ban A.H. 707/28 January A.D. 1308 that Amir Hasan Sijzi visited Shaykh Nizam ad-din Awliya at Ghiyathpur. Impressed by the Shaykh's discourse to the audience assembled there, he decided to prepare a record of the Shaykh's utterances. He went on with his plan quietly for some time but one day he could not help disclosing it to the Shaykh. The Shaykh asked to see what had been written, and glanced through the pages with approbation. Later the Shaykh revised some of its pages and filled the lacunae. The work was completed in five thin fascicles under the rubric **Fawa'id al-Fu'ad** (Morals for the Benefit of the Heart, or Morals for the Heart). This is how an authoritative version of the discourses of Shaykh Nizam ad-din Awliya came to be compiled. No other collection of his sayings—available or extinct—was seen or approved by the Shaykh himself.

A new genre of Sufi literature was thus introduced by Amir Hasan. Literature produced earlier was either metaphysical in content or had dealt with mystic litanies and lucubrations that could be understood only by the initiated. With **Fawa'id al-Fu'ad,** Sufi literature entered a new phase and assumed a more lively, realistic, and concrete form related to actual circumstances. It made Sufi teachings accessible to a broad audience of Indian Muslims.

Assessed chronologically, the **Fawa'id al-Fu'ad** contains an account of the Shaykh's meetings from 3 Sha'ban A.H. 707/28 January A.D. 1308 to 19 Sha'ban A.H. 722/2 September A.D. 1322. The period covered by each of the five fascicles is as follows:

1. 3 Sha'ban A.H. 707/27 January A.D. 1308 to 29 Dhu'l-Hijja A.H. 709/18 June A.D. 1309 (34 meetings)
2. 29 Shawwal A.H. 709/1 April A.D. 1310 to 13 Shawwal A.H. 712/11 February A.D. 1313 (38 meetings)
3. 27 Dhu'l-Qa'da A.H. 712/26 March A.D. 1313 to 21 Dhu'l-Hijja A.H. 713/8 April A.D. 1314 (17 meetings)
4. 24 Muharram A.H. 714/10 May A.D. 1314 to 3 Rajab A.H. 719/23 August A.D. 1319 (67 meetings)
5. 21 Sha'ban A.H. 719/7 October A.D. 1319 to 20 Sha'ban A.H. 722/3 September A.D. 1322 (32 meetings)

In all, the book contains a record of 188 meetings of the Shaykh, collected over a period of about 15 years. Thus out of about 5,475 days only 188 days of discourse have been covered here. The Shaykh had worked in Delhi for more than a half a century. The combined fascicles provide the account of but a very small period of his mystic activity in the capital city of the Delhi sultanate.

This record of meetings spans the reign of four Sultans of Delhi—ʿAla ad-din Khalji (695–715/1296–1316), Mubarak Khalji (716–720/1316–1320), Khusrau Khan (720/1320), and Ghiyath ad-din Tughluq (720–725/1320–1325). Shaykh Nizam ad-din breathed his last on 18 Rabiʿ al-Akhir A.H. 725/3 April A.D. 1325 at the age of about eighty-two years, slightly more than three years after the last meeting recorded in **Fawaʾid al-Fuʾad.** It shows that the Shaykh's memory, his power of presentation, and judgment remained intact until almost the very end of his life.

Shaykh Nizam ad-din Awliya's position in the history of Islamic mysticism in South Asia is unique in certain respects. He transformed institutional Sufism, which initially aimed at individual spiritual salvation and training, into a movement for mass spiritual culture. This led to the proliferation of hospices (**khanqahs**) in the country and the adoption of common lingua franca for the communication of ideas, and brought about a significant change in the nature of mystic literature. It shifted the focus of mystic interest from abstract thought to concrete conditions of life and discipline. It was a historic development, the background of which was thus explained by the Shaykh himself to the historian Ziya ad-din Barani:

> God in His almighty wisdom has given a special characteristic to each age, which is manifested in the distinct ways and manners of the people of that age. Hence the temperament and disposition of the people of one generation seldom resembles that of their predecessors. This (assessment) is based on (past) experience. The essence of discipleship is to sever ties with all that is not Him, and to immerse oneself in spiritual practices leading to Him. . . . The saints of old did not admit anyone to their discipline unless they saw that that person had cut himself off completely from the world. But from the time of Shaykh Abu Saʿid Abul Khayr . . . to the age of Shaykh Saif ad-din Bakharzi and from the time of Shaykh Shihab ad-din Suhrawardi to the age of Shaykh Farid al-Haqq wad-Din . . . crowds of people, among them kings and nobles and men of

> fame, together with others, flocked there. Out of fear of the Day of Judgment, they threw themselves under the protection of these lovers of God. The saints of old admitted them all, elite and non-elite alike, into their discipline. . . . Shaykh Abu Saʿid, Shaykh Saif ad-din Bakharzi, Shaykh ad-din Suhrawardi and Shaykh Farid al-Haqq wad-din . . . have admitted, like myself, all [types of] people [into their discipline]. . . . I always hear people saying that many of those who have been initiated into my discipleship abstain from sin, offer congregational prayers, and busy themselves in supererogatory prayers and litanies. If I were to tell them in the very beginning about the conditions of discipleship and not bestow upon them the mystic garment (**khirqa**) of repentance and blessing . . . they would be deprived of the (benefit of the) good acts that they (now) perform.[9]

It is in the light of this development that **Fawaʾid al-Fuʾad** assumes great significance in the history of institutional Sufism in the Asian subcontinent. The discussions set forth in its pages are meant to be intelligible to the common man, those nonelites for whom the Shaykh had thrown open the door of his spiritual discipline.

That individual assemblies have a definite space-time context and are related to the milieu in which they took place may be appreciated if the discussions are related to the sociopolitical developments of the time. An instance will suffice to explain. Amir Khusrau thus informs us about the wealth brought by Malik Kafur from his Deccan campaign:

> On Tuesday, the 24 Muharram (A.H. 710), a black pavilion was erected on Chautra-i Nasiri, like the Kaʾba on the navel of the earth. The kings and princes of Arabia and Persia took up their places around it. The Maliks, who had been sent on the expedition from the Capital, came before the Emperor . . . and presented the spoils. Elephants of the size of Marwa, Safa, Tur and Bu Qabis, horses that raised a dust [cloud] out of the sea like western winds, and treasures under which a thousand camels would have groaned, were all displayed.[10]

The next day, on 25 Muharram A.H. 710, Shaykh Nizam ad-din Awliya addressed his audience follows, according to Amir Hasan:

> Conversation turned to MISERS WHO HOARD THEIR WEALTH: the more they make, the more they want. The master observed: "God the Almighty and Exalted has created different sorts of persons. For instance, if there were an individual for whom ten **dirams** sufficed to meet his daily needs and one day he happened to acquire more, he would not feel secure till he had spent that surplus. At the same time, there might be another person of such a temperament that however must be gained the more he wanted. In neither instance can the individual control his instincts; it is a matter of divine will."
>
> After that he advised: "True comfort comes from EXPENDING GOLD AND SILVER. Hence no one can find comfort unless he expends the silver in his possession. For instance, if someone wants to wear fine clothes or to eat delicious food or to gratify some other desire, he cannot succeed without expending silver. Hence it is obvious that the true comfort in having gold and silver is to expend it."
>
> Then he repeated his point. "The real purpose of amassing gold and silver is to use it for the benefit of others."

The Shaykh continued to stress the problem of wealth and its proper use till he had brought home to his audience the dangers involved in its accumulation. He pointed out how in his youth half a **tanka** had "clung to the skirt of his heart and disrupted its concentration."

The Shaykh had his own peculiar ways of instruction. He did not advise any visitor directly. He referred to the individual's problems indirectly and suggested remedies through anecdotes and parables. The value of anecdotes in **Fawa'id al-Fu'ad** can be appreciated only if one keeps in mind this practice of the Shaykh. Even the Sultan of Delhi, ʿAla ad-din Khalji, was aware of this method of the Shaykh. Once he sent Malik Qara Beg and Qazi Mughis ad-din to the Shaykh to inquire about the welfare of an army he had sent to the South. He instructed his messengers to report to him "every story and incident" that they heard from the Shaykh.[11] The didactic value of anecdotes in his conversations cannot be overemphasized. Every story had a moral for the audience. Once, while discussing how one felt really free and unfettered if he did not expect anything from anybody, he gave the story of a saint known only as Shaykh ʿAli. He was stitching his frock with his legs outstretched. Without prior intimation the Caliph (of Baghdad) came to meet him. The minister to the Caliph stepped forward and asked Shaykh ʿAli to fold his legs as the Caliph was coming. Shaykh ʿAli ignored all this and as the Caliph was about to leave, he caught hold of his hand and also the hand of his minister, saying: "Look! I have folded my hands and therefore I can stretch my legs."[12]

Admonishing his disciples against prayers offered with a distracted mind, the Shaykh related the following story:

> Shaykh Hasan Afghan was a disciple of Shaykh Baha ad-din Zakariya. He heard the call for prayers in the bazaar and stopped there to offer prayers. On finishing his prayers he came to the leader of the congregational prayers (**Imam**) and told him in a low voice: "Respected sir, you began the prayers and fell in with you. You went from here to Delhi, bought some slaves, and then returned to Multan. Next you went to Khurasan with these slaves. I got my neck twisted trying to catch up with you. What has all this to do with prayer?"[13]

Amir Hasan Sijzi, the compiler, was not paid his salary for some time and was distressed and worried on that account. The Shaykh related the following story of a Brahman:

> Though the Brahman was very wealthy, the chief magistrate of that city fined him, seized all his possessions and reduced him to poverty. That Brahman became destitute. He was hard pressed to make ends meet. One day he came across a friend. "How are you?" asked the friend. "Well and happy," replied the Brahman. "How can you be happy?" retorted the friend; "everything has been taken from you." "With me still," replied the Brahman, "is my sacred thread (**zunnar**)."[14]

As he heard this story, Amir Hasan's anxiety over his own circumstance disappeared.

All through **Fawaʾid al-Fuʾad** one finds the Shaykh demonstrating the accumulated wisdom of his mystical training through parables, stories, and anecdotes. Specific reference to a visitor's problem may not be there, but the story itself indicates the nature of the problem he was dealing with.

**Fawaʾid al-Fuʾad** became the basic text of the Chishti mystic ideology. The moral and spiritual principles adumbrated here provided élan to the mystic movement in India and the Chishti centers were organized throughout the country on their basis. The basic principles of the Shaykh's ideology may be thus summarized:

1. Service of humankind is the *raison d'être* of religion. It has higher spiritual significance than mere formal adherence to rituals and practices. He explained it thus:

> Devotion to God is of two kinds: **lazmi** (obligatory) and **muta'addi** (supererogatory).[15] In the **lazmi** devotion, the benefit which accrues is confined to the devotee alone. This type of devotion includes prayers, fasting, pilgrimage to Mecca, recitation of religious formulae, turning over the beads of the rosary, and the like. The **muta'addi** devotion, by contrast, brings advantage and comfort to others; it is performed by spending money on others, showing affection to people, and by other means through which one strives to help fellow human beings. The reward of **muta'addi** devotion is incalculable.[16]

The Shaykh narrated numerous anecdotes to bring home to his audience the significance of this concept of religion, a concept that had revolutionary dimensions. Hardly any visitor left his hospice without experiencing a sense of relief in his heart. The Shaykh had heard in a spiritual trance that no work would be more highly rewarded on the Day of Judgment than "bringing happiness to the human heart."[17] In the eyes of God no spiritual exercise, no penitence, no prayer, no vigil had greater significance than removing the misery of fellow human beings, bringing consolation to distressed hearts, and helping the downtrodden.

With this approach to religion, Shaykh Nizam ad-din made the Sufi movement a humanitarian activity to remove sin and suffering from society. If we recall Toynbee's standard that "the practical test of a religion, always and everywhere, is its success or failure in helping human souls to respond to the challenges of suffering and sin,"[18] then we are led to acknowledge that Shaykh Nizam ad-din Awliya's role in the religious history of South Asia was of immense significance.

The Shaykh's approach to religion emanated from his concept of God. For him God was an all-embracing Reality present in his ethical, intellectual, and aesthetic experience. He lived for the Lord alone. His cosmic emotion, rooted in his faith in God as the Supreme Nourisher, empowered his mystic mission. He believed in following the ways of the Lord of the Creation. Divine bounty does not discriminate between one individual and another. When the sun rises it gives light and warmth to all people, whether they live in palaces or in huts. When it rained, the poor and rich alike benefitted from the downpour. Once Shaykh Muʿin ad-din Chishti of Ajmer was asked to explain the highest form of religious devotion which endeared man to God. He said: "Develop river-like generosity, sun-like bounty and earth-like hospitality."[19]

Shaykh Nizam ad-din Awliya demonstrated the significance of this advice as an inspiring motive in his own life. Once he mentioned a story of the Prophet Abraham to illustrate this approach. The Prophet Abraham never took his meals without some guest joining him. He sometimes went for miles in search of a guest. One day he was alone with a polytheist. He hesitated giving food to this man till the Divine admonition came to him: "Abraham! How is it that we can give life to this man yet you cannot give him food?!"[20] The message was clear: A traveler on the Path was expected to transcend all barriers of cult, race, language, and geography in dealing with his fellow creatures.

2. Shaykh Nizam ad-din Awliya believed that if one learned "to live for the Lord alone," love, peace, and amity would prevail in this world. Human relationships would become effable and affectionate. Human beings are "like children of God on earth" and one who seeks His pleasure must strive for the welfare of all people, regardless of any consideration. "Living for the Lord alone" meant a fundamental change in the human approach to life and its problems. When one was inspired by this ideal, whatever one did or focused on became devotion to God. It would lead the individual to sublimate other motivations. The moral of the following anecdote, the miraculous element apart, is to stress how one can live for the Lord alone, subordinating both sex and hunger to higher ideals:

> A saint lived by the bank of a river. One day this saint asked his wife to give food to a dervish residing on the other side of the river. His wife protested that crossing the water would be difficult. He said: "When you go to the bank of the river tell the water to provide a way for you due to respect for your husband who never slept with his wife." His wife was perplexed at these words and said to herself: "How many children have I borne by this man. Yet how can I challenge this directive from my husband?" She took the food to the bank of the

river, spoke the message to the water, and the water gave way for her passage. Having crossed, she put food before the dervish, and the dervish took it in her presence. After he had eaten, the woman asked: "How shall I recross the river?" "How did you come?" asked the dervish. The woman repeated the words of her husband. On hearing this the dervish said: "Go to the water and tell it to make way for you out of respect for the dervish who never ate for thirty years." The woman, bewildered at these words, came to the river, repeated the message, and the water again gave way for her passage. On returning home, the woman fell at her husband's feet and implored him: "Tell me the secret of these directives which you and the other dervish uttered." "Look", said the husband. "I never slept with you to satisfy the passions of my lower self. I slept with you only to provide you what was your due. In reality I never slept with you, and similarly, that other man never ate for thirty years to satisfy his appetite or to fill his stomach. He ate only to have the strength to do God's will."[21]

3. Shaykh Nizam ad-din Awliya taught the sublimation of desires through nourishing cosmic emotion. This gave real spiritual equanimity and poise to one who practiced it. The Shaykh never tried to curb an individual's natural aptitudes. Rather, he sublimated them through the development of counter-attractions. One of his beloved disciples was the famed court poet Amir Khusrau. From his early life Amir Khusrau had been interested in romantic poetry. When he joined the Shaykh's discipline, he thought of giving it up. The Shaykh, however, encouraged him not to obstruct the natural flow of his emotions.[22] In the course of time, and due to the Shaykh's influence, the great poet did change his amorous fancies into cosmic emotion. What was material and mundane became spiritual and cosmic. Similarly, the Shaykh's nephew Khwaja Rafiʿ ad-din was interested in archery and somatic arts. The Shaykh did not prevent him from pursuing his hobbies.[23] Instead, he made him commit the Qur'an to memory and thereby gave a different orientation to his personality.

4. The Shaykh believed that one could not live a life of divine significance without firmly rejecting all materialistic attractions (**tark-i dunya**).[24] This did not mean leading the life of a recluse or denying to oneself all the good things of this world. Rather, it meant the rejection of that attitude of mind which involved man in material struggles in such a

way that he ceased to look at the divine significance of life and frittered away his energies in petty material pursuits. Like Wordsworth he felt:

> Getting and spending we lay waste our powers.
> Little we see in nature that is ours.

He explained his views in this regard as follows:

> Rejection of the world does not mean that one should strip oneself of clothes or put on a loin cloth and sit idle. Instead "rejection of the world" means that one may put on clothes and take food. What comes (unasked) should be accepted but not hoarded. One should not place one's heart on anything. Only this is rejection of the world.[25]

To illustrate the same point we find him drawing a distinction between "appearance and reality": What a certain saint did to provide for the needs of his wife (and family) may have appeared as worldliness, but in reality it was not.[26]

The Shaykh thought that possession of private property deepened a person's links with the material world and blocked the energizing currents of spiritual life. Each individual should subsist on the basic minimum and distribute the rest among the needy and the poor. Real happiness, according to Shaykh Nizam ad-din, lay not in accumulating money but in spending it.[27] He thought that, with respect to material attractions, there were three types of persons. "First, those who want worldly goods and spend their days in its search. . . . Secondly, those who consider the world to be their enemy and speak disdainfully about it. Thirdly, those who consider the world as neither an enemy nor a friend and do not refer to it either with enmity or friendship. They are the best of all."[28]

5. Shaykh Nizam ad-din Awliya was a firm believer in pacifism and nonviolence. Violence, he said, created more problems than it solved. In forgiveness and large-hearted tolerance lay the supreme talisman of human happiness. "If some man places a thorn in your way," he said, "and you place another thorn in his way, there will be thorns everywhere."[29] He advised his disciples to be good even to their enemies and very often he would recite the following verses of Shaykh Sayf ad-din Bakharzi:

> He who is not my friend—may God be his friend,
> And he who bears ill-will against me, may his joys (in life) increase.
> He who puts thorns in my way on account of enmity,
> May every flower that blossoms in the garden of his life, be without thorns.[30]

Not only in action but also in thought the Shaykh preached an approach of large-hearted forgiveness. In patience and tolerance he saw the secret of social well-being. He used to say: "[If] one man vents his wrath on another and the second man is patient, the virtuous attitude belongs to him who is patient and not to him who gives vent to his wrath."[31] He advised his disciples against suppression of anger because suppression forces the virus into other channels of thought and action. "Forgive the person who has committed a wrong and thus eliminate your anger," was his advice.[32] One day a person reported to him: "People speak ill of you from the pulpits and elsewhere. We cannot bear hearing it any longer." The Shaykh replied: "I forgive them all; you, too, should forgive them."[33]

Forgiveness rather than retribution was the real way to peace and happiness in social relations. The Shaykh said:

> If there is a contention between two persons—say, between me and some other person, its solution is this: I, for my part, should cleanse my heart of all ideas of revenge. If I succeed in doing that, the opponent's desire to do some harm to me would also be lessened.[34]

6. The Shaykh analyzed the basis of human exchange as reflecting three possible types of relationship with other human beings: (a) He may be neither good nor bad to others. This is what happens in the nonliving world (**jamadat**). (b) He may do no harm to others but only what is deemed good. (c) He may do good to others, and yet if others harm him, still remain patient and not retaliate. This last option was the one adopted by "truthful persons."[35] It was an approach grounded in the Sufi interpretation of human nature. The Shaykh used to say that there is **nafs** (the animal soul) and **qalb** (the human soul). **Nafs** is the abode of mischief, animosity, and strife, while **qalb** is the center of peace, resignation, and good will. If someone acting under the influence of **nafs** is dealt with by one acting under the direction of **qalb**, the strife would end. On the other hand, if **nafs** is met by **nafs**, there will be no end to

contentions and enmities.[36] Since every human action covers the stages of *knowing, feeling,* and *willing,*[37] all programs of reform should be initiated at the stage of *knowing.*

7. Complete trust (**tawakkul**) in God and resignation to His will leads to blissful contentment in life.[38] It helps the individual in breaking the trammels of society and living a life that can be called one's own.

8. Miracle-mongering had no place in the spiritual discipline of Shaykh Nizam ad-din Awliya. He considered performance of miracles a sign of spiritual imperfection. In **Fawa'id al-Fu'ad** there are no references to miracles performed by the Shaykh. He has, however, mentioned the miracles of others, not to demonstrate their spiritual powers but to illustrate some principle or to bring home some moral. "They have divided the Path," he once remarked, "into a hundred stages of which the capacity for displaying miracles is the seventeenth; if a mystic is stopped at this stage, how will he cross the remaining eighty-three stages?"[39]

9. The Shaykh had very definite and specific rules about his mystic discipline: (a) No one devoid of learning could be appointed a **khalifa** (deputy) to carry on the work of spreading the order;[40] (b) no **khalifa** was permitted to visit the courts of kings or to accept grants from them;[41] (c) no **khalifa** could accept any government job, even a judgeship;[42] (d) the **khalifa** was to live on **futuh**[43] (solicited gifts); (e) nothing received by way of **futuh** was to be hoarded. The structure of the Chishti mystical ideology stood on these principles, and the Shaykh tried to build morally autonomous personalities in his disciples in accordance with the principles enunciated in **Fawa'id al-Fu'ad.**

## Shaykh Nizam ad-din Awliya: Ancestry and Education

Shaykh Nizam ad-din Awliya's ancestors originally belonged to Bukhara but the pressure of Mongol invasions drove them to India. When Chingiz Khan attacked Bukhara he ruthlessly massacred its inhabitants. "More than thirty thousand men," writes Vambery, "were executed and the remainder were, with the exception of the very old people amongst them, reduced to slavery, without any distinction of rank whatever; and thus the inhabitants of Bokhara, lately so celebrated for their learning, their love of art, and their general refinement, were brought down to a dead level of misery and degradation and scattered to all quarters. But a few escaped the general ruin."[44] Among these few who managed to escape Mongol savagery were some ancestors of Shaykh Nizam ad-din Awliya.

Khwaja ʿAli and Khwaja ʿArab—paternal and maternal grandfathers of the future Shaykh—reached India and settled at Badaon, a quiet place where people who did not want to involve themselves in government service preferred to live. The use of the suffix **Khwaja** before their names was perhaps due to their association with the **silsilah-i Khwajagan,** the precursor of the Naqshbandi order. It was in Badaon that Khwaja ʿArab gave his daughter—Bibi Zulaikha—in marriage to Khwaja ʿAhmad, son of Khwaja ʿAli. Nizam ad-din was born of this couple.

Badaon is one of those North Indian cities where Muslim settlements had appeared long before Turkish arms reached there.[45] At least ten years before its conquest by Ghurids Maulana Razi ad-din Hasan Saghani,[46] the famous author of **Mashariq al-Anwar,**[47] was born in Badaon. It appears that Muslim cultural institutions had already struck deep roots in that region. Subsequently many scholars, poets, saints, and literati from Central Asian lands also found shelter there. Due to its strategic position,[48] it came to enjoy a reputation second only to Delhi.

Shaykh Nizam ad-din Awliya was born on the last Wednesday of the month of Safar[49] circa the year 640–41/1243–1244.[50] He was given the name Muhammad, but became known by his surname, Nizam ad-din.[51] According to Muhammad Jamal Qiwam ad-din,[52] Nizam ad-din was a posthumous child—a statement that is not corroborated by any other source. ʿAli Jandar says that he was a suckling babe (**shir khwar**) at his father's demise.[53] Amir Khurd vaguely hints that he was in his infancy,[54] while according to Jamali he was five years of age when his father died.[55] Because ʿAli Jandar's statement is recorded on the authority of the Shaykh himself, it deserves credence. The Shaykh had heard about the circumstances in which his father had died from his elder sister. According to her, Bibi Zulaikha had dreamt that someone asked her to make a choice between her son and her husband as one of them was destined to die. Bibi Zulaikha chose the son. Soon afterward Khwaja Ahmad fell ill and passed away.[56] Nizam ad-din was raised by his mother, a lady of fervent piety. It was she who inculcated in her son a spirit of resignation and contentment.

Badaon was the real nursery where the thought and emotions of the future Shaykh were nurtured. It had a serene spiritual atmosphere that appealed to Nizam ad-din's retiring and peace loving nature. In his later years, whenever he heard the name of Badaon uttered, his mind conjured up pictures of days gone by. Sometime in 1319 Amir Hasan Sijzi, the author of **Fawa'id al-Fu'ad,** returned from Badaon with the royal army and reported to the saint that he had visited there the graves of his father, his teacher Maulana ʿAla ad-din Usuli, and others. Tears flowed from the eyes of Shaykh Nizam ad-din as he paid silent homage to their memory. He loved Badaon—its fauna and flora, its fruits and gardens, its men and manners, its language and literature. The way he addressed his servant Iqbal as **Lalla**[57] and favored the Purbi dialect shows the influence of Badaon on his diction. Dara Shukoh reports that in moments of spiritual exhilaration the Shaykh used to say: "The promise and pledge that I made to God (on the Day of Creation) was in Purbi rhyme."[58] He became nostalgic and tears appeared in his eyes when he thought about the Badaon of his day.

Nizam ad-din lived in Badaon for about twenty years,[59] and completed his early education there. These were days of abject penury and hard struggle. His widowed mother was financially broken but spiritually impregnable. She provided an emotional and moral prop for her son.

Names of two teachers of his from Badaon have come down to us—Shadi Muqri and Maulana ʿAla ad-din ʿUsuli. Shadi Muqri was an experienced and able teacher who knew how to teach the Qur'an and create in boys an interest in memorizing it. He himself could recite the Qur'an according to its seven recognized methods of recitation.[60] Originally the slave of a Hindu,[61] he secured emancipation in later life and became the pupil of Khwaja Muqri, a scholar-saint of Lahore. It was generally believed that whoever received elementary instructions in the Qur'an from Shadi Muqri eventually succeeded in committing the Holy Book to memory. Though Nizam ad-din did not commit the Qur'an to memory until he had moved to Delhi—many years after leaving Badaon—he ascribed this achievement to the blessings of Shadi Muqri.

Maulana ʿAla ad-din Usuli was a pious, dedicated, and erudite scholar of Badaon. His life was spent in penitence and penury, holding fast to traditions of scholarship in extremely indigent circumstances. Often he starved for days but never disclosed it to anybody and carried on his instructional work, though hunger and thirst made his mouth dry and choked.[62] Young Nizam ad-din's mind was deeply influenced by his example. He used to refer to him very affectionately as "my teacher."[63] He learned from him the value of dedicating one's life to higher ideals, regardless of material discomfort. The author of **Shawamil al-Jumal** says that unique to Shaykh Nizam ad-din Awliya was that his thought and personality had been shaped by but one spiritual mentor (Shaykh Farid) and one teacher (Maulana ʿAla ad-din).[64]

Maulana ʿAla ad-din Usuli possessed the humility of a real scholar. He looked on teaching as a cooperative work in which both teacher and student should participate for their common benefit.[65] When Nizam ad-din finished studying **Qaduri,**[66] Maulana ʿAla ad-din declared him qualified for putting on his head "the turban of scholarship" (**dastar-i fazilat**). In those days this declaration was usually made in a function that resembled present-day convocation ceremonies. Nizam ad-din reported this to his mother in a depressed mood because it was difficult for the family to arrange for the turban and the feast. His mother assuaged his worry by promising to arrange everything needed. A carder quickly cleaned the cotton; the mother and her slave-girl prepared the spindles and a weaver in the neighborhood wove a sheet of four yards within a couple of days. Bibi Zulaikha washed the cloth without putting any starch in it. Together with forty crumbs, she gave it to her son to take it to Maulana ʿAla ad-din. The Maulana added to it something from his own pocket and arranged a feast to which the scholars and saints of Badaon were invited. The feast being over, the ceremony began. Nizam ad-din placed the turban before his teacher, who stood up and, holding one corner in his own hand with the other in the hands of his pupil, started tying it on his head. At every winding of the turban Nizam ad-din, out of gratitude, prostrated himself before his teacher. A notable saint of Badaon, ʿAli Maula, who was a guest of honor on this occasion, was touched at this reverential bearing of Nizam ad-din and remarked in Hindivi: **"Aray Maulana! Yeh bada hausi"** (Oh Maulana! He will be a great man). Maulana ʿAla ad-din asked him the reason for his prediction. He replied: **"Ju mundasa bandhay, wa pain pasray?"** (Who, after wearing the **dastar,** prostrates himself before a teacher?). This humility augured a bright future. "The other sign of future greatness," added ʿAli Maula, "was that his turban had no thread of silk in it."[67]

It appears that Maulana ʿAla ad-din Usuli was basically a teacher of **fiqh** (Islamic Law). Two books mentioned in connection with his instruction to Shaykh Nizam ad-din are **Hidaya**[68] and **Qaduri.**

Notwithstanding the abject poverty in which the family passed its time in Badaon, his mother readily agreed to move to Delhi when her son placed his head at her feet and sought her permission to go there[69] in order to benefit from its better academic opportunities. Shaykh Nizam ad-din was less than twenty years of age when he left Badaon. It seems probable that he never again returned to his home town.

*Early years in Delhi*

Shaykh Nizam ad-din, along with his mother and sister, had to face appalling poverty in Delhi. Circumstances forced him to change his residence from one quarter to the city to another. Homelessness combined with destitution made his life a painful struggle against heavy odds. Nevertheless he pursued his studies with single-minded devotion. In those days two loaves of bread could be had for a **jital,** but often he did not have a single **jital** to buy the bread.[70] His mother and sister patiently bore the pangs of starvation and hunger. When there was nothing in the house to eat, his mother would say: "Nizam ad-din! Today we are the guests of God."[71] Young Nizam derived inexplicable spiritual solace from this remark and always longed to hear it from her. If for several days there was no shortage of food in the house, he would get impatient for the day when his mother would utter the sentence.[72]

*His mother*

Shaykh Nizam ad-din's mother was a remarkable lady in many respects—pious, inured to suffering and resigned to the will of God. She was born with a silver spoon in her mouth but when the circumstances of her life changed, she bore with patience the frowns of misfortune. She molded the thought and personality of her son and illustrated by her example that endurance and moral excellence are possible even in the midst of adverse circumstances. Her one great concern in life was to provide her son the best possible education. Continuous fasts and endless struggle shattered her health and she did not live long enough to see her son at the height of his glory. Whenever she happened to look at the feet of her son, she remarked: "Nizam! I see signs of bright future in you. You will be a man of destiny some day." One day on hearing this remark the Shaykh asked: "But when will this happen?" "When I am dead," replied his mother.[73]

Every month when the Shaykh saw the new moon, he offered felicitation to his mother by placing his head at her feet. Once when he thus greeted her, she said: "Nizam! At whose feet will you put your head next month?" The Shaykh burst into tears. "To whose care will you entrust me?" he asked. "Tomorrow I will tell you," replied the mother. She then directed him to go and sleep at the house of Shaykh Najib ad-din. In the small hours of the morning the male servant came rushing and said that his mother had called him. Nizam ad-din hurried to the house. "Where is your right hand?" asked his dying mother. He stretched out his hand. She took it in her hand and said: "O God, I entrust him to Thee." So saying Bibi Zulaikha breathed her last. The Shaykh used to say that if she would have left a house full of gems and jewels, it would not have given his bereaved heart as much solace and satisfaction as did these few words.[74] Throughout his life he felt himself to be living under the protection and care of God.

Though Bibi Zulaikha appears to have lived in Delhi for but a few years, she lies buried in its outskirts, her grave being scarcely a mile away from the Qutb Minar in a small village known as Uchchin. It was the practice of Shaykh Nizam ad-din throughout his life that whenever he had any problem he went to the grave of his mother and prayed to God there.[75]

*Problem of Accommodation*

Frequent change of residence was a great strain on the nerves of the Shaykh, who was anxious to spend his time in studies, meditation, and prayer. One day, while he was sitting on the bank of Hauz-i Qutlugh Khan and memorizing the Qur'an, a **darwesh** came to him and advised him to leave Delhi and settle elsewhere. A number of alternatives came to his mind: He should go to Patiali, the home town of Amir Khusrau; he should settle at Basnala, near Delhi; he should go to Bihar to the **khanqah** of Shaykh Khizr Paradoz[76] and teach his children; and so on. He even went to Basnala but could not find a house for rent or lease despite three days' strenuous search and returned to Delhi disappointed. According to Muhammad Jamal Qiwam ad-din, he wanted some place near the river where he could busy himself in meditation.[77]

*Ghiyathpur*

Due to some mysterious prompting, Nizam ad-din decided to settle at Ghiyathpur, a desolate village some miles from the capital. When Kaiqubad settled at Kilugarhi (ca. 1288–1289), huge crowds began to throng there.[78] In search of a quieter place, the young Nizam ad-din thought of leaving this locality too. One day an extremely handsome man came to him. The man, who had an otherworldly look on his face, expressed strong disapproval of Nizam ad-din's desire to settle away from society. He recited a verse meaning: "The day that you appeared like moon, did you not know that the world would point its fingers towards you?" He further told Nizam ad-din to behave in such a way that he would not be put to shame before the Prophet on the Day of Judgment. He exhorted the future Shaykh to have the courage to be busy with God and also to look after His creatures.[79] Nizam ad-din hesitated, and meanwhile brought the mysterious stranger some food to eat. The latter refused to eat. Then Nizam ad-din, impressed by the visitor's determination, made up his mind to remain at Ghiyathpur. As soon as he declared his resolve to continue residing there, the stranger took a bit of food and left.[80] Thus Ghiyathpur became the seat of the Shaykh's mystic activity.

However, he lived a life of extreme penury, eking out an existence that would have broken a less determined person. When starvation became endless, a bowl (**zanbil**) was put at the door. People could put anything to eat in it.[81] At the time of breaking fast, the bowl was taken in and emptied on the dinner-cloth. A beggar once happened to pass by. He thought that the food on the cloth was leftovers from dinner. Scooping it all up, he left. Nizam ad-din smiled and said: "It appears that there is still imperfection in our work and for that reason we are being kept in hunger."[82]

*Teachers in Delhi*

Nizam ad-din had reached Delhi during the Ilbarite period, perhaps during the time of Sultan Nasir ad-din Mahmud (1246–1266). Delhi was then a rendezvous of scholars, poets, mystics, and craftsmen of distinction from distant parts of the Muslim world.[83] He must have had opportunities to meet many scholars of repute, and this contact accounts for his extensive knowledge of standard works on different branches of Muslim learning.[84]

Of his formal teachers in Delhi, the names of Khwaja Shams ad-din and Maulana Kamal ad-din Zahid have come down to us. One of his teachers who is referred to only once in **Durar-i Nizami** was Maulana Amin ad-din Muhaddith.[85] He died just before Shaykh Nizam ad-din decided to settle at Ghiyathpur. Another teacher, whose name is not mentioned, lost the esteem of Shaykh Nizam ad-din when he saw him exceedingly elated and happy at his son's appointment as **qazi** of some village. When his son, donning the dress of a **qazi,** came to see him, Shaykh Nizam ad-din happened to be there. The father said: "God be praised! What I had for years longed for, God has bestowed on you today." Nizam ad-din felt that receiving education from a teacher with such materialistic ends in view was not worthwhile and so he lost no time in leaving him.[86]

Nizam ad-din learned the **Maqamat**[87] of Hariri from Maulana Shams ad-din and committed its forty sections to memory. But the Maulana could not influence the thought or character of Nizam ad-din, as he was extremely greedy. Balban had appointed him **Mustaufi-i Mumalik** (auditor general) and in that capacity he had hoarded huge wealth. In his later years the then Sultan ordered the confiscation of all his property. When the government officers reached his house to attach his property, Nizam ad-din happened to be there. The Maulana was extremely grieved at the government order. The young pupil, who had developed a different attitude toward worldly goods, did not have the audacity to advise his teacher but he humbly submitted that he should remain resigned to the divine will. The Maulana did not utter a word in reply but when Nizam ad-din took leave of him, he said: "You should pray for the return of my wealth to me lest its deprivation tortures me." Nizam ad-din was sorry to see his teacher so deeply in love with material wealth.[88]

The teacher who did make a real impact on the mind of Nizam ad-din was Maulana Kamal ad-din Zahid, a distinguished Traditionist of Delhi, pious, erudite, and unassuming. He was a pupil of Maulana Mahmud ibn Abi al-Hasan Asʿad al-Balkhi,[89] a pupil of Maulana Razi ad-din Hasan Saghani, the author of **Mashariq al-Anwar.** When Balban came to know about his piety and scholarship, he called him to his court and requested him to accept the duty of leading his prayers. "Our prayer is all that is left to us," replied the Maulana. "Does he want to take that also from us?" Balban was dumbfounded and did not pursue his request further.[90]

Nizam ad-din received instructions in **Mashariq al-Anwar**[91] from Maulana Kamal ad-din Zahid and committed it to memory.[92] On 22 Rabiʾal-Awwal 679/21 July 1280, he granted a certificate to his pupil. It was written on a manuscript of the **Mashariq al-Anwar.** This certificate shows that: (1) Nizam ad-din was looked upon as a front-rank scholar by the great Traditionist, who speaks about his scholarship in eloquent terms; (2) his spiritual qualities also were recognized by Maulana Zahid, who requests him in this inscription to pray for him and his descendants; (3) if the date of the grant of his certificate is correctly transcribed by copyists, Nizam ad-din must have been about forty-three years of age at that time and must have already completed his formal education.[93] Among the Traditionists there is a convention that a certificate is very much sought after from scholars who had received instruction from any one in the direct chain of narrators or compilers of **ahadith.** Since Maulana Kamal Zahid was a pupil of the author of **Mashariq al-Anwar,** he would have considered it a privilege to receive **ijaza** from him even at such an advanced age. The words of respect used for the Shaykh by Maulana Zahid make it abundantly clear that the recipient of the certificate was a fully mature person with an established reputation. Incidentally, it shows that Shaykh Nizam ad-din's academic interests continued for at least two decades after his initiation into the discipline of Shaykh Farid.

Maulana Kamal ad-din Zahid inculcated in Shaykh Nizam ad-din Awliya a deep love for the Traditions of the Prophet and initiated him also into the principles of critique relating to the Science of Traditions (**ʿilm-i Hadith**). Traditions of the Prophet remained the most absorbing subject of study for him throughout his life. It appears from **Durar-i Nizami** that some of the sessions of his assemblies were exclusively devoted to elucidation and explanation of the Traditions of the Prophet, and Qazi Muhi al-Kin kashani particularly participated in these discussions.

On the whole, Maulana ʿAla ad-din Usuli of Badaon and Maulana Kamal ad-din Zahid of Delhi were the two teachers who inspired the Shaykh most. The two special fields of academic interest for Nizam ad-din were **fiqh** (Law) and **hadith,** and in these he was indebted to Maulana Usuli and Maulana Zahid, respectively.

An essential part of the method of instruction in those days was a system of seminars and debates that deepened the foundations of a student's scholarship and developed his power of expression. Nizam ad-din distinguished himself as an excellent debator and became known as Nizam ad-din **Bahhath** (the debator) and Nizam ad-din **Mahfil Shikan** (the breaker of assemblies).[94] Whatever the academic value of this power of debate and discussion, Nizam ad-din did not have any occasion to use these faculties in his life. In fact, the Chishti mystic tradition was opposed to casuistry and discussion. If Nizam ad-din learned anything from his experience of debates in his school days, it was its utter futility in changing the outlook and character of the other person.

## Shaykh Nizam ad-din Awliya: Discipleship and Succession

*At the feet of Shaykh Farid of Ajodhan*

It was in Badaon that Nizam ad-din had first heard the name of Shaykh Farid ad-din Ganj-i Shakar (1173–1265).[95] Shaykh Farid's **Jamaʿat khanah** at Ajodhan had gained renown as one of the premier centers of spiritual activity in South Asia. Since Ajodhan (later known as Pakpattan)[96] was also a meeting place of roads from different directions, those who passed through there, whether kings and nobles, soldiers, scholars, merchants, or sundry others, often visited the saint and sought his spiritual blessings.

As destiny would have it, when Nizam ad-din reached Delhi, he happened to stay in the neighborhood of Shaykh Najib ad-din Mutawakkil, younger brother of Shaykh Farid and himself a simple, pious, and sincere **darwish.** It was in his company that Nizam ad-din passed the most formative period of his life. On completing his formal education in Delhi, he requested Shaykh Najib ad-din to pray for his appointment as **qazi,** which was the highest ambition of a scholar in those days. The Shaykh gave no reply. When he repeated his request, Shaykh Najib said: "Don't be a **qazi.** Be something else."[97] At that time he could hardly have appreciated the significance of this remark. He must have felt somewhat disappointed, but later in life, when a more purposeful sphere of activity opened up before him, he realized the wisdom of Shaykh Najib's remark.

The decision to proceed to Ajodhan was taken suddenly. According to Jami, he was one night busy in prayers in the Jama' Masjid of Delhi. In the early hours of the morning he heard a **muezzin** (one who calls to prayer) reciting the following verse from the Qur'an:

Has not the time arrived
For believers that
Their hearts in all humility

Should engage in the remembrance of God?
(LVII:16)

It had a powerful impact on Nizam ad-din and he left for Ajodhan without any provision for the journey.[98] He was twenty years of age when he reached Ajodhan.[99] On being conducted into the presence of Baba Farid, who was now nearing his nineteenth year and had attained an all-India stature, Nizam ad-din became nervous. The Shaykh welcomed him by reciting a couplet meaning:

The fire of your separation has burnt our hearts.
The storm of desire to meet you has ravaged our lives.[100]

With great effort Nizam ad-din mustered courage to say that he was very eager to kiss the feet of the Shaykh. The old saint noticed his nervousness and remarked that "every newcomer is nervous"[101] in order to sooth his excited nerves. He then instructed his senior disciples, who looked after the management of the **Jamaʿat khanah,** to provide a cot for him. Nizam ad-din hesitated in sleeping on the cot as many **huffaz** (those who had committed the Qur'an to memory), devotees, and saints much senior to him in age and experience were sleeping on the ground. When Maulana Badr ad-din Ishaq was apprised of his hesitation, he sent a message: "Will you do as you wish or will you obey the orders of the Shaykh?" Nizam ad-din quietly submitted and slept on the cot.[102]

Nizam ad-din was then initiated into the discipline. Contrary to his usual practice, the Shaykh did not ask him to have his head shaved (**mahluq**). Nizam ad-din himself had long curly hair and in his heart of hearts did not want to get his head shaved, but when he saw others with shaven heads, he felt something attractive in them and approached his master for permission to get his own head shaved. The permission was readily granted.[103]

Shaykh Nizam ad-din once told his audience that he had visited his master thrice in three years[104] and had stayed there for several months each time. During these three visits the aging saint completed his spiritual training.

The first conflict in Nizam ad-din's mind after gaining admission into the discipline of Shaykh Farid was whether to complete his education or to give it up and turn solely to the culture of his soul. "I never ask anybody," Baba Farid told him, "to give up studies. Knowledge also is necessary for a **darwesh.** So do this [spiritual work] and that [studies] also, till such time as one of them gets an upper hand over the other."[105]

Baba Farid instructed Nizam ad-din in some basic texts; propounded the basic and fundamental principles of the order; illustrated through his own conduct the type of life that a mystic was expected to lead; eliminated all traces of that intellectual arrogance which had quietly entered his mind when he won laurels in the highest academic circles of Delhi; embellished his inner life with all the qualities necessary for a mystic entrusted with the stupendous task of looking after the spiritual well-being of others; and then appointed him, a young man who had hardly attained the age of twenty-three years, his own chief successor.

How Shaykh Farid's intuitive intelligence (**nafs-i gira**) reached every crevice and corner of discipline's character may be gauged from the following incident. One day the Shaykh was teaching **ʿAwarif al-maʿarif** to his disciples. His manuscript had some errors of transcription and so he had to proceed slowly, correcting the mistakes and removing the inaccuracies. Nizam ad-din interrupted the Shaykh and said that Shaykh Najib ad-din Mutawakkil had a good manuscript of the book. Shaykh Farid was annoyed and irritated. "Has this **darwesh** no capacity of correcting a defective manuscript?" he exclaimed repeatedly. When Nizam ad-din realized that his master had disapproved of his remarks, he fell at Shaykh Farid's feet and humbly begged for forgiveness. But Shaykh Farid was in no mood to forgive. Nizam ad-din was overcome with deep grief. In extreme depression he even thought of commiting suicide and went into the wilderness, weeping and crying. Shaykh Farid's son, Shihab ad-din, who was his friend, interceded on his behalf and secured the Shaykh's pardon. Shaykh Farid called Nizam ad-din to his presence and remarked: "All this I have done for your perfection. . . . A pir (spiritual master) is a dresser of brides."[106] He then bestowed his special cloak on him.[107] On the face of it Shaykh Nizam ad-din's remark seems innocent, but Baba Farid's intuitive intelligence found in it a trace of that intellectual arrogance which distinctions and laurels in the academic circles of Delhi might have produced in him. He resorted to this admonition in order to eliminate it.

One day a classmate with whom Nizam ad-din had had academic discussions in Delhi happened to meet him in Ajodhan. The classmate was staying in an inn and had a servant to attend to his needs. Seeing Nizam ad-din in grimy and tattered clothes, he exclaimed: "Maulana Nizam ad-din! What misfortune has befallen you? Had you adopted teaching work at Delhi, you would have become a leading scholar of this age, enjoying affluent circumstances." Shaykh Nizam ad-din said nothing in reply but reported the matter to Shaykh Farid. "What would be your answer to such a question?" asked the Shaykh. "As the Shaykh directs," replied Nizam ad-din. "When you meet him next," replied Baba Farid, "recite the couplet, meaning

> You are not my traveling companion. Go, take your own path.
> May prosperity be your portion in life and misfortune mine."

The Shaykh further asked Nizam ad-din to get a tray of food from the kitchen and take it on his head to his friend. The friend came to see Shaykh Farid and was so charmed by his mystic ways that he decided to join his discipline.[108]

There were a number of delicate hints and suggestions of psychological significance involved in the way Shaykh Farid dealt with this matter. Their import was not lost on Nizam ad-din.

One day an old man came to Shaykh Farid and, while introducing himself, reminded the Shaykh that they had previously met in the **khanqah** of Shaykh Qutb ad-din Bakhtiyar Kaki. The old man was accompanied by his son, who was uncouth and insolent. He entered into an acrimonious discussion with the Shaykh and began to shout loudly. Nizam ad-din and the saint's son Maulana Shihab ad-din were at the door. When they heard the boy talking rudely to the saint, Maulana Shihab ad-din entered the room and slapped the boy on his face. The boy was about to strike at Maulana Shihab ad-din when Nizaṃ ad-din grabbed him by the hand. The Shaykh intervened, ordering his son to please the visitors. The Maulana gave some money to father and son, whereupon both left the **Jamaʿat khanah** happy and satisfied.[109]

Each one of these incidents of the **Jamaʿat khanah** of Shaykh Farid had a lesson for Nizam ad-din. No one could lead others on the path of spiritual discipline unless he was adequately educated in religious sciences and had developed an insight into shariʿat law. Arrogance and conceit were unknown to mystic life. Nobody was to leave the portals of the khanqah displeased or hurt. Shaykh Farid permitted his young disciple to write amulets and give them to people.[110] One day he picked up a hair that had fallen from the Shaykh's beard and obtained his permission to use it as amulet.[111]

Baba Farid fully realized the conditions of abject penury in which Nizam ad-din lived in Delhi. Once when he sought the Shaykh's permission to leave for Delhi, he gave him a gold coin (**ghiyathi**) for his expenses. Later Nizam ad-din came to know that this was the last coin in Shaykh Farid's house. At the iftar time Baba Farid had nothing to break his fast with. Nizam ad-din placed his master's gift at his feet. It was accepted with the remark: "I have prayed to God to grant you a portion of earthly goods." Nizam ad-din was worried at this lest worldly comforts destroy his spiritual personality. The Shaykh removed his anxiety by observing: "Don't be afraid. This will not entangle you in any trouble or calamity."[112] On 13 Ramadan 664/18 June 1266 Shaykh Farid conferred his **Khilafat Nama** on Nizam ad-din and granted him permission to enrol disciples. He prayed to God for his bright future and said: "You will be a tree under whose soothing shadow people will find comfort."[113] Overwhelmed by the kindness of his spiritual master, Nizam ad-din submitted:

> You have bestowed great honor on me and have nominated me your successor. This is a great treasure for me. But I am a student and dislike worldly connection and have looked at it with disdain. This position is very high and beyond my capacity to shoulder. . . . For me your kindness and favor is enough.

"This task will be efficiently performed by you," rejoined the Shaykh. But when he found Nizam ad-din still hesitant, Baba Farid had to insist, and in great excitement declared:

> Nizam! Take it from me; though I do not know if I will be honored before the Almighty or not, I promise not to enter paradise without your disciples in my company.[114]

Nizam ad-din had not the courage to utter a word further. He accepted the Shaykh's order and left for Delhi. Soon afterward Baba Farid, whose health had completely broken down as a result of continuous fasts, vigils, and penitences, fell seriously ill. A few days before his death Sayyid Muhammad Kirmani reached Ajodhan from Delhi. The saint lay on a cot inside his small room, while his sons and disciples were busy discussing at the door the problem of his successor. Sayyid Muhammad Kirmani expressed his desire to see the Shaykh but was not allowed. However, he pushed open the door of the room and fell at the feet of the Shaykh. The Shaykh opened his eyes and affectionately asked: "How are you, Sayyid? How and when did you come here?" "This very moment," replied Sayyid Muhammad. In the course of his conversation he referred to Shaykh Nizam ad-din and conveyed his respects. On hearing Shaykh Nizam ad-din's name, the Shaykh eagerly enquired: "How is he? Is he happy?" The Shaykh then entrusted all the articles of mystic regalia—prayer carpet, cloak, and staff—to Sayyid Muhammad with instructions to convey them to Shaykh Nizam ad-din. It was a great disappointment for the sons of the Shaykh.[115]

## Shaykh Nizam ad-din Awliya: Leadership and Lifestyle

### *At the Head of the Chishti Order*

It was at the age of twenty-three that Shaykh Nizam ad-din Awliya was appointed as his **khalifa** (successor) by Shaykh Farid and was directed to settle in Delhi and work for the expansion of this **silsilah,** or mystical order. It was a stupendous challenge to work in the capital of the empire without being involved in **shughl** (government service) or consorting with kings; to provide guidance to the disciples of the Great Shaykh spread far and wide; to push forward the work of the **silsilah** in regions still beyond the reach of the Delhi Sultans; and to evolve an effective mechanism to deal with those associated with the order. Shaykh Nizam ad-din not only rose to the occasion, he infused a new spirit into the Chishti organization. Addressing him Amir Khusrau once said:

> You have put the beads of Shaykh Farid in a rosary.
> It is on this count that your title has become Nizam (stringer of pearls).

In the course of time, as the result of Shaykh Nizam ad-din's efforts, the entire country came to be studded with **khanqahs** of the Chishti order. According to Muhammad Ghauthi Shattari, Shaykh Nizam ad-din sent 700 deputies (**khalifahs**) to different parts of the country and

> in a short time the fame of his spiritual excellence, his concern for his disciples and his interest in their spiritual culture, reached every corner of the land and every ear, and his **khalifahs** reached every province of the country to train the novice and to make perfect the initiated.[116]

### *The Khanqah*

The **Khanqah** of Shaykh Nizam ad-din Awliya stood by the side of the river Jamuna, whose cool refreshing breeze added to the serenity of its atmosphere. It comprised a big hall in the center and small rooms on its two sides. An old banyan tree stood in the courtyard, somewhat away from the center, but its branches provided shade to a part of the roof also. A veranda surrounded the courtyard, but its parts adjoining the hall were walled up for providing accommodation to senior inmates. Opposite the main gate was the gate room with a door on either side. A few men could sit there comfortably without obstructing the passage of others. Near it was the kitchen.

The Shaykh lived in a small room of wooden walls on the roof of the hall. During the day he had his rest in one of the small rooms in the main building. A low wall ran round the roof, but on the side of the courtyard the wall was raised higher to provide shade for the Shaykh and his visitors when they sat talking in the morning hours.

From early morning till late into the night, men from all walks of life and all strata of society—princes, nobles, officers, learned men and illiterates, villagers and town folk—came to pay their respects to the Shaykh. There were persons who came for a short visit just to meet the Shaykh and seek his blessings. There were others who lived in the **khanqah** permanently or temporarily and were of different categories: (1) elder disciples of the Shaykh, like the Kirmani family, the descendants of Maulana Badr ad-din Ishaq, and others; (2) nephews of the Shaykh who were under his guardianship; (3) disciples who came from different places and stayed there for different periods; and (4) those who managed the **khanqah** affairs, like Iqbal, Mubashshir, and others. Some of them had their families living in houses in the neighborhood while they themselves spent most of their time looking after the establishment. Iqbal, who looked after the **futuh** and managed the open kitchen (**langar**), had a house close by; Maulana Burhan ad-din Gharib supervised the preparation and distribution of food in the kitchen but had his house in the vicinity.[117]

Food was distributed to the visitors and inmates round the clock. Though the Shaykh lived on the upper story, he was not unaware of what went on in the **Jamaʿat khanah** below: While one window overlooked the Jamuna river, another opened directly onto the courtyard near the entrance.

The kitchen was a huge establishment, sufficient to supply food to thousands of people every day. Its vastness is indicated in the following story from the Lodi hagiographer Jamali. A pious saintly woman in the neighborhood who earned her livelihood by spinning thread sometimes sent him some flour. Once the Shaykh asked his disciple Kamal ad-din to mix it with water and put it in some vessel to boil. Just when the process of cooking was going on, a **darwesh** appeared and shouted: "If you have anything to eat, do not hold it from me." The Shaykh asked him to wait a little as the pot was boiling, but he was impatient. The Shaykh got up and, winding his sleeves round his hands, picked up the boiling pot and brought it to the **darwesh.** The **darwesh** lifted the pot and smashed it on the ground with the words: "Shaykh Farid had bestowed his spiritual blessings on Shaykh Nizam ad-din. I break the vessel of his material poverty." It is said that thereafter enormous **futuh** (unasked-for gifts) began to pour into his **khanqah.**[118] According to Shaykh Nasir ad-din Chiragh-i Delhi, so much **futuh** came to him that it appeared as if a tributary of Jamuna had been bearing gifts afloat![119]

Since **futuh** also included edibles, the kitchen stores were always overflowing with articles of food. According to the rules of the **khanqah,** these provisions could not be kept in the store for longer than a week. The Shaykh's instructions were to clean and sweep the stores every week, lest there arise an atmosphere of hoarding or accumulation that countermanded the spirit of resignation to God's will.

The author of **Qiwam al-ʿaqaʾid** gives us some idea of the menu served in the **khanqah.** During the time of Sultan ʿAla ad-din Khalji, when rationing and control rules were in force, the Shaykh's establishment also came under scrutiny. A number of spies visited the **khanqah** to watch how much food was prepared and distributed. When the Shaykh came to know of their intentions, he instructed his attendants to increase the number of items on the menu! It appears that Sultan ʿAla ad-din Khalji later exempted the **khanqah** from the regulations in general effect.[120]

*Musical Assemblies*

**Samaʿ** (lit., **majalis-e samaʿ**, or assemblies of listening, but for Sufis a special kind of listening was required, namely, listening to spiritual music in a collective gathering organized for that purpose) was a regular feature of the **khanqah** of Shaykh Nizam ad-din Awliya.[121] Mystic music was introduced and popularized in Delhi by Qazi Hamid ad-din Nagauri.[122] According to Maulana Burhan ad-din Gharib, an intoxicated mystic (**majdhub**) had predicted about Shaykh Nizam ad-din Awliya that he would give effulgence to the Qazi's work.[123] It was in the closing years of his life that Ghiyath ad-din Tughluq, under pressure from the ʿ**ulama,** placed certain restrictions on music parties in public. The Shaykh's routine was not disturbed and **samaʿ** remained spiritual nourishment for him throughout his life. The public was so enchanted by his **samaʿ** gatherings that, according to Amir Khurd:

> Any verse or tune which affected the Shaykh during the audition would become popular among the people for a long time, and the young and the old, the nobles and commons, at their meetings and in the quarters and lanes of the city, would enjoy them through the blessings of the Shaykh.[124]

The Shaykh was, however, very strict in enforcing certain conditions for audition parties.[125] One day he came to know about the use of musical instruments by some of his disciples. He disapproved of it and said: "Of what use are singers and musical instruments to a man who is a stranger to cosmic emotions?"[126]

*The **Jamaʿat khanah*** as a welfare center

The **Jamaʿat khanah** of the Shaykh served as a welfare center for the entire locality. It helped and supported numerous groups living in the neighborhood. To give some concrete examples: One day some houses in Ghiyathpur caught fire. It was a very hot summer day. The Shaykh rushed to the roof of his house barefoot and stood there till the fire was completely extinguished. He then deputed Iqbal to count the houses that had been burnt. He sent to every house two silver coins (**tankas**), two trays of food, and one pitcher of cold water. In those days two silver coins sufficed for buying all the essentials for a household.[127]

Another day the Shaykh saw an old woman drawing water from a well near the river Jamuna. He stopped and inquired from the woman: "Since the Jamuna is so near, why do you take the trouble of drawing water from this well?" The woman replied: "I have an old, destitute husband. We have nothing to eat. The water of the Jamuna is very tasty and induces hunger. Because it quickens our appetite, I do not take water from the river." The Shaykh was deeply shaken at this explanation. Returning to the **khanqah,** he summoned Iqbal and said: "Lalla! In our Ghiyathpur there is a woman so poverty-stricken that she does not drink Jamuna water for fear of getting hungry. Go to her house, find out her daily needs, and every month without fail give her that amount."[128] On another occasion, hearing about an imminent Mongol invasion, large numbers of people from adjacent areas flocked to the **khanqah** of Shaykh Nizam ad-din. They sought refuge within its walls, and the Shaykh did not disappoint them. He provided both food and shelter to these people. At the same time, disciples who had come to see him from distant places were asked to shorten their stay in the **khanqah** and to return home.[129]

### *Daily Routine*

Shaykh Nizam ad-din Awliya followed an extremely busy but highly regulated schedule. His program was adjusted according to the time fixed for the obligatory prayers (**namaz**). Since he fasted almost regularly he woke up in the wee hours of the morning when those who fast throughout the day eat something. He took very little at that time and when the attendant, Khwaja ʿAbd al-Rahim, insisted on his taking more, he replied with tears in his eyes: "So many poor and destitute people are sleeping in the corners of mosques and on the platforms of shops! They have nothing to eat for dinner. How can this food go down my throat?"[130]

In the morning hours the Shaykh met visitors on the roof of the **khanqah.** He offered his mid-day prayers in the community hall below. After the prayers, he retired to his room on the upper story and continued to meet visitors there. After offering afternoon prayers (ʿ**asr**), he again granted interviews and continued to meet with people up to sunset.

At the time of breaking the fast (**iftar**), the Shaykh again came down to the community hall. He ate a piece of bread with some vegetable and distributed the rest to those present. During the summer days soon after breaking his fast he would go to his room upstairs. In winter days he would retire to his room on the ground floor. He granted interviews to the visitors till the time for night prayers (**ʿisha**). Dinner was served upstairs. The Shaykh himself took very little but asked others to enjoy the dinner. The night prayers were offered in congregation in the hall below. Thereafter the visitors left and the Shaykh returned to his room upstairs. There he busied himself in his devotions for some time. Then he would sit down on his cot for rest and a rosary would be brought to him by his personal attendant. Amir Khurd informs us that at that time none except Amir Khusrau could remain in the presence of the saint. The poet, who was always full of reports, news, and reviews, would talk about different matters as the Shaykh approvingly nodded his head. Sometimes the Shaykh would ask: "What more, O Turk?" and Khusrau would expound on different matters. At this time the Shaykh also met some of his relations. When all had left, Iqbal would come and bring some water for ablution and retire. The Shaykh then bolted the door. Nobody had access to him thereafter, but inmates could see the light in his room burning through the silent hours of the night.[131] Most of his time at night was spent in vigil. He once told a disciple that in the small hours of the morning some verses would come to his mind and fill his soul with joy. Blessed with good eyesight, he could easily read closely written manuscripts by candle light.[132]

Though the Shaykh followed his schedule meticulously, he was always available to visitors who came to him at odd hours. One day he told Amir Hasan Sizji, the compiler of **Fawaʾid al-Fuʾad:** "It is customary among Shaykhs that no one goes to them except between sun-rise (**ishraq**) and mid-day (**zuhr**) prayers. But it is not so with me. Anybody can come at any time:

In the lanes of taverns and the inns of vagabonds
There is no restriction—come, sit and be at home."[133]

The Shaykh never maintained good health.[134] Vigils and fasts had their effect on his well-being. He nevertheless lived to the ripe old age of eighty-three and, barring his final illness, retained an acute intelligence and remarkable comprehension of problems.

*Attitude towards the State*

Shaykh Nizam ad-din's spiritual mentor Shaykh Farid Ganj-i Shakar had clearly warned his followers: "If you desire elevation in your spiritual ranks, keep away from hereditary princes."[135] Shaykh Nizam ad-din sincerely acted on this advice and firmly instructed his senior disciples: "You will not go to the door of kings nor will you seek rewards from them."[136]

The Shaykh himself gave a wide berth to the rulers of his day and neither visited their courts nor accepted their grants. Sultan Jalal ad-din Khalji offered him some villages, which he declined to accept.[137] The Sultan then sought an interview with the Shaykh but was turned down. He then thought of a surprise visit. "My house has two doors," warned the Shaykh; "if the Sultan enters by one I will make my exit by the other."[138]

While the Shaykh closed his door to Sultans, he could not stop nobles and merchants, government officials and army officers, as well as others from visiting him and from seeking his blessings. The Shaykh was, however, in his highest spirits among the poor and the destitute. When thronged by nobles and soldiers, he sadly remarked: "These people waste the time of this **faqir.**" Nevertheless many upper-class Muslims, including princes and nobles, joined his spiritual discipline.[139]

When ʿAla ad-din Khalji came to power (in A.D. 1296), Shaykh Nizam ad-din Awliya's fame and popularity was as its apogee. All sorts of people—elites and nonelites—visited his hospice and sought his blessings. Some courtiers cleverly hinted to the Sultan that the saint's popularity could turn into a political danger. The Sidi Maula incident could be noted as confirmation of this suspicion.[140] To ascertain the saint's intentions, ʿAla ad-din wrote a letter to him offering to be guided by his advice in all matters. The Shaykh did not even care to open this letter, which was brought by Khizr Khan. "We **dervishes** have nothing to do with the affairs of state," he replied. "I have settled in a corner away from the men of the city and spend my time in praying for the Sultan and other Muslims. If the Sultan does not like this, let him tell me so. I will go and live elsewhere. God's earth is vast enough."[141] This reply convinced the Sultan that the Shaykh had no political ambitions. In the course of time he came to develop great faith in the Shaykh.[142]

The author of **Qiwam al-ʿAqaʾid** supplies interesting details in this regard. The Sultan made all sorts of investigations and probes—he sent spies to the **khanqah,** enquiring about visitors, about the food served there, about the general atmosphere of the **Jamaʿat khanah.** Eventually he was satisfied that the Shaykh had nothing worldly about him and was working for the spiritual enlightenment of the Muslims of his time. He then requested Shaykh Nizam ad-din to admit his two sons—Khizr Khan and Shadi Khan—into his discipline. To honor the Shaykh he arranged a big feast in which the princes personally served the food. The mother of these princes also sought the Shaykh's blessings.

ʿAla ad-din's son and successor Mubarak Khalji, however, became suspicious and ill-disposed toward the Shaykh[143] because Khizr Khan was his disciple. He spoke ill about the Shaykh in open court (**durbar**), trying to incite people to assassinate him at the same time that he tried to stop nobles from visiting him. Since the Shaykh enjoyed immense popularity, it was not possible to take any direct action against him. The extent to which nobles ignored the Sultan's wishes may be gauged from the example of Amir Khusrau, a court poet of Sultan Mubarak. Notwithstanding the Sultan's hostile attitude toward the saint, he did not hesitate to praise his spiritual mentor in **Nuh Sipihr,** an epic poem written expressly for the Sultan. It was natural to presume that the saint would have resented the Sultan's animosity, and credulous piety of the age attributed to the Shaykh's curses—which he never uttered against anyone—the assassination of Mubarak Khalji. (The latter event was, in fact, due to a Parwari coup.)

It was under the influence of the ʿ**ulama** that Ghiyath ad-din Tughluq objected to the audition parties of the Shaykh.[144] He even summoned the Shaykh to a religious council (**mahzar**) to explain his position. As the Tughluq Sultan had come to power by mobilizing religious support, he could not possibly reject out of hand the opposition of the ʿ**ulama** to Sufi audition parties. Yet the details of the episode, as given by Amir Khurd, show no ostensible hostility of feelings between the Sultan and the saint. The atmosphere in which the proceedings of the **mahzar** were conducted, especially the disregard the externalist scholars showed to the Traditions of the Prophet cited by the Shaykh in support of his practice, did disappoint and even depress Nizam ad-din, but it was the ʿ**ulama** and not the Sultan whom he criticized. The story that the Sultan had sent a message to the Shaykh from Bengal ordering him to quit Delhi before the royal party's return, and the Shaykh's alleged remark "Delhi is still far off,"[145] both seem highly improbable. The Sultan's death took place due to the fall of a wooden pavilion hastily constructed by his son to celebrate his return. The Sultan did not die immediately, but during the period that he was seriously ill and lay in bed in a state of semi-consciousness, it is unlikely[146] that the Sultan would have sent any message to the Shaykh or that the latter would have replied to it cryptically foreboding disaster for the monarch.

## SHAYKH NIZAM AD-DIN AWLIYA: DEATH AND INFLUENCE

### *Death of the Shaykh*

Shaykh Nizam ad-din Awliya breathed his last on 18 Rabiʿ al-Thani A.H. 725/3 April 1325. Shaykh Rukn a-Din Abul Fath, the famous Suhrawardi saint of Multan, led his funeral prayer. He was laid to rest, as he had desired, in an open space.[147] Sultan Muhammad bin Tughluq built a dome over it.[148] The **Jamaʿat khanah** mosque near the tomb is wrongly attributed to Khizr Khan.[149] It was constructed by Firuz Shah Tughluq, who specifically refers to it in his **Futuhat.**[150]

### *Place in Mystic History*

Shaykh Nizam ad-din Awliya occupies a unique place in the history of institutional Sufism in South Asia. During the 665 years that have elapsed since his death, kings, conquerors, nobles, scholars, saints, and all segments of the population—Hindus and Muslims alike—have visited his tomb in search of blessings and benediction. The spiritual organization that he set up flourished in almost all parts of India—from Kashmir to Kerala, from Lahore to Lakhnauti. Malwa, Gujarat, Rajputana, and kingdoms of the Deccan saw his spiritual order in full bloom. Hundreds of khanqahs in south India owe their affiliation to his order. Long before the Deccan experiment of Muhammad bin Tughluq he sent Khwaja ʿAziz ad-din to Deogir to propagate the Chishti discipline.[151] Subsequently Shaykh Burhan ad-din Gharib, Maulana Fakhr ad-din Zarradi, Amir Hasan Sijzi, Sayyid Yusuf (father of Sayyid Muhammad

Gesu Daraz), and others migrated to the Deccan and played an important role in organizing the Sufi movement there.[152] The founder of the Bahmanid Kingdom, ʿAla ad-din Hasan Bahman Shah, considered his throne to be a gift from Shaykh Nizam ad-din. It is said that when Hasan saw the Shaykh in Delhi, the latter gave him a breadcrumb pressed on one of his fingers, commending it as the banner of his future Sultanate.[153] When fortune brought Hasan to the throne, the first thing that he did was to send Shaykh Burhan ad-din Gharib five maunds of gold and ten maunds of silver to be distributed among the needy and the poor as a blessing on the soul of Shaykh Nizam ad-din Awliya.[154] Several compilations of the conversations of Shaykh Burhan ad-din Gharib[155] popularized the traditions of Shaykh Nizam ad-din in the south. Later, Sayyid Muhammad Gesu Daraz of Gulbarga wrote a number of books—among them commentaries, summaries, and translations—that articulated the thought of both Shaykh Nizam ad-din and earlier saints to whom he had looked for inspiration and guidance.[156]

In Bengal the saints of Laknauti and Pandua were his spiritual descendants. Shaykh Nur Qutb-i Alam, who became the focal point for the spiritual life of the people of Bengal, was a spiritual descendant of Akhi Siraj,[157] himself a disciple of Shaykh Nizam ad-din Awliya. Sayyid Ashraf Jahangir Simnani, Maulana Husam ad-din Manikpuri, and a host of other saints of Bengal and Bihar were spiritually connected with Shaykh Nizam ad-din Awliya.[158] Books taken from Shaykh Nizam ad-din's library by Maulana Akhi Siraj formed the nucleus of the first Chishti center in Bengal.

In Gujarat, Shaykh Sayyid Hasan, Shaykh Husam ad-din Multani, and Shah Barak Allah—three distinguished disciples of Shaykh Nizam ad-din Awliya—played an important role in spreading the mystic ideology of Shaykh Nizam ad-din Awliya. Subsequently, Shaykh Kamal ad-din ʿAllama, Shaykh Siraj ad-din, Shaykh Rajan, and Shaykh Yahya Madani kept the torch of the Chishti **silsilah** burning in Gujarat.[159]

In Malwa, Shaykh Wajih ad-din Yusuf, Shaykh Kamal ad-din, and Maulana Mughis ad-din, three gifted disciples of Shaykh Nizam ad-din, dedicated their lives to the propagation of Chishti principles and practices.[160] There was hardly any part of Hindustan that was not visited by disciples of Shaykh Nizam ad-din Awliya, and the majority of them initiated brisk activity for spreading the mystic ideals embodied in **Fawaʾid al-Fuʾad.**

Eminent saints of other spiritual orders also paid eloquent tribute to the Shaykh, lauding, above all, his dedication to the service of others. Shaykh Rukn ad-din Multani of the Suhrawardiya referred to him as "King of Religion";[161] Shaykh Sharaf ad-din Yahya Maneri of the Firdausiya acknowledged his stage of mystic consciousness to be one where sleep and wakefulness had become equivalent;[162] and in the **khanqah** of Shaykh Ahmad Maghribi of Ahmadabad respectful references were often made to the same Chishti standard bearer, Shaykh Nizam ad-din Awliya.[163]

*The Scholar*

Shaykh Nizam ad-din was, by all standards, an erudite scholar of his age. He had learnt at the feet of distinguished scholars from Badaon and Delhi; he had kept himself abreast of all developments in the academic and intellectual life of the capital city of the Delhi Sultanate. To the last days of his life he retained his interest in books and spent some hours at night in quiet study, making summaries, taking down notes, and writing his own comments. During the very early years of his stay in Delhi, his only property was his books; they were transported on the heads of people to the mosque. It appears that the Shaykh had endowed his library not only for his own use but also for the use of his disciples since, as mentioned above, books from his library were taken by Akhi Siraj to Lakhnauti.

The only composition from the pen of Shaykh Nizam ad-din Awliya that has reached us is an Arabic **khutba** that is "still recited in the pulpits at many Indian mosques." Dr. M. G. Zubaid Ahmad remarks about this **khutba** that it "has been much appreciated throughout India on account of the elegance of the style coupled with the heart burning expression of a lover's zeal and enthusiasm for the Divine love, contained therein. . . . Its style is elegant and at the same time sublime."[164]

Shaykh Nizam ad-din's scholarship was reflected in his academic discussions. It was a well-integrated and thoroughly assimilated knowledge. He was known among his contemporaries not only for his piety but also for his scholarship. In fact, it was his scholarship that attracted to his fold eminent intellectuals like Maulana Fakhr ad-din Zarradi, Maulana Shams ad-din Yahya, Maulana Wajih ad-din Pa'ili, and Shaykh Nasir ad-din Chiragh-i Delhi, among others.

Shaykh Nizam ad-din's special field of interest was **hadith** (Traditions of the Prophet). He was esteemed by the scholars of Delhi as a great **muhaddith,** and his cogent, clear exposition of Prophetic Traditions was admired by specialists. In view of his keen interest in **hadith,** Amir Khurd has devoted a separate section to this topic in **Siyar al-awliya,** as has the author of **Durar-i Nizami.**

It appears that the Shaykh also used to set aside some days for exclusive discussions about **hadith.**[165] Qazi Muhyi ad-din Kashani was a regular participant in his lectures on **hadith.** As he had committed the Mashariq al-Anwar to memory,[166] he may be credited with having more than two thousand traditions of the Prophet at his fingertips. His knowledge of **hadith** and, what is more, his anxiety to make people follow the Path of the Prophet (**sunnah**) meticulously in every detail of life, is evident from **Fawa'id al-Fu'ad.**

*Personal Impact*

Shaykh Nizam ad-din Awliya was one of the most charismatic personalities of his age. A scholar with deep insight into religious sciences—particularly the Qur'an and the **hadith**; a saint whose vigils and fasts cast an aura of serene spirituality round his face; a humanist who spent all his time attending to the problems of the downtrodden and the destitute; a pacifist who believed in nonviolence and returning evil with good—the Shaykh represented in his person the highest traditions of morality, mysticism, and religion. For more than half a century his **khanqah** in Delhi was a sanctuary of peace for people in search of spiritual solace. His mission in life was to cultivate a personal relationship with the Creator by expounding a worldview that transcended, and encouraged others to transcend, every narrow and parochial consideration.

Tall and handsome, fair in complexion, with a fully grown beard, curly hair, and red, sleep-laden eyes,[167] he had an aura of spiritual calm and majesty surrounding his face. Such a glow radiated from him that it dazzled the vision of others, leading them to keep their eyes fixed to the ground.[168] Amir Khusrau felt so nervous in his presence that he went out again and again to regain his composure.[169]

Throughout the day Shaykh Nizam ad-din attended to the problems of other people: He assuaged their woes, he reduced their worries, he lifted their drooping spirits. One day Khwaja 'Aziz ad-din told the Shaykh about an after-dinner conversation at a feast he had attended.

People there had said that Shaykh Nizam ad-din had no worries in life because whatever others longed for came to him unasked. On hearing this the Shaykh remarked:

> Nobody in this world has more worries than I. So many people come to me, confiding in me their woes, their worries. All these accounts of misery and sorrow sear my heart and weigh down my soul.[170]

Instead of expounding on the lofty principles of mysticism as nuanced by great Sufi theorists, he illustrated in his person the accumulated wisdom of the mystic tradition. He used to say that what the **ʿulama** proclaim through speech, the Sufis express through their behavior.[171] He immensely enhanced the impact of his teachings through frequent recourse to self-scrutiny and self-criticism. He would find something wrong with himself even when others were intent to do wrong to him. One day a visitor treated him with great rudeness and insolence. He remained cool and patient throughout. When the person finally left, he told the audience that perhaps the visitor had been sent by God to correct him: Since large numbers of people came and placed their heads at his feet, it tended to create some pride in him. By contrast, people such as the just departed detractor cleansed the heart of pride![172]

Khalji imperialism had brought in its wake vices and profligacy in social life. Pimps, prostitutes, ruffians, vagabonds, **ibahatis**,[173] magicians, gamblers—all sorts of people plied their abominable trade. Amir Khusrau has described in some detail the moral depravity and promiscuity prevalent at this time.[174] The Shaykh threw himself headlong into the work of moral reform and regeneration.

One day a man was caught in the **Jamaʿat khanah** carrying a knife, probably with the intention of doing harm to somebody. The inmates bound him and wanted to reprimand him severely. The Shaykh intervened. Summoning the man before him, he elicited his solemn promise that he would not injure anybody. Then the Shaykh dismissed him with some money.[175] In this way did he use his quiet and persuasive methods[176] to extricate people from the quagmire of sin and immorality. The Sultan, by contrast, adopted Draconian methods to deal with libertinism and licentiousness. The Sultan forced prostitutes to marry,[177] while the Shaykh sent them subsistence money to wean them away from their abominable trade.[178] The Sultan ordered drunkards to be beaten with sticks and thrown into wells specially dug for that purpose in front of the Badaon Gate; the Shaykh attracted them to a moral life[179] through his large-hearted tolerance, which hated the sin and not the sinner. "If we ignore the sinner and the miscreant, who will look after them?" Such was the approach of the Chishti saints, and Shaykh Nizam ad-din sincerely adopted it.[180] Referring to the two entirely antithetical methods of reform and reclamation adopted by the Shaykh and the Sultan, the contemporary historian Ziya ad-din Barani writes:

> On the one side, Sultan ʿAla ad-din for the security and welfare of his state had by terror, force, punishments, insistent severities, chains and imprisonment, forbidden intoxicants and other prohibited things that are the means to sinfulness and wickedness. . . . On the other hand, Shaykh Nizam ad-din had during those very days opened wide the doors of his discipleship. He gave the patched frock (**khirqa**) to sinners, administered the oath of repentance to them and accepted them as his disciples. . . . The consciousness of being a discipleship of the Shaykh prevented people from doing things forbidden. . . . Men and women, old and young, shopkeepers and the general public, slaves, servants and boys of young age began saying their prayers. Probably most disciples of the Shaykh considered the post sunrise (**ishraq**) and forenoon (**chasht**) prayers necessary. . . . The hearts of elites and nonelites became inclined towards good (thoughts) and good deeds. . . . The inclination of the Shaykh's disciples . . . favored towards books on the mystic path (**suluk**). . . . The **Fawa'id al-Fu'ad** of Amir Hasan found many purchasers because it contained the conversations of Shaykh Nizam ad-din.[181]

Shaykh Nizam ad-din Awliya continued his moral mission with the same dedication for about a decade after the death of Sultan ʿAla ad-din Khalji. During this period his overriding concern was to reduce human misery and to extricate people from sin and immorality. He remained indifferent to the political upheavals of the Delhi Sultanate. During his lifetime three major dynasties and a dozen rulers appeared on the throne. Each disappeared like an iridescent bubble, while he continued to proclaim moral principles that have endured the test of time.

Though more than six centuries separate his epoch from ours, a world of historic memories looms large at the mere mention of his name. The life story of Shaykh Nizam ad-din Awliya provides an alternative vision to the political intrigues of the period, just as the pomp and panoply of the court, the din and clatter of arms on the battlefield, contrast with the meditative saint, now laughing, now crying, ever at prayer with the One, happiest in discourse with the poor.

## Amir Hasan Sijzi, The Compiler

Amir Hasan ʿAlaʾ-i Sijzi, the compiler of **Fawaʾid al-Fuʾad,** was a devoted disciple of Shaykh Nizam ad-din Awliya. On account of his poetic excellence he was known as the "Saʿdi of Hindustan,"[182] and all the great Indo-Persian poets, including Amir Khusrau and Faizi, paid their tribute to his muse. The contemporary historian Zia ad-din Barani, who knew him intimately, had this to say about him:

> The second incomparable poet of ʿAla ad-din's reign [in addition to Amir Khusau] was Amir Hasan Sijzi. He has plenty of works in prose and verse and has been a model in perspicuity and fluency of speech . . . he has composed many ecstatic **ghazals** of great fluency, . . . (he) was adorned with many praiseworthy qualities and moral virtues. I have seldom seen any one like him in subtle and witty conversation in assemblies, in ready knowledge concerning the Sultans, great men and scholars of Delhi, in firmness of reason, judgment and mystic way of life, in contentment and sincere faith, in living happily and passing his days happily without worldly goods, and in keeping aloof from all worldly ties. . . . Owing to the firm faith which Amir Hasan had in Shaykh Nizam ad-din, he has collected in a few volumes the exact words he heard from the Shaykh in his assemblies during the period of his discipleship. To this work he has given the name of **Fawaʾid al-Fuʾad.** In these days **Fawaʾid al-Fuʾad** has become a work of guidance for sincere disciples. Amir Hasan has some **diwans** as well as numerous works in prose and a large number of **mathnawis.** He was such a pleasant companion, witty, carefree, considerate, cultured and polite, that I have found more joy and happiness in his company than in the company of any one else.[183]

Born in Badaon in 652/1254,[184] Hasan received his early education in his native town. Later he moved to Delhi, where he completed his education. He was hardly thirteen years of age when he started composing amorous verses. His collection of poems (**diwan**) breathes poetic sensitivity of a very high order. In fact, in Hasan poetry becomes what Carlyle calls "musical thought"—thought that sings itself, emotions that dance in rhythm, and feelings that move in tune and time as naturally as the heart beats. Shaykh Nizam ad-din Awliya used to compare the poetic talent of Khusrau and Hasan with the following analogy: "Our Khusrau is like a saltish river, while Hasan is like a sweetish rivulet."[185]

Both Barani and Amir Khurd have referred to his prolific literary output, but unfortunately most of his writings have perished. Besides **Fawa'id al-Fu'ad,** the following compositions of Hasan have survived:

1. A **diwan** (collection of poems) edited by Mas'ud 'Ali Mahvi and published from Hyderabad (A.H. 1352).

2. A prose elegy on the death of Prince Muhammad, copied by Yahya Sirhindi[186] and by 'Abd al-Qadir Badaoni[187] in their works.

3. A book of mystic aphorisms, **Mukh al-Maani,** available only in manuscript,[188] though its contexts were appreciatively noted by Shaykh Nizam ad-din Awliya.[189]

It appears that in his early years Hasan led a life free from either self-restraint or moderation; he perhaps indulged in drinking also. It is very significant that in the opening discussion of **Fawa'id al-Fu'ad** the Shaykh talks about repentance and sin, declaring that one who has committed no sin and one who has sincerely repented from past sins have equal position on the Sufi Path. Keeping in view the Shaykh's methods of instruction, we may regard this discussion as motivated by a desire on the part of Nizam ad-din to console Hasan's heart after he had repented.

Perhaps it was awareness of Hasan's libertine youth that led later writers to build up fascinating but fantastic stories about his repentance. Jamali, the author of **Siyar al-'Arifin,** says that once, when the Shaykh was returning from Mehrauli after visiting the mausoleum of Khwaja Qutb ad-din Bakhtiyar Kaki (the master of his master, Shaykh Farid ad-din), he saw Hasan drinking wine with his companions on the bank of the Hauz-i Shamsi. Hasan, says Jamali, was an acquaintance of the Shaykh and had known him from his Badaon days. Inebriated and blustering, he looked at the Shaykh, and recited verses meaning:

We know each other as friends;
If association exercises any effect, where is it?
Your piety has not diminished my sinfulness;
What is more powerful—your piety or my sinfulness?

The Shaykh took pity on his condition and remarked: "Society does have its effect." This brief comment of the Shaykh touched Hasan's heart. Falling at the feet of the Shaykh, he repented of his sins and joined the band of disciplines at Ghiyathpur. According to Jamali, Hasan was seventy-three years of age at that time.[190] Sometimes a verse of Hasan, meaning

O Hasan! you have repented at an age
When the capacity for sinning was no longer in you.

is also cited to prove that he repented only at an advanced age.

There are, however, several difficulties in this account. (1) Hasan could not have been seventy-three years of age at this time because we find him accompanying the royal army in later years. How could a septuagenarian be employed in the army and also take part in a long, difficult campaign, such as that in the Deccan surely was? (2) If the year 707/1307–1308, with which **Fawa'id al-Fu'ad** begins, or even a year earlier[191] be taken as the date of the change in Hasan's life-style, it is difficult to accept the claim that he was publicly drinking wine at **Hauz-i Shamsi,** for ʿAla ad-din Khalji had issued strict prohibitionary orders, and it is inconceivable that a member of the court could have flouted them with impunity. (3) There could have been no contact between the Shaykh and Hasan dating back to Badaon days since the Shaykh left Badaon for Delhi in circa 652/1254–1255, the very year that Hasan was born.

There is a quite different Hasan who emerges from the pages of **Fawa'id al-Fu'ad.** He is not as old as Jamali would have us believe. He was continuously employed in the army, perhaps as an ordinary army officer. He lived in the cantonment area, an area the fresh air and cleanliness of which the Shaykh also liked.[192]

The **Fawa'id al-Fu'ad** contains some interesting references to Hasan's life: (1) One day he apologized to the Shaykh for his inability to go to the mosque to offer congregational prayers as there was no one to look after his books and papers in his absence. (2) There were occasions in his life when he was in financial difficulties due to delay in the payment of his army salary. He sought the Shaykh's permission to accept unasked for money proffered by a friend. (3) The Shaykh prescribed litanies to him gradually, but only after ensuring that whatever had been suggested earlier had become a normal routine for Hasan. This indicates that Hasan's nature took time to be made fully amenable to the litanies and practices the Shaykh prescribed for his disciples and, as we noted above, the Shaykh never overburdened a disciple with spiritual practices and litanies beyond his capacity. (4) Hasan set free his household slave Malih as a result of the Shaykh's teachings.

Hasan's literary achievements were beyond doubt. He was a fulgent poet, an impressive prose writer, and a brilliant conversationist. He could transform the Shaykh's conversations into a work of art, but he had to sacrifice the exuberance of his literary art at the altar of the Shaykh's anxiety for a straightforward and truthful recording of his conversations. The style of **Fawa'id al-Fu'ad** is impressive because of its utter simplicity; except for the paeans to the Shaykh that open each section, it eschews any attempt at embellishment or rhetorical force. This was due to the Shaykh's intervention: Since he frequently checked the record of Hasan and filled the lacunae, truthful recording became Hasan's forte. No one has ever challenged the statements attributed to Shaykh Nizam ad-din in **Fawa'id al-Fu'ad.**

Impelled by profound love and respect for his master, Hasan undertook this work, little knowing that he was creating a tradition in mystic literature or introducing a new genre for the communication of mystic ideas and practices. Other disciples were inspired by his example, and themselves made a number of collections of the Shaykh's conversations. Among the most noteworthy are the following:

1. **Durar-i Nizami,** by ʿAli Jandar
2. **Malfuzat,** by Khwaja Shams ad-din Bihari[193]
3. **Anwar al-Majalis,** by Khwaja Muhammad[194]
4. **Hasrat Namah,** by Ziya ad-din Barani[195]
5. **Tuhfat al-Abrar wa Karamat al-Akhyar,** by Khwaja ʿAziz ad-din Sufi.[196]

Except **Durar-i Nizami**[197] no other **malfuz** is available now. ʿAli Jandar had written one further book, **Khulasat al-Lata'if,**[198] but it is extinct. The **Durar-i Nizami** throws valuable light on the life, thought, and personality of Shaykh Nizam ad-din Awliya. It reveals the extent of his interest in **hadith** literature. With economy of language, ʿAli Jandar has presented the moral and religious teachings of the Shaykh. Yet **Fawa'id al-Fu'ad** reflects greater understanding of the depth of the Shaykh's thought and combines brevity of expression with repeated, unflagging insight. As its arrangement is *ad hominem* and the discussions vary in both length and content, each section reflects a natural and realistic flow. While the **Durar** presents systematized information, covering a number of important religious problems, **Fawa'id al-Fu'ad** offers a record of the general meetings of the Shaykh in which the direction of discussion changes frequently. Its unplanned, often unexpected twists are as authentic as they are captivating. Except for **Fawa'id al-Fu'ad,** no other collection of his conversations was seen or approved by the Shaykh. Referring to the way **Fawa'id al-Fu'ad** was compiled, Shaykh Burhan ad-din Gharib once informed his audience in the Deccan that whenever the Shaykh narrated any anecdote and Hasan happened to be there, the former would turn his face toward the latter, suggesting that it could and should be noted down.[199]

Two early biographical accounts of Shaykh Nizam ad-din Awliya that also contain references to his teachings are **Qiwam al-'Aqa'id** and **Siyar al-Awliya.**

**Qiwam al-'Aqa'id**[200] was compiled by Muhammad Jamal Qiwam in 755/1354 when Sultan Abul Muzaffar Bahman Shah (r.1347–1358), the first Bahmanid Sultan, was on the throne. The author was the grandson of Shaykh Shams al-'Arifin, a disciple of Shaykh Nizam ad-din Awliya. The **Qiwam al-'Aqa'id** supplies some interesting bits of information and brings into focus the respectful attitude of Sultan 'Ala ad-din Khalji and his nobles toward the Shaykh. Until the present Introduction, this biography has not been used to supplement other sources in reconstructing Shaykh Nizam ad-din Awliya's life. Despite its systematic format, **Qiwam al-'Aqa'id** fails to cover every aspect of the Shaykh's life. Chiefly it records the author's recollections about the master as he was remembered, with great affection and respect, by his disciples in the Deccan.

The most comprehensive biography of the Shaykh, setting forth also his views on a variety of topics, was compiled by Sayyid Muhammad bin Mubarak Kirmani, known as Amir or Mir Khurd. Compiled between 752–790/1351–1382, it was titled **Siyar al-Awliya.**[201] Amir Khurd's ancestors were closely associated with both Shaykh Farid ad-din Ganj-i Shakar and Shaykh Nizam ad-din Awliya. The author himself was a disciple of the Shaykh and had close personal contact with almost all the principal **khalifahs** and relatives of the Shaykh. The **Siyar al-Awliya** incorporates also brief accounts of the elder saints of the Chishti **silsilah.** It is the most reliable and authentic record of the life and ideology of Chishti masters, particularly Shaykh Nizam ad-din Awliya and his spiritual descendants. The author has freely drawn from **Fawa'id al-Fu'ad** in reconstructing the ideological profile of the Shaykh. The last part of **Siyar al-Awliya** deftly consolidates Nizam ad-din's views on significant religious topics.

Other **malfuzat,** such as **Rahat al-Qulub, Rahat al-Muhibbin,** and **Afzal al-Fawa'id,** have been attributed to Shaykh Nizam ad-din Awliya. They are apocryphal in nature. Shaykh Nizam ad-din Awliya protests in **Fawa'id al-Fu'ad** about the genuineness of this literature. Even a hurried comparison of any or all of them with the tone and tenor of **Fawa'id al-Fu'ad** reveals what a vast chasm separates the content and methodology of the real **malfuzat** from simulacra.[202]

Some of the **malfuzat** of the spiritual successors of Shaykh Nizam ad-din Awliya contain valuable information about the Shaykh. Particular reference may be made to **Khair al-Majalis,**[203] the conversations of his principal successor, Shaykh Nasir ad-din Chiragh-i Dehli, compiled by Hamid Qalandar. In the Deccani a family of three brothers—Hammad, Rukn ad-din, and Majd ad-din, sons of Maulana 'Imad Kashani—prepared several collections of the conversations of Shaykh Burhan ad-din Gharib, a senior disciple of Shaykh Nizam ad-din Awliya. Hammad wrote **Ahsan al-Aqwal,**[204] Rukn ad-din prepared **Nafa'is al-Anfas,**[205] and **Shama'il al-Atqiya,**[206] while **Ghara'ib al-Karamat**[207] and **Baqiyat al-Ghara'ib**[208] were compiled by Majd ad-din. Since Shaykh Burhan ad-din Gharib had to work out the principles of his **silsilah** in a new milieu, he was nostalgic about Delhi and remembered with love and respect the traditions of Shaykh Nizam ad-din Awliya. As was inevitable, he culled considerable information about mystic teachings from **Fawa'id al-Fu'ad.**[209]

The **Jawami' al-Kalim,**[210] conversations of Sayyid Muhammad Gesu Daraz of Gulbarga, compiled by his son Sayyid Muhammad Husaini, contains some very valuable pieces of information about the Shaykh, his physical features, his daily habits, and his spiritual practice. Gesu Daraz's information supplements the facts provided in **Fawa'id al-Fu'ad,** and it is also of value in assessing the impact of **Fawa'id al-Fu'ad** on the religious attitudes of later generations.

Hasan was not merely a pioneer in the field of compiling **malfuzat;** he set in motion a tradition that was accepted by founders of all other spiritual orders in India, among them the Suhrawardis, the Firdausis, and the Shattaris. It led to the production of similar literature about the utterances of mystic teachers of other affiliations in different parts of India, from Multan to Pandua, from Delhi to Daulatabad. Though some prior attempts had been made to compile records of saintly discourse,[211] these compilations did not attain the level of **Fawa'id al-Fu'ad** because they mixed conversations with biographical details, often confusing contemporary assessments with the evaluation of posterity. It was left to Hasan to introduce a new genre of Sufi literature, and to introduce it into South Asia. It was a genre in which many imitated his pioneering effort but none surpassed his final product.

The present English translation of **Fawa'id al-Fu'ad** by Professor Bruce B. Lawrence is an excellent rendering of the Persian original. With his insight into the intricacies of religious thought[212] and his extensive knowledge of Muslim mystical literature in South Asia,[213] he is eminently qualified to undertake this task. He has accomplished it with remarkable success. His translation captures the spirit of the original. It conveys the thought of a great South Asian Sufi master with freshness as well as clarity. It will certainly find a place among some of the finest English translations of Persian classics.

## NOTES

1. **Futuhat-i Firuz Shahi,** ed. with English tr. and notes S. A. Rashid and M. A. Makhdoomi (Aligarh, n.d.), p. 17.
2. A village, but a few miles from Delhi, where the Shaykh had settled. He later built a hospice there. Remnants of this hospice may be seen near Humayun's tomb. See Bayazid Biyat, **Tadkhira-i-Humayun wa Akbar,** ed. M. Hidayat Hosain (Calcutta, 1941), p. 234.
3. **Tarikh-i Firuz Shahi,** ed. Sir Syed Ahmad Khan (Calcutta, 1862), pp. 343–47.
4. Ibid., p. 360; Amir Khurd, **Siyar al-Awliya,** Chirangi Lal edition (Delhi, A.H. 1302), p. 308.
5. **Siyar al-Awliya,** p. 278.
6. Ibid., p. 308.
7. *Lectures* (Lahore, 1890), p. 270.
8. Manuscript in personal collection.
9. **Hasrat Namah,** as cited in **Siyar al-Awliya,** pp. 346–47.
10. **Khaza'in al-Futuh,** ed. M. W. Mirza (Calcutta, 1953), p. 112; Eng. tr. M. Habib, *Campaigns of Ala uddin Khalji* (Madras, 1931), p. 79.

11. Barani, **Tarikh-i Firuz Shahi,** p. 331.
12. Conversation dated 5 Shawwal A.H. 707.
13. Conversation dated 26 Shawwal A.H. 707.
14. Conversation dated 23 Rabiʿ al-thani A.H. 710.
15. The opposition between *lazmi* and *mutaʿaddi* is adopted from grammatical terminology, the *mutaʿaddi* verb being transitive, i.e., the action exercising an effect upon an object, and the *lazmi* being intransitive, i.e., its action being confined to the subject. Sir Hamilton Gibb once wrote to me: "The transference of these terms to mystical devotion is, in fact, remarkably apt." In the present context, it seems expedient to provide the most evident meaning "obligatory" and "supererogatory," though the secondary meanings would not have been lost on the Shaykh's followers, namely, if one did what was required it aided only the individual, while if one did what exceeded requirements it benefited others, and also ultimately oneself.
16. Conversation dated 3 Muharram A.H. 708.
17. **Siyar al-Awliya,** p. 128.
18. *An Historian's Approach to Religion,* Gifford Lectures, 1952–1953, p. 296.
19. **Siyar al-Awliya,** p. 46.
20. Conversation dated 27 Zil Hijjah A.H. 718.
21. Conversation dated 7 Dhu'l-Qaʿda A.H. 710.
22. **Siyar al-Awliya,** p. 301.
23. Ibid., p. 203.
24. Conversations dated 2 Rabiʿ al-Akhir A.H. 711; 25 Dhu'l-Hijja A.H. 711.
25. Conversation dated 5 Shawwal A.H. 707; see also **Siyar al-Awliya,** pp. 543–545. Rumi gives a similar explanation when he says:

> What is the (material) world? (Nothing but)
> becoming neglectful of God.
> It is not wealth, sons or wife (which one
> considers material wealth).

26. Conversation dated 15 Muharram A.H. 715.
27. Conversation dated 18 Rabi' al-akhir A.H. 718.
28. Conversation dated 18 Rabiʿ al-akhir A.H. 718.
29. Conversation dated 26 Rabiʿ al-awwal A.H. 712.
30. Ibid.
31. Conversation dated 16 Jumada al-ukhra A.H. 715.

32. **Siyar al-Awliya,** pp. 552–56.
33. Conversation dated 2 Safar A.H. 713.
34. **Siyar al-Awliya,** p. 555.
35. Conversation dated 14 Rajab A.H. 720.
36. Conversation dated 20 Rabiʿ al-awwal A.H. 714.
37. The Shaykh calls them **khatra, ʿazimat,** and **faʿl.** Conversation dated 5 Jumada al-awwal A.H. 708. See also **Siyar al-Awliya,** pp. 565–67.
38. Conversation dated 10 Rabiʿ al-akhir A.H. 710.
39. Conversation dated 12 Safar A.H. 714.
40. **Siyar al-Awliya,** p. 288.
41. Ibid., p. 295.
42. Ibid.
43. Ibid., pp. 560–61.
44. Arminius Vambery, *History of Bokhara* (London, 1873), p. 130.
45. K. A. Nizami, *Religion and Politics in India during the Thirteenth Century* (Bombay, 1961), pp. 76–77.
46. For details of his life, see conversation dated 29 Jumada al-ukhra A.H. 713.
47. A famous collection of the traditions of the Prophet that was taught in Indian *madrasahs* during the medieval period, it has survived in numerous manuscripts. See M. G. Zubaid Ahmad, *The Contribution of India to Arabic Literature* (Allahabad, 1945), p. 292.
48. Khusrau, **Wast al-Hayat** (Aligarh, 1920), p. 78. For a brief account of Badaon during the early Sultanate period, see K. A. Nizami, *Tarikhi Maqalat* (Delhi, 1965), pp. 39–44.
49. **Siyar al-Awliya,** p. 387.
50. No early authority has given the year of his birth; the Shaykh himself did not remember it. It may, however, be worked out on the basis of some facts of his life. He went to Ajodhan to see Baba Farid when he was twenty years of age. He visited his spiritual mentor three times, once every year, before he breathed his last in 664/1265. Calculated on this basis, the date of his birth would be 641–642/1243–1244.
51. It is not clear when and how the suffix **Awliya** came to be added to his name. Because it is the plural of **wali,** its use may appear odd. In the preface to the fifth fascicle of **Fawaʾid al-Fuʾad,** Hasan refers to him as **Sultan al-Awliya.** It may be that later generations dropped **Sultan** and continued **Awliya** with his name. In his commentary on Shah Wali Allah Dihlawi's **Qaul al-Jamil** (Kanpur A.H. 1291, p. 135), his son Shah ʿAbd al-ʿAziz says that the use of a plural for an individual indicates emphasis

on that quality. The Qur'an calls Prophet Abraham **Ummat.** In mystic circles Khwaja ʿObeid Allah is called **Ahrar,** Ka'ab is called **Ahbar,** though these are all plural terms.

52. **Qiwam al-ʿAqa'id,** Ms. Osmania University Library, pp. 11–12. The author was the son of Shaykh Shams al-ʿArifin, a disciple of Shaykh Nizam ad-din Awliya. He completed this work in 755/1354.

53. **Durar-i Nizami,** Ms., ff. 113–ab.

54. **Siyar al-Awliya,** p. 95.

55. **Siyar al-ʿArifin,** p. 59.

56. **Durar-i Nizami,** Ms. ff 13–ab; **Siyar al-Awliya,** p. 96. His grave in Badaon near the Sagar Tank is a popular place of pilgrimage. Hafiz Rahmat Khan, the Rohila chief, built a mosque and an enclosure around it. The grave of Khwaja ʿAli Bukhari is also within that enclosure.

57. **Siyar al-Awliya,** p. 319; **Jawamiʿ al-Kalim,** Kanpur A.H. 1356.

58. **Hasanat al-ʿArifin,** Ms. Nadwat-ul-Ulama, Lucknow No. 202, p. 21.

59. **Durar-i Nizami** (Ms). Jamali's statement (**Siyar al-ʿArifin,** p. 50) that he left Badaon at the age of twenty-five is not correct.

60. Conversation dated 27 Rabiʿ al-awwal A.H. 716.

61. Ibid.

62. **Siyar al-Awliya,** p. 419. For the extremely indigent circumstances of his life, see **Khair al-Majalis,** ed. K. A. Nizami (Aligarh, 1959), pp. 190–91.

63. Conversation dated 15 Ramadan A.H. 716.

64. Abul Faiz Minallah, **Shawamil al-Jumal dar Shama'il al-Kumal,** Ms. Rauza Shaykh's Collection, Gulbarga, p. 25. Written in A.H. 878/A.D. 1473.

65. Conversation dated 15 Ramadan A.H. 716.

66. Abul Hasan Ahmad b. Muhammad al-Qaduri (972–1037) was a distinguished author on Muslim jurisprudence.

67. **Khair al-majalis,** p. 191.

68. A famous book on Muslim Law, it was compiled by Maulana Burhan ad-din Abul Hasan ʿAli Marghinani (1135–1197).

69. **Qiwam al-ʿaqa'id,** Ms. p. 14.

70. **Siyar al-Awliya,** p. 113.

71. Ibid.

72. Ibid.

73. Ibid., p. 150.

74. Ibid., p. 109.

75. Ibid.

76. Ibid., p. 112.

77. **Qiwam al-ʿAqaʾid,** Ms. p. 20.

78. Conversation dated 27 Shaʿban A.H. 715; **Qiwam al-ʿAqaʾid,** Ms. p. 21.

79. Conversation dated 27 Shaʿban A.H. 715; **Qiwam al-ʿAqaʾid,** Ms. p. 22; **Siyar al-Awliya,** p. 111.

80. Conversation dated 27 Shaʿban A.H. 715.

81. **Siyar al-Awliya,** pp. 113–14.

82. Ibid., p. 114.

83. **Futuh al-Salatin,** Madras ed. pp. 114–15.

84. In **Fawaʾid al-Fuʾad** alone he refers to works of Iman Ghazzalim, Iman Nasiri, Zamakhshri, ʾAin al-Quzat, Marghinani, etc., which shows his familiarity with medieval religious thought of all shades and opinions.

85. **Durar-i Nizami** (Ms.); **Siyar al-Awliya,** p. 66.

86. **Durar-i Nizami** (Ms.).

87. A classical work on Arabic literature compiled by Abu Muhammad al-Qasim al-Hariri (1054–1122).

88. **Durar-i Nizami** (Ms.).

89. **Siyar al-Awliya,** p. 105.

90. Ibid., p. 106.

91. **Mashariq al-Anwar** is a collection of the Traditions of the Prophet based on **Sahih Bukhari** and **Sahih Muslim.**

92. **Siyar al-Awliya,** p. 101: **yad giraft.**

93. Fifteen years had passed since Baba Farid's death and Nizam ad-din had by then established his reputation as a mystic teacher. That Nizam ad-din had continued his education after he was initiated into the discipline of Shaykh Farid is clear from a remark of the great saint (**Siyar al-Awliya,** p. 107). This happened when Shaykh Nizam ad-din was only twenty years of age. It appears from this certificate of Maulana Kamal Zahid that for twenty-three years after that he continued to pursue his studies.

94. **Siyar al-Awliya,** p. 101.

95. For details about his life and teachings, see K. A. Nizami, *The Life and Times of Shaykh Farid-uʾd-din Ganj-i Shakar* (Aligarh, 1955).

96. For Pakpattan, see M. Abdullah Chaghtai, *Pakpattan and Baba Farid* (Lahore, 1968).

97. Conversation dated 23 Ramadan A.H. 708; **Siyar al-Awliya,** p. 169.

98. **Nafahat al-Uns** (Lucknow, 1915), p. 452.

99. **Siyar al-Awliya,** p. 106. Amir Khurd gives the day but not the year. Later writers have added the year on the basis of their calculation. It appears from **Qiwam al-ʿAqaʾid** that his mother was alive at this time and he had undertaken this journey to Ajodhan with her permission (Ms., p. 16). She died soon after his return from Ajodhan (ibid., p. 18).
100. Conversation dated 18 Shawwal A.H. 708; **Siyar al-Awliya,** p. 107.
101. **Siyar al-Awliya,** p. 107.
102. Ibid.
103. Ibid.
104. Conversation dated 10 Dhuʾl Hijja A.H. 709.
105. Ibid.
106. Conversation dated 9 Ramadan A.H. 708.
107. **Siyar al-Awliya,** p. 239.
108. Ibid.
109. Conversation dated 28 Jumada al-ula A.H. 716.
110. Conversation dated 26 Rajab A.H. 718.
111. Conversation dated 7 Dhuʾl-Qaʿda, A.H. 710.
112. **Siyar al-Awliya,** pp. 131–32.
113. Ibid., pp. 116–17.
114. Ibid., p. 348.
115. Ibid., pp. 121–22.
116. Muhammad Ghauthi Shattari, **Gulzar-i Abrar** (Ms.), and also its Urdu translation, **Adhkar-i Abrar** (Lahore, 1975), p. 83.
117. All these details may be found in **Siyar al-Awliya** in the accounts of the persons concerned.
118. **Khair al-Majalis,** p. 257.
119. **Khair al-Majalis,** p. 257.
120. **Qiwam al-Aqaʾid,** Ms. pp. 163–65.
121. On the importance of **samaʿ** for Shaykh Nizam ad-din and other early Chishti masters, see Bruce B. Lawrence, "The Early Chishti Approach to **Samaʿ**," in *Islam and India: Festschrift for Aziz Ahmad,* ed. M. Wagle (New Delhi: Vikas, 1980), pp. 69–93.
122. Conversation dated 18 Shawwal A.H. 720.
123. Rukn ad-din Dabir ʿImad Kashani, **Nafaʾis al-Anfas,** Ms. Nadwat ul Ulama Library No. 73, p. 23. For other copies of **Nafaʾis al-Anfas** as also for a detailed, insightful exposition of the parallels between its composition and the composition of **Fawaʾid al-Fuʾad,** see Carl W. Ernst, "The Textual Formation of Oral Teachings in the Early Chishti Order," Ms. pp. 19–21, to be included in his forthcoming monograph

on Sufism and history at Khuldabad, "Eternal Garden: Mysticism, History and Politics at a South Asian Sufi Center" (Albany, N.Y.: SUNY Press, forthcoming). In this same connection, see **infra** notes 204–09.

124. **Siyar al-Awliya,** p. 512.

125. See Conversation dated 19 Dhu'l-Hijja A.H. 720 for details.

126. Conversation dated 2 Safar A.H. 713; **Siyar al-Awliya,** p. 522.

127. **Jawami' al-Kalim,** p. 123.

128. Ibid.

129. **Siyar al-Awliya,** pp. 276–77; Conversation dated 9 Ramadan A.H. 719.

130. **Siyar al-Awliya,** p. 128.

131. Ibid., p. 126.

132. Ibid., p. 383.

133. Conversation dated 26 Safar A.H. 712.

134. **Khair al-Majalis,** p. 257.

135. **Siyar al-Awliya,** p. 75. The attitude of the early Indo-Muslim mystics toward the state has been discussed by me in a series of articles published in *Islamic Culture,* October 1948 to January 1950.

136. **Siyar al-Awliya,** p. 295.

137. Ibid., p. 114.

138. Ibid., p. 135. The printed text gives 'Ala ad-din, which seems to be a copyist's error for Jalal ad-din.

139. **Tarikh-i Firuz Shahi,** pp. 343–46; the author of **Qiwam al-'Aqa'id** devotes one full chapter (ch. VI) to the faith of nobles in the Shaykh.

140. Barani, **Tarikh-i Firuz Shahi,** pp. 209–12; **Futuh al-Salatin,** p. 316.

141. **Siyar al-Awliya,** pp. 133–34.

142. Barani, **Tarikh-i Firuz Shahi,** p. 332.

143. Details of the strained relations may be read in *Islamic Culture,* Oct. 1949, pp. 316–18; and K. A. Nizami, **Salatin-i Delhi Kay Mazhabi Rujhanat** (Delhi, 1958), pp. 289–97.

144. For details regarding the **sama'** controversy, see **Siyar al-Awliya,** pp. 527 et seq. For the legal aspect of the problem, see Maulana Fakhr ad-din Zarradi's excellent treatise, **Usul al-Sama'** (Jhajjar; Muslim Press, A.H. 1311).

145. *Tarikh-i Mubarak Shahi* (p. 96) is the earliest work to refer to this remark of the Shaykh.

146. Some uncritical writers, like Sleeman (*Rambles and Recollections* II, p. 45) and Cooper, (*The Hand Book of Delhi,* p. 97), have cast asper-

sions on the character of the Shaykh and have involved him in a conspiracy against the Sultan with the prince. This is all a figment of their imagination. No one who has the slightest knowledge of the Shaykh's character can entertain such ideas. Mzik, Bohrah, and others have exposed the absurdity of this charge. See also Nizami, **Salatin-i Dehli Kay Mazhabi Rujhanat,** pp. 314–20.

147. **Siyar al-Awliya,** p. 154.

148. Ibid.

149. **Siyar al-ʿArifin,** p. 74. Following Jamali many later writers have repeated this mistake.

150. **Futuhat-i Firuz Shahi,** ed. S. A. Rashid and M. A. Makhdoomi (Aligarh, n.d.), p. 17.

151. **Siyar al-Awliya,** p. 198.

152. See *History of Medieval Deccan,* ed. Ḥ. K. Sherwani and P. M. Joshi (Hyderabad, 1974), Vol. II, Ch. 2: K. A. Nizami, 'Sufi Movement in the Deccan,' pp. 175–99.

153. Tabatabaʾi, **Burhan al-Maʾathir,** ed. G. Yazdani (Hyderabad, 1936), p. 12; Nizam ad-din, **Tabaqat-i Akbari** (Calcutta, 1911), III, p. 6; Firishta, **Tarikh** (Lucknow, A.H. 1281, I, p. 274.

154. **Tarikh-i Firishta,** I, p. 277. For Chishti-Nizami centers during the Bahmanid rule, see M. Suleman Siddiqi, *The Bahmani Sufis* (Delhi, 1989).

155. See **infra** notes 204–09 for detailed citations of these works.

156. For his works, see K. A. Nizami, "Gesu Daraz," *Encyclopaedia of Islam* (new ed.), I:1114–16. Of particular significance are his commentaries on **ʿAwarif al-Maʿarif, Sharh Taʿarruf,** and the **Tamhidat.**

157. **Siyar al-Awliya,** pp. 289–90; Muhammad Bulaq, **Rauza-i Aqtab** (Delhi, 1887), pp. 48–49.

158. For details, see K. A. Nizami, **Tarikh-i Mashaʾikh Chisht,** 2nd ed. (Delhi, 1980), Vol. I, pp. 253–58.

159. For details, see Syed ʿAbdul Hayy, **Yad-i Ayyam** (Lucknow, 1983), pp. 84–86; and Nizami, **Tarikh-i Mashaʾikh Chisht,** Vol. I, pp. 262–66.

160. See Ghauthi Shattari, **Gulzar-i Abrar,** Ms.; and Nizami, **Tarikh-i MaShaykh-i Chisht,** Vol. I, pp. 266–68.

161. **Siyar al-Awliya,** p. 139.

162. Zain Badar, **Maʿdan al-Maʿani** (Bihar, A.H. 1301, p. 405).

163. **Tuhfat al-Majalis,** Ms. I.O.DP. 977, ff. 24 ab.

164. *The Contribution of India to Arabic Literature* (Allahabad, 1945), pp. 184–86. In **Fawaʾid al-Fuʾad** (conversation dated 15 Muharram A.H.

710) Shaykh Nizam ad-din Auliya is clearly reported to have said that he wrote no book. This **khutba** does not fall within that category. The Shaykh was also fond of jotting down brief notes, comments, and views on books, as Amir Khurd has repeatedly mentioned.

165. See **Durar-i Nizami,** Ms.

166. **Siyar al-Awliya** p. 101.

167. For his features and other details of his personality, see **Siyar al-Awliya** and **Jawami' al-Kalim.**

168. **Siyar al-Awliya,** p. 130.

169. **Nafa'is al-Anfas,** Ms. Nadwat al-Ulama, Lucknow, p. 12. According to **Siyar al-Awliya** (p. 260), Maulana Husam ad-din Multani became wet with perspiration in his presence.

170. **Khair al-Majalis,** p. 105.

171. **Siyar al-Awliya,** p. 323.

172. Conversation dated 15 Muharram A.H. 710.

173. People who had legalized incest. See I. H. Qureshi, *Administration of the Sultanate of Delhi* (Karachi, 1958), pp. 254–58.

174. **Khaza'in al-Futuh,** pp. 19–21.

175. Conversation dated 20 Rabi' al-Awwal A.H. 716.

176. **Siyar al-Awliya,** p. 323; Conversation dated 16 Jumada al-Akhir A.H. 715.

177. **Khaza'in al-Futuh** (Calcutta, 1953), pp. 16–20; **Tarikh-i Firuz Shahi,** pp. 342–44.

178. **Jawami'al-Kalim,** p. 123. For the highly favorable, and also highly unusual, attitude of Shaykh Nizam ad-din toward women, see Bruce B. Lawrence, "Asceticism and Sexuality: The Dilemma of South Asian Sufi Masters," forthcoming in Vasudha Narayan, ed., *Asceticism in South Asia* (University of Georgia Press). Almost the entire paper examines stories from **Fawa'id al-Fu'ad** about women, concluding that though Shaykh Nizam ad-din was celibate, he deeply empathized with the women he knew, from his mother and sister to female visitors to his **khanqah.**

179. **Siyar al-'Arifin,** p. 87.

180. **Siyar al-Awliya,** p. 52.

181. **Tarikh-i Firuz Shahi,** p. 343 et seq.

182. Barani, **Tarikh-i Firuz Shahi,** p. 360. Shaykh Nasir ad-din Chiragh is reported to have remarked that both Khusrau and Hasan strove to imitate Sa'di yet did not succeed because whatever Sa'di wrote was due to overflow of cosmic emotion (**Khair al-Majalis,** p. 143). For an alternative view, suggesting how Hasan exceeded Sa'di in the pathos

of some of his finest **ghazals,** see Bruce B. Lawrence, "Thematic Antecedents for the Urdu Ghazal in the Sufi Poetry of the Sultanate Period," in *Studies in the Urdu Gazal and Prose Fiction,* ed. Muhammad Umar Memon, (Madison, Wis.: 1979), pp. 61–100, but espec. 79–84.

183. **Tarikh-i Firuz Shahi,** pp. 359–60.

184. **Diwan-i Amir Hasan,** Introduction, p. 25.

185. ʿAbd al-Haqq Muhaddith, **Musannifin wa Musannifat-i Hind,** Ms. Nadwat al-Ulama Library, Lucknow, No. 70, p. 8.

186. **Tarikh-i Mubarak Shahi,** pp. 44–51.

187. **Muntakhab al-Tawarikh,** Vol. I, p. 131 et seq.

188. Ms. in Azad Library, Aligarh. For a descriptive note, see K. A. Nizami, **Tarikhi Maqalat** (Delhi, 1966), pp. 166–69.

189. Conversation dated 3 Muharram A.H. 712.

190. **Siyar al-ʿArifin,** p. 87.

191. It appears from a reference in the *FF* (Conversation dated 28 Shawwal A.H. 708) that a little more than a year before he started recording the conversations of the Shaykh, he had joined his discipline.

192. Conversation dated 21 Dhuʾl Hijjah A.H. 713.

193. **Siyar al-Awliya,** p. 318.

194. Ibid., p. 200.

195. Ibid., pp. 346–48.

196. Ibid., p. 202.

197. Mss.: (i) personal collection, (ii) Buhar collection, Calcutta, (iii) Salar Jung Museum, Hyderabad (61/5 99). An imperfect Urdu translation was also published by Sayyid Muhammad Yasin ʿAli Nizami in 1332/1913.

198. **Siyar al-Awliya,** p. 449.

199. **Nafaʾis al-Anfas,** Ms. Nadwat al-Ulama, Lucknow, p. 13.

200. A unicum Ms. exists in Osmania University Library. Dated 791/1388, it is perhaps the earliest available manuscript of any source for the life of the Shaykh.

201. Published by Chiragi Lal, Delhi, 1302/1885, and reprinted in Islamabad, Pakistan 1398/1978.

202. For the most superb general introduction to this problem, see Mohammad Habib, "Chishti Mystics Records of the Sultanate Period," *Medieval India Quarterly* I (1950); 1–42; reprinted in *Politics and Society during the Early Medieval Period: Collected Works of Professor Mohammad Habib,* Vol. I, ed. K. A. Nizami (New Delhi, 1974), pp. 385–433. For an extended study of differences between **Fawaʾid al-Fuʾad** and **Afzal al-fawaʾid,** apocryphally attributed to Amir Khusrau, see Bruce B.

Lawrence, "**Afzal al-fawa'id**—A Reassessment," in *Life, Times and Works of Amir Khusrau Dehlavi,* ed. Z. Ansari (New Delhi, 1975), pp. 119–31.

203. Edited by K. A. Nizami (Aligarh, 1959).

204. Library Salar Jung Museum, Mss. (478 and 1479); Ms. personal collection.

205. Ms., Nadwat ul Ulama, Lucknow. As noted above, the compiler has frankly admitted his indebtedness to the biographical genre launched in India by Hasan Sijzi (pp. 3–4). Two other lithograph editions of this text exist in my personal collection.

206. Published Ashraf Press, Hyderabad A.H. 1347; Ms. personal collection.

207. Ms. in Salar Jung Museum 43/876.

208. **Rauzat al-Auliya,** p. 5.

209. For fuller information on the dependency and differentiation between these two Chishti masters, see Carl W. Ernst, "Eternal Garden: Mysticism, History and Politics at a South Asian Sufi Center" (Albany, N.Y.: SUNY Press, forthcoming), especially ch. II.b on Burhan ad-din's establishment and teaching.

210. Published Intizami Press, Hyderabad 1356/1937.

211. For the most notable examples other than Jalal ad-din Rumi, **Fihi ma Fihi,** ed. Badi' al-Zaman Furuzanfar (Tehran, 1338/1959) and trans. A. J. Arberry, *Discourses of Rumi* (London, 1961), see the following:

1. **Halat-O-Sukhanan-i Shaykh Abu Sa'id Fazl-ullah b. Abil Khair al-Maihani** by Muhammad b. Abu Ruh Lutfullah in or about A.H. 540/1145–1146 (Ms. in British Museum);
2. **Asrar-ut-Tauhid fi Maqamat-i Shaykh Abi Sa'id,** by Muhammad b. Munawwar in A.H. 547/1178 (ed. Ahmad Bahmanyar, Tehran, 1934).
3. **Malfuzat-i Najm al-Din Kubra** (ob. A.H. 618/A.D. 1221)—Ms. in Asiatic Society of Bengal.

212. See *Shahrastani on the Indian Religions* (The Hague, 1976).

213. See *Notes from a Distant Flute: the Extant Literature of Pre-Mughal Indian Sufism* (Tehran, 1978).

# TRANSLATOR'S INTRODUCTION

Shaykh Nizam ad-din Awliya, whose person pervades *Morals for the Heart,* is at once a Muslim mystic and a mystic of transcreedal, which is to say universal, stature. Professor Khaliq Ahmad Nizami of Aligarh Muslim University, in his Introduction, documents better than could anyone else the markings of Shaykh Nizam ad-din as a Muslim saint or Sufi master of South Asia. The purpose of this preface will be to highlight the saint's contribution to mysticism on the universal plane.

It is an elusive purpose because it must be communicated through words and, still worse, through printed words. The nature of mysticism is such that it plays with words but never accords them more than provisional value. Tolstoy understood the truth of this axial ambiguity when he wrote in his novel *Resurrection* that "mysticism without poetry is superstition."[1] Because poetry represents the thin edge of discourse, at once the distillation of language and the compression of meaning, it has special force for most mystics, including those Muslim mystics known as Sufi masters.

The other form of language that attracts mystics is narrative. Lessons of enduring moral value have greater force when encoded in tales than when announced as rules of behavior. The most esteemed mystics are usually storytellers in religious garb; they project their teaching, as also themselves, through third-person narratives.

Shaykh Nizam ad-din was a superb storyteller and at the same time a lyricist of the highest order. Before focusing on the forms of his self-expression, however, we must recall that he shared with all other mystics a sense of what William James properly identified as the ineffability of mystical experience. Anyone could talk of mystical experience, but words were no substitute for the experience itself, an experience without verbal markers. As John E. Smith has shrewdly observed, "The paradoxes of mysticism . . . should lead us to stress the mystical claim that there never can be a surrogate for the goal at which the mystic aims. . . . For the most part, the function of [mystical] writing, when it is not addressed to the initiated, may be taken as evocative and indexical."[2]

Shaykh Nizam ad-din understood very well that words, including his own words, were intended to be evocative rather than declarative, indexical but never comprehensive. Even those who were initiated into his tradition, the Chishti **silsilah,** a chain of spiritual masters going back to the Prophet Muhammad through his cousin and son-in-law ʿAli, even these initiates could not understand the special relationship that he or any other saint had with the One. The distinction is evoked in one of the earliest entries in **Fawaʾid al-Fuʾad:**

> Discussion turned to THE DIFFERENCE BETWEEN SAINTHOOD (**walayat**) AND SAINTDOM (**wilayat**). The master (Shaykh Nizam ad-din) explained: "The saint possesses both **walayat** and **wilayat** at the same time. **Walayat** is that which masters impart to disciples about God, just as they teach them about the etiquette of the Way. Everything such as this which takes place between the Shaykh and other people is called **walayat.** But that which takes place between the Shaykh and God is called **wilayat.** That is a special kind of love (**mahabbat**), and when the Shaykh leaves the world, he takes his **wilayat** with him. His **walayat,** on the other hand, he can confer on someone else, whomever he wishes, and if he does not confer it, then it is suitable for God Almighty to confer that **walayat** on someone. But the **wilayat** is the Shaykh's constant companion; he bears it with him (wherever he goes)."[3]

What Shaykh Nizam ad-din did impart to others, through verse and narrative, was an extraordinary sense of Islam as drama, as the drama of human existence, at once exalting and threatening everyone who dared plumb the depth of meaning called God. Such drama became evident not only in prayer and meditation, fasting and self-denial, but also in the consideration of life's most mundane essentials. In the case of the recorder of Nizam ad-din's words, the poet-courtier Amir Hasan Sijzi, one of those essentials was his monthly salary. When it was paid on time, he was able to meet his social obligations as well as to enjoy the company of the Shaykh. When its payment was delayed, Hasan suffered anxiety and distress, emotions that the Shaykh, with his sensitive temperament, immediately grasped, even as he also grasped the relaxation that overcame Hasan when his delayed salary was finally paid. To imbue such mundane matters with divine significance would seem to require extraordinary imagination. Shaykh Nizam ad-din possessed such an imagination. This is the story that he told Amir Hasan on one occasion after the courtier's salary that had been in arrears was at last paid:

> There once was an Israelite ascetic. For years he had scrupulously obeyed God. Then one day a message came to the prophet of that time: "Go tell that ascetic: 'What do you gain from those discomforts caused by your strict observance? I have not created you but for chastisement!' " As soon as the prophet had given this message to the ascetic, the ascetic got up and began to twirl around. "Why," asked the prophet, "did this disclosure make you so happy that you've started dancing?" "At least He has remembered me," replied the ascetic, "he has taken me into account. I have experienced His reckoning, for:
>
> Even though He says He'll kill me,
> That **He** says it can't but thrill me!"[4]

The story contains numerous instructive insights. Its two principal actors, the ascetic and the prophet, act in inverse relationship to their usual roles: The prophet gets the message but not the point of the message. He conveys the message to the ascetic who, instead of being crushed by his seeming rejection and undergoing still further penance, accepts it as a pretext for celebration. That inversion of roles then leads the listener/reader to reflect on the real point of the story: The Almighty can disclose His will to whomever He wants by whomever He chooses to whatever ends He deems appropriate. A prophet does not have a special claim on God because of his prophecy. An ascetic does not have a special claim on God because of his asceticism. What does matter is openness to the divine will, the ability to hear that God and not some other, including one's own self-seeking inner voice, is speaking. When one does at last recognize the mark of the Unseen, as does the Israelite ascetic in the above story, then whatever that mark be one should rejoice. The Israelite ascetic does indeed rejoice, not only dancing but also uttering a verse that summarizes the paradox of this dalliance between the creature and the Creator:

> Even though He says He'll kill me,
> That **He** says it can't but thrill me!

Not even death is to be feared when God is the "killer."

The larger message that Shaykh Nizam ad-din communicates to Amir Hasan is the same as that which God through the prophet communicates to the Israelite ascetic: Do not pride yourself on what you have or do not have. Whether experiencing material deprivation or comfort and well-being, listen for the voice of God. It will not always tell you what you want to hear, but if it is His voice, you have been blessed, and that blessing, and that alone, should make you thrilled.

Other readers might find still other meanings in the above story than the ones I have adduced. What they will not find is what the story meant to Amir Hasan himself. A faithful disciple, he is attempting to transmit the Shaykh's message to all readers, rather than to restrict its relevance to himself and his immediate circumstance. He provides the pretext for the Shaykh's intervention. Often he does not hesitate to follow up with further questions to the Shaykh. Yet he claims attention only as a mediator or facilitator of Nizam ad-din's wisdom. He never inserts his own views as an alternate source of insight or as a special claim to authority.

Narratology has absorbed the attention of theorists from both history and literature. In **Fawa'id al-Fu'ad** we have perhaps the locus classicus of Indo-Muslim narrative history. Can we then learn something additional about Amir Hasan's recording of Shaykh Nizam ad-din's discourses by reviewing the strong pro-narrative arguments of the nineteenth-century French historiographer Augustin Thierry, or the more recent debate between the French linguists Emil Benveniste and Roland Barthes? Let us try. Thierry differentiated narrative from commentary or dissertation, viewing it as a powerful mimetic strategy that reactualizes the past at the same time that it compels the narrator, insofar as possible, to "disappear from the story and let the facts speak for themselves." Benveniste, following Thierry, distinguishes between the primary narrative of events (**histoire**) and the secondary intervention of a narrator (**discours**). For Benveniste there is a truth to be discovered, and he advocates the recoverability of events as they really occurred (**histoire**), apart from and beyond their distortion by a narrator (**discours**).

Barthes, however, scoffs at the possibility of erasing distortion. No narrator can render herself or himself invisible from the process of narration. Every **histoire** is implicated by **discours.** In Barthes' view, therefore, the interpretive task was botched by late nineteenth-century continental historians: Trying to distance their labor from the flawed subjectivity of their predecessors, they invoked the name of science and waved the flag of objectivity. What resulted was a distinction between content and narration—but it is a false distinction that dissolves on close inspection. For the narrator is always present: There has to be both the tale and the telling, the narrated story as well as the act of narrating it. Never, never can one send a package without paper; there is no **histoire** without **discours.**[5]

Such an analysis would be of value if we were confronted with stable artefacts of the sort imagined by both Barthes and his opponents. Do we have a discrete, delimited text? Do we find a univocal relationship framing both narrative and narrator? The answer to both questions is no. While **Fawa'id al-Fu'ad** represents Shaykh Nizam ad-din's discourses as narrated by Amir Hasan, there is no simple linear or dyadic relationship between text and author. It is not the issues but rather the parameters that are too narrow in the European historiographic debate about narratology. Both sides presuppose, almost reflexively, a single text and a single narrator. Even were there to be multiple texts and a series of narrators, there would still be a diachronic space and a hieratic model of relationship governing all points of reference.

Such is not the case in **Fawa'id al-Fu'ad.** Here we confront a four-way interaction that both complicates and streamlines the narrative process. There is, first, the saint whose experience with God is beyond words; it is ineffable. That unbridgeable chasm of silence supersedes all the words that hint at what remains a zone of privilege shared only by the saint and God. Second, there are the words of the saint communicated to his followers. As Professor Nizami makes clear in his Introduction, only a fraction of those verbal directives were remembered and later transmitted to posterity through a literary medium. Third, there is the assiduous recorder/compiler, who is also a faithful disciple, and who struggles to capture not only the form but the flavor of those pearls that tumble from the saint's lips in his hearing. All three of these elements confer a legitimacy of sorts on **Fawa'id al-Fu'ad,** but they remain necessary rather than sufficient conditions for its accuracy. By themselves they would still leave ample room for distortion of either fact or emphasis, distortions that are mirrored in later attempts by other Sufi adepts to employ this popular genre. Unlike Thierry, they did not believe that there could be a pure, recoverable text, but also unlike Barthes, they did not believe that all subjective markings should be labeled "distortion" and simply accepted as part of the historical process of transmission.

What exceptionalizes **Fawa'id al-Fu'ad** is not only its undisputed position as the first compilation of saintly discourses to have been preserved in the Asian subcontinent but also the repeated intervention of the saint himself—whether to amplify, to delete, or to correct the words of his recording disciple. Shaykh Nizam ad-din was concerned about the accuracy of what would be registered as his teaching on Islam and the mystical Path. He did not defer to Amir Hasan's poetic license, even though he accepted the latter's initiative and trusted his sincerity. It was the saint himself who negotiated the final text with his compliant recorder.

We are given few glimpses into this creative editorial process in the actual text of **Fawa'id al-Fu'ad** yet they are sufficient to conclude that the telling and retelling, the recording and revising of these assemblies uniquely succeeded in communicating the **walayat** of Shaykh Nizam ad-din. **Fawa'id al-Fu'ad** succeeded as a mystic lodestone during the saint's lifetime, and it has continued to enjoy success since then for countless others beyond the immediate circle of Chishti adepts for whom it was initially intended.

Perhaps nothing can better illustrate the compatibility verging on symbiosis between the saint and the recorder than the special role of verse throughout the pages of **Fawa'id al-Fu'ad.** Almost all the verses are in Persian, although the two in Arabic have special significance and require further comment. One is an elaborate poem in Arabic that a **qawwal** (a musician who performs at **majalis-e sama'**, or mystical audition parties) had recited before Shaykh Baha al-Din Zakariya, the chief Suhrawardi saint of the Punjab and a spiritual rival of Shaykh Farid al-Din, Nizam ad-din's master. The principal function of this poem in **Fawa'id al-Fu'ad** is to demonstrate that even the most intensely lyrical paean on behalf of Shaykh Baha al-Din did not distract Nizam ad-din from his incipient attraction to the other major saint of thirteenth-century Punjab, Shaykh Farid al-Din. The verse also demonstrates incidentally the extraordinary facility of Amir Hasan not only in composing poetry but also in rendering verse from one language (Arabic) into verse in another (Persian). The full poems, transcribed into Roman letters and versified in English, read as follows:

Arabic, **rajaz**

**bi-kulli subhin wa-kulli ishraqin**
**tabkika ʿayni bi-damʿi mushtaqin**
**qad lasaʿat hayyatu ʾl-hawa kabdi**
**fa-la tabiba liha wa-la raqin**
**illa ʾl-habiba ʾlladhi shughiftu bihi**
**fa-ʿindahu ruqyati wa tiryaqi.**

At dawn, again and again, each evening,
My eyes, due to love of you, keep weeping.
My liver, bitten by the snake of desire,
No doctor nor charmer has the means of curing.
For none but he who inflames me with desire
Can, if he chooses, quench that raging fire.

And Hasan, rendering the last four lines into a Persian quatrain, makes it:

**az mar-e ghamash gazida daram jigare**
**k-ora nakunad hec fusune asare**
**juz dost ki man shefta-e ʿishq-e o yam**
**afsun-e ʿilaj-e man ci danad digare.**

My liver's been pinched by a serpent's deadly bite
Which no spell, however potent, can hope to right.
Only that one whose love distracts and destroys me
Can cast a spell that heals, for who else knows my plight?[6]

As clever as is the above sequence of Arabic and Persian verse, it does not begin to have the theological impress of Shaykh Nizam ad-din's distinctive outlook to the extent that does the other major Arabic poem appearing in **Fawaʾid al-Fuʾad.** Like the above, this second Arabic poem is not of Shaykh Nizam ad-din's composition but it is quoted by him approvingly in the following passage:

> He next spoke briefly about THE ASCENSION OF THE PROPHET. A dear one who was present asked: "How did the Ascension take place?" The master—may God remember him

with favor—replied: "From Mecca to Jerusalem was the Night Journey (**isra**; Q.17.1), from Jerusalem to the first heaven was the Ascension (**mi'raj**), and from the first heaven to the place of 'two bows' length' (Q.53:7) was the Ascent (**'iraj**)." Then that dear one elaborated his question, asking: "Some claim that the Ascension was bodily, others that it was spiritual. How can it be both?" On the blessed tongue of the master—may God remember him with favor—came this verse:

"Imagine the best, ask not for details!"

"In matters of religion," he added, "one must have faith; one should not show excessive zeal in either asserting or examining them." Then he recited the following two couplets in full, adding that it was a beloved present that evening who had composed them in a moment of inspiration:

He came to me, wrapped in the cloak of night
Approaching with steps of caution and fright.
Then what happened, happened; to say more fails.
Imagine the best, ask not for details.

The Arabic, transcribed, reads as follows:

**ja'ani fi qamisi 'l-layli mustataran**
**yuqaribu 'l-khatwa min khawfin wa-min hadharin**
**fa-kana ma kana mimma lastu adhkuruhu**
**fa-zunnu khayran wa-la tas'alu 'an al-khabari.**

This is the major reference to the Ascension of the Prophet Muhammad in the pages of **Fawa'id al-Fu'ad.** Its exposition in such dramatic verse conveys an impression of awe. The reader, like the dear one in the original assembly, is left to "imagine the best." Who was it who came in the cloak of night but Muhammad? To whom else would he come "with steps of caution and fright" but the Almighty? It is a poem that both suggests and holds back, at once revealing and concealing the truth. It is also worth noting that only in a poem could one hope to capture the mystery of that moment called the **mi'raj-i nabi,** the Ascension of the Prophet. For Iranians as for Indians, miniature art could be pressed into the service of literary production, and it is to demonstrate their complementary function that a Safavid miniature of the Ascension, repainted in Mughal India, is included on the cover of this translation. Though neither poetry nor art can exhaust the surfeit of meaning in such numinous events, each succeeds to the extent that it draws the imagination beyond the seemingly miraculous to that higher realm of reality so crucial to mystics. Once again Tolstoy's dictum seems apt: "Mysticism without poetry is superstition."

Love fares even worse without poetry than does mysticism. It becomes hackneyed babbling at best, at worst crude self-deception. Some of the most poignant passages of **Fawa'id al-Fu'ad** contain Persian verses that Shaykh Nizam ad-din utters on the topic of love. I would not have attempted to render these verses, or any other verses from **Fawa'id al-Fu'ad,** into English verse were it not for the extraordinary generosity of an overseas colleague, Professor Christopher Shackle of the School of Oriental and African Studies, London. Professor Shackle had read some of my earlier translations of **Fawa'id al-Fu'ad.**[7] A skilled translator of Punjabi verse, he was convinced that translations from Persian into English verse were not only possible but desirable. He read through all my prior efforts and then crafted a full forty pages of his own efforts. I worked through each of Professor Shackle's translations, in some cases agreeing with him, in others coming up with further possibilities of my own not previously imagined. At each point I benefited from his initiative, his expertise and, above all, his friendship. Without the unusual collegial exchange that he prompted, I might never have had the courage to finish the fourteen-year labor of translating **Fawa'id al-Fu'ad** into English. Had I finished it on my own, what would have resulted would not have included English versifications of Persian and Indo-Persian poetry.[8]

A sample of poems where the saint evokes the nature of love will illustrate the nature of our combined labor.[9] Throughout the saint's discourses love is more often equivalent to pathos, above all the pathos of human engagement with God as transcendent Beauty. Most verses imply the conceit of being able to express through the ear that which cannot be experienced by the eye. Among Indo-Persian poets who have tried to encapsulate this theme, perhaps none has exceeded Qazi Hamid ad-din Nagauri, a thirteenth-century Suhrawardi saint much esteemed by the Chishti masters.[10] It is the following quatrain from Qazi Hamid ad-din that transfixed Shaykh Nizam ad-din as also other Sufi masters:

**An ʿaql kuja ki dar kamal-e to rasad**
**Van ruh kuja ki dar jalal-e to rasad**
**Giram ki to parda bar girifti zi jamal**
**An dida kuja ki dar jamal-e to rasad**

I first rendered it as follows:

Where is the intellect to perceive Your perfection?
Where is the soul to attain Your majesty?
I want you to remove the veil from the face of beauty.
But where are the eyes to behold Your beauty?

Later, in response to Shackle's attempt to find an appropriate rhyme on -ness, stringing "perfectness," "awesomeness," and "loveliness," I felt obliged to create my own:

Where's the mind to grasp Your sovereignty?
Where's the soul to mirror Your majesty?
Beauty's face, I know, You could unveil
But where are eyes to behold Your beauty?

At first, I wanted to change the rhyme scheme to 2-3-4 but Shackle's effort convinced me to try again with the 1-2-4 rhyme scheme of the original poem. I differ with Shackle principally in the word choice of "beauty" rather than "loveliness" to render **jamal.** Either could fit but is there not more of an edge to -ty than -ness for a final rhyme in American English? It seems so to my ear, yet it is for each reader of both the Indo-Persian and our attempted translations to make the preferred choice for herself or himself.[11]

The most difficult passages, for Shackle as for me, are those that play on the instrumental necessity of death. In both Persian and Indo-Persian Sufi poetry a theme that complements the extraordinary, yet unattainable, beauty of the divine Beloved is the requirement of death. Death is required yet not as a natural process; rather it is affirmed as a necessary, voluntary, even welcome sequel to unqualified love. The primary exemplar of "love to the point of physical death" is Mansur al-Hallaj. A literal martyr to love, who lost his limbs before being beheaded, burned, and his ashes tossed on the Tigris River, his memory is hallowed by all those Sufis who symbolically also commit themselves to losing selfhood on the path of love.

The Indo-Persian difference from classical Persian verses on the same theme may be seen by comparing verses quoted by Shaykh Nizam ad-din with those of earlier Sufi masters. Among those who eloquently attest to the Hallajian pattern of unstinting love issuing in voluntary death is Shaykh Najm al-Din Daya in his famed **Mirsad al-ʿibad.** Consider his lyrical reflection on Hallaj:

**Bar atesh-e to besozam**
**Gar sukhtan-e manat besazad**
**Gufti ke bibaz jan cun mardan**
**ʿashiq che konad ke jan nabazad**

Hamid Algar translates this poem as follows:

Let me burn on thy love's fire
If for me to burn pleases thee.
Thou said, "Lose thy life in manly style";
What is a lover to do, except lose his life?[12]

The sense of commitment in these verses is balanced by a delayed acquiescence to the Beloved. The bold acknowledgement of the Beloved's demand is followed by a rhetorical question rather than a blanket submission: **ʿashiq che konad ke jan nabazad?** But the final verse of this same narrative on Hallaj in **Mirsad al-ʿibad** removes all doubt about the sacrifice required on behalf of love:

**ʿishq amad o shud chukhunam andar raq o pusht**
**Ta kard mara tahi o pur kard az dost**
**Ajza-ye wojud-e man hame dost girift**
**Nami ast az man bar man o baqi hame ust.**

Again Algar's rendition captures the above in blank verse:

Love came and like blood ran through my flesh and veins
Emptied me, then filled me with the Friend.
The Friend took from me every part of my being,
Of me, a name remained to me; the rest is all HE.

In this final verse, love is all-consuming and transforming yet the concrete sense of being killed by the Beloved remains attenuated, as is the sense of constant renewal through love. Indo-Persian Sufis preferred the image of physical death through the sword to extinction on flames, and in the poetry they selected, as in the poetry they wrote, the dagger as well as the sword loom large. Consider the following verse. Like most of the above, it comes from Persian rather than Indo-Persian, being credited to the little known Khorasanian mystic Shaykh Ahmad-e Jam

(d. 1141). The verse, like the name of Ahmad-e Jam, was celebrated in the subcontinent chiefly among the Chishtiya brotherhood:

**kushtagan-e khanjar-e taslim-ra**
**har zaman az ghaib jane digar ast.**

I first attempted to render it in blank verse:

Those who are slain by the dagger of submission
Each moment from the Unseen receive a new life.

Shackle then found a rhyme that worked:

On all the victims of submission's knife
Each moment the Unseen bestows new life.

And I, following him, discovered another:

All those by the knife of submission killed
Each moment from God with new life are filled.

The verse requires familiarity with the Sufi antonyms of **fana** (annihilation) and **baqa** (permanence). Within that referential field, **fana** is tantamount to loss of self, surrender to the Beloved, who is the Transcendent Creator, who is God. Total surrender equals self-effacement or death; hence those who submit are slain by the dagger of submission. They do not die, however, for in each moment that they die, beyond death they experience **baqa**—"persistence" or "permanence." It is a permanence vouchsafed by the same one who demands death and it is a permanence continuously renewed. **Each** moment from the Beyond or the Unseen or God, the "slain" receives a new soul, which is to say, new life in Him. The pivotal image that empowers this verse is the dagger or knife of submission. It is pivotal because its agent is ambiguous: Is it God, or is it the submission to Him, that produces death? To the extent that the act of submission induces a response it is unimportant who or what the agent of death is, but the beauty of the couplet is its ability to play on the ambiguity as also the dyad of **fana/baqa** and thereby inspire would-be Sufi adepts.

Apart from the hermeneutics of cross-cultural meanings in vastly different contexts, how does one render such a couplet into American English? It is in order to sharpen the focus of the original for an American audience that I have followed Shackle in providing rhyme where there was no rhyme. Indeed, I have exceeded Shackle's initiative by doubling the rhyme, rhyming not only two verbs at the end but also two nouns in the middle of this highly charged couplet. In other aspects also Shackle's approach has improved my own earlier efforts: first, the linking of the initial to the sequel line, and second, the generalizing of **baqa** from "a life" to "life."

Even more graphic, at once more poignant and more lyrical, than the couplet of Shaykh Ahmad-e Jam on death is the following anonymous verse, extant, as far as I know, only through its citation by Shaykh Nizam ad-din in **Fawa'id al-Fu'ad:**

> **dari sar-e ma vagarna dur az bar-e ma**
> **ma dost kushim o to nadari sar-e ma.**

My first effort produced:

> Take heed of me,
> Else begone from me.
> Though I kill my friends,
> Still you heed me not.

Shackle rendered it as:

> Take heed of me, or else "Begone" I say.
> My friends I kill, but no heed you will pay.

Antiphonally I discovered:

> Take heed of me, or else "Begone" I say.
> Though my friends I kill, still no heed you'll pay.

Numerous are the critics who have commented on the fondness of Persian poets for word or phoneme repetitions, but in this short verse it is carried to extremes: **dar-sar-gar-bar** in line one are followed by **dar-sar** in line two. The message is all the more powerful because the voice speaking from Beyond is understood to be the divine Beloved. Rather than the passive voice of the submissive lover, which dominates Persian poetry, here we have the active voice of the jealous lover. How can one recapture the force of this unusual imagery? Moreover, **ma** is accented twice in each line, each time in a stress position. Initially I rendered **ma** as "me" (though literally it means "us"), with a nod to "be" (in begone), while Shackle expanded the rhyme to include the terminal say/pay rhyme. In my rejoinder, I retained his suggestion and added a further kill/still, in order to stress the thematic point of this intricate rhyme: The Friend/God kills His friends, still they remain unaware that He requires death or **fana** (as the prelude to larger life or **baqa**).

Without a sense of the cultural idiom being invoked, the reader might misread this verse as an instance of divine sadism. For those steeped in the Indo-Persian Sufi tradition, however, it becomes a further, exquisite reminder of the high demands that Love makes on the would-be lover.

When so much is at stake, even the selection of a single word becomes crucial, especially when the poet is striving to communicate the flavor of that longed-for death! Usually one does not find either a poet or a mystic reflecting on the difficulty of choosing particular words, but Shaykh Nizam ad-din, the master whose presence animates **Fawa'id al-Fu'ad,** makes just such a disclosure. It occurs only once, at the point when the Shaykh alludes to the intensity of desiring God, which he experienced in a dream. He had been speaking about the taste that is evoked in Sufis through **majalis-e sama'** (or musical assemblies). "It resembles a fire set ablaze," he observed, and then goes on to remark: "Once something appeared to me in a dream, and I uttered this verse:

> O Friend, you have slain me with the **hand** of anticipation!
> And again, I repeated in my dream:
> O Friend, you have slain me with the **wound** of anticipation!
> But when I woke up, I remembered that the correct form of the verse went like this:
> O Friend, you have slain me with the **sword** of anticipation!"

For Professor Shackle, it seemed more appropriate to render the above as:

> You have slain me, my friend, with the **hand** of this waiting.
> **wound**
> **sword**

This marks one of the few instances where I did not modify my prior translation in response to Shackle's suggested rendition. In this case, the Persian is very direct:

> **Ai dost ba-dast-e intizaram kushti.**
> **ba-zakhm-e**
> **ba-tegh-e.**

Not only is the friend so invoked clearly the divine Beloved, but the invocation must come in the initial position, with a capital letter, if one is to capture the immediacy of Shaykh Nizam ad-din's dream. He is, after all, addressing God about his innermost spiritual state or **wilayat:** Like the earlier verse that had literally killed his grand-**pir,** the master of his master, this verse connotes the deadliness of the game of love when played at the advanced level of Sufi shaykhs. For Nizam ad-din, unlike Qutb al-Din, the point of death is not submission (**taslim**) but expectancy or waiting (**intizar**). To non-Sufis that may sound like a quibbling, minor distinction but to a Sufi it suggests the subtlety with which Nizam ad-din is at once conjoined to, and separated from, his predecessor: Qutb al-Din literally expired during **samac,** while Nizam ad-din found that its "fire" propelled him toward the metaphysical goal of his quest without requiring his immediate physical extinction. Killed by anticipation, he nonetheless lived, but he lived for others rather than for himself.

Still, it was important to note in the above verse that the instrument of killing was the **sword** not the **hand,** which would be too anthropomorphic, and not the **wound,** which would be too bodily. The "right" word to convey the Shaykh's innermost spiritual condition is **sword,** for it alone accents both the Friend's intervention and the instrument of psychological extinction.

It is perhaps fitting to end all this talk of killing and dying with the first couplet cited above from **Fawa'id al-Fu'ad.** It reflects one of those instances where I not only differed from Shackle but also from myself, that is to say, I could not decide which of two translations fits the sense of the original Indo-Persian:

**u sukhan az kushtan-e man mikunad**
**man ba-hamin khush ki sukhan mikunad.**

My first attempt was to say:

Though He speaks of killing me,
**He** speaks to me—how thrilling!

But Shackle preferred:

When He speaks, I know He says He'll kill me—
That He speaks is still enough to thrill me.

I tried to imitate his rhyme scheme in a shorter meter:

Even though He says He'll kill me,
That **He** says it can't but thrill me.

Perhaps it is to be expected that after having poured over texts and contexts, meanings and interpretations, for so long, I would at last find myself unable to choose between options. For many reasons, I continue to find myself in a quandary over the above couplet. Even though both renditions convey the sense of the Indo-Persian original, they weight differently the trope of killing. My alternate couplet, like so many others, was inspired by Shackle's attempt. I found his longer meter too awkward to imitate or to retain, yet I remain unhappy with the shorter meters that mark my own efforts. Both reach for the immediacy of the pungent image in the original without, however, capturing its easeful flow. Most days I still prefer my original effort, though I encourage the reader to consider both Shackle's alternative and my own second effort. Better still, you may attempt to construct a fourth option from your own muse. Such are the games, seemingly frivolous but metaphysically freighted, that we begin to play when we enter into the multifaceted world of Shaykh Nizam ad-din Awliya.

I was first introduced to this extraordinary figure and to other Sufi masters of Sultanate India through Professor Khaliq Ahmad Nizami. Professor Nizami agreed to write the Introduction with the same warmth and energy and insight that have characterized his illustrious scholarly career. Like his namesake, Shaykh Nizam ad-din, what he says in writing discloses but a fraction of his true being; only those who have been privileged to know him know also his spiritual and intellectual depth. He is, moreover, generous to a fault. He has assisted me in countless ways over the past two decades, and I hope he will accept from me the dedication of our combined labor to his family—his wife, his sons, his daughter, his in-laws, and now his grandchildren—all of whom have sustained the productivity of his scholarly career, just as they have contributed to the joy of my visits to Aligarh. No one succeeds without the help of others, and it is due to the Nizami family that **Fawa'id al-Fu'ad** has become *Morals for the Heart,* with the hope that it may bring to English readers some of the solaces and satisfactions, the spontaneity and charm that it evokes for countless South Asians, whether they have access to the original Persian text or to one of several Urdu renditions.

There exists no critical edition of the Persian text of **Fawa'id al-Fu'ad,** even though Muhammad Latif Malik has collated five Persian lithographs, together with a single Urdu translation, in his Lahore edition of 1966. Malik has also provided a concise overview of Shaykh Nizam ad-din's life.[13] In most cases it is his edition that has formed the basis for my translation, but I have also benefited from alternate readings in both the Newal Kishore (Lucknow) edition of 1326/1908 and the Mujtabai (Delhi) edition of 1334/1916. The major difference between the lithographs, apart from some crucial poetic passages, is the dating of particular assemblies; unless otherwise indicated, I have preferred the choice of datings given by Malik. One of the ironies of modern printing is the failure to print sufficient copies of Muhammad Latif Malik's edition of **Fawa'id al-Fu'ad:** Sold out within a year of its appearance, it has never been reprinted. I was first introduced to the Malik edition through the good offices of Simon Digby, a nonpareil British scholar whose keen interest in my work has been a continuous source of inspiration during the interim years since our first meeting in 1976. I have consulted for my own translation of **Fawa'id al-Fu'ad** the copy of the Malik edition made available through the Joseph Regenstein Library of the University of Chicago. So rare are copies of the Malik edition that at a recent conference in London (December 1990), two faculty members from the School of Oriental and African Studies complained that no copy of that edition of **Fawa'id al-Fu'ad** was to be found in their library!

The title of the book is itself a marvel, providing one more instance of Amir Hasan's genius. Not only does it effect a pleasing rhyme of consonant and vowel sounds through the repetition of f-a-d, but the second word **fu'ad** has a special ring for Sufis. In depicting the heart, Shaykh Najm al-Din Daya notes that **fu'ad** is among its inner aspects, at once the mine of witnessing (**ma'dan-e mushahadat**) and the abode of vision (**mahall-e ru'yat**), echoing the Qur'anic dictum: "The **fu'ad** did not lie concerning what it saw" (Q.53:13).[14] Not only the Shaykh and Amir Hasan but also other Chishti adepts were probably aware of, and delighted in, these denotations of **fu'ad.**

In order to enlighten the hearts of English readers of this translation, I have facilitated reference to the Shaykh's numerous morals by capitalizing stressed topics throughout the text. While one may consult the index for systematic perusal of major themes, there is also a delight in discovering Shaykh Nizam ad-din's insights by random reference, and it is to that end that there appear woven through the English translation phrases like IMMERSING ONESELF IN GOD and THE IMPORTANCE OF GIVING SOMETHING, or else names of prominent persons, like SHAYKH SAYF AL-DIN BAKHRAZI and MAULANA NUR TURK. Endnotes are provided, but mostly to assist other scholars or would-be students of Islamic mysticism: The worldview of the Shaykh himself should become clear from the main text, at least to the extent that text-derived clarity is possible, since by nature all texts, like the "mere" words of which they are composed, remain provisional, their many meanings elusive.

# Nizam Ad-Din Awliya

## MORALS FOR THE HEART

Conversations of Shaykh Nizam ad-din Awliya
recorded by Amir Hasan Sijzi

---

In the name of the God full of Compassion, ever Compassionate.

These essences of the Unseen, which adorn the One beyond doubt, derive from that treasure-house of affirmation, that storage-bin of certitude, the upright master, he whose name (i.e., Muhammad) is linked to the Qur'anic dictum: "We have not sent you except as a mercy to the universe" (Q.21:107), he who is the king of the poor and worthy, Shaykh Nizam of Truth, of Law, of Guidance, of Faith—may God provide for the Muslims through the lengthening of his life. Amen.

Having collected everything which I heard from that candle of the angelic assembly, I have written down the distillation of his blessed discourse and what it means—at least to the extent that I understood it. Since the heart of the spiritually aroused will benefit from it, I have named this work **Morals for the Heart (Fawa'id al-Fu'ad)**. God alone is our helper; on Him do we rely.

## FASCICLE I (Hereafter I)

### I. Assembly 1
### Sunday, 3 Sha'ban A.H. 707 (27 January 1308)

The hopeful sinner Hasan 'Ala Sijzi, who is the compiler of this discourse, obtained the benefit of kissing the feet of that king of the universe and wellspring of compassion. Praise be to God that on that day, after he had discussed the necessity of saying prescribed prayers plus the early morning prayer and making six prostrations and also saying the evening prayer as well as performing a fast on the brightest white days,[15] he spoke as follows: "THE PENITENT IS EQUIVALENT TO THE UPRIGHT,[16] since the upright is he who never drinks throughout his life or commits a single sin, while the penitent is he who has sinned and then repented of his sin. The two are equivalent," he noted, "in accordance with this Tradition of the Prophet Muhammad—may peace be upon him: 'A person who repents of his sin is like someone who has never sinned.' " He then explained what was meant: "That sinner who becomes aware of his sin and subsequently repents, turning to obedience—every moment he is conscious of the need to obey, and it is possible for one particle of that comfort which he finds in obedience to reduce to ashes all his sinful excesses."

Discussion turned to THE MEN OF GOD and how they OUGHT TO REMAIN HIDDEN till God Almighty Himself has decided to reveal their identity. The master then told a short anecdote about Khwaja Abu'l-Hasan Nuri[17]—may God illumine his grave. "O God," he once prayed, "hide me in Your country among Your servants." From the Beyond he heard a voice: "For God nothing is hidden, nor is God Himself ever hidden!" In the same connection, the master went on to tell another story. "In the vicinity of Nagaur there lived a saint known as Hamid ad-din Suwali[18]—may God grant him mercy and forgiveness. He was asked, 'How is it that after their death some of the saints are never remembered by name while in the case of others, their posthumous fame spreads to the end of the earth? What causes this disparity in the states of saints?' Hamid ad-din answered: 'He who strives to become famous during his lifetime—after he dies his name will be forgotten, while he who conceals his identity during his lifetime—after he dies his name will resound throughout the world!' "[19]

Discussion next turned to THE GREAT SHAYKHS and their PROGRESS to stages BEYOND that of GOD'S DEPUTIES (**abdal**).[20] The master told about a man who, on entering the hospice (**khanqah**) of Shaykh ʿAbd al-Qadir Jilani[21]—may God sanctify his lofty secret—saw a person sitting at the doorway with broken hands and feet. The fellow was in a wretched condition. Approaching the Shaykh, the visitor told him what he had seen and requested the Shaykh to intercede on behalf of this fellow. "Fie!" exclaimed Shaykh ʿAbd al-Qadir; "he has been disrespectful." "What did he do wrong?" asked the visitor. "He is one of God's deputies," explained the Shaykh. "Day before yesterday he, together with two of his companions, were winging through the air. As they approached the space above our **khanqah,** one of the companions, out of respect, detoured to the right; the other, out of respect, detoured to the left, but this wretched fellow, being disrespectful, flew over the **khanqah**—and came plummeting to the ground!"

In the same connection the master began to discuss how ONE OUGHT TO BE RESPECTFUL TO THE **PIR** (Spiritual Master) and give answers that are pleasing to him. Once, on the eve of the ʿ**id** celebration, Khwaja Junayd Baghdadi[22]—may God sanctify his lofty secret—was sitting in his **khanqah.** Four men from the Unseen came to pay their respects to him. Turning to one of them, he asked, "Where will you go in the morning to say your **ʿid** prayers?" "To Blessed Mecca" was the reply. "And you?" he asked the second. "To Exalted Medina" was the reply. "As for you?" he queried the third. "To the Sanctified House, that is, Jerusalem," was the reply. "And what about you?" he demanded of the fourth. Bowing down before Junayd, the fourth replied, "I will remain in Baghdad in the service of the master [i.e., Junayd]." To the fourth visitor Junayd exclaimed, "It is you who are the most devout, you are the most knowledgeable, you are the most virtuous of all!"

The conversation next turned to PURIFICATION. "To perfect his soul," explained the master, "man must do four things: eat little, talk little, sleep little, and also socialize little."[23] To illustrate the true nature of effort and exertion, he recited the following verse:

Although God guides us in our faith,
Still efforts must be made by men.
The deed-books read on Judgment Day
Must have their entries here first penned.

### I. Assembly 2
Friday, 8 Shaʿban, A.H. 707 (4 February 1308)

After prayer I obtained the benefit of kissing the master's feet. I had had a slave named Malih.[24] Out of deference to the master—may God perpetuate his blessings—and in gratitude for the privilege of discipleship, I had set him free and offered prayers on his behalf. At the same time this slave approached the feet of the eminence of both worlds and was honored to make the oath of allegiance to him. Praise be to God!

On this occasion the master—may God prolong his blessings—observed that "THERE IS NO SUCH THING AS SLAVERY AND DOMINION IN THE WAY; all who enter properly into the world of love do God's work." To explain what he meant he told the story of a certain master from Ghazni. He had a slave named Zairak and that Zairak was extremely righteous and virtuous. When the time of death approached for that saint, his disciples asked: "Who will sit in your place?" "Zairak," he replied. Now that master had four sons, Ikhtiyar, Ajlad, Ahba, and Ajla. Zairak said, "O Khwaja, your sons will not allow me to succeed you. Every moment they will vent their anger on me." "Set your heart at ease," replied the saint. "If they cause you any trouble, I will defend you from their evil machinations." In short, when the saint was joined to the realm of divine mercy, Zairak succeeded him. The sons of the saint began to foment trouble. "You are our slave! What right do you have to sit in our father's place?" When their harassment became intense, Zairak went to the grave of the saint, pleading, "O master, you said: 'If my sons vex you, I will defend you from their evil machinations.' Now that they are berating me, you must honor your promise." Having said this, he returned home. Within a few days unbelievers attacked the vicinity of Ghazni. The inhabitants went out to do battle with them. All four of the saint's progeny also joined in the fray, and all four of them died the death of martyrs. And Zairak continued to abide in that place without further commotion.

The aforementioned Malih, after he had taken the vows of discipleship, offered two cycles of prayer. "What was your intention in offering these two cycles of prayer?" asked the master. "To expel everything other than God," replied Malih.

### I. Assembly 3
### Friday, 15th of Shaʿban, A.H. 707 (11 February 1308)

After prayer I obtained the benefit of kissing the master's feet. A **juwaliq** (i.e., a kind of itinerant dervish)[25] entered and sat down for about an hour, then got up and left. The master—may God remember him with favor—said, "Among this group of people very few had access to the presence of Shaykh Baha ad-din Zakariya—may God have mercy on him.[26] But into the presence of Shaykh al-Islam Farid ad-din—may God have **abundant** mercy on him—every sort of dervish and other kind of person would come." After that, he observed that IN THE MIDST OF EVERY GROUP of people (ʿ**ami**) there IS ONE OF GOD'S ELECT (**khassi**).[27] And in this connection he told a story about Shaykh Baha ad-din Zakariya. "The Shaykh traveled much. Once he came upon a group of **juwaliqs,** and sat down among them. A light appeared in that group. As his eyes focussed on it, he saw that the light emanated from a member of that group. Slowly he approached the man. 'What are you doing in the midst of this group?' he asked. 'Zakariya!' retorted the man. '[I am here] that you may know that in the midst of every group of people there is one of God's elect!' "

In the same vein the master told a further story. "Once a saint arrived in the midst of a group of this sort (i.e., **juwaliqs**). He saw one of them recite the whole Qurʾan in two cycles of prayer. The saint was amazed. He said to himself: 'In circumstances of the kind this man experiences, it is rare to find such a level of obedience, for not everyone can persist in this (spiritual) task (of memorizing and reciting the Qur'an).' After a short while he left the **juwaliqs.** When ten years had elapsed, he happened to encounter the same group again. That dervish whom he had seen before was still performing the very task which had amazed him. 'Now have I witnessed the truth of this axiom,' he declared, 'that in the midst of every group of people there is indeed one of God's elect!' "

I. Assembly 4
Friday, 22nd of Sha'ban, A.H. 707 (18 February 1308)

After prayer I obtained the benefit of kissing his feet. The master said: "Between the prayers of evening and nightfall do you make the six prostrations that I have commended to you?" "Yes," I replied. After the fast of the bright white days, he asked again whether I had performed these prayers. I said that I had. After the mid-morning prayer, he asked once more. "I have done it," I repeated, "and after four inclinations I said the prayer of good fortune." "Today," he replied, "good fortune upon good fortune has been added to you." Praise be to God for all those blessings!

I. Assembly 5
Friday, the 5th of Ramadan, A.H. 707 (2 March 1308)

Before prayer I obtained the benefit of kissing the master's feet. "What is THE PREEMINENT FORM OF NONCANONICAL PRAYER?" he asked. Then he explained that, according to the decree of Maulana Zahir ad-din Hafiz—may God Almighty grant him peace—it was the **namaz-i tarawih** [a lengthy prayer consisting of twenty prostrations]. "Every evening," recalled the master, "he would also urge me to read three sections of the Qur'an, so that after ten consecutive evenings I might complete the whole of the Qur'an and obtain the benefit of performing this task. At his command, after the congregational prayer, I would retire to observe the **namaz-i tarawih.** 'Good!' he would exclaim to me; 'That is a commendable thing for you to do!' "

Afterward, in the same connection, the master told a story about Shaykh Baha ad-din Zakariya—may God have mercy upon him. One evening he turned to those who were present (in his hospice) and asked, "Who among you this evening will say two cycles of prayer, and in one cycle will recite the whole of the Qur'an?" Among those present no one could fathom the sense of what the Shaykh was saying. Shaykh Baha ad-din then stepped forward. In one cycle of prayer he recited the entire Qura'an plus four additional sections; then in the second cycle he recited the **Surat al-Ikhlas** (Q.112) and finished his prayer.

On the same theme the master told still another story about Shaykh Baha ad-din Zakariya—may God have mercy upon him. The latter would say: "Whatever I have been told about the prayers and invocations of saint and devotees—I have observed them all, but one thing I have not been able to do, and that is this: It has been related to me that a certain saint from the break of dawn till the rising of the sun would recite the entire Qur'an. However much I have wanted to do the same, I could not."

In the same context he told one further anecdote. "Qazi Hamid ad-din Nagauri[28]—may God have mercy upon him—was once circumambulating the Ka'ba. He saw a certain man whom he began to track: Wherever that saintly person would walk, Qazi Hamid ad-din would follow in his footsteps. The **pir,** on realizing what was happening, asked Qazi Hamid ad-din—may God have mercy upon him: 'Why are you practicing external conformity? Conform yourself to what I am really doing.' 'What is that?' asked Qazi Hamid ad-din. 'Every day,' replied the **pir,** 'I recite the entire Qur'an 700 times!' Qazi Hamid ad-din was stupefied. To himself he thought, 'But it is the meaning of the Qur'an which he calls to mind and imagines that he is reciting its words!' The **pir** craned his head toward the Qazi and remarked, 'I recite literally, **not** figuratively!' "

When the master—may God remember him with favor—had finished this story, Aghaz ad-din 'Ali Shah—may God Almighty grant him peace—who belonged to the inner circle of his disciples, asked, "Is this not a miracle (**karamat**)?" "Yes," replied the master, "it **is** a miracle. Every action which the intellect can decipher—that is one thing, but every action which it is impossible for the intellect to unravel—that is a miracle."

After a while the conversation turned to THE OBEDIENCE OF THE SHAYKHS. The master noted that Shaykh Abu Sa'id Abu'l-Khayr—may God have mercy upon him—used to say: "Whatever I have been told about the prayers of the Prophet Muhammad—peace and blessings be upon him—I have observed. I have even gone to this extent: When I heard that the Prophet—peace and blessings be upon him—once performed the inverted prayer (**namaz-i ma'kus**), I went and, tying a rope around my feet, suspended myself upside down inside a well and performed my prayers in this posture."

As he finished telling this story, the master turned toward this humble servant, and commented, "Whoever achieves his objective through virtuous action is the beneficiary of divine grace . . . yet it is still incumbent on man to exert himself!"

## I. Assembly 6
### Friday, 5th of Shawwal, A.H. 707 (30 March 1308)

After prayer I obtained the benefit of kissing the master's feet. Conversation turned to RENUNCIATION AND SOLITUDE and during that period he told of a dervish who practiced extreme poverty and physical deprivation. Due to continuous hunger his stomach became distended. He was walking down a road one day when our friend Khwaja Muhammad Tapuh placed a grain (of barley) before him. "I have already eaten garlic dregs today," replied the dervish. "Due to the feeling of total contentment I experienced, I have no need today of this grain (of barley)." After that the master—may God remember him with favor—marveled at the dervish's zest for righteousness. "What contentment! What power! What patience!" he exclaimed.

In the same connection he went on to speak about CONTENTMENT AND DESIRING NOTHING OTHER THAN GOD. "There was a saint named Shaykh ʿAli," he noted; "One day he was sewing his patched garment (**khirqa**) with one of his legs outstretched before him, and as he was quilting, the fold of the patched garment covered the outstretched leg. The successor (to a notable saint), happened to arrive at this time, according to reports, but Shaykh ʿAli did not budge from his place. Remaining in the same position, he invited the successor to come in. The successor entered and, greeting Shaykh ʿAli, sat down. Shaykh ʿAli returned his greeting, but the attendant who was accompanying the successor said, 'Shaykh, fold your legs.' Shaykh ʿAli ignored him. Two or three times the attendant repeated his injunction. Later, as the successor was about to leave, Shaykh ʿAli clasped the hand of the attendant and that of the successor, 'Look!' he exclaimed, 'I have folded my hands; hence I do not need to fold my legs! That is to say, I am not now desiring, nor have I ever desired, anything from you. I grasp nothing; I have folded my hands. So if I choose not to fold my legs, that is my right!' "

For a while the conversation turned to THE BASIS FOR SPIRI-

TUAL PROGRESS, that is, the kernel of meaning. In this connection the master noted that a man once presented himself to Khwaja Ajall Shirazi—may God grant him mercy and forgiveness—and the Khwaja conferred discipleship on him. The new disciple expected Khwaja Ajall to instruct him on the invocations and prayers he ought to observe. "Whatever you do not find agreeable for yourself," declared the Khwaja, "do not wish it to happen to others; wish for yourself (only) what you also wish for others." In short, that man went away and after a while returned, presenting himself again to Khwaja Ajall Shirazi—may God have mercy upon him. "On such-and-such a day," he submitted to the Khwaja, "I waited upon you, hoping that you might tell me a prayer or invocation (that I could repeat), but you told me nothing. Today I am also expectant." "On that day," replied the Khwaja, "what were your instructions?" The disciple was stupefied; he did not answer. The Khwaja smiled and said, "On that day I told you that whatever was not pleasing to yourself was also not pleasing to another, and (that you ought to) wish for yourself the same thing that you wish for another. You did not remember that instruction. Since you have not learned the first lesson, how can I give you another?"

After that the master told the following story about a certain chaste saint. Many times he used to say that all virtuous deeds, such as prayers, fasting, invocations, and saying the rosary are a cauldron, but the basic staple in the cauldron is meat: Without meat you do not experience any of these virtuous deeds. Finally they asked that **pir**: "Many times you have used that analogy, but now explain it." "Meat," replied the saint, "is RENOUNCING WORLDLINESS, while prayer, fasting, invocation, as well as repetition of the rosary—all such virtuous deeds presuppose that the one who does them has left the world and is no longer attached to any worldly thing. Whether he observes or does not observe prayer, invocations, and other practices, there is no cause for fear, but if friendship with the world lingers in his heart, he derives no benefit from supplications, invocations, and the like."

After that the master observed: "If one puts ghee, pepper, garlic, and onion into a cauldron and adds only water, the end result is known as pseudo-stew. The basic staple for stew is meat; there may or may not be other ingredients. Similarly, the basis for spiritual progress is leaving the world; there may or may not be other virtuous practices."

The master then began to speak about what RENOUNCING WORLDLINESS actually entailed. "Renouncing worldliness does not mean, for instance, that one becomes naked, wearing only a loin cloth and sitting (in solitude). Renouncing worldliness means, instead, to wear clothes and to take food while at the same time keeping in continuous use whatever comes to hand, feeling no inclination to hoard and no attachment to material objects. That [disposition alone] is tantamount to renouncing worldliness."[29]

### I. Assembly 7
### Friday, 19th of Shawwal, A.H. 707 (13 April 1308)

After prayers I obtained the benefit of kissing the feet of the master. Conversation focused on THE MANNERS OF SUFIS, THE SIGNS OF THE SHAYKHS AND THEIR TECHNICAL TERMS. The master observed: "Shaykh Jamal ad-din Bistami—may God have mercy upon him—used to be the Shaykh al-Islam and spiritual overlord of Delhi. He was well informed about the customs and manners of Sufis, as is evident from the following anecdote. Once a water jug was brought to him and it had four handles. Another saint was present and he said, 'This is called "the jug of Luqman." ' 'Why do they call it "the jug of Luqman" '? inquired Shaykh Jamal ad-din Bistami. The other saint fell silent. Shaykh Jamal ad-din then told this story. 'There was once a saint known as Shaykh Luqman Sarkhasi—may God have mercy upon him. His virtues were numerous, as is evident from the following anecdote. It has been related that Shaykh Luqman once missed the Friday prayer or failed to follow one of the divine injunctions, and God knows the truth of what really happened, but in any case, the **ʿulama** of that city came out to question him. People told him: "The **ʿulama** of the city are coming to investigate you." "Are they coming by horseback or on foot?" asked the saint. "On horseback," was the reply. At that time Shaykh Luqman was sitting on a wall. "By the order of God Almighty," he intoned, "move!" and the wall immediately moved.

"As for 'the jug of Luqman,' it evolved as follows: Shaykh Luqman once asked a disciple to bring him a jug of water. The disciple fetched a jug but it had no handle. 'I must have a jug which I can pick up,' protested the saint. The disciple made a handle on the same jug and brought it back to the saint. Smiling, Shaykh Luqman observed, 'You may clasp this jug but where am I to take hold of it? Go, make a jug with two handles and bring it back.' The disciple went and fashioned two handles on to the jug and presented it to the saint, clasping one handle with one of his hands, the other handle with the other hand. Again, Shaykh Luqman protested, 'You are holding on to both handles. Where am I to clasp it? Go! Make a jug with three handles.' The disciple went and made three handles, but when he returned to the Shaykh, he clasped two handles himself, one in each hand, while the third handle pointed toward his own chest! Smiling, Shaykh Luqman demurred, 'Go, make four handles.' And the disciple, after making four handles, once again returned, presenting the jug to the saint, who at last accepted it. Hence it is that the four-handled jug is called 'the jug of Luqman.' "[30]

I. Assembly 8
Friday, 26th of Shawwal, A.H. 707 (20 April 1308)

After prayers I obtained the benefit of kissing the master's feet. Conversation turned to PRAYER AND THE SPIRITUAL AWARENESS (**huzur**) OF PRAYER LEADERS. The master observed that the indispensable precondition for spiritual awareness is that the prayer leader absorb the meaning of what he prays in his heart.

After that he told about a certain Muslim who was among the disciples of Shaykh Baha ad-din Zakariya—may God have mercy upon him. "The disciple was known as Hasan Afghan. The man was a pillar of saintliness, so much so that Shaykh Baha ad-din Zakariya used to say: 'If tomorrow they ask me to bring forward one person from my household (**dargah**) as a representative to face judgment on behalf of all the others, I would select Hasan Afghan.' Once this same Hasan was passing through a town and arrived at the mosque in time for prayer. The Imam led the prayer and the people followed along. Khwaja Hasan also joined in. When the prayers were completed and the congregation had dispersed, he slowly went up to the Imam and said, 'Respected sir, you began the prayers and I fell in with you. You went from here to Delhi and bought some slaves, came back, then took the slaves to Khurasan, and afterward left there for Multan. I got my neck twisted trying to catch up with you. What has all this to do with prayer?!' "[31]

Then, to explain his saintliness further, the master said, "Once they were building a mosque in such-and-such a place. Khwaja Hasan arrived there. To the people constructing it he said, 'Be sure to make the prayer niche pointing to Mecca (**mihrab**) here, for orientation to the Kaʿba (**qibla**) is in this direction.' Having said this, he pointed to a particular spot. A scholar was present there. He disagreed, saying, 'No, orientation to the Kaʿba is in another direction.' Many words were exchanged between them. Finally Khwaja Afghan said to the scholar, 'Face that direction which I indicated and note it well.' The scholar complied with the saint's demand and verified that the Kaʿba was indeed in the same direction that Khwaja Hasan had indicated."

After that the master began to explain THE SPIRITUAL STATES OF KHWAJA HASAN. "He was illiterate. He could not read. People would come to him and, placing a piece of paper and a tablet before him, would begin to write some lines, a sample of poetry, a sample of prose, some in Arabic, some in Persian; of every sort they would write some lines. And in the midst of these lines they would include a single line from a verse of the Word of God. Then they would ask Khwaja Hasan, 'Of all these lines, which is from the Qur'an?' He would point to the Qur'anic verse, saying, 'It is this!' 'But you don't read the Qur'an,' they would protest. 'How can you tell that this is a Qur'anic verse?' He would reply: 'I see a light in this line that I do not see in the other lines of writing.' "

Also, in connection with THE SPIRITUAL STATE OF SAINTS, the master began to speak of immersion in prayer. "There was a man named Khwaja Karim," he noted. "In his early life he was a clerk in Delhi but in his last years he turned away from worldly preoccupations and became one of those united with God (**wasilan**). Many times he used to say, 'As long as my grave is in Delhi, no unbeliever will conquer the city.' "

The master then explained KHWAJA KARIM'S TOTAL AWARENESS OF GOD DURING PRAYER. "Once at the time of evening prayer, he was completely absorbed in prayer before the city gate. But in those days there were civil disturbances and no one was permitted to mill around the gate in the evening. That Khwaja Karim was absorbed in prayer. His friends were standing by the gate. 'Quickly,' they entreated him, 'come into the city!' The gatekeepers also tried to urge him on. In short, when Khwaja Karim finished his prayer and returned from there, they asked him, 'Did you not hear some voices?' 'No,' he replied. 'How strange that you did not hear our insistent urgings!' they commented. 'Strange?' retorted Khwaja Karim, 'What would be strange is for someone to be truly in prayer and **still** hear the urgings of others!' "

After that the master observed that Karim, once he set his face toward God Almighty, never laid his finger on any coin or currency. And about leaving the world and its pleasures, he noted: "One must have a high spiritual resolve and not be preoccupied with the defilements of the world, nor be held in tow by sensual desires." Then these two lines of poetry came to his blessed lips:

For one brief moment stand back from the lusts you bear,
And let a thousand witnesses[32] come forward there.

### I. Assembly 9
Thursday, 10th of Dhu'l-Qa'da A.H. 707 (3 May 1308)

I obtained the benefit of kissing the master's feet. "How is it that you come today," he asked, "since the time for recording conversations had been fixed as Friday?"[33] "This blessing appeared to be especially auspicious today," I explained, "and every time that the opportunity for such a blessing appears I try to obtain the benefit of kissing the master's feet." "You have done well," he replied. "Whatever comes from the Unseen is for the good."

After that he began to talk about THE INFLUENCE OF COMPANY. "The company of others has a powerful influence," he observed, and then he went on to speak at great length about RENOUNCING WORLDLINESS. During this time upon his blessed tongue came the query: "Is there any one who, by removing himself from a putrid object, has not undertaken a noble task?"

### I. Assembly 10
Friday, 11th of Dhu'l-Qa'da A.H. 307 (4 May 1308)

I obtained the blessing of kissing the master's feet. Present on this occasion were several of the dear ones (i.e., members of the inner circle of the Shaykh's disciples), such as Maulana Wajih ad-din Pa'ili, Maulana Husam ad-din Hajji, together with Maulana Taj ad-din, his friend, and Maulana Jamal ad-din as well as other friends. Food was brought in, and the master said, "Everyone who is not fasting—please eat!" Since these were the bright days, most of the group were fasting. When food was put before them, only two or three people who were not fasting took some. At this point the master commented, "When friends arrive, one should put food out for them. ONE OUGHT NOT TO ASK, 'ARE YOU FASTING?' because if someone does not wish to fast, he will eat of his own accord. Moreover, it is wise not to ask, 'Are you fasting?' because if someone replies 'I am fasting' (and he is not), he is skirting the edge of hypocrisy. On the other hand, if he is actually firm and sincere in his fasting, there is no room for hypocrisy, and yet because he replies, 'Yes, I am fasting,' instantly his obedience, which had been a secret, is divulged on the public ledger. Should someone answer, 'I am partially fasting,' he has told a lie, and as for the person who remains quiet, he shows contempt for the questioner!"

I. Assembly 11
Monday, 21st of Dhu'l-Qa'da A.H. 707 (14 May 1308)

I obtained the benefit of kissing the master's feet. The subject of conversation was THE BLESSING which is CONFERRED BY THE FEET OF SAINTLY MEN. He asserted: "Every spiritless place [where they have trod] has been scented by their feet. Consider the congregational mosque of Delhi—how many feet of saints and holy men have trod upon it and for that very reason how much comfort is to be found there!"

At that time he spoke of Mahmud Kabir. "He is reported to have said: 'One morning I saw a saint who came and went from the space above the multicolored beams of the Friday mosque, that is, the space above the balcony of the central prayer niche (**mihrab**)—he came and went from there like an ant: in great haste but without the least confusion. Back and forth he went from one to the other. I stood looking at him from afar. As dawn approached, he descended from those beams. I came forward and greeted him. "Did you see me?" he asked. "Yes," I replied. "Don't tell anyone!" he enjoined me.' "

At this point I interjected: "Most of the SAINTS CONCEAL THEIR SPIRITUAL STATES—why is that?" Replied the master: "If they disclose their secret, you would shift the abode of confidentiality to another person. Suppose someone tells your secret to someone else, and then that person makes it public. Would you ever again divulge a secret to the first person?"

"How is it," I asked, "that Khwaja Abu Sa'id Abu'l-Khayr—may God have mercy upon him—often gave voice to words from the Unseen?" "At the time that saints are overcome by desire (for God)," explained the master, "due to their intoxication (**sukr**), they say something, but that person who is perfected (**kamil**) lets out no kind of secrets." After that a line of verse came twice to his blessed lips:

God's heroes drain a thousand seas . . . yet thirst.
God's heroes drain a thousand seas . . . yet thirst.

He then observed that it requires great patience to honor the divine secrets and those who do are wholly men of sobriety (**sahw**). "Which is the higher stage," I asked, "the stage of the men of intoxication or that of the men of sobriety?" "The stage of the men of sobriety," replied the master. And God knows best.

## I. Assembly 12
### Wednesday, 14th of Dhu'l-Hijja, A.H. 707 (5 June 1308)

I obtained the blessing of kissing the master's feet. The topic of conversation turned to THE ACCEPTANCE OF ANOTHER'S GIFT. From his blessed tongue came the declaration: "One should honor any devotion or invocation that comes from a man infused with divine grace, for in so doing, one will find a different kind of comfort. Some invocations," he went on, "I have made incumbent on myself but others I have received from my master, that is, Shaykh Farid ad-din—may God sanctify his lofty secret. At those times when I use both kinds of invocations, what a difference is there in the respective comforts they provide! It is as great as the distance between heaven and earth!"

Conversation turned to LEAVING OF CHOICE that is, not pursuing a work of your own volition. Asked the master: "Why should a man who has been given wisdom by another call himself wise?"

Then he told a story about Shaykh Abu Sa'id Abu'l-Khayr—may God have mercy upon him. One Friday he came out of his hospice (**khanqah**) in order to participate in the congregational prayer. "Which is the way to the Friday mosque and how does one go there?" he asked his disciples. One of those present said, "This is the way." Others asked him, "How many times has the Shaykh participated in congregational prayer, and still he doesn't know the way to the mosque?" "I know the way," replied Shaykh Abu Sa'id, "but I ask all the same, in order that in every circumstance I am dependent on the wisdom of another!"

After that the master exhorted those present about LEAVING COUNTRY, LOVE OF HOME, PROPERTY, AND THE LIKE. He also recited the following verse:

Take to the rocks and deserts like a beast,
And leave your home for cats and mice to feast.
Since Jesus' food from heaven was conveyed,
In heaven too a home for him was made.
Homes merely built to guard one's food-supply
Are like the nests where bees and insects lie!

I. Assembly 13
Sunday, 3rd of Muharram, A.H. 708 (23 June 1308)

I obtained the blessing of kissing the master's feet. The topic of discourse was DEVOTION (TO GOD). "There are two forms of devotion," he explained; "One is mandatory, the other is supererogatory. Mandatory devotion is that from which the benefit is limited to one person, that is, to the performer of that devotion, whether it be canonical prayers, fasting, pilgrimage to Arabia, invocations, repetitions of the rosary, or the like. But supererogatory devotion is that which brings benefit and comfort to others, whether through the expenditure of money or demonstration of compassion or other ways of helping one's fellow man. Such actions are called supererogatory devotion. Their reward is incalculable; it is limitless. In mandatory devotion one must be sincere to merit divine acceptance, but in supererogatory devotion even one's sins become a source of reward! May God grant success!"

I. Assembly 14
Thursday, 7th Muharram, A.H. 708 (27 June 1308)

I obtained the benefit of kissing the master's feet. Discussion turned to THE DIFFERENCE BETWEEN SAINTHOOD (**walayat**) AND SAINTDOM (**wilayat**). The master explained: "The saint possesses both **walayat** and **wilayat** at the same time. **Walayat** is that which masters impart to disciples about God, just as they teach them about the etiquette of the Way. Everything such as this which takes place between the Shaykh and other peoples is called **walayat**. But that which takes place between the Shaykh and God is called **wilayat.** That is a special kind of love, and when the Shaykh leaves the world, he takes his **wilayat** with him. His **walayat**, on the other hand, he can confer on someone else, whomever he wishes, and if he does not confer it, then it is suitable for God Almighty to confer that **walayat** on someone. But the **wilayat** is the Shaykh's constant companion; he bears it with him (wherever he goes)."

In this connection the master told the story of a certain saint who sent one of his disciples to call on another saint and to determine what had transpired on the face of the earth that night. The disciple sent back word that at night Shaykh Abu Saʿid Abuʾl-Khayr—may God sanctify his lofty secret—had expired at Mayhana (in Khurasan). The same saint sent someone else to enquire who it was on whom They had conferred his

**walayat.** "I have no news of that," he answered; "all that has been made known I have disclosed to you." Subsequently, word was received that They had conferred that **walayat** on Shams al-ʿarifin. That very night the saint, with his disciple, went to the door of Shams al-ʿarifin. Before they could say anything, Shams al-ʿarifin declared: "How many Shams al-ʿarifins does God have? On **which** Shams al-ʿarifin have They conferred the **walayat** of Abu Saʿid Abuʾl-Khayr?"

After that the master told a story about Shaykh Najib ad-din Mutawakkil—may God have mercy upon him, the brother of Shaykh al-Islam Farid ad-din—may God sanctify his lofty secret. When he first went to school to acquire a formal education, the teacher asked: "Are you Najib ad-din Mutawakkil?" "I am Najib ad-din **mutaʾakkil,** that is, the compulsive consumer," he replied; "how can any one be **mutawakkil,** that is, utterly reliant (on God)?" Then the teacher asked, "You **are** the brother of Shaykh al-Islam Farid ad-din, are you not?" "In appearance I am," replied Najib ad-din, "but how can any one be truly his brother?"

After a while conversation turned to THE CAPACITY FOR FORGIVENESS AMONG MEN INFUSED WITH DIVINE GRACE, men who see the true state of those claiming to serve the saints. "There was once a master full of grace and charity," noted the master. "From time to time he would send Qazi ʿAin al-Quzat Hamadani—may God show him mercy and forgiveness—some money to expend as the saint saw fit. Now it happened that on a certain occasion Qazi ʿAin al-Quzat wanted something from another person, and he obtained what he wanted. That master heard about it and was displeased. He sent to Qazi ʿAin al-Quzat a messenger who chided the saint: 'Why do you need to get anything from someone else, and why do you waste this bounty on others?' Qazi ʿAin al-Quzat—may God have mercy upon him—wrote the following reply: 'Look out for the welfare of the afflicted, in order that someone else might obtain this bounty. Do not act like those of whom it has been said: "God has been merciful to us, so has the Prophet, but one (of our fellow Muslims) has not been merciful to us!" ' Nor should you act like that group one of whose members said:

Come, gardener, open wide the garden gate but
Once I and my love have entered, then slam it shut!"

That same day Amir Chahju, nephew of the writer, became a disciple (of Shaykh Nizam ad-din) and made the profession of allegiance, and Shams ad-din, his brother, was also shaved, as was a grandson of Shaykh

Jamal ad-din Hansawi[34]—may God have mercy upon him. And Mawlana Burhan ad-din Gharib[35]—may God Almighty give him peace—also had the hair of both his head and his beard shaven in renewing his vows of allegiance to the master. Shaykh ʿUthman Siwistani wanted a cap and obtained it, while Shams ad-din was presented with a cloak (**khirqa**). Many a day was passed in peace due to what happened on that day.

It was on the same occasion that the master told a story about Shaykh Badr ad-din Ghaznawi—may God have mercy upon him. When he used to come into the presence of Shaykh al-Islam Qutb ad-din Oushi—may God sanctify his secret—he would lower his head and the Shaykh would recite the following verse:

Indeed the lamp grows dim so quick
When once the oil has left its wick.

I. Assembly 15
Wednesday, 6th of Jumada al-ula, A.H. 708 (24 October 1308)

Having returned to Delhi with the imperial army from Khizrabad, I obtained the benefit of kissing the master's feet. The topic of conversation turned to MEN OF THE UNSEEN, their capacity to intuit events and to exercise high spiritual resolve in acts of devotion and striving. At this time the master told about a youth named Nasir in Badaun. "It has been reported about him that he once said, 'My father became a person united with God (**wasil**). One night they summoned him before the door to our house. He came out. From inside I heard the exchange of greetings, and then I heard my father say, "I will bid farewell to my children and family." But they replied: "The moment is fleeting." After that I learned nothing more about where they or my father went.' "

On the same occasion he told a story about Shaykh Shihab ad-din Suhrawardi—may God have mercy upon him. He wrote a book in which he recalled: "In our time there was a youth named Qazuni. Ten of the Unseen used to gather in his home. Once people were lined up for ritual prayer, and one of the men of the Unseen was the prayer leader. Those present heard a loud Qur'anic recitation and repetition of the rosary, together with the rest of the prayer service. But they did not see him; only Qazuni did." Shaykh Shihab ad-din went on to note: "One of those men of the Unseen put a small bead into the hand of Qazuni; it is a bead which has come down to me and which is still in my possession."

On the same occasion the master told another story. "There was a man named ʿAli, the door of whose prayer cell men of the Unseen regularly visited. Each time they would exchange greetings, and this went on for some time till one day they came and greeted ʿAli as usual: 'Peace be upon you!' But Khwaja ʿAli replied: 'O men of the Unseen, you are always saying "Peace" and speaking out loud but you never become visible!' After he spoke thus, he never again heard their voices."

At this point I interjected: "But was not Khwaja ʿAli rude to speak in this manner?" "Indeed, he was," replied the master, "and it was for this very reason that he was deprived of the future benefit of their presence." After that, the master explained: "Men of the Unseen first speak with, and listen to, a devout person; then they meet him, and only at the end do they vanish with him!"

How can words express what exhilaration and comfort was derived from the master's telling of this story!

### I. Assembly 16
Tuesday, 19th of Jumada al-ula, A.H. 708 (6 November 1308)

I obtained the blessing of kissing the master's feet. He began to discuss SPIRITUAL PROGRESS (and backsliding). "The traveler is constantly on the way to perfection," he explained, "that is, so long as he is progressing in the Way, he is in hope of perfection."

"There is the traveler, the standstill, and the retreater," he later noted. "The traveler is the one who treads the Path; the standstill is the one who stops along the Way."

At this point I interjected, "Can the traveler become the standstill?" "Yes," replied the master. "Every time that the traveler lapses in his obedience, he becomes stationary. If he quickly resumes his work and repents, then he may again become a traveller. If, God forbid, he remains at a standstill, then he may become a retreater or backslider."

He went on to enumerate the seven stages of spiritual backsliding: (1) turning away; (2) veiling; (3) multiplying the veil(s); (4) wasting the excess; (5) forfeiting the basis; (6) hardening (of the heart); and (7) enmity.

"Say there are two friends," explained the master; "they are the lover and the beloved, each absorbed in love of the other. If the lover, either by what he does or fails to do, displeases the Beloved, the Friend shuns him, that is, the Friend **turns away** from him in aversion. Then the lover must immediately apologize and continuously repent. If he does, the Beloved will become content with him. But if the lover persists in his error and refuses to apologize, the turning away becomes a **veil** between them; it is the Beloved who puts a veil between them. Then the lover must repent, yet if he delays further, **the veil multiplies.** What happens beyond this point? If the Friend becomes separate from His friend, and the latter still does not repent, the latter will **waste the excess merit** which has accrued to him from all his supererogatory devotions and prayers and other actions. If he still does not repent and persists in that foolishness, then he **forfeits the basis,** that is, the comfort in obedience, which has preceded the accumulation of excess. If even at this point he falls short of complete repentance, there is a **hardening of the heart**—that is, the Friend separates Himself even in His heart. If he remains obdurate in his failure to repent, the hardening of the heart turns to **enmity.**

God forbid that we ever enter that [fearful state] either in thought or in reality!

## I. Assembly 17

Monday, 25th of Jumada al-ula, A.H. 708 (15 November 1308)

I obtained the blessing of kissing the master's feet. Conversation turned to THE VIRTUE OF GIVING FOOD TO OTHERS. On the blessed tongue of the master came these words: "There is no merit attached to providing food for your own people." Then he began to talk of Khwaja ʿAli, the son of Khwaja Rukn ad-din, the venerable Chishti saint—may God bestow His favor upon both of them. He was taken captive during the onslaught of the infidel Mongols. They brought him before Chinghiz Khan. At the time one of the disciples of that noble dynasty (of Chishti saints) was present, not only present but in a position of authority (at the Mongol court). When he saw that Khwaja ʿAli had been taken prisoner, he was dumbfounded. To himself he thought, "How can I procure his release? In what way should I mention his name before Chinghiz Khan? If I say that he comes from a noble family and is himself a saint, what will Chinghiz Khan care? And if I mention his obedience and devotion, that, too, will have no effect."

After pondering a long time, he went before Chinghiz Khan and announced, "The father of this man was a saint who gave food to people. He ought to be set free." "Did he give food to his own people," asked Chinghiz Khan, "or to people who were strangers?" "Every one provides food for his own people," replied the courtier, "but the father of this man gave food to strangers." Chinghiz Khan was very pleased with this reply. "A saint," he noted, "is someone who gives food to God's people," and immediately he ordered them to set Khwaja ʿAli free. He also gave the saint's son a cloak and apologized for having detained him. "In every religion," concluded the master—may God remember him with favor—"giving food (to others) is a commendable action."

Conversation next turned to THOUGHT, RESOLVE, AND ACTION. "First," noted the master, "there is thought, that is, it is the first thing to enter the heart. After that comes resolve, that is, a person fixes his heart on that thought. Finally, there is action, that is, a person implements that resolve.

"For ordinary people," he went on, "as long as they do nothing, they obtain no result, but for the elect, even to consider doing something is to be held accountable for it.[36] A member of the elect should flee to God every moment of his life: since thought, resolve, and action are all the creation of God, he should seek refuge in God under all circumstances."

After that the master told a story about Shaykh Abu Saʿid Abuʾl-Khayr—may God show mercy upon him. "No thought goes through my mind," Abu Saʿid once confided, "but that I am suspected of having implemented it, even if I, in fact, have never acted on that thought." Once a wholly upright dervish came to his **khanqah.** Shaykh Abu Saʿid recognized his perfection and knew what sort of man he was. At the time of **iftar** (i.e., breaking of the fast), Shaykh Abu Saʿid Abuʾl-Khayr asked his daughter to bring the saint a bottle of water. She was his youngest daughter, yet with perfect courtesy and extreme respect she offered water to the saint. Shaykh Abu Saʿid was delighted at his daughter's conduct. The thought crossed his mind: "Who will be the fortunate fellow to catch this daughter in his snare?" After this thought had crossed his mind, he asked Hasan Muʿazz, his attendant in the **khanqah,** to go to the bazaar. "Go, find out what is the talk of the town!" he instructed the servant. Hasan went to the bazaar and returned. Approaching Shaykh Abu Saʿid Abuʾl-Khayr, he said, "Today in the bazaar I heard talk that no ear can bear to hear." "Speak!" ordered the Shaykh. "How can I tell you what I heard?" pleaded Hasan. "You **must** say what you heard!" commanded the Shaykh. "In the bazaar," replied Hasan, "one man was saying to another, 'Shaykh Abu Saʿid Abuʾl-Khayr wishes to ensnare his own daughter!' " The Shaykh laughed and said, "And so they would call me to account even for that thought of mine?"

When the master—may God remember him with favor—had completed this story, I submitted: "Is it to be presumed from this story that

Shaykh Abu Sa'id Abu'l-Khayr was the most virtuous man of his times?" "Yes, indeed!" replied the master.[37] The servant derived great comfort from this response of the master.

Conversation next turned to THE PERPETUATION OF REPENTANCE. On the blessed tongue of the master came these words: "If someone quaffs the wine of repentance, every moment his friends and associates appear to him as a stumbling block, and every moment as he is quaffing that wine, friends and associates, at the place where they experience desire, continue to query and test him, so that the man never ceases drinking. What does this mean? That there remains in his heart an inclination (to sin), and only when he repents of **that** thought does his heart become fully cleansed, with the result that no friend or acquaintance can impede him.

"Everyone to whom men impute sin and iniquity," continued the master, "it means that at the root of that person's heart there is still a slight inclination to sin and iniquity. When a penitent person is able to remove his heart totally from that which is unworthy, no memory of offense or disobedience will cling to his heart. In this will be indication that he has found 'the perpetuation of repentance'; that is, when the penitent grounds himself in repentance, he will not wish for any sin nor will he even recollect the word 'iniquity.' If, however, he still has an inclination to crime and corruption, every moment he will face new impediments, and at the same time recollect past lapses and impieties."

The topic of THE HYDERIS[38]—may God have mercy upon them—came up. "The founder of that group," noted the master, "was a Turk (Qutb ad-din Hyder) who possessed great spiritual powers. During the Mongol onslaught, the infidels of Chinghiz Khan turned toward India. At that time Qutb ad-din counseled his friends, 'Flee, for these people will overpower you!' 'What are you talking about?' they asked him. 'They have brought a dervish along with them,' he explained, 'and they have kept him hidden. That dervish is coming (here) now. In a dream I have wrestled with that same dervish, and he threw me to the ground. The truth of the matter is that they also will overpower you, so flee!' Having said this, he himself retired into a cave and did not reappear. And what he had predicted came to pass."

When the master had finished telling this story, I asked, "Did not this group shape pellets of iron into necklaces as well as rings and bracelets, claiming it to be the prescribed custom of their founder?" "Yes, they did," he replied. "Qutb ad-din did such things, but it was to indicate his spiritual state. In that spiritual state he could pick up burning hot iron, and shape it around his neck into a necklace or around his hand into a bracelet; the iron in his hand became like wax. The Hyderis still exist, and their members still wear such necklaces and bracelets, but where is that spiritual state (which the founder possessed)?"

And then conversation turned to this delicate subject: THAT ALONE IS LIFE WHICH THE SAINT SPENDS IN MEDITATING ON GOD. The master told an illustrative story. "There was a saint named Merk Grami. A dervish once came to visit him, and that dervish had the special power (**karama**) of realizing in a waking state whatever it was he had seen in his dream. Once he was overcome with longing to go to the place where Merk Grami was. On the way he stopped for the night and had a dream in which he heard that Merk Grami had died. What could he do now? 'At the least,' he thought to himself, 'I can pay a visit to the place where he had been buried.' On arriving at the home town of Merk Grami, he asked, 'Where is Merk Grami's grave?' 'He is alive and well,' everyone replied; 'why do you ask about his grave?' The dervish was stunned. 'How could my dream be wrong?' he wondered to himself. When at least he came into the presence of Merk Grami, they exchanged greetings and (before the saint could speak) Merk Grami told him: 'The dream you had was correct, for though I usually spend the night meditating on God, last night I was thinking about something other than Him. From the world beyond came this cry: "Merk Grami has died. May God help him!" ' "

### I. Assembly 18
Thursday, 13th of Jumada al-thani, A.H. 708 (3 December 1308)

[A long discussion of FASTING, with detailed reference to Prophetic precedents and their interpretations. It concludes:] "If some one fasts continuously," explained the master, "the pain of fasting becomes easy for him; the reward is greater, however, for the person on whose soul the act of fasting weighs more heavily. Hence the fast of David is this: 'One day you fast without interruption, the next day you break the fast.' "

### I. Assembly 19
Wednesday, 19th of Jumada al-thani, A.H. 708 (9 December 1308)

I obtained the benefit of kissing the master's feet, and touched my head to the ground in front of him. "After performing the afternoon prayer," he observed, "you should recite ten cycles of prayer, together with five pauses for greeting, and in these ten prayer cycles, you should also recite the Chapter of Sincerity (**Surat al-Ikhlas**) ten times. This form of prayer is called the prayer of Khizr. Why is it known as the prayer of Khizr? Because whoever performs this prayer continuously is assured of meeting Khizr."

[There then follows a description of CYCLES OF QUR'ANIC RECITATION, which, when appended to the canonical prayer, are especially efficacious.]

## I. Assembly 20

Thursday, 27th of Jumada al-thani, A.H. 708 (17 December 1308)

I obtained the blessing of kissing the master's feet, and conversation turned to THE EXERCISE OF SUBLIME PATIENCE AT THE TIME OF DEATH. "Whoever exercises patience at the time of death is able to accomplish a rare and noble thing," observed the master; "by contrast, everyone who indulges in lamentation and raises his voice on behalf of the departed person does an ignoble thing. In this connection he noted that Hippocrates the physician reportedly had twenty sons, and all twenty of them died one day when a roof collapsed on them. When news of this reached Hippocrates the physician, the expression on his face did not change even slightly."

"And look at Majnun" continued the master; "when he was informed that Layla had died, he said, 'Woe is me! Why did I take as a friend someone who was to die?' "

After that when evening came—and it was Friday evening—a woman presented herself to the master and professed allegiance to him. He then began to comment on THE NUMEROUS BENEFITS that accrue FROM THE VIRTUE OF WOMEN. He called to mind a woman from Indraprasta named Fatima. She had been such a model of chastity and virtue that Shaykh al-Islam Farid ad-din—may God sanctify his lofty secret—used to say repeatedly of her: "That woman is a man whom the Creator has sent to earth in the bodily form of a woman!"

The master then declared that dervishes who ask saintly women and saintly men to intercede on their behalf invoke saintly women first because they are so rare. "When a wild lion comes into an inhabited area from the forest," he explained, "no one asks: 'Is it male or female?' Similarly, the sons of Adam, whether they be men or women, must devote themselves to obedience and piety." After discussing the virtue of the pious and telling (more) stories about them, he concluded with these lines of poetry:

If good I'm judged, as one of them I'm reckoned.
If bad I be, through them I am forgiven.

I. Assembly 21
Saturday, 13th of Rajab, A.H. 708 (5 January 1309)

I obtained the benefit of kissing the master's feet. "With whom do you keep company most frequently?" he asked. I mentioned the names of some pious friends. "I, too, keep their company," he replied, and the following couplet came to his blessed lips:

With lovers sit to feel a lover's pain.
From all others your distance e'er maintain.

Having said this, he then mentioned a dictum attributed to Shaykh Abu Saʿid Abuʾl-Khayr—may God have mercy upon him: "It is the custom among Shaykhs that when they are informed about someone's condition, they ask: 'With whom does he keep company?' From that it also becomes evident to what class of people he belongs."

Conversation turned to THE VIRTUE OF LAYLAT AL-RAGHAʾIB (The Night of Supererogatory Devotions). "Devotions is the plural of devotion," observed the master; "that is to say, many things transpire on that night." From his blessed lips came this pronouncement: "Whoever says the prayers prescribed for Laylat al-Raghaʾib will not die that year." He then told the story of a man who never missed the observance of prayer during Laylat al-Raghaʾib. "The year in which he died," explained the master, "ended on the day of Laylat al-Raghaʾib, and before he was able to perform the prayers appropriate to that night, he expired."

The topic of discourse shifted to THE PRAYER OF KHWAJA UWAYS QARANI—may God be pleased with him. "This prayer falls on the third, fourth, and fifth of the month of Rajab," observed the master; "but according to others, it occurs on thirteenth, fourteenth, and fifteenth of Rajab, while still others fix it on the twenty-third, twenty-fourth, and twenty-fifth of Rajab."

He then proceeded to amplify the virtue accruing from this prayer, and he told the following story about an esteemed scholar named Maulana Zayn ad-din who taught in a certain **madrasa.** He was an unusual man. To every question that was asked of him he would give a categorical answer; and when debate on scholarly issues would arise, people would ask him for an opinion. "I cannot read nor have I ever been a student of anyone," he used to say. "But on becoming an adult, I once observed the prayer of Khwaja Uways Qarani and I prayed: 'O God, I have reached maturity, and yet I have had no formal education. Give me knowledge as a miracle (**karama**).' God Almighty, due to the blessing of this prayer, bestowed knowledge on me, so that every problem on which there is a difference of opinion I can give the correct interpretation and explain it in full detail."[39]

"At the end of Rajab," the master went on to note, "there also occurs a PRAYER FOR LONG LIFE." And in this connection he told a story about Shaykh Badr ad-din Ghaznawi—may God grant him mercy and forgiveness. He used to pray this prayer regularly, but according to the report of Shaykh Nizam ad-din, the son of Shaykh Zia ad-din Panipati—may God have mercy upon him, in the year when Shaykh Badr ad-din Ghaznawi—may God grant him mercy and forgiveness—died he failed to recite the prayer for long life. "Why did you not say that prayer this year?" he was asked. "Nothing more remains for me from my life," he replied, and the same year he expired.

### I. Assembly 22
### Tuesday, 23rd of Rajab, A.H. 708 (15 January 1309)

I obtained the benefit of kissing the master's feet. He began to expound upon THE KAʿBA, ITS BUILDING AND DEMOLITION. From his blessed lips came the observation: "The Kaʿba was twice destroyed, as the Prophet—blessing and peace be upon him—had predicted: 'They will destroy the Kaʿba twice, and the third time it will be borne up to heaven, where it will stay till the Day of Resurrection. At that time, they will bring idols and place them in the Kaʿba. Women from the tribe of Rawasi will come, and just as they begin kicking at the idols, the Kaʿba will be borne away to heaven.' "

I. Assembly 23
Thursday, 11th of Sha'ban, A.H. 708 (2 February 1309)

I obtained the blessing of kissing the master's feet. There was a matter on which I needed the master's guidance. "Is it not essential," I asked him, "for a disciple to apply himself continuously to obedience and devotion, making every effort to recite both invocatory and petitionary prayers? And if he also studies the books of the Shaykhs, will he not be busy rather than idle?" He then made a special gesture of honor toward me, bestowing on me a cap and cloak. "Praise be to God, the Lord of the universe!" he declared.

I. Assembly 24
Thursday, 25th of Sha'ban, A.H. 708 (16 February 1309)

I obtained the blessing of kissing the master's feet. The topic of conversation turned to RECITING THE QUR'AN AND STAYING UP THROUGHOUT THE NIGHT. At that time there was a group observing the all-night prayer vigil in the mosque. "If one stayed up all night in one's home," I asked, "what would be the result?" "To recite one portion of the Qur'an at home," he replied, "is better than to recite the whole of the Qur'an in a mosque!"

After that he told the story of a man who in bygone days used to stay awake throughout the night and perform prayers in the congregational mosque of Damascus; he hoped that such conspicuous devotion would secure his appointment as Shaykh al-Islam.

At this point tears began to flood the eyes of the master—may God remember him with favor.[40] "The first thing you must do (as a disciple)," he pleaded, "is to turn your back on becoming Shaykh al-Islam or master of a Sufi hospice!"

He then began to tell the story of a certain grocer—may God have mercy upon him—who fasted for twenty-five years. He informed no one about his practice; even the members of his own household did not know that he was fasting. If he was at home, he would lead people to believe that he had eaten at his shop; and if he was at his shop, he would lead people to believe that he had eaten at home.

"The basis (for spiritual endeavors) must be A SOUND INTENTION," observed the master, "because while people note what you do, God Almighty takes note of what you intend to do. When your intention is fixed on God, then a little amount of work will be greatly rewarded."

In this connection he told a story about the Friday mosque in Damascus. It had a huge endowment (**waqf**). The administrator of that place was such a powerful person that he was almost equivalent to a second emperor. Indeed, if the emperor had a monetary need, he would take out a loan from the endowment administrator. Now it happened that a dervish who hankered after those endowment funds began to practice obedience and devotion in the congregational mosque of Damascus, in the hope that he might gain fame and be offered that religious trust. For some time he busied himself with acts of obedience, and yet no one mentioned his name. Then one evening the power of his obedience caused him to repent of his hypocrisy. He made a pact with God Almighty: "I will worship You for Your sake alone. I am not making this pact in order to obtain control of that trust." He continued to busy himself with acts of obedience, omitting no detail and performing everything with sound intention. Before long some people approached him to take the job of administering the mosque endowment. "No," he told them. "I have left that. For a long time I had been very desirous of such a position, and it is only because I have left it that they now offer it to me!" In short, he continued to busy himself with God Almighty and did not become tainted by engaging in the occupation of trust administrator.

### I. Assembly 25
Friday, the 9th of Ramadan, A.H. 708 (1 March 1309)

I obtained the blessing of kissing the master's feet. One of those present told the story of a man who was extremely virtuous, and also eager to enter the service of dervishes. I told him: "Why do you not attach yourself to the master (i.e., Shaykh Nizam ad-din)?" He replied: "I once went there with the intention of professing the oath of allegiance to him. When I saw the spread out tablecloths and the burning candles, however, I decided to direct my commitment elsewhere, and left."

The master—may God remember him with favor—on hearing this story, turned to those present and asked: "Where are these tablecloths? Where are the candles?" Then he smiled and added: "Since the time was not right for him to benefit from the oath of allegiance, they appeared to him just as he described them." At this point the servant interjected:

"Why would tablecloths and candles be THE BASIS FOR directing one's COMMITMENT elsewhere?" On his blessed lips came this response: "Some make a commitment on very trivial grounds; others bring to discipleship a firm faith and unshakable constancy."

The master then began to talk about HONORING THE COMMAND OF ONE'S SPIRITUAL GUIDE (**pir**). "Once Shaykh al-Islam Farid ad-din—may God sanctify his lofty secret—wrote a prayer in his own hand," he recalled. " 'Can someone commit this to memory?' he asked. I detected that by this query he meant that I should memorize it. I offered my services. 'If I order the servant to memorize,' he instructed, 'you should be prepared to read that prayer back to me.' 'Let me read it once in the presence of the Shaykh,' I replied, 'and I will have memorized it.' 'Read,' he ordered. As I began reading, I corrected the Arabic in one place. 'Read it this way,' he directed, even though the way I had first read it also made sense. In the same short span of time I committed the prayer to memory. I submitted to him, 'I have memorized the prayer. If you give the command, I will recite it.' 'Recite,' he ordered. And so I recited, and that Arabic which the Shaykh had commanded I also recited.[41]

"When I later came out from his presence, Maulana Badr ad-din Ishaq—may God show mercy and forgiveness to him—said to me, 'You have done well to read this Arabic as the Shaykh had directed.' I replied: 'If the founder of this branch of knowledge and others who were expert in its principles were to come and tell me: "Arabic is not to be read the way you read it," I would still read it as the Shaykh had directed!' Maulana Badr ad-din was pleased. 'This respect for the authority of the Shaykh which you have shown,' he noted, 'is not to be found in any of the rest of us.' "[42]

Conversation turned to PROPER CONDUCT (of the disciple) TOWARD THE MASTER. "I have heard from the lips of Shaykh al-Islam Farid ad-din—may God sanctify his lofty secret," recalled the master, "that during his lifetime he himself had committed an act of arrogance toward his spiritual master, Shaykh Qutb ad-din—may God sanctify his lofty secret. And it happened in his way: 'Once I asked permission from the Shaykh (i.e., Qutb ad-din) to go into seclusion and perform an inverted fast for forty days (**chilla**). "There is no need to do this," replied Shaykh Qutb ad-din—may God sanctify his lofty secret; "it will give you notoriety. Moreover, no such practice has been transmitted from our masters." I replied: "The luminous moment (**waqt**) of God's presence is upon me, and I have no intention of seeking notoriety.

I will **not** do this for the notoriety of it." Shaykh Qutb ad-din fell silent. After this, for the rest of my life, I was ashamed of what I had said, and I have repeatedly repented of my hasty, disrespectful reply.' "

When he had finished telling this story, the master—may God remember him with favor—confessed: "I, too, have been guilty of committing an unintentional act of arrogance against my spiritual master. And it happened in this way: One day Shaykh Farid ad-din had a copy of **ʿAwarif al-Maʿarif** before him, and he was using it to provide morals (**fawaʾid**) for his disciples. But the copy had been written by a weak hand: The script was faint and contained numerous errors. I had once seen another manuscript of the **ʿAwarif al-Maʿarif** in the possession of Shaykh Najib ad-din Mutawakkil—may God have mercy upon him. 'Shaykh Najib ad-din has a clean copy,' I blurted out. This remark greatly offended my master. For an hour he kept asking: 'Has the dervish *no* power to correct a defective manuscript?' The first one or two times these words came to his blessed lips I did not know to whom he was speaking. If I had realized that he was referring to me, I would have immediately implored his forgiveness, but I remained oblivious to the fact that I was the one whom he had in mind. After my master had repeated this question several times, Maulana Badr ad-din Ishaq—may God grant him mercy and forgiveness—turned toward me: 'The Shaykh is addressing this remark to you,' he said. I rose, bared my head and threw myself at the Shaykh's feet. 'As God is my witness,' I pleaded, 'I had not realized that the esteemed master was referring to me in this question. I had seen another manuscript and was reporting that fact; I had absolutely nothing else in mind.' But however much I apologized, I saw that it did not diminish the Shaykh's rage. When at last I arose from there, I did not know what I was doing. May it never happen that any one else experiences the anguish that befell me that day! Tears overwhelmed me. Distraught and bewildered, I walked around till I arrived at the edge of a well. I thought to myself, 'Better to be a dead beggar than to go on living with the bad name that this indiscretion has given me!' In this state of anxiety and confusion, I wandered toward the desert, weeping and lamenting. Only God Almighty knows what state had overcome me at that moment.

"Fortunately, the Shaykh had a son named Shihab ad-din. He and I were very close friends. On hearing what had happened to me, he approached Shaykh Farid ad-din and interceded on my behalf. The Shaykh relented; he sent his servant Muhammad to fetch me. I came and placed my head at his blessed feet. He was pleased. The next day, summoning me to his presence, he showered me with words of compassion and comfort. 'I have done all this for the perfection of your spiritual state', he explained. And on that same day from his noble lips came these words:

'The spiritual master is the groom for his disciple.' Then he ordered that I be presented with a robe of honor and special clothes. Praise be to God, the Lord of the universe!"

### I. Assembly 26

Saturday, the 23rd of Ramadan, A.H. 708 (15 March 1309)

I obtained the benefit of kissing the master's feet. He began to talk about THE EFFORT REQUISITE TO OBEDIENCE. Upon his blessed lips came these words: "When a man first practices obedience, every moment weighs heavy on him and appears to be difficult. But it may happen that through the sincerity of his effort, God Almighty bestows success on him and makes that work seem easy, and then every work which had at first seemed onerous to him will be completed with dispatch."

The master next told a story about Shaykh Najib ad-din Mutawakkil—may God have mercy upon him. "Many times he wanted to set to writing a compilation of Sufi anecdotes, but his income was so tight that he could not manage to purchase the instruments for writing and also to pay wages for a scribe; if a scribe did become available, he could not afford to pay him, or if he somehow found the means to pay him, he could not obtain additional funds to buy paper and the other provisions necessary for writing. Then one day a scribe named Hamid came to him. Shaykh Najib ad-din told him: 'For a long time now I have wanted to commit to writing a compilation of Sufi anecdotes, but I have not found the means to accomplish that objective.' 'What are your present resources?' asked Hamid. 'I have one **diram** [a silver coin equivalent to about 4 cents],[43]' replied Shaykh Najib ad-din. Hamid took that one **diram** and bought paper with it. Now everyone knows how little paper one **diram** can buy, and Hamid had not finished writing on that paper before Shaykh Najib ad-din received another charitable donation, with which he purchased more paper and the other necessities for writing. Money for the scribe's salary also came to hand. More and more charitable donations continued to arrive, and as a result the book was quickly and satisfactorily completed. The point is: Even a work begun with difficulty will be completed, as long as one persists."

Conversation then turned to THE DURATIVE VIRTUES OF SHAYKH NAJIB AD-DIN MUTAWAKKIL. "One day I was sitting in his presence," recalled Shaykh Nizam ad-din, "and at that time I was wrapped up in myself. Turning to him, I said: 'Read the **Surat al-Fatiha** once that I may become a judge (**qazi**).' Shaykh Najib ad-din Mutawakkil remained silent. I thought that he had not heard me. 'Read the **Surat al-Fatiha** once more for me,' I repeated, 'that I may become a judge.' Still he did not reply. A third time I asked him to read that **surah** on my behalf. 'Do not become a judge!' he snapped. 'Become something else!' " "Look what an aversion he had to this work," commented the master—may God remember him with favor. "He would not even read the **Surat al-Fatiha** to help me obtain it."

The master next began to speak about FORGIVENESS. "There is a tradition to the effect that the disciple should keep one **diram** in reserve in his purse. When a time of need arises, he can take that one **diram** from his purse and spend it. But if that **diram** is lodged in the fold of his purse and he can not put his hand on it, he may become worried that he has lost it. Every moment that he is distraught on this account God Almighty will forgive him."

Then the master—may God remember him with favor—explained: "This tradition has been related about a saintly person who had but one **diram,** for if the man had several **dirams** and lost one, he would not have become distraught, but someone who had only one **diram** and lost that **diram** would indeed be distraught, and God Almighty would forgive him." This meaning was disclosed on the same day that the master conferred on me a robe of honor and special clothes. Praise be to God, the Lord of the universe!

### I. Assembly 27

Thursday, the 28th of Ramadan, A.H. 708 (20 March 1309)

I obtained the blessing of kissing the master's feet. He conferred this blessing while seated on the second floor balcony of his **khanqah.** There was a staircase nearby. When I prostrated myself before him, he indicated that I should go sit at the head of the stairs. I did. The wind was constantly blowing the door shut, and so I held it open with one hand. This had been going on for about an hour when the Shaykh happened to glance at me and saw that I was holding the door open. "Why don't you let go?" he asked. Prostrating my head to the ground, I replied, "But I have been holding the door open." "Yes," he observed, "you **have** been holding onto the door, and holding onto it firmly!" From his blessed lips there then came this explanation: "Shaykh Baha ad-din Zakariya—may God have mercy upon him—often used to say, 'You should not tarry at every door and entrance. Hold onto one door and hold onto it firmly!' "

He next told the story of an ecstatic saint who was once standing by the gateway to the city at the time of morning prayer. When they opened the gate, people came rushing out and scattered in every direction; to the right, to the left, and straight ahead, each person went his own way. The ecstatic, when he saw this, said: "They are all mad. Since everyone goes in a different direction, they will not arrive at one place. But if they all took the same path, they would arrive at the desired destination."

The master then began to discuss EATING LITTLE FOOD, and detailed the benefit and harm of that for someone with a full stomach. At the conclusion there came to his blessed lips these words: "It is not usually acceptable for someone with a full stomach to eat. But there are two exceptions. If a person has just received a guest, even though he has already eaten his fill, he may, for the sake of hosting his guest, eat something further. Also, if a person has been fasting during Ramadan and cannot afford to prepare the predawn meal for himself, since he knows that after dawn there also will be nothing for him to eat, it is acceptable for him to eat more than his fill should he be invited to a friend's house."

The topic of discourse shifted to THE POWER OF INVOCATORY PRAYER. The master observed: "If someone is seized with an illness or bodily affliction so severe that no medical remedy can remove it, he should follow the following schedule on Friday: After offering his other prayers and before the time of evening prayer, he should do nothing else except engage in the continual remembrance (**dhikr**) of these three names. Whoever says these three names in sincerity—O God, O Source of Compassion, O Ever Compassionate—will find immediate release from his ailment."

### I. Assembly 28
### Saturday, the 18th of Shawwal, A.H. 708 (30 March 1309)

I obtained the blessing of kissing his feet. That day I informed him of MY WISH TO COMPILE THESE DISCOURSES. It happened as follows: The time was auspicious, and he granted me a private audience.

"With your permission," I said, "I would like to ask something of you." "Permission is granted," he replied. "For more than a year," I explained, "I have been continuously in your service. Every moment that I have obtained the blessing of kissing your feet, I have also derived counsels (**fawa'id**) from your elegant words. What exhortation and advice and inducement to obedience, what stories about the saints and their spiritual states have I heard from you! Every kind of soul-inspiring discourse has fallen on my ears, and I wanted to make that the foundation for my own life—indeed, to use it as a guide on the Path for this broken person, at least to the extent that I could record with the pen what I understood. Also, I have heard the Shaykh say many times that the novice must consult a book on the Sufi masters and their guidelines for spiritual progress. Since no collection has been made of the inspiring teachings of the master's predecessors, I have compiled those of your blessed words which I have heard and till now I have not shown them (to anyone), awaiting your command, that I might do what you want in this regard."

After the master—may God remember him with favor—had heard this request, he replied: "At the time that I entered the service of Shaykh al-Islam Farid ad-din—may God sanctify his lofty secret, I had the same idea in mind: Whatever I heard from his auspicious mouth, I wanted to note it down. The very first day that I had the privilege of entering his presence, the initial words I heard from his blessed lips were the following verse:

> What is absence from You? A fire, heart upon heart burning!
> And yearning for You? A tide, soul after soul upturning!

After that I had wanted to confess to him the strong desire that I had to kiss his feet. But the awe I felt in his presence made me hesitate. I could only manage to say this much: 'The yearning to kiss your feet has overwhelmed me.' When he saw the effects of awe in me, these words came onto his blessed lips: 'To everyone who enters, there is a sense of awe.'

"In short, from that day every time the Shaykh spoke, whatever I heard from him I wrote down. On returning to my room, I would put his discourse in proper order. I kept on writing down what I heard till one day I informed him of this activity. After that, whenever he told a story or offered a guideline, he would check to see if I was present. If, on some occasion, I did not happen to be present, the directive which he had given in my absence he would repeat again later in my presence."

And then added the master—may God remember him with favor:

"I witnessed a miracle (**karama**). At that very time a stranger gave me some sheets of white paper bound in a volume. I accepted them from him and recorded the morals (**fawa'id**) of Shaykh al-Islam. At the top of each page I would write: 'Glory be to God! Praise be to God! There is no god but God! God is Great! There is no might nor power but with God the Magnificent, the Sublime!' And then I would record the discourse of the Shaykh as I had heard it, and to this day that compilation is still with me."

After relating all these events, the master asked me: "Did you bring those sheets of paper with you?" "Yes," I replied. "Let me see them!" he directed. I brought out six folios of the manuscript which I had been compiling and put them in his blessed hands. He examined and approved them. "You have written well!" he remarked, and every passage where he would pause he would exclaim: "Good! Good!" One or two places were left blank. "Why are there these blank spaces?" he would ask. "I did not recall the remainder of this discourse," I submitted. With care and kindness he would explain to me the remainder of those discourses till all the entries were complete. Praise be to God, the Lord of the universe, for the master's nurturing compassion to this broken person!

Conversation next turned to the GRACE AND MERCY OF THE SUBLIME CREATOR. "Opposite to the thought of the creature is the work of the Creator," explained the master, and then he told the story of a Caliph who was among the prominent Caliphs in Baghdad. He imprisoned a youth. The mother of that youth came and pleaded with the Caliph for the release of her son. "I had given the command that he is to be held in confinement," replied the Caliph, "and so long as there is one surviving member of my family your son will remain a prisoner." When she heard this, the woman began to cry. Turning her face skyward, she petitioned: "This is the command of the Caliph; what is Your command?" The Caliph heard her plea and had a change of heart. He issued a command for her son to be released and then, purchasing a horse, gave it to the boy. He further commanded the boy to ride the horse throughout Baghdad, with servants preceding him and proclaiming: "This is the gift of God against the will of the Caliph!"

The master then began to discuss THE CAPACITY OF THE SPIRITUAL MASTER TO GIVE AND THE CAPACITY OF THE DISCIPLE TO RECEIVE. He told the story of a certain man named Yusuf who was among the disciples of Shaykh al-Islam Farid ad-din—may God sanctify his lofty secret. "One time Yusuf came before the Shaykh and began to complain: 'I have been in your service for many years. Everyone but me has received something from the Shaykh's beneficence. It ought to be that I am honored before all the others.' This and similar things he said.

"There has been no shortcoming on my part," replied Shaykh al-Islam Farid ad-din. "There must be preparedness and capability on your part. I do all that I can, but if God Almighty does not give the capacity, what can anyone else do?" As he was talking, the Shaykh noticed a young lad sitting in the assembly. "Come here," he said. Now opposite where the Shaykh was sitting there was a pile of bricks. The Shaykh directed the lad to bring him a brick. He went, fetched a brick, and set it before Shaykh Farid ad-din. Sitting nearby was a friend who had come to see the Shaykh. The Shaykh told the lad to go, fetch another brick, and place it before the friend. The lad went and did as he was told. "Go now and fetch still another brick and place it before this friend," said Shaykh Farid ad-din, pointing to Yusuf. The lad went and, bringing back **half** a brick, set it in front of Yusuf. "What have I to do with this?" asked the Shaykh. "I did what I could, but when you continue to have the same capacity today as you had before, what is there left for me to do?"[44]

I. Assembly 29
Monday, 20th of Shawwal, A.H. 708 (11 April 1309)

I obtained the benefit of kissing the master's feet. He started to tell a story about Shaykh ʿUthman Khairabadi[45]—may God have mercy upon him. From his blessed lips came the pronouncement: "Shaykh ʿUthman was a very saintly person. He also wrote a commentary on the Qurʾan." He then went on to note that the Shaykh resided in Ghaznin, where he used to prepare a vegetable stew of turnips, beets, and such things. After putting all the ingredients in a pot, he would boil them. The resulting stew was very tasty.

Afterward, in explaining divine favor, the master recited the following verse:

> God upon the shepherd puts a prophet's crown.
> Else how could shepherds as prophets gain renown?

He was referring here to the Prophet Moses—peace be upon him—and his relationship with Khizr. And then he began to expound upon the spiritual states of Shaykh ʿUthman. "If someone came and gave him a counterfeit **diram** in order to buy some of his stew, he would take it: Even though he knew it to be counterfeit, he would say nothing to the buyer. And if someone gave him a **diram** which was good currency, he would also take it and give the person stew. Hence people assumed that Shaykh ʿUthman did not know the difference between counterfeit and good money. Many used to come and give him false currency. He would accept it as good money and give them food. At the time of his death, Shaykh ʿUthman looked skyward and prayed: 'O God, you know better than anyone that people gave me false currency and I accepted it as good. I have not taken offence at what they did. If there has come to You from me false devotion, then in Your mercy please do not take offence at what I have done.' "

The master told one further anecdote about Shaykh ʿUthman Khairabadi. Once a dervish who was the master of his spiritual state (**sahib-e hal**) came to Shaykh ʿUthman and asked for some food from his cauldron. Shaykh ʿUthman dipped his ladle into the pot, and when he pulled it out, there were only pearls! Exclaimed the dervish: "What can I do with this?" Shaykh ʿUthman put the ladle back into the pot, and this time he scooped out gold! "These are but pebbles and gravel," groused the dervish. "Pull out something that I can eat!" A third time Shaykh ʿUthman dipped his ladle into the pot and scooped out the same vegetable stew that he had been boiling. Observing Shaykh ʿUthman's self-disclosure of his spiritual state, the dervish declared, "You must no longer stay here (i.e., in the world)." Within a few days Shaykh ʿUthman—may God have mercy upon him—expired and left this world.

"When a dervish discloses something of such magnitude," observed the master—may God remember him with favor," it is not suitable for him to remain in the world, as Hakim Sanai has said:

> Display not that beauty which burns men's souls right through.
> Once displayed, though, go cast upon those flames wild rue.
> For what's that beauty of yours but your drunkenness?
> And what's that wild rue but your very existence?[46]

After that the master explained: "It is because saints disclose the divine secret due to their drunkenness that they are called 'exponents of intoxication' (**sukr**), in contrast to the prophets, who are called 'exponents of sobriety (**sahw**)'. Sanai not only alluded to their drunkenness; he also implied that when one discloses the divine secret, one should not delay leaving the world. Hence he said:

For what's that beauty of yours but your drunkenness?
And what's that wild rue but your very existence?

"Disclosing divine secrets and performing miracles (**karamat**)," concluded the master, "are actually a hindrance in the Path. For true devotees the real task is to be firm in the pursuit of love." And praise be to God for that (counsel)!

### I. Assembly 30
### Monday, 23rd of Dhu'l-Qa'da, A.H. 709 (13 May 1309)

I obtained the blessing of kissing the master's feet. A youth entered the assembly. "Your grandfather was a disciple of which spiritual master?" asked the master—may God remember him with favor. "He was a disciple of Shaykh Jalal ad-din Tabrizi—may God have mercy upon him," replied the youth. "Shaykh Jalal ad-din Tabrizi—may God have mercy upon him—initiated very few disciples," commented the master, "as did Qazi Hamid ad-din Nagauri—may God have mercy upon him."

Maulana Burhan ad-din Gharib—may the purity of God encompass him—was present at this assembly. "The spiritual preeminence of both these saints has been certified by God and also by you," he observed. "Why did they not initiate more disciples?" "Their spiritual preeminence cannot be judged defective because they enrolled or did not enroll but a few disciples," replied the master—may God remember him with favor.[47] "It is like this: Suppose there are two men. Both are endowed with evident qualities of manhood. The one has produced offspring while the other has not. Is the one without children for that reason defective in his manhood?" And he continued to elaborate on this matter. "The relationship of a prophet to his community provides a comparable example. On the Day of Judgment, when they bring forward the believers and righteous persons of each prophet, that is, those who comprise his community, one community will have few people, another many. As for that prophet whose community consists of but one person

—will it then be said that there is some shortcoming or defect in him? No! And the same will be said of THE SPIRITUAL STATES OF **PIRS** AND THE NUMBER OF THEIR DISCIPLES."

### I. Assembly 31
### Sunday, 29th of Dhu'l-Qa'da, A.H. 709 (19 May 1309)

I obtained the blessing of kissing the master's feet. Conversation turned to MUSIC (**sama'**) and THE ECSTASY (**wajd**) THAT IT INDUCES. Upon his blessed lips came the statement: "Among the ninety-nine Beautiful Names of God which Muslims recite is **al-wajid,** and it is valuable to know the meaning of **al-wajid,** that is, 'the one who is self-sufficient!' "

After that he observed that the meaning of **al-wajid** is also derived from **wajd** "ecstasy" (experienced in music) and hence, **al-wajid** means "the one who induces ecstasy." **Shakur,** too, is one of the ninety-nine Beautiful Names and normally **shakur** means "one who gives thanks" but with reference to Him it means "He who accepts the gratitude of (His) creatures." In a similar vein, **al-wajid** is usually taken to mean "one who is the master of ecstasy" but this would be an inaccurate assertion with respect to God the Holy and Sublime Creator. Hence **al-wajid** means "the one who induces ecstasy."

Discussion then turned to SHIHAB AD-DIN SUHRAWARDI—may God have mercy upon him—who NEVER LISTENED TO MUSIC (**sama'**). The master noted that Shaykh Najm ad-din Kubra—may God be merciful and gracious unto him—used to say: "All of the best possible graces have been bestowed on Shaykh Shihab ad-din Suhrawardi . . . except the taste for music."

After that the master expounded on the absorption of Shaykh Shihab ad-din Suhrawardi in his work. "Once Shaykh Awhad Kirmani[48]—may God have mercy upon him—came to visit Shaykh Shihab ad-din. The latter folded up his prayer carpet and placed it under his knees, which among the great Shaykhs is a sign of extreme deference. When evening came, Shaykh Awhad Kirmani asked for music. Shaykh Shihab ad-din summoned some musicians and arranged for a musical gathering. Then he himself retired to a corner where he engaged in obedience to God and remembrance (**dhikr**) of Him. Shaykh Awhad Kirmani and the other participants in the musical assembly became absorbed in the music. The next morning one of the **khanqah** servants came to Shaykh Shihab ad-din—may God have mercy upon him—and said: "There was a musical gathering here last night, and every moment that group was afraid that they might be bothering you." "Was there music?" asked Shaykh Shihab ad-din. "Yes!" exclaimed the servant. "I was not aware of it," replied the Shaykh.

"You see," commented the master—may God remember him with favor, "they did not think that Shaykh Shihab ad-din would be so absorbed in the moment and so intent on the remembrance (**dhikr**) of God that he could remain oblivious to the overpowering affect of music. Every time that a musical assembly would gather in his **khanqah** and the participants would recite the Qur᾿an, Shaykh Shihab ad-din would hear it, but the actual musical performances, with all their attendant commotion, he would not hear. Just imagine how absorbed he was in his spiritual discipline!"

The master then began to talk about THE SAINTS' TOMBS OF LAHORE. "Many saints have been laid to rest there," he observed. "Have you seen Lahore?" he asked me. "Yes," I replied, "I have seen it and visited some of the saints' tombs there, such as that of Shaykh Husayn Zanjani—may God have mercy upon him—and other saints."

On his blessed lips came these words: "Shaykh Husayn Zanjani and Shaykh ʿAli Hujwiri[49]—may God bless both of them—were disciples of the same master, and that **pir** was the pole (**qutb**) of his age. Husayn Zanjani had lived in Lahore for a long time when their common **pir** said to Khwaja ʿAli Hujwiri, 'Go settle in Lahore.' ʿAli Hujwiri protested: 'But Shaykh Husayn Zanjani lives there.' 'Go!' said the **pir,** repeating his injunction. ʿAli Hujwiri dutifully left and proceeded to Lahore. He arrived there in the evening. The next morning he heard them reading the funeral prayer for Shaykh Husayn!"

The topic of discourse turned to POETRY. "Some of the Shaykhs have written a lot of good verse," commented the master, "especially Shaykh Awhad Kirmani and Shaykh Abu᾿l-Saʿid Abu᾿l-Khayr and other notable saints. Shaykh Sayf ad-din Bakharzi, who had mastered all branches of learning, was also a commendable poet. His disciples used to come before him, complaining, 'Every Shaykh has left some book or composition. Why don't you write down something?' Shaykh Sayf ad-din Bakharzi would reply: 'Every verse of my creation is equivalent to a book!' "[50]

[Amir Hasan then elaborates some variations of the canonical morning prayer, together with additional Qur᾿anic readings, that he has observed. He reports these special devotions to his master. Moved to tears, Shaykh Nizam ad-din tells him about similar variations of the morning prayer which he had said at the direction of Shaykh al-Islam Farid ad-din.]

I. Assembly 32
Thursday, the 11th of Dhu'l-Hijja, A.H. 709 (31 May 1309)

I obtained the blessing of kissing the master's feet. Conversation turned to PROPER CONDUCT IN THE SAINT'S ASSEMBLY, that is, how to enter the presence of the **pir** and locate the right place to sit down. "Proper conduct," observed the master, "is that a person who enters the saint's assembly should sit down in whatever empty place he espies. It is not fitting, at the moment that one comes to visit the **pir**, to be thinking: 'Whom should I sit ahead of or behind?' Wherever a person sees an opening he should sit down, since every visitor is on the same footing."

The master then went on to give an example from Tradition: "Once the Prophet—blessings and peace be upon him—was sitting in a particular place and his friends had formed a circle around the spot where he was sitting. Three people arrived. One saw an opening in that circle, and coming forward quickly, sat down there. The second saw no place in that circle and sat down outside it. The third person looked away from there and left. An hour passed. The Prophet—blessings and peace be upon him—said: 'During this hour Gabriel—peace be upon him—has come and told me: "God Almighty says that whoever arrives at a circle (of pious people), finds a place there, and sits down among them, We will see that he is given refuge in Our presence. As for the person who does not find a place in such a circle, We will take upon Ourselves his shame, and on the Day of Judgment We will not disgrace him. But as for that person who looks away and leaves, Our mercy will be similarly deflected from him." ' "

In conclusion, the master declared: "Proper conduct is that whoever comes into an assembly and finds an empty place should sit down there, and if there is no place, then he should sit down outside the circle. Under no circumstances should he sit down in the middle, for whoever sits in the middle of a circle will be cursed."

I. Assembly 33
Sunday, the 21st of Dhu'l-Hijja, A.H. 709 (10 June 1309)

I obtained the honor of kissing the master's feet. He began to speak about reciting the Qur'an and the deeper perception of Truth that comes from reading and chanting it. From his blessed lips came the statement: "When the reader of the Qur'an experiences a taste (for God) and derives a sense of peace from a particular verse, he should keep repeating that verse and prolong the sense of peace.

"In the practice of QUR'AN RECITATION AND LISTENING (TO MUSIC)," he went on, "the devotee experiences a sense of spiritual bliss which may be manifest as celestial lights, mystical states, and physical effects. Each of these three derives from three worlds: the present world, the angelic sphere, and the potential realm, this last being intermediate between the first two. And these three manifestations of spiritual bliss may occur in one of three places: the spirits, the hearts, or the bodily limbs. At first celestial lights descend from the angelic sphere on the spirits, then mystical states descend from the potential realm on the hearts, and finally physical effects from the present world alight on the bodily limbs. In other words, during the state induced by listening to music, celestial lights descend from the angelic sphere upon the spirits. What subsequently appear in the heart are called mystical states, because it is from the potential realm that they descend on the hearts. Next, crying, movement, and agitation appear, and they are called physical effects because they alight from the present world on the bodily limbs. Praise be to God, the Lord of the universe."

Conversation then turned to ALMSGIVING. The master noted that when five conditions are present at the time of almsgiving, then without doubt the alms will be acceptable (to God). Of those five conditions two precede the giving of alms, two accompany the act of giving, and one comes after alms have been given. As for those which precede, one of them is that that which he gives be legally permissible. The second is that he intends to give it for the benefit of a virtuous person, one who will not expend alms corruptly or lavishly. In other words, he gives it to deserving people. Of the two conditions that accompany the act of giving, one is that he give with humility, cheerfulness, and an expansive heart. The second condition is that he give in secret. That single condition which comes after the giving is that he not discuss what he has given; he should mention it to no one.

"There are two meanings to the word **sadaqa**," observed the master. "It may mean either 'almsgiving' or 'a bride's dowry.' The first meaning has already been explained, while the second pertains to the portion of her inheritance which a woman is given before marriage. Both meanings emphasize the sincerity (**sidq**) of love which is attached to the respective actions. For instance, that which will be bequeathed to a woman (as dowry) must appear to her as an expression of sincere love, and for that reason it is called **sadaqa.** Similarly, whoever gives something in the way of Truth must always give it out of sincere love, and hence, almsgiving, too, is called **sadaqa.**"

The master then told a story about THE COMMANDER OF THE FAITHFUL ABU BAKR SIDDIQ [i.e., the sincere one]—may God be gracious unto him. "Abu Bakr had 40,000 dinars, all of which he presented to the Prophet of God. The following poem attests to his generosity:

> For closeness with the Prophet did he crave,
> And sucked the serpent's poison in the cave.
> Forty thousand dinars did he offer,
> As well his thorn-stitched quilt for love he gave.

It happened thus: One day Abu Bakr took the 40,000 dinars in his possession and gave all of them to Prophet—blessing and peace be upon him. 'What about your offspring and other members of your household?' asked the Prophet—peace and benediction be upon him. 'Sufficient is (faith in) God, along with His prophet,' replied Abu Bakr.

"After that ʿUmar Khattab—may God be gracious unto him—came, and just as Abu Bakr Siddiq had offered all the money in his possession, so ʿUmar gave half of what he possessed to the Prophet—peace be upon him. 'How are you providing for your children and family?' asked the Prophet—blessing and peace be upon him. 'I have given half to you,' replied ʿUmar, 'and the other half is for the members of my household.' On the basis of their respective gifts, Muhammad then made a decision about who would succeed him as the leader of the Muslim community."

The master proceeded to tell one further story about THE GENEROSITY OF ABU BAKR SIDDIQ. "That same day that he presented the Prophet—peace be upon him—with 40,000 dinars he also offered him the shirt and outer garment he was wearing. At that moment the angel Gabriel—peace be upon him—came to the Prophet—peace be upon him—wearing a similar shirt and outer garment. 'Why are you dressed in these clothes?' asked Muhammad—peace be upon him. 'O Prophet,' responded Gabriel, 'today all the angels have been ordered to dress like Abu Bakr Siddiq, wearing a shirt and outer garment similar to his.' " At this juncture the master—may God remember him with favor—repeated the verse:

Forty thousand dinars did he offer,
As well his thorn-stitched quilt for love he gave.

Continuing on the subject of SINCERITY (**SIDQ**), the master told the story of a man who had twenty-five gold dinars. "I will go on the pilgrimage to the Kaʿba," he said to himself, "and I will give this money to the shrine attendants and residents of that place." And with this intention in mind, he set out on his journey. Along the way he was confronted by a fearless vagrant. Drawing a sword, the thief threatened to slay the traveler. The latter took off the money belt he was wearing and threw it in front of the thief. "Why do you want to kill me?" he asked. "I have a money belt." Incredulous, the vagrant seized the belt and poured out the gold coins. There were twenty-five dinars. Picking them up he put them in front of the traveler, saying, "Take them back and go in peace, lest your truthfulness bring down the wrath of God upon me!"

The master also commented on the meaning of FORGIVENESS (**tasadduq**) AND NOT REDEEMING THE COST OF A BAD PURCHASE: "Once the Commander of the Faithful ʿUmar—may God be gracious unto him—had bought a horse, and that horse grew so lean that it looked like a skeleton. The Commander of the Faithful ʿUmar—may God be gracious unto him—wanted to have the person who sold him that horse buy it back at the same price as the original purchase. When the Prophet—blessings and peace be upon him—came to hear of this matter, he intervened, saying, 'You ought not to make a seller redeem what he has sold you, even when you discover that what he sold you was, in fact, of bad quality.' "

After that the master began to talk about THE MERIT OF FEEDING OTHERS. "A saint has said," he explained, "that one **diram** spent for food set before friends is better than twenty **dirams** expended on alms."

He also told this story about the merit of feeding others. "There was once a dervish of high spiritual attainment who approached the chief minister of Bukhara, saying, 'I have a request to make of the ruler of the city. Please intercede on my behalf and urge him to grant my request.' 'In what connection do I know you,' asked the chief minister, 'that I should intervene on behalf?' 'I have a claim upon you,' replied the man. 'What claim?' asked the chief minister. 'Once you laid out some food for guests. I came and sat at your table and ate some of your food. I have this claim upon you.' The chief minister, when he heard this, immediately got up, went to the ruler of the city and obtained a favorable response to the man's request."

Next the conversation turned to THE COMMERCIAL TRANSACTIONS OF SUFIS, that is, THEIR BUYING AND SELLING. Shaykh Badr ad-din Ishaq—may God grant him mercy and forgiveness—once gave a servant some **shatranj** (a dish of vegetables) and said, "Take this to the bazaar and sell it!" After that he remarked: "To be a dervish is to sell." Someone asked him: "What kind of selling is appropriate for dervishes?" He replied: "They never bring anything back home with them. Whatever price the product fetches in the market, they sell it at that price!"

### I. Assembly 34
Monday, the 29th of Dhu'l-Hijja, A.H. 709 (18 June 1309)

I obtained the blessing of kissing the master's feet. He began to speak of THE SPECIAL VIRTUES AND SPIRITUAL ATTAINMENTS OF IBRAHIM ADHAM—may God have mercy upon him. "For nine years he lived in a cave," noted the master, "and there was a stream running through that cave. He sat by the stream and devoted himself to God Almighty till one evening it became very cold, in fact, freezing cold. He thought he was going to perish. In the darkness he stretched out his hand and felt a leather garment. He pulled it around his shoulders and made himself warm. As the new day began to dawn, he discarded that garment, and when his vision gradually cleared, he saw dragons! He closed his eyes; he lowered his head; he began to tremble. It was while he was in this state of fright that Ibrahim Adham—may God have mercy upon him—heard a voice: 'We have saved you from destruction through destruction!' That is to say, from possible destruction by the fierce cold we rescued you through dragons, which also could have destroyed you!"[51]

After that the master recalled the incident of another dervish who had experienced a similar miracle (**karama**). He had fallen into a pit and there was no rope to pull himself out. He was on the brink of destruction. Suddenly he saw something resembling a rope which had been lowered from above into the well. He recognized it as a way to save himself. He grabbed it and was pulled out of the water. When his vision gradually cleared, he saw that it was a lion which had lowered his tail into the pit! Again, he heard the same message: "We have saved you from destruction through destruction!"

And he continued to speak of THE MIRACLES (**karamat**) OF SAINTS. "There was once a blind saint. An adversary came and sat down in front of him, wanting to test the saint. To himself he thought, 'Since this person is blind, there must also be some defect in his inner person!' Turning to the blind man, the adversary started to ask, 'What is the sign of a saint?' But as he was asking the question, a fly came and alighted on his nose. The man swatted it away. But it came back. He swatted it away again. A third time this happened, and in the meanwhile he managed to ask his question. 'The least of the signs of a saint,' replied the blind man, 'is that no fly alights on his nose!' "

The master then began to explain the importance of PAYING ATTENTION TO A MORSEL OF FOOD AND ITS EFFECTS. "There was once a youth who presented himself to Ibrahim Adham—may God have mercy upon him—and became the latter's disciple. So totally immersed in the worship of God was he that Ibrahim Adham became amazed at his obedience and devotion. The saint scolded himself, saying: 'This lad is just beginning (the life of a Sufi) and yet his feats of obedience put me to shame!' After that, an inner light flashed within Ibrahim Adham: 'All those accomplishments are Satanic! That youth is eating food unlawfully earned, and hence Satan is flourishing through his acts of obedience!' When this situation was made known to Ibrahim Adham, he said to that lad: 'Take your nourishment from the same food that I am eating.' And the youth did as he was directed. The food appropriate for dervishes which Ibrahim Adham was eating he paid for by carrying and selling wood. The youth began to eat food purchased by the same kind of labor. That baseless obedience he formally practiced was gradually displaced by his new devotion, even to the extent that he began to say the canonical prayers with genuine effect. Finally he accomplished the true work of Sufis and returned to his origin, that is, he attained salvation at death."

Added the master: "It was for the benefit of his disciple that Ibrahim Adham disclosed this secret which is the secret of all secrets in attaining blessings. Every Shaykh must perform a similar function. But," he concluded, "total sincerity (**sidq**) is necessary to obtain even a small amount of true devotion."

Next the master spoke about THE REWARD FOR SELF-DENIAL. "Shah Shuja Kirmani—may God's mercy be upon him—did not sleep for forty years. After forty years, he fell asleep one night and saw Almighty God in his dream. After that time, he made plans to sleep, so that he might again enjoy such a dream. One day a voice from the

Unseen proclaimed: 'That felicitous dream that you had was a reward for your continual wakefulness during forty years!' "

The master then spoke about THE ACCUMULATION AND EXPENDITURE OF WORLDLY GOODS. "The Tradition of the Prophet—peace be upon him—has been handed down in two versions: (1) Permissible earnings would be accepted and interdicted earnings would lead to torment and punishment in the next world; or (2) both permissible and interdicted earnings would lead to torment and punishment. Now torment and punishment as the consequence of interdicted earnings is self-evident, but torment due to permissible earnings requires explanation: The wage earner would be required to stand erect in the noonday sun of Resurrection; he would be made to give an account of what he had earned, from what sources, and with what result. This Tradition, namely, that one would be accountable for both permissible and interdicted earnings, has been attributed to the Commander of the Faithful, ʿAli—may God show favor on him."

The master next began to talk about SPIRITUAL MASTERS WHO DID NOT ACCEPT MONEY. "There were conditions attached to accepting and expending money," he explained. "One should accept money only if one thought it was merited. For instance, if the person to whom the money is offered is an **ʿalawi,** the giver might give it to him believing that he belongs to the family of the Prophet—peace be upon him. But if one who is proffered money is not an **ʿalawi,** then it would be unlawful for him to accept."

In this connection conversation turned to WHAT A SPIRITUAL MASTER IN NEED SHOULD DO. The master observed: "He should not ask for anything, nor should there be any intention to ask, nor the expectation that something would be offered. But, if without intending to receive or expecting to be offered, he receives something, then it is permissible for him to accept." He told a story to illustrate this point. "A pious man used to say, 'I will never ask anyone for anything, nor do I expect to receive anything from anyone.' Yet if someone offered him something, he did not hesitate to accept, even if the giver was the Devil himself!" The master then smiled, noting that the holy man had said something to this effect in order to make it known to what extent he did not care who was the giver or from where the money was offered. His chief concern was to indicate that he expected nothing from no one.

The master next commented on one of the major traits of the Prophets—blessings and peace be upon all of them, namely, THAT AT THE TIME OF HIS DEATH EACH PROPHET WAS GIVEN THE

CHOICE OF STAYING LONGER IN THIS WORLD, OR DEPARTING AT ONCE. When the last moment arrived for the Prophet Muhammad—peace be upon him—it occurred to ʿA'isha—may God be pleased with her—that she should enquire whether the Prophet—may peace be upon him—wanted to linger a few more days with his companions or wanted instead to depart to the next world. Pondering this issue, she visited the Prophet—peace be upon him—and looked intently at him. The Prophet—may blessing and peace be upon him—declared: "May I depart with the Prophets, the Righteous, the Martyrs, and the Virtuous, O Most Merciful of Those who grant mercy!"

This concludes the part of **Morals for the Heart** (**Fawa'id al-Fu'ad**) which I wrote within a period of one year and five months, from the beginning of Shaʿban, A.H. 707, to the end of Dhu'l-Hijja, A.H. 709. And if God the Exalted and Glorious wills, whatever more I hear of the precious words proceeding from the master I will record in the same fashion. "With assistance from God Almighty, Hasan may meet with success."

## Fascicle II (Hereafter II)

In the name of God full of Compassion, ever Compassionate.

These lofty pages and fragrant breezes have been gathered from the blessed speech and pious breath of that upright master, the Pole of the Poles on earth, the Seal of the Saints in both worlds, Shaykh Nizam of Truth, of Guidance, of Faith—may God provide for the Muslims through the lengthening of his life. Amen. In like manner, I had previously recorded some bits and pieces and, binding them together, called that volume, **Morals for the Heart (Fawa'id al-Fu'ad)**. I am hopeful that the reader, together with the writer, will achieve the collective benefit of both worlds—if God the Unique wills it.

I give to friends these pages, for now my book is done.
Of those who hope count Hasan ʿAla Sijzi as one.

### II. Assembly 1
Wednesday, 29 Shawwal, A.H. 709 (1 April 1310)

I obtained the benefit of kissing his feet. Conversation turned to LEAVING THE COMPANY OF PEOPLE. On his blessed lips came the remark: "In the days of my youth I had sat and fraternized with people. Always the doubt lingered in my mind: 'How can I escape from these persons?' Even though they were scholarly men and I, too, was engaged in research, aversion (to their company) haunted me. So much so that many times I would say to my friends, 'I don't want to be among you. I have been like your guest for a few days, nothing more.' " Interjecting, I asked the master, "Did this take place before you became attached to Shaykh al-Islam Farid ad-din—may God sanctify his lofty secret?" "Yes, it did," he replied.

### II. Assembly 2
Wednesday, 27th of Dhu'l-Qaʿda, A.H. 709 (28 April 1310)

I obtained the good fortune of kissing his feet. Conversation turned to DISCIPLES' VISITING THEIR MASTER. The central issue was: How often should they make such visits? From his blessed lips he recounted: "Three times, once each year while he was alive, I had gone to visit Shaykh al-Islam Farid of Truth, of Law, of Faith (Farid ad-din)—may God sanctify his lofty secret." And then he added, "After his death I had gone seven other times, or was it six? In all likelihood I had gone seven times. Yes, to the best of my recollection, during his lifetime and after his death, I visited him a total of ten times."

After that he observed that Shaykh Jamal ad-din Hansawi had made seven visits from Hansi, and then he spoke about Shaykh Najib ad-din Mutawakkil and his visits. "After his first visit, at the time of departing, he requested the Shaykh to recite the first chapter of the Qur'an (**Surat al-Fatiha**), in order that he might return again, and again have the benefit of kissing his hand. The Shaykh replied, 'There is no need to recite the **Fatiha.** You will come again many times.' After that he did return eighteen more times, and on the nineteenth visit he asked the Shaykh to recite the **Fatiha** as he had on his first visit. 'At that time,' pleaded Shaykh Najib ad-din, 'you had replied, "I will come and visit you many times again." From then till now I have visited nineteen times. I request you to recite the **Fatiha** that I might visit one more time, and make the total number of my visits twenty.' Shaykh Farid remained silent. Shaykh Najib ad-din assumed that Shaykh Farid had not heard what he said. He repeated his request. Still the Shaykh did not reply. Finally he got up and left. After that the two never met again."

Then the conversation turned to Shaykh Baha ad-din Zakariya—may God have mercy upon him. The blessed master spoke about the meeting of Shaykh Baha ad-din with the Shaykh of Shaykhs, Shihab ad-din Suhrawardi—may God continually sanctify his lofty secret. "He had been with Shaykh Shihab ad-din but seventeen days when, on the seventeenth day, Shaykh Shihab ad-din conferred on him his blessings (and dismissed him as a fully empowered disciple). After Shaykh Baha ad-din had come to Hindustan (and been there for some time), he determined that he should return (to Baghdad) and visit his Shaykh. But on the way he was intercepted by Shaykh Jalal ad-din Tabrizi—may God have mercy on him. Shaykh Jalal ad-din turned back Shaykh Baha ad-din, saying, 'It is the command of the Shaykh of Shaykhs that you return.' " After that the master spoke at length about the saintliness of Shaykh Baha ad-din. "In but seventeen days," he declared, "Shaykh Baha ad-din obtained the blessings that other disciples had not acquired in years. So rapid was his success that some of the older disciples took offense, complaining, 'We have spent so many years in the saint's presence and yet we had no such favors conferred on us.' Their murmurings reached the ears of Shaykh Shihab ad-din. He made this reply to them: 'You brought wet wood. How can wet wood catch fire? But Zakariya brought dry wood. With one puff he went up in flames!' "

### II. Assembly 3
### 13 Dhu'l-Hijja, A.H. 709 (14 May 1310)

I obtained the good fortune of kissing his feet. Conversation turned to OBEDIENCE AND PREOCCUPATION WITH GOD. The master observed: "Everything which exists exists between two states of nonexistence. That which is set between two states of nonexistence must itself partake of nonexistence, as occurs in the days known to women. If one day blood appears, the second day cleanness, and the third day blood again, then that cleanness must also be reckoned as blood." After that on his blessed lips came the saying: " 'Existence between two nonexistences [i.e., preexistence or **azal** and postexistence or **abad**] is like the intermittent period of cleanness between two days of bleeding in menses [i.e., it is illusory and impermanent].' The point is this: Since one's earthly life must be reckoned as nonexistence, what reliance can be placed on it? And why should one pass this brief period in idleness and neglect?"

After that he told the story of a saint who was constantly preoccupied with God. "He never fraternized with people. He was once asked: 'What is the matter with you? Why do you never seek out anyone and always avoid the company of others?' That saint gave this reply: 'Before this period I did not exist for thousands of years, and after this again I will not exist. Such a brief period of life that I am granted between two nonexistences—why should I waste it by seeking out people and engaging in useless matters? Would to God that I may expend this gift of life in that which pleases God!' "

Maulana Mahmud Awadhi—may his piety endure—was present. The master asked him: "Where are you staying?" "In the house of Maulana Burhan ad-din Gharib—may his virtues persist," he replied. On the master's lips came this line of verse:

Be pure and unmarred wherever you are.

After that he observed: "Every day some part of the earth asks other parts of the earth in language that expresses their respective conditions, 'Today has any person who remembers God (**dhakiri**) tread upon you, or any grief-stricken person, or someone pain-afflicted?' Most reply 'no,' but if the reply is 'yes,' then that portion of the earth on which such a holy one has tread assumes pride of place over the others."

II. Assembly 4

Wednesday, 25th of Dhu'l-Hijja, A.H. 709 (26 May 1310)

I had the benefit of kissing his feet. That day the master had just returned from attending funeral prayers for a dear friend. He began to speak of the spiritual states of the deceased. "He was an upright man, of high morals, and he expended money for noble ends. He never meddled in others' affairs. Even though he had never taken someone's hand, that is, never become his disciple, he tread the path of righteousness."

After that on his blessed lips came the remark: "When a man acquires knowledge, he becomes noble, but when he acts obediently, his work becomes still better. And in this matter he needs a spiritual guide so that he may break both (idols), that is to say, when he subjects both knowledge and work to a higher goal, he becomes proud of neither and does not suffer from reliance on them."

In this connection he then spoke of that deceased friend. He had heard that at the time of his death he was alone. Neither relative nor stranger waited on him. There was only him and God. What a tremendous spiritual boon!

Then he told a story about SHAYKH SHIHAB AD-DIN KHATIB HANSAWI. "He used to pray in private, imploring the Almighty, 'O God, I have fulfilled all the promises I made you. I am hopeful that you, for your part, will grant me this one wish, that at the time of my death no one will be with me, neither the angel of death nor any other angel. Just you and me.' " And after this the master continued, "This Shihab ad-din was a very special dear one. Every evening he would recite **Surat al-Baqara** before going to sleep. 'One night,' as he tells the story, 'I had no sooner finished reciting this **surah** than I heard a voice coming from the corner of my room:

Take heed of me, or else "Begone" I say.
Though my friends I kill, still no heed you'll pay.

The people of my household were fast asleep. I was astonished. Who could have spoken these words? Especially since there was no one in the house from whom such lines could have come forth.

Take heed of me, or else 'Begone' I say."

The master, when he arrived at this verse, began to cry. He was engulfed in tears, so much so that he could not finish his account of Shaykh Shihab ad-din. Weeping, he kept saying, "This was the message delivered to Maulana Shihab ad-din. He experienced hardships, he underwent trials, yet he died as he wished."

The master then spoke of SAMA' AND THE PEOPLE OF SAMA'. "**Sama'**," he remarked, "is a proving ground for men of spiritual prowess." Conversation then turned to the question: "HOW DOES FAITH WORK?" He observed: "The unbelievers at the time of death will experience punishment. At that moment they will profess belief but it will not be reckoned to them as belief because it will not be faith in the Unseen. If the believer repents at the time of death, that repentance of his will be accepted; only the faith of the unbeliever at death remains unacceptable."

## II. Assembly 5
### Sunday, 15th of Muharram, A.H. 710 (14 June 1310)

I had the benefit of kissing his feet. Conversation turned to THE BOOKS OF THE SAINTS AND THE MORALS THAT THEY CONTAIN. A dear one was present. He remarked: "A man once showed me a book in Awadh, and he claimed that your eminence had written it." The master—may God remember him with favor—retorted, "He spoke a lie. I have written no book."

After that he observed that Shaykh 'Ali Hujwiri, when he was writing *The Unveiling of What Has Been Hidden* (**Kashf al-Mahjub**),[52] put his name at the beginning of the book, and then again in two or three other places. Why did he draw attention to his name in this manner? Because, as he himself explained, he had earlier written some verses in Arabic and not included his name. Then a young man had taken these same verses and written them in **his** name. Later [on account of this plagiarism] that man died without faith.

When he had completed this story, the master remarked: "THE TIME OF DEATH is a difficult time, and it is also difficult to know whether one will die as a believer or an unbeliever." After that on his blessed lips came this observation: "The sign of sincerity of faith is this, that the dying person at the moment of death becomes yellow, his forehead dotted with sweat." In this vein he spoke about his mother. "My mother at the time of her death expired with these very signs of good fortune on her face."

After that he turned toward those present and instructed them: "TO PRESERVE ONE'S FAITH one should perform two prostrations in the following manner after the sunset prayer. In the first inclination after the **Fatiha** one should recite **Surat al-Ikhlas** seven times and **Surat al-Falak** once. In the second inclination one should recite **Surat al-Ikhlas** seven times and **Surat al-Nas** once. And after that one should prostrate one's head and say three times, 'O Living and Eternal God, keep me steadfast in faith.' "

Concerning the blessing of this prayer sequence, he told a story. "I heard the following story from Khwaja Ahmad ibn Shaykh Muʿin ad-din Sijzi[53]—may God sanctify his lofty secret. And this Khwaja Ahmad was a very upright person. He testified: 'I had a companion who was a professional soldier. He used to perform these two prostrations of prayer regularly. Once, however, we were traveling in the vicinity of Ajmer at sunset. The time for evening prayer (right after sunset) arrived, but we were afraid of thieves. Thieves indeed did appear. I at once finished saying the three prescribed and the two customary prayers, then hurried toward the city. That friend, despite being harassed by thieves and fearful of them, still performed the two supererogatory prayers for preserving the faith. Much later, I received information that that young man was about to die. In order to verify his circumstances [i.e., his spiritual state] at death, I went to the place where he was on the verge of expiration. He died as he should have died.' " Then the master—may God remember him with favor—commented: "Khwaja Ahmad told the story of the death of that young man in such a manner that if they ask me before the Throne of Judgment, I, too, will testify that he died with untarnished faith. Praise be to God, the Lord of the universe."

After that he told another story about the two prostrations that are performed after evening prayer. "In this same connection I had a friend, a classmate, named Maulana Taqi ad-din. An upright man and also a scholar, he used to perform the two extra prostrations of prayer (for maintaining faith) after every evening prayer. In the first inclination, after **Surat al-Fatiha** he would recite **Surat al-Buruj** (Surah 75) and in the second inclination, after **Surat al-Fatiha** he would recite **Surat al-Tariq** (Surah 76). After his death," continued the master, "I saw him in a dream, and I asked him, 'What did God Almighty do with you?' He replied: 'When the record of my deeds had been reviewed, the command went forth: "We forgive him on account of these two prostrations of prayer!" ' "

One of those present asked: "Did you call this the Prayer of Light?" "No," replied the master, "this is called the Prayer of Towers (**buruj**). What is called the Prayer of Light consists of those two prostrations in the first of which one recites **Surat al-Anʿam** (Surah 6) from the beginning up to the verse ending with "they deride" (v.4) and in the second of which one recites from "do they not see that we destroyed, and so forth" (v.5) up to "they deride" (v.9).

After that he told still another story as an INDUCEMENT TO PRAY THE TWO EXTRA PROSTRATIONS FOR FAITH AFTER SUNSET AND ALSO AT SUNRISE. "When evening comes an angel alights on the roof of the Kaʾba and announces: 'O servants of God and followers of Muhammad! God Almighty has given you a night and before you there lies another night, that is, the night of the grave. In order to claim the treasure from that second night, you must perform a work in this night. And the work is this, that you do two prostrations of prayer. In both prostrations after **Surat al-Fatiha,** recite five times **Surat al-Kafirun** (Surah 109). Similarly, when day breaks the same angel appears on the rooftop of the Sacred House (Jerusalem) and announces: 'O servants of God and followers of Muhammad! God Almighty has given you a day and before you lies another day. That second day is the Day of Resurrection. In order to claim the treasure from that second day you must perform a work in this day. And the work is this, that you do two prostrations of prayer. In both prostrations, after **Surat al-Fatiha** recite five times **Surat al-Ikhlas** (Surah 112).' "

After that on his blessed lips came this remark: "Shaykh Jamal ad-din Hansawi—on whom be God's mercy and forgiveness—used to narrate a Tradition (of the Prophet Muhammad) in this connection. I do not remember the exact words of the Tradition, but its meaning corresponds to what I have just recounted."

Conversation then turned to REMEMBERING THE DEATH OF SAINTS AND THEIR SPIRITUAL STATE AFTER DEATH. In this connection he observed: "Saints on the verge of death are like a person having a dream, and it is as if the beloved is lying in bed beside him. At the moment that that sleeper departs this life, it is as if he is suddenly startled awake from his dream, and that Beloved for whom he had searched throughout his life, he sees lying beside him in his own bed. Imagine the joy and delight that he experiences!"

One of those present asked: "Are there saints who are blessed with the vision (of their Beloved) even in this world?" "Yes," replied the master, "but this favor that he is granted here briefly is disclosed to him there in its fullness. It is like the sleeper who when he wakes up finds his Beloved in his very own bed, as has been indicated in the following Tradition: 'People are asleep, but when they die they awake.' That is to say, all human beings are now asleep, but when they die they wake up. In other words, each person, to the extent that he is immersed in something here, when he dies the very thing that he sought will be given him."

After that he continued to speak about THE DEATH OF SAINTS. He told this story: "I had a friend in Badaun. His name was Ahmad. He was very upright and pious and possessed of the qualities of God's deputies (**abdal**). Though he was illiterate, every day he devoted himself to understanding juridical issues and their implementation. And he would ask everyone he met about them. When I was on my way to Delhi, he also came to Delhi. One day we met in public. As soon as he saw me, he began to pummel me with legal queries. Then he asked about the health of my mother. He already knew about the affliction from which she had been suffering, but no one had told him about her death. I took it on myself to tell him that my mother had been blessed with God's mercy, that is, she had died. 'May **you** live a long life' was his rejoinder. But then he became bothered and vexed. He began to cry." The master —may God remember him with favor—when he came to this point in the story also began to cry. So convulsed was he with tears that I could not make out what he was trying to say. In the midst of his weeping, these verses came upon his blessed tongue. I do not know whether they were connected to the story of that Ahmad or whether he recited them by association. The poem was this:

Alas, my heart, your careful planning ill served
To keep even one night for union reserved.
But united to you or not, O friend, I
Witness at least this separation preserved![54]

After that he remarked, "Some time later this Ahmad departed from the abode of this world. On the night after his death I saw him in a dream. Just as he had during his lifetime, he began asking me questions about the law and its application. 'Why are you asking me about this now?' I protested. 'While you were alive that was a commendable vocation, but surely not after death!' In response he asked me: 'Do you really think that the saints of God are dead?' "

While the master was telling this story, a **juwaliq** entered the room. And he began to utter some shameful remarks that are inappropriate for a saintly assembly. The master—may God remember him with favor—said nothing. In short, he lived up to the expectations that the **juwaliq** had of him. After that he turned to those present and emphasized: "This is what has to be done (in such circumstances). Just as many persons come, place their head at my feet, and offer something, so there ought to be people like this who come and speak unabashedly. It is through such acts that the saint can offer penance for those other acts."

Then he told a **JUWALIQ** STORY. "Once a confused one of their number came to me and began mumbling many senseless things. I did not reply. At last he exclaimed: 'For as long as the world exists may my offensiveness and your forbearance persist!' "

After that he related how one of these fearless fellows burst into the presence of Shaykh Farid ad-din—may God sanctify his lofty secret—and protested: "Why is it that you have set yourself up as an idol?" The Shaykh replied: "I have not done this. God has done it." The **juwaliq** insisted: "No, **you** have done it." "I have not done this. God has done it," repeated the Shaykh. That interloper, when he finally heard what the Shaykh had been saying, was overcome with shame. Getting up, he left at once.

After that the master told still another story in this connection. "Once some **juwaliqs** came into the presence of Shaykh Baha ad-din Zakariya—may God have mercy on him. The Shaykh had a very low regard for this group. Upon their arrival the **juwaliqs** expected the Shaykh to give them something. He did not. They went outside and began to quarrel. As they made an uproar, they also began picking up bricks. The Shaykh ordered the door to be closed. After it was closed, the **juwaliqs** began to heave bricks against it. A little while later Shaykh Baha ad-din Zakariya declared: 'I am occupying this place at the command of Shaykh Shihab ad-din Suhrawardi. I did not come here of my own accord. It was a man of God who bade me come here.' He then ordered them to open the door of his hospice. When they did, the **juwaliqs** fell on the ground, prostrating themselves before the Shaykh. Then they got up and left."

After that the master—may God remember him with favor—observed: "The first time that Shaykh Baha ad-din ordered the door closed, it was out of human instinct, but he also was not sure of the spiritual quality of that moment. But after a little while [when his mind had become clear], he ordered the door to be opened."

Concerning such SHIFTS IN SPIRITUAL STATES, the master told a final story. "In the Battle of Uhud many companions of the Prophet—may God be pleased with them—were slain. When the fighting was over, Gabriel—peace be upon him—came and said; 'O Muhammad, you too lie down with your slain companions, until the heat of anger has passed from you.' "

## II. Assembly 6
### Wednesday, 25th of Muharram, A.H. 710 (24 June 1310)

I obtained the good fortune of kissing his feet. Conversation turned to MISERS WHO HOARD THEIR WEALTH: The more they make, the more they want. The master observed: "God the Almighty and Exalted has created different sorts of persons. For instance, if there were an individual for whom ten **dirams** sufficed to meet his daily needs and one day he happened to acquire more, he would not feel secure till he had spent that surplus. At the same time, there might be another person of such a temperament that however much he gained the more he wanted. In neither instance can the individual control his instincts; it is a matter of divine will."

After that he advised: "True comfort comes from EXPENDING GOLD AND SILVER. Hence no one can find comfort unless he expends the silver in his possession. For instance, if someone wants to wear fine clothes or to eat delicious food or to gratify some other desire, he cannot succeed without expending silver. Hence it is obvious that the true comfort in having gold and silver is to expend it."

Then he repeated his point. "The real purpose of amassing gold and silver is to use it for the benefit of others." In this connection he remarked: "From the outset I have never set my heart on collecting anything. I have never sought worldly goods. And once I attached myself to Shaykh al-Islam Farid ad-din—may God sanctify his lofty secret—I began to serve a person who, having opted for total, unconditional renunciation, had no regard for either this world or the next."

Then he remarked: "Before becoming Shaykh Farid ad-din's disciple, I had difficulty finding even the minimum means of livelihood. (Physical) contentment was not my lot. Then one day in the evening a passerby gave me half a **tanka.**[55] I said to myself: 'Evening has already arrived, and whatever I needed was taken care of earlier. I will keep this and spend it in the morning.' When night came, I busied myself in prayer and meditation, but that half **tanka** clung to the skirt of my heart and disrupted my concentration. When I saw what had happened to my spiritual state, I exclaimed: 'O God, when will morning come so that I may dispense with that coin?' "

## II. Assembly 7
Wednesday, 5th of Safar, A.H. 710 (4 July 1310)

May God receive the following custom with favor and accord it success—I obtained the benefit of kissing the master's feet.

Conversation turned to THE MERIT[56] OF SAINTS. Some of them can even fly! In this connection the master told a story. "In Badaun there lived a preacher. His pulpit was attached to a wall in which there were niches. The niches were about the height of a man above the pulpit, and they were so configured that no man could sit in them. Once, however, in a fit of ecstasy that preacher leapt from the pulpit and landed in one of those niches—seated!"

In the same vein he told a related story. "There was once a yogi who came to Uchch. Attempting to convert Shaykh Safi ad-din Gazaruni, he engaged him in heated debate. 'Come!' he said to the Shaykh, 'show me your superiority.' '**You** show me your superiority,' retorted the Shaykh; 'since it is **you** who are trying to convert, it is up to **you** to demonstrate your superiority.' The yogi soared from the ground into the air, till his head touched the ceiling. Then he came straight back to the ground. Turning to the Shaykh, he crowed, 'Now, **you** show me your superiority.' Shaykh Safi ad-din Gazaruni turned his face toward the heavens, imploring: 'O God, you have given this superiority to a stranger. Please grant me some miracle of like quality.' After that the Shaykh soared from his place. He flew toward the **qibla,** that is, in the direction of Mecca. Then he headed north. Reversing himself, he flew south, finally landing in his original place. Then he sat down. The yogi was awestruck. Placing his head at the feet of the Shaykh, he said: 'I cannot display such power. I can merely go straight up from the ground and come back down. I can't turn in mid-air and fly to the right or the left, while you, you can turn in whatever direction you wish. This is God's work. It is divinely inspired. What I do is both false and futile.' "

To illustrate further this sort of intentional movement, the master told the following story. "Once there was a philosopher who paid a visit on the Caliph and brought his books with him. He hoped to divert the Caliph from the path of God. The Caliph was, in fact, beguiled by the philosopher's erudition. News of their meeting was conveyed to Shaykh Shihab ad-din Suhrawardi—may God sanctify his lofty secret. The Shaykh, as he reflected on the situation, said to himself: 'If the Caliph were to be won over by this philosopher, a host of people would be condemned to darkness.' Having said this, he arose and went to the palace of the Caliph. By the time he arrived, the Caliph had already become engaged in conversation with that philosopher. The Shaykh's arrival was announced. He was invited into the Caliph's quarters. On entering, the Shaykh saw the Caliph with that philosopher. 'What are you discussing at this moment?' he queried. 'We are just engaged in chitchat,' replied the Caliph. Both he and the philosopher concealed the fact that they had been discussing a point of philosophy. The Shaykh persisted. 'I asked: "What are you discussing?" '

"When the Shaykh continued to importune them, that philosopher announced: 'We are just now engaged in discussing the natural movement of the sky. There are three kinds of movement: natural, voluntary, and involuntary. Natural movement is that movement that occurs by its inherent nature, such as when someone drops a stone from his hand, it immediately falls to the ground. Voluntary movement is that which is self-controlled; it will move in a particular direction according to its own intent. Involuntary movement is that which always relates to someone else's action. For instance, if someone threw a stone into the air, that would be involuntary movement (from the viewpoint of the stone). But when its upward arc decreased, as it would each moment in accordance with its size, it would fall to the ground, and that descent would be called a natural movement. Now we have reached the point in our discussion where we can understand the movement of the sky as natural.'

" 'No,' objected the Shaykh. 'It is not so. The movement of the sky is involuntary.' 'How can that be?' asked the philosopher and the Caliph. 'There is an angel of this form, with these features, and he it is who makes the sky move by the command of God—may He be honored and glorified. A Tradition has depicted this very process.' The philosopher began to laugh. Then the Shaykh approached the Caliph and that philosopher. Leading them from the covered room where they had been sitting, he took them outside. The Shaykh looked up to the sky and began to pray: 'O God, that which you have revealed to your humble servants, reveal now also to these persons.' Then, turning to that Caliph and that philosopher, he told them: 'Look to the sky.' They both turned their eyes heavenward and saw that angel whom the Shaykh had described and whom God had directed to move the sky. Then the Caliph rejected the philosopher's teaching and remained firm in his faith as a Muslim. Praise be to God, Lord of the universe."

### II. Assembly 8
### Monday, 27th of Rabiʿ al-awwal, A.H. 710 (11 August 1310)

I had the good fortune of kissing his feet. He began talking about THE SPIRITUAL STATES OF SHAYKH AL-ISLAM FARID AD-DIN—may God sanctify his lofty secret. He told the assembly that the Shaykh usually broke his fast with sherbet, which was brought to him in a bowl with some raisins in it. Mixing it with water in a large cup, he distributed half or two-thirds of it among those present in his assembly. He reserved the one-third or so that was left over for himself, but even of that he would give some to select persons, and it was considered auspicious for those thus favored. In between the breaking of fast and the saying of prayers, they would bring in two loaves of bread. The bread weighed less than two pounds and was basted with a layer of fat. Breaking one of the loaves in pieces, he distributed those pieces to those around him. The other loaf he would eat himself, though even out of that he offered some to select persons. Then he performed the evening prayer and remained totally absorbed in God till dinner. For dinner they laid a table, setting out every kind of food. After dinner the Shaykh did not eat again till the moment of breaking fast the next evening.

After that he spoke about an affliction of the bowels that befell Shaykh al-Islam. Eventually he died from this illness. The master—may God remember him with favor—remarked, "One evening at bedtime I was attending him. I saw that a cot had been laid for him. The same rug on which he sat during the day they stretched over the cot, even though that rug did not reach as far as his feet. For that portion of the cot on which rested his blessed feet they brought a patch of cloth, but if he pulled it up during the night, the bottom part of his cot would remain uncovered. They also brought a staff which he had been given by Shaykh Qutb ad-din Bakhtiyar Kaki—may God sanctify his lofty secret—and placed it at the head of the cot. The Shaykh, placing his head on that staff, would take rest, but frequently he would reach up to touch, and also to kiss, that staff."

After that the master observed: "One day during this illness he instructed me and some friends to go to such-and-such a room, remain awake through the night and pray for his recovery. We did as he instructed. I, together with my friends, went to that room. There was a balcony off that room, and I went to that balcony, taking some food with me. I remained in that same place praying throughout the night. When morning came, we went and, standing before the Shaykh, reported to him how we had followed his instructions: We had remained awake and at prayer throughout the night. The Shaykh reflected for awhile, then said, 'Your prayer has had no effect on my health.' I hesitated to answer, but a friend named ʿAli Bihari, who was standing behind me, spoke up. 'We are deficient. Only the blessed essence of the Shaykh is perfect. How can prayers of the defective on behalf of perfect ones find a favorable response?' Since the Shaykh did not seem to hear what he had said, I repeated the words of this friend. He then turned to me and announced: 'I have asked God that whatever you seek from Him you may obtain.' And he gave me his staff."

I interjected at this point, asking: "Were you present at the time of Shaykh al-Islam's death?" His eyes teemed with tears as he replied: "No, he sent me to Delhi in the month of Shawwal. He died on the fifth of the month of Muharram. But he did remember me at the time of his death and sent this message: 'I, too, was not present at the death of Shaykh Qutb ad-din Bakhtiyar Kaki—may God sanctify his lofty secret. I was in Hansi at that time.' " As he disclosed this chronology, the master—may God remember him with favor—began to cry out loud. So poignant was his distress that others present were moved to empathize with him.

He continued: "The illness of the Shaykh had reached an advanced stage when the month of Ramadan came upon us. He was too sick to fast. They brought a watermelon. They cut it up, putting the pieces before the Shaykh. He began to eat and at one point extended a piece of watermelon to me. I wanted to eat it. In my heart I resolved to fast continuously for two months to atone for the Ramadan fast that I was about to break. For where else could I obtain the benefit that would accrue to me for having eaten something provided by the Shaykh from his own hand? I was on the verge of eating the watermelon when he intervened. 'Don't!' he declared. 'It is possible for me to have a dispensation from observing the Law, but it is not permissible for you. You must not eat.' " Someone then asked about the age of the Shaykh. "He lived to be 93," replied the master.

On that particular day he continued to speak only about Shaykh Farid ad-din, and in listening to his discourse, those present experienced an indescribable taste of the divine presence. When evening came, he said the late evening prayer and then gave me a special prayer rug. Praise be to God, the Lord of the universe!

### II. Assembly 9
### Saturday, 10th of Rabiʿ al-Akhir, A.H. 710 (6 September 1310)

I obtained the benefit of kissing his feet. Conversation turned to PETITIONARY PRAYER. He said: "One must pray before misfortune occurs." In Arabic he elaborated this point. "When misfortune descends as prayer ascends, the two meet in the air. At the point where they collide, if prayer is more powerful, then misfortune turns back, thwarted; otherwise, misfortune descends and prevails!"

In this connection he told a story about THE INVASIONS OF THE INFIDEL TARTARS. "When the Mongols reached Nishapur, its ruler summoned Shaykh Farid ad-din ʿAttar—may God sanctify his lofty secret, and asked the Shaykh to petition God. 'The time for petitionary prayer has passed,' replied Shaykh Farid ad-din. 'Now is the time for contentment.' That is to say, misfortune is descending from God. Now you must be content with what God has ordained." Then the master added, "After misfortune descends, one should still offer petitionary prayer. Although it cannot prevent misfortune, it can still lessen the hardship of one's affliction."

In the same vein he spoke about PATIENCE AND CONTENTMENT. "Patience is this," he said, "that when something odious happens to you, you bear with it and do not complain. As for contentment, that is when something odious happens to you and you do not regard it as odious, but instead act as if that misfortune had never befallen you!"

"The theologians," he went on, "deny this meaning of contentment. They maintain that it is inconceivable that something odious might afflict a person without that person perceiving it as odious. The rejoinder to their denial is this," he explained. "Many times it happens that a traveler will have a thorn lodge in his foot. His foot may even begin to bleed, but he is hurrying along so fast, and is so preoccupied with reaching his destination, that he does not take notice of what has happened to his foot. Only later does he become aware of pain. Also, there are many instances of a soldier having been wounded, but because he is so engaged in combat, at first he remains unaware of his wound. Only on returning home does he realize what has happened to him. Now, if you reflect on the lesson of these incidents in which pain goes unnoticed, you will understand how much more that same reflex characterizes one who is preoccupied with meditating on God.

After that he spoke about QAZI HAMID AD-DIN NAGAURI—may God be merciful to him. "He was sitting in a certain place when a man came to punish him for wrongs he had allegedly committed. That man rained blows on Qazi Hamid ad-din, hitting him a thousand times. Yet the Qazi let out no cry nor did any sign of pain appear on his face. Afterward, when they brought him to the political tribunal, he was asked, 'How is it that you experienced no pain from this beating?' 'At the moment that I was being pummeled,' replied Qazi Hamid ad-din, 'my beloved was keeping watch over me. Under his gaze no pain could reach me.' " Then on the tongue of the master—may God remember him with favor—came this blessed utterance: "If such protection is provided under the gaze of a human beloved, how much more protected is one under the gaze of the divine Beloved?"

Conversation next turned to TRUST. The master observed that there are three stages of trust. (1) The first is the relation of a client to his advocate. That advocate is both knowledgeable of the law and well disposed toward him. The client has faith in the outcome, saying to himself, "I have a lawyer who both knows his business and is my friend." In short, the client has trust, even though from time to time he may ask that advocate a question or suggest to him that he argue the case in a particular manner or offer a specific motion. Such is the first stage of trust for a Sufi adept: He also has trust, but at the same time he asks favors of God. (2) The second stage of trust is the relationship of a nursing child to its mother. It also has trust but it does not question. Never does it say to its mother: "Give me milk at such-and-such a time." When hungry, it simply cries. It does not implore. It does not say: "Give me milk." Its heart has total confidence in the compassion of its mother. (The same is true for the Sufi adept at the second stage of trust.) (3) As for the third stage, it is this: that the adept conducts himself like the corpse in the hands of a washerman. That corpse asks no questions. It does not move on its own. It responds to every wish and to every initiative of the washerman. This is the third stage of trust. It is the highest, and its attainment represents a lofty spiritual station for the Sufi adept.

During that same assembly they brought in food, and one of those present began to tell a joke. "I was in such-and-such a place. Though I was full, they brought out **tutmaj** and I couldn't resist eating it." This and other amusing anecdotes he narrated. The master—may God remember him with favor—smiled, and in keeping with the mood of that occasion, he told a further story. "Once I had gone to see Shaykh Jamal al-din Khatib Hansawi—may God have mercy upon him! It was the time of morning prayer in winter. Shaykh Jamal ad-din, turning toward me, recited the following verses:

> On winter days how well we've fed
> On ghee-cooked stew and crisp-baked bread!

I said in Arabic: 'One who is absent [from this world] remembers what is absent [from him].' Shaykh Jamal ad-din nodded and said: 'I will ask my servants to bring whatever is available.' Even as he spoke, they brought in trays. Referring to this food and to the tablecloth they spread out for it, he told a story. 'Once there was a man named Muhammad. He came and sat down in the presence of Shaykh al-Islam Farid ad-din—may God bless his lofty secret. When they brought in a loaf of bread, they couldn't find a tablecloth or linen on which to set it. Shaykh Farid ad-din instructed them to put it on the ground. That Muhammad thought to himself. "How good it would be were there a cloth!" The Shaykh, with his index finger, drew a design on the ground and declared to that man: "O Muhammad, know that this is a tablecloth!" ' " "That Muhammad," added the master, "was still a spiritual novice."

## II. Assembly 10

Friday, 23rd of Rabiʿ al-akhir, A.H. 710 (19 September 1310)

I obtained the benefit of kissing his feet. In this week I was distressed because there had been an interruption in my salary payment. As soon as I called on the master, he began to tell me the following story. "There used to be a man who was a great saint. Many times I would meet him and he would tell me some words of wisdom. Due to his preeminence I never asked his name, yet every time I encountered him he would tell me another story. Once when he met me, he exclaimed: 'God willing, you will be the kind of person on whom people can depend without fail.' " After the master—may God remember him with favor—had told this story, he commended to me what the saintly stranger had said. "That is the final word, the final word," he stressed.

Then he added: "On another occasion that same man, on meeting me, told me this story. 'In Lahore there lived a distinguished saint named Shaykh Zindadil.[57] On the day of ʿ**id**, after people had said their prayers, that Shaykh looked to the heavens and cried out: "Today is ʿ**id.** Every servant has received from his master some ʿ**id** gift. Please give me also an ʿ**id** gift." He had no sooner finished speaking than a piece of silk cloth descended from heaven. On it were inscribed these words: "We have freed your soul from the fire of hell." When people realized the high degree of that man's spiritual state, they flocked to him, trying to kiss his hand or feet. In the meantime, a friend of that Shaykh came to visit him. "From God Almighty you have received an ʿ**id** gift," he remarked; "now give **me** some ʿ**id** gift." That Shaykh, on hearing this request, gave his friend the piece of silk cloth. "Go!" he told him. "This is your ʿ**id** gift. Tomorrow I will confront the fire of hell!" ' "

After that the master—may God remember him with favor!—told one more story. "On another occasion a man who had come to call on me shared this anecdote with me. Listen to the following tale. There was once an urban Brahman. Though he was very wealthy, the chief magistrate of that city fined him, seized all his possessions, and reduced him to poverty. That Brahman became destitute. He was hard pressed to make ends meet. One day he came across a friend. 'How are you?' asked the friend. 'Well and happy,' replied the Brahman. 'How can you be happy,' retorted the friend, 'since they have seized everything that you possess?' 'With me still,' replied the Brahman, 'is my sacred thread (**zunnar**).' "

On finishing the story, the master—may God remember him with favor—asked me. "Did you understand the context of this story?" "Yes," I replied, "I did." For on hearing this story, I felt an inner contentment. I realized that the master had told the story to calm the heart of this helpless creature. He added, "You should never experience distress on account of the interruption of your salary or the nonattainment of worldly goods. If the whole world passes you by, don't fret; you must maintain love of God at all times." Praise be to God that I was able to grasp the context for this moral instruction that the master gave me!

### II. Assembly 11
### Friday, 24th of Jumada al-ula, A.H. 710 (19 October 1310)

I obtained the benefit of kissing his feet. During the preceding night I had had a dream. I explained it to the master. "In this dream Amir ʿAlam Walwalji[58] appeared and gave me some sweets." The master—may God remember him with favor—asked: "Were you once attached to him as his disciple?" "Yes, I was." "Then he was sending you something from the Unseen," replied the master. "On another Thursday evening he may give something else from the Unseen, something that you cannot begin to imagine."

II. Assembly 12

Monday, 24th of Jumada al-ula, A.H. 710 (19 October 1310)

It was the eleventh day since I had seen that dream in which I had been promised some still greater blessing. In short, during that assembly he spoke at length about THE SPIRITUAL GREATNESS OF AMIR ʿALAM WALWALJI. In connection with praising him, he spoke about a saint who dispensed spiritual favor that had been given to him by Khwaja Ajall Shirazi—may God have mercy on him. "Once that saint ascended the pulpit and a great throng waited on his words, among them Amir ʿAlam Walwalji. As that saint began to preach, he proclaimed: 'O Muslims, take note and remember well that what spiritual prowess I have received from Khwaja Ajall Shirazi. Tonight I want to transmit that prowess to my own (spiritual) heir.' He commanded Amir ʿAlam Walwalji to come forward. He did, and after he had ascended the pulpit, the saint ejected blessed saliva from his mouth, and into the mouth of Amir ʿAlam Walwalji."

II. Assembly 13

Sunday, 29th of Jumada al-akhira, A.H. 710 (23 November 1310)

I obtained the good fortune of kissing his feet. Conversation turned to THE SPIRITUAL BENEFIT OF THE MONTH OF RAJAB. "In this month," observed the master, "many petitions are answered, and four nights in this month have an especially holy property. One is the first night, another is the first Friday, a third is the evening of the fifteenth, and the fourth is the evening of the twenty-seventh, which is the night of the Ascension (of the Prophet Muhammad).

After that he spoke about SUPEREROGATORY PRAYERS. "Such supererogatory prayers," he observed, "replace the obligatory prayers that the believer has missed." He then alluded to the Greatest Imam, Abu Hanifa—may God have mercy on him. "It was his practice," said the master, "that for every obligatory prayer he missed he would say in its stead five supererogatory prayers."

## II. Assembly 14
### Saturday, 13th of Rajab, A.H. 710 (6 December 1310)

I obtained the benefit of kissing his feet. Conversation turned to HOLDING FIRM TO [THE ABSOLUTION THAT COMES FROM] REPENTANCE. On his blessed tongue came this pronouncement: "Once the novice has pledged allegiance to his spiritual master, all the sins that he previously committed are forgiven." In this connection he told a story. "There was a man named Siraj ad-din who lived in the town of Awhar. Once I visited there and went to his home. He and the other residents of Awhar had become disciples of Shaykh Farid ad-din—may God sanctify his lofty secret. But on that particular day some of the residents of that town had become annoyed with the family of the wife of that Siraj ad-din. There was an unpleasant exchange of harsh words. The relatives of Siraj ad-din were accused of having committed some grave offenses. His wife spoke up for herself. "Those things of which you accuse me," she observed, "please reflect on them: Did they occur before or after we pledged allegiance to Shaykh Farid ad-din? [For if they occurred before, which she clearly felt they did, then she was forgiven by Shaykh Farid ad-din and exempt from being punished for them]." The master—may God remember him with favor—when he arrived at this point in the story commented: "How nice she spoke—this wife of Siraj ad-din!"

## II. Assembly 15
### Tuesday, 29th of Rajab, A.H. 710 (22 December 1310)

I obtained the benefit of kissing his feet. A visitor came and asked him to intercede for his well-being. The master replied: "You should recite **Surat al-Jumʿa** (Q.62) every evening for relief from material duress." Then he remarked: "Every Friday evening Shaykh al-Islam Farid ad-din—may God sanctify his lofty secret—would recite **Surat al-Jumʿa.** 'I recite it because I must,' he used to say, 'but I never recite it for myself. I recite it for others, since it is my conviction that the believer must be grateful for whatever he has been given.' "

In this same assembly he also told the following story. "Once I came upon a group dressed in the manner of Sufis. One was saying to the other. 'I saw such-and-such in a dream.' The other explained: 'That is an auspicious dream. You will earn much money, you will acquire many goods, you will abound in the comforts of life.' I wanted to intervene and protest; 'O Khwaja, whose clothes are those that you wear? People in such clothes do not offer dream interpretations like this.' But then the thought occurred to me: Who am I that I should make such a rebuke? I said nothing and left."

When the master—may God remember him with favor—had finished this story, the man who had come to request intercessory prayer for relief from material duress said: "Alas, O esteemed master, we human beings know no relief from seeking goods, comfort, even affluence." The master—may God remember him with favor—smiled and then replied: "You are correct. But I did not tell this story about you. I told it to disclose my own frame of mind!"

## II. Assembly 16
Thursday, 6th of the blessed month of Ramadan
in the favored community, A.H. 710
(27 January 1311)

I obtained the good fortune of kissing his feet. That day I, together with some senior friends, renewed our oath of allegiance to the Shaykh. In this connection he told us a story. When the Prophet—blessings and peace be upon him—resolved to conquer Mecca, he sent ʿUthman—may God be pleased with him—ahead, with a message for the Meccans. While he was still in Mecca, a rumor reached the Prophet—peace be upon him—that ʿUthman had been killed. The Prophet—peace be upon him—when he heard this, summoned his companions. "Come!" he told them, "renew your oath of allegiance to me so that we can make war against the Meccans. His companions renewed their oath. At that time the Messenger—blessing and peace be upon him—was reclining against the trunk of a tree. They call this "the oath of benediction" (**baiʾat al-ridwan**). Among those who came before him was a companion named Ibn Akuʿ. He also made the oath of allegiance. The Messenger—on whom be peace—asked, 'Have you not renewed your oath once before?' 'Yes, I have,' replied Ibn Akuʿ, 'and at this moment I am glad to renew it again.' The Messenger—on whom be peace—extended him the hand of allegiance." After that the master remarked: "If a disciple wants to renew his oath of allegiance but his Shaykh is not present, he may take the garment of his Shaykh and, placing that garment before him, make his oath of allegiance to it. Don't be surprised," he added, "that Shaykh al-Islam Farid ad-din—may God sanctify his lofty secret—renewed his allegiance to Shaykh Qutb ad-din many times in this fashion, and I have followed his example."

Then he began to discuss THE BEAUTY OF RELIANCE (ON ONE'S SHAYKH). "Shaykh Rafiʿ ad-din, who was the Shaykh al-Islam of Awadh, told me that he had a close relative who had been a disciple of Khwaja Ajall Shirazi—may God have mercy on him. Once that disciple was accused of serious offenses and, having been convicted, was led to the place of execution. The executioner wanted to situate him so that he was facing toward the **qibla** (the direction of the Kaʿba in Mecca). The disciple also wanted to face Mecca but that was the opposite direction from the tomb of his master, so he would have had to die with his back to his **pir.** He at once turned around and stood facing the tomb of his master. 'Here,' insisted the executioner, 'everyone dies facing Mecca. Why do you want to be different?' 'Look,' replied the condemned disciple, 'It is up to me to choose the direction that I want to face at death; you just get on with your job.' "

In this connection he told another story. "I was once on a trip. One day, after having traveled a long distance, I began to feel ill. Even though I had been riding, I felt thirsty. I rode to the edge of a pond and dismounted from my horse. I wanted to scoop up some water and drink it. My heart became faint; I began to experience stomach cramps. And then, as I was on the verge of losing consciousness, these words came on my tongue: 'O Shaykh! O Shaykh!' After awhile I regained consciousness and found myself overwhelmed with confidence, confidence about the meaning of my life's work. I nurtured the hope that at the end of my life I would surrender myself into the hands of my Shaykh, just as I had imagined that I was about to do earlier—if God Almighty wills."

## II. Assembly 17
Sunday, 23rd of the blessed month of Ramadan,
A.H. 710 (13 February 1311)

I obtained the good fortune of kissing his feet. Conversation turned to VISITING GRAVES. "When my mother—may she be blessed—fell ill, she asked me several times to visit the tomb of a certain martyr or a certain saint," he recalled. "I would obey her command, and when I returned home, she would say; 'My illness is better, my affliction has eased.' " In the same vein he told another anecdote about the time that Shaykh al-Islam Farid ad-din—may God sanctify his lofty secret—fell ill. He commanded me, with some friends, to visit the graves of a few martyrs who were buried in the vicinity. On our return he remarked: "Your visit produced no effect on me, that is, it didn't relieve my distress." I was speechless. But a friend of mine named 'Ali Bihari spoke up, even though he was standing further away from the Shaykh. 'We are deficient,' he pleaded. 'Only your essence is perfect. How can the prayers of the deficient produce an effect on those who are perfect?' This remark did not register with the Shaykh, however; he seemed not to have heard what 'Ali Bihari said. I repeated the same remark. Turning to me, he said: 'I have asked God to provide you with whatever you seek from Him!'[59]

"Later on that occasion he gave me his staff, saying, 'You and Badr ad-din Ishaq—on whom be mercy—go and busy yourselves remembering God in such-and-such a room.' We both went there and all through the night busied ourselves in remembering God. When I returned to the Shaykh's presence, he remarked: 'It was good, that is, I feel better.' " The master then told another story about Shaykh Farid ad-din. "Once he said to me: 'You and your friends go and recite **Surat al-Fatiha** a thousand times and then tell your friends to go and tell their friends to do the same.' We went and did as he had commanded. Everyone recited **Surat al-Fatiha** as many times as he could, one 5,000, another 4,000, some less, some more. I recited it 10,000 times, intoning a certain number each day, about 1,000 more or less, until I reached 10,000."

After that I asked the master: "Did this take place on account of Shaykh Farid ad-din's illness?" "No," he replied; "it took place before then. Its purpose was to help the reciters attain what they wished from God Almighty."

## II. Assembly 18
### Monday, 7th of Dhu'l-Qa'da, A.H. 710 (28 March 1311)

I had the benefit of kissing his feet. He was reading the commentary of Imam Nasiri—on whom be mercy, and so he told a story about the Imam. "Once he experienced an affliction, and he became so ill that he had a stroke of apoplexy. His relatives and friends thought that he had died. They [performed the funeral prayer and] put him in the grave, but when evening came he regained his consciousness. 'They have put me in the grave,' he thought to himself, and in that state of bewilderment and helplessness he remembered that everyone who is in distress and recites **Surat al-Yasin** (Q.36) forty times finds relief from God Almighty. He began to recite **Surat al-Yasin.** When he had finished intoning it thirty-nine times, he began to see a result. A grave robber, hoping to steal his shroud, had begun to remove the dirt over his grave and had already reached his tomb. The Imam realized that this was a grave robber. The fortieth time that he recited **Surat al-Yasin** he recited it softly so that the thief would not hear him and continue opening the tomb. In short, when he had finished reciting **Surat al-Yasin** the fortieth time, Imam Nasiri quietly stepped out of his tomb. The grave robber, upon seeing him, was overcome with fright and expired on the spot. The Imam regretted his sudden demise, and said to himself: 'I should have been quiet and let him steal my shroud. From now on I must leave the graveyard discreetly.' Even as he repented for having emerged so abruptly from his tomb, it occurred to him that when others espied him unawares, they, too, might panic and become distraught. That night he reentered the city very cautiously, and announced in a loud voice: 'I am so-and-so and because of an attack of apoplexy I was mistakenly buried.' As he said this, he moved from place to place so that people would not think that something impossible had all of a sudden occurred."

Conversation next turned to SAINTS SO IMMERSED IN REMEMBERING GOD THAT THEY TAKE NO HEED OF FOOD OR SLEEP, DOING WHAT THEY DO ONLY FOR HIS SAKE. He told the story of a saint who lived by the bank of a river. "One day this saint asked his wife to give food to a **darwesh** residing on the other side of the river. His wife protested that crossing the water would be difficult. He said: 'When you go to the bank of the river tell the water to provide a way for you due to respect for your husband who never slept with his wife.' His wife was perplexed at these words and said to herself: 'How many children have I borne by this man. Yet how can I challenge this directive from my husband?' She took the food to the bank of the river, spoke the message to the water, and the water gave way for her passage. Having crossed, she put food before the **darwesh,** and the **darwesh** took it in her presence. After he had eaten, the woman asked: 'How shall I recross the river?' 'How did you come?' asked the **darwesh.** The woman repeated the words of her husband. On hearing this, the **darwesh** said: 'Go to the water and tell it to make way for you out of respect for the **darwesh** who never ate for thirty years.' The woman, bewildered at these words, came to the river, repeated the message, and the water again gave way for her passage. On returning home, the woman fell at her husband's feet and implored him; 'Tell me the secret of those directives which you and the other **darwesh** uttered.' 'Look,' said the saint, 'I never slept with you to satisfy the passions of my lower self. I slept with you only to provide you what was your due. In reality, I never slept with you, and similarly, that other man never ate for thirty years to satisfy his appetite or to fill his stomach. He ate only to have the strength to do God's will.' "

After this the master—may God remember him with favor—told a story about the exemplar of saints, SHAYKH QUTB AD-DIN BAKHTIYAR KAKI—may God sanctify his lofty secret. "Shaykh Qutb ad-din had twin sons," said the master. "One of them died in childhood. The other reached maturity, but did not resemble the Shaykh nor did he display any of his spiritual aptitude." In this connection on the blessed and eloquent tongue of the master came the following remark: "Shaykh al-Islam Farid ad-din was the true son of Shaykh Qutb ad-din—may God illumine both their graves!" Continuing the story about Shaykh Qutb ad-din, he noted that "when the younger son of the Shaykh died, those attending the funeral came to his house afterward. They found the Shaykh's wife mourning the death of her child. On hearing her loud outcries, the Shaykh began wringing his hands in distress. Shaykh Badr ad-din Ghaznavi—may God be merciful and kind to him—was present. Coming close to Shaykh Qutb ad-din, he asked: 'What is the cause of your distress?' 'Not till this moment,' replied Shaykh Qutb ad-din, 'did I remember that I should have prayed to God to grant my son long life! Had I requested it, he would have answered my prayer.' " The master—may God remember him with favor—remarked: "See how deeply he was absorbed in remembering the Friend: He took no note of either the life or the death of his son!"

Then he began to speak about PETITIONARY PRAYER. "The servant, when he implores God in prayer, should not recollect any sin nor any act of obedience. To dwell on good deeds while beseeching God might be seen as boasting and the prayer of the boastful remains unanswered. On the other hand, if his sin distracts him while he beseeches God, his prayer will be weakened. Instead, one ought to focus on the mercy of God while beseeching Him for favor, and one must remain firm in the conviction that God will answer the believer's prayer—if He, God Almighty, wills." He also instructed that "the servant in offering petitionary prayer should keep both hands open. His hands should be so close to one another that they actually touch, and they should be raised so high that it seems as though the servant is about to receive some gift.

"But," he concluded, "the point of petitionary prayer is to comfort the heart of the believer, for only God Almighty knows what is best for His servants."

The master—may God remember him with favor—also spoke about THE FAITH OF DISCIPLES (IN THEIR MASTERS). He told the story of a neighbor in the city where he used to live. "His name was Muhammad. Every year he suffered from a painful intestinal tumor. When I resolved to visit Shaykh al-Islam Farid ad-din—may God sanctify his lofty secret—my neighbor asked me to tell the Shaykh about his affliction, about how much he suffered, and also about how much he needed an amulet from him. When I arrived at Ajodhan, I called on the Shaykh and, after telling him about this man's illness, asked him for a curative amulet. 'Write it yourself,' was his reply. At his behest I prepared the amulet and then delivered it into his holy hand. After examining it, the Shaykh gave it back to me and said: 'Present it to your neighbor.' Upon my return home I gave the amulet to that man, and for the rest of his life he never again suffered from intestinal tumors." One of those present asked: "What did you inscribe on the amulet?" "I wrote some appropriate invocations," replied the master, "such as 'God alone heals, God alone suffices, God alone forgives.' The rest I don't remember."

Concerning THE BEAUTY OF THE DISCIPLES' RELIANCE (ON THEIR MASTERS), he also said: "Once when I was present in the assembly of Shaykh al-Islam Farid ad-din, I saw a curl fall from his beard and alight on his chest. I said: 'If the Shaykh permits, I have a request to make.' 'What is it?' he asked. 'A curl has fallen from your beard,' I replied. 'If you permit, I want to keep it as an amulet.' 'It is yours,' he replied. Picking up that curl with the utmost respect, I folded it in my garment and took it home." As he recounted this event, the eyes of the master—may God remember him with favor—welled up with tears. "What amazing effects I have seen from that single, blessed curl!" he exclaimed. "From that time on whoever experienced grief or despair and would come to me asking for an amulet, I would give them that curl. They would take it with them and keep it till they were relieved of their affliction. Then they would return it to me. One day, however, a friend of mine, Taj ad-din Minai, came and asked me for the amulet because his young son had fallen sick. I had kept that amulet in a certain niche. I looked and looked for it there, but could not find it. I looked in other niches, thinking that I might have misplaced it. But I could not find it anywhere. My friend had to return home empty-handed. Soon after, his young son died from that illness. Later another person came to me, asking for the amulet. Out of habit I looked in the niche where I used to keep it, and to my surprise, it was there!" Then the master—may God remember him with favor—remarked: "It was because the son of my friend was destined to die that I could not find that life-saving amulet!"

### II. Assembly 19
Wednesday, 6th of Dhu'l-Qa'da, A.H. 710 (27 March 1311)

I obtained the good fortune of kissing his feet. He began talking about POETRY AND PROSE. From his blessed mouth came this pronouncement: "Every eloquent turn of phrase that one hears causes delight but the same thought expressed in prose when cast into verse causes still greater delight. A similar judgment applies to chanting: Every phrase that causes delight, if you are able to hear it changed, how much greater still is your delight!"

At this point I interjected: "Is there nothing which touches the heart so deeply as listening to devotional music (**sama'**)?" "For those who tread this Path desiring the Divine," replied the master, "the taste which is evoked in them through **sama'** resembles a fire set ablaze. If this were not the case, where would one find eternity (**baqa**), and how would one evoke the taste for eternity?" As he spoke, the master's eyes began to fill with tears and he let out a deep sigh. "Once something appeared to me in a dream," he continued, "and I uttered this verse:

'O friend, you have slain me with the **hand** of anticipation!'

And again, I repeated in my dream:

'O friend, you have slain me with the **wound** of anticipation!'

But when I woke up, I remembered that the correct form of the verse went like this:

'O friend, you have slain me with the **sword** of anticipation!' "

### II. Assembly 20
Tuesday, 13th of Dhu'l-Hijja, A.H. 710 (3 May 1311)

I obtained the benefit of kissing his feet. Conversation turned to SINCERITY OF DISCIPLESHIP. He told the story of an army officer who was also a disciple of the Shaykh of Islam Farid ad-din—may God preserve his lofty secret. "His name was Muhammad Shah. Whenever he wanted to see the Shaykh, he would visualize him in a dream, and wherever he wanted to go the Shaykh would appear to him from that direction. Once he resolved to go to Hindustan. At night, while he was focused on that resolve, the Shaykh appeared to him in a dream. Someone was going to Ajodhan. When he woke up, he said to himself: 'I, too, must go that way.' Note! He had heard no word from the Shaykh nor did he receive any confirmatory sign from him. He had merely seen this person going to Ajodhan. Yet he at once abandoned his resolve to go to Hindustan, and proceeded instead to Ajodhan. Along the way he experienced much comfort and ease of mind.

"This Muhammad Shah Ghuri," observed the master—may God remember him with favor—"was a dear friend. In the last years of his life, he made the pilgrimage to Mecca and no one ever heard anything more of him."

## II. Assembly 21
### Saturday, the 11th of Muharram, A.H. 711 (30 May 1311)

I obtained the benefit of kissing his feet. He began to speak about a noted Shaykh. "Once someone came into his presence, desiring to become his disciple. He professed obedience to the Shaykh, and the Shaykh, in turn, gave him the cloak emblematic of discipleship. This was the expected protocol in such matters. Afterward, however, word came to the Shaykh that that disciple had been guilty of unseemly conduct, reverting to grave sins of the sort that he had committed before becoming a disciple. On hearing this, the Shaykh went at once to that disciple's house. 'Come,' he told him, 'come and live in my house. Do whatever you do in my house. I will cast a cloak over you, veiling your sins.' When the disciple heard this, he threw his head at the feet of the Shaykh. He renewed his oath of allegiance, and from that moment on became fully and firmly repentant. Praise be to God the Lord of the universe!"

After the master had finished this story, I asked: "Is it fair to say that the master oversees all the spiritual states of the disciple? Even if he does not witness the actual deeds of his disciples, so that he knows firsthand what they do, does he still oversee the realm of their commitment (to him), so that disciples can trust him to know whether their commitment remains firm, or whether it has become lax?" "Yes," replied the master, "commitment is the cornerstone in this work, just as in the visible world the cornerstone is faith. In the same way that the disciple must have firm faith in the oneness of God—may He be exalted and praised—and in the prophecy of Muhammad—on whom be peace —so he must have a total commitment to the authenticity of his master (**haqq-i pir**). A believer, when he is firm in his faith, does not become an unbeliever due to one sin. By the same token, a disciple, when he is firm in his commitment, cannot be labeled an apostate if he suffers a single lapse in conduct. Rather, he continues to hope that the blessing which accrues from reliance on the master will restore him to moral probity."

Conversation next turned to RECITING THE QUR'AN AND THE BLESSINGS DERIVED FROM MEMORIZING IT. I asked: "If one cannot memorize the Qur'an, is it still permissible to read from it when chanting?" "Of course," he replied, "for in the eyes also there is a portion of divine favor." After that he told a story. "The Great Shaykh —may God sanctify his lofty secret—would say to everyone who approached him wanting to memorize the Qur'an: 'First memorize **Surat al-Yusuf** (Q.12), for everyone who has memorized **Surat al-Yusuf** will be granted a blessing from God Almighty such that he will be assured of memorizing the whole Qur'an one day."

In this connection he noted: "The Prophet—may peace be upon him—once said: 'Everyone who has the intention to memorize the entire Qur'an, even if he does not succeed by the time of his passing from this world, will be visited by an angel in his grave. The angel will give him an orange from heaven. Once he consumes that orange, he will feel as though he has memorized the entire Qur'an, and tomorrow on the Day of Judgment he will be accorded the status of one who **has** memorized the Qur'an!' "

Then he began to speak about scholars who had the qualities of dervishes, so evident were their high moral standards. "I have known three such scholars," he observed. "The first was Maulana Shihab addin Meeruti, the second Maulana Ahmad Hafiz, the third Maulana Kaithala."

He spoke about Maulana Ahmad as follows. "He was a **hafiz,** one who had memorized the Qur'an. He was truly a man of God. Once he told me that he intended to visit the tomb of the Great Shaykh—may God sanctify his lofty secret. I met him on the outskirts of Sarsi. He told me: 'When you approach the grave of the Great Shaykh, convey my greetings and tell him that I do not seek this world. It has enough seekers already. Nor do I seek the world to come. I only want what is expressed in the Tradition: "Let me die a Muslim and be joined with the righteous." ' "

He then told a story about the saintliness of Maulana Kaithali. "He seemed to enjoy the blessing of a spiritual master, even though he had not bound himself to any one. He enjoyed the company of many pious persons and men of God. The very first time that I met him, his speech, as also his demeanor, indicated that he was among those joined to God (**wasilan-i haqq**). Something came to mind, and I asked him. He answered that that was related to this, and this to that. In short, he explained the whole matter to me." The master—may God remember him with favor—as he was telling this story, became teary eyed. "Imagine," he said, "if I had taken that same problem to a hundred learned jurists, not one of them could have solved it!"

Also, concerning THE VIRTUES OF MAULANA KAITHALI, he told a further story. "Once the Maulana had come to see me. Mubashshir, my servant, was then still a youth and, due to some indiscretion, he had been beaten with a stick. The Maulana displayed signs of pain such that one might have thought that he, not Mubashshir, had been beaten with a stick. He began to cry, lamenting that this lad had suffered pain due to his (the Maulana's) stinginess." The master—may God remember him with favor—said: "Due to the compassion and empathy of the Maulana, my heart was overwhelmed with pathos!"

He told still another story about his saintliness, a story that he heard from the Maulana himself. "One year there had been a famine in Delhi. It occurred during the reign of Qutb ad-din Hasan. Passing through the cloth market, I became hungry and bought some food. I said to myself: 'I should not eat this food alone.' I sought someone with whom to share it. I saw a dervish wearing a Sufi cloak. He passed before me, patched garment and all. I called out to him. 'O Khwaja! I am a dervish and you, too, are a dervish. I am poor and you, too, appear to be poor. There is this bit of food. Come, let us share it!' The dervish agreed. We went to the vicinity of a restaurant, and began to eat. During the meal I looked at the dervish and said, 'O Khwaja! I owe twenty **tankas** [i.e., almost $400]. I must repay that debt.' 'Eat your food with a clear heart,' he replied. 'I will give you twenty **tankas**.' " Maulana Kaithali said: "I thought to myself: 'From where will this man with his threadbare cloak find twenty **tankas** to give me?' In short, when we finished eating, he got up and motioned me to follow him. He went to a mosque, behind which was a grave. Standing at the head of that grave, he said something and, with a small stick he had in his hand, he slowly began to strike that grave a couple of times. As he did so, he said: 'This dervish needs twenty **tankas.** Provide it for him.' Having said this, he turned to me and announced: 'The master will provide. You will get twenty **tankas.**' " Maulana Kaithali said: "When I heard this message, I kissed the hand of that dervish and, bidding him farewell, proceeded toward the city. I was bewildered: 'From where would I obtain those twenty **tankas?**' Someone had given me a letter which I was supposed to deliver to a certain house. A Turk was sitting on the balcony of his home, as I passed by in search of this other house. Seeing me, he called out and sent his servants to fetch me into his presence. That Turk showered me with kindnesses. Yet, however much I tried, I could not recognize him. That Turk persisted: 'Are you not that scholar who in such and such a place performed so many services on my behalf?' I kept saying: 'I did not assist you anywhere.' That Turk replied: 'But I do know you. Why do you keep concealing yourself from me?' In short, he kept saying many things like this. Finally, he produced twenty **tankas** and, with profuse apologies(!), pressed them into my hand."

Continuing to speak about the saintliness of Maulana Kaithali, the master—may God remember him with favor—noted: "The fact that he did not eat food alone showed that he followed every laudable practice, and possessed many more virtues besides!" After that he told the story about his death. "Once I was traveling in the vicinity of Sarsi. I heard that a caravan had been held up here and that many Muslims had been slain at the hands of Hindus. Among those slain had been a scholar named Kaithali. He had been reciting the Qur'an and they had slain him in the act of recitation." The master—may God remember him with favor—paused. "I could not help but think that that man must have been Maulana Kaithali. The next day I went to the place where the slain had been buried and after reciting **Surat al-Fatiha,** I began to make inquiries. It was that same Maulana Kaithali who had died a martyr's death—may God open up to him a boundless mercy!"

### II. Assembly 22
Wednesday, the 3rd of Rabiʿ al-awwal, A.H. 711 (20 July 1311)

I obtained the benefit of kissing his feet. On this occasion I was coming to see him after one month. Never before had I been absent for so long a period of time. Two or three other friends were present when I kissed his blessed feet. The master—may God remember him with favor—turned toward me. "At the very moment that you arrived," he exclaimed, "we were discussing the virtuous!" In embarrassment I lowered my hand again to the ground. After that he commented: "Khwaja Shams al-Mulk—may God have mercy on him—followed the custom that if a student absented himself from class or a friend came to see him after a long interval, he would ask: 'What have I done that you no longer come?' " After that the master smiled and added, "If he wanted to make a joke, Khwaja Shams al-Mulk would say something like: 'What have I done that you no longer come, that I might do it again?' " Then the master remarked: "When I had been absent and come after a long interval, it occurred to me that he would say something in the same vein to me. Instead he addressed me with the following couplet:

I ask but this: that occasionally
You should come and cast a glance upon me.

When he had finished reciting this verse, the master—may God remember him with favor—became tearful, so much so that he aroused empathy in those present. One friend observed: "I have heard tell that in those days when you visited Khwaja Shams al-Mulk, he would show great respect for you, even to the point of inviting you to sit with him in a special place on his balcony." "Yes," replied the master, "on that balcony where he used to sit no one else would sit beside him except Qadi Fakhr ad-din Naqila or Maulana Burhan ad-din Baqi. When he would summon me to sit there, I would protest, but to no avail. He would not accept my demurral, and instead would make a place for me near him." One of those present asked, "He had an official position at that time, did he not?" "Yes," replied the master—may God remember him with favor; "he was then the state auditor. It was in this connection that Khwaja Taj ad-din Zira recited the following verse:

O judge, your friends' desires have been fulfilled indeed:
You're now the state auditor of all India."

I interjected: "To be sure, the piety and erudition of Khwaja Shams al-Mulk are well known, but how do we know that he was attached to the dervishes or harbored any affection for them?" The master—may God remember him with favor—replied: "His faith was exemplary. He who showed such respect for me thereby showed his firm commitment (to all those who tread the Path). Praise be to God, Lord of the universe!"

II. Assembly 23
Wednesday, the 24th of Rabiʿ al-awwal, A.H. 711 (10 August 1311)

I obtained the blessing of kissing his feet. On that day some other friends had come with me to pay their respects to him. "Did you come together?" he enquired. "Each one came separately from his home," I replied, "but we arrived here at the same time." "To come separately is better," he observed, "as Shaykh al-Islam Farid ad-din—may God sanctify his lofty secret—used to say, 'To come one by one is better than inviting the curse of the evil eye (when you come as a group).' "

Then he began to speak on the POWER OF THE EVIL EYE AND THE POWER OF MAGIC. He noted: "The power of neither is neglible, that is, each has a marked effect. The Muʾtazilites denied this notion. They used to say: 'The effect of magic and the effect of the evil eye when they seem to appear in a given circumstance are, in fact, illusory. They do not do what people claim that they do.' "

With reference to magic, the master began to speak about THE DISTINCTION BETWEEN PROPHETIC MIRACLES (**muʿjizat**) and SAINTLY MIRACLES (**karamat**). "There are four kinds of miracles," he observed. "They are: **muʿjizat, karamat, maʿunat,** and **istidraj. Muʿjizat** are linked to the prophets, since they have been given perfect knowledge. As conduits of revelation, what they cause to appear are known as **muʿjizat.** As for **karamat,** such miracles are distinctive to saints. They also have perfect knowledge and can perform sinless acts. Saints differ from prophets, however, because the former, unlike the latter, are overcome, that is, they are directed by God only in particular moments, and hence what they make appear are **karamat.** As for **maʿunat,** they are the property of ecstatic beings (s.**majnun,** pl.**majanin**), who exhibit neither perfect knowledge nor sinless actions. From time to time they can cause a contravention of nature, and when they do, that is known as **maʿuna.** As for **istidraj,** that pertains to a group of people who are not believers, such as magicians and others like them, and when they cause something unusual to happen, that is called **istidraj.**"

Then the master began to enumerate MODES OF KNOWLEDGE. "There are three modes," he explained. "The first is sensory, the second cognitive, the third intuitive. The sensory mode is experienced through what we eat and smell, the cognitive through knowledge, whether self-evident or acquired, while the intuitive is similarly divided: It can be either self-evident or acquired. However, he who has access to intuitive, which is to say divine, knowledge, knows instinctively what others must acquire through the exercise of their cognitive faculties." After that he remarked: "How can one acquire direct cognition through the intuitive mode? **That** is the work of prophets and saints. And what are the qualities of those who have such immediate access to divine knowledge? They contrast with the qualities of those who labor in the cognitive mode and take delight in solving a problem through the exercise of cognitive reasoning, whether self-evident or acquired. For such, the road to intuitive knowledge is blocked." To illustrate this point, he told the story of a pious person who used to say: "Something from the Unseen has alighted upon my heart. If God Almighty wills, I may write it down with a pen. After that, he wrote much, but the last comment that he wrote was this: 'No matter how much I write, I cannot capture with the pen what I had intended to write!' "

Then from his blessed lips came this pronouncement. "A sinner even in the state of sin remains obedient in three senses. First, he knows that what he does is not correct. Second, he knows that God Almighty sees and knows what he does. Third, he still hopes for restitution. All three of these postulates form the basic creed for those who are obedient." After that he noted: "The Asharites teach that the unbeliever who converts just prior to death dies a believer, while the believer whom—God forbid!—professes disbelief just prior to death dies an unbeliever." In this connection he alluded to Khwaja Hamid Suwali—may God have mercy upon him. "The Khwaja knew a certain Hindu in Nagaur of whom he used to say repeatedly: 'This man is a saint.' " Next the master told a story about Imam Abu Hanifa. "Once he was asked whether unbelievers would reside in hell permanently or not. 'No,' he answered; 'they will not.' 'How is that?' they asked. 'On the Day of Resurrection,' he replied, 'when unbelievers will face punishment and affliction, they will embrace faith but that faith will not benefit them. Because they had no faith in the Unseen, when they do embrace Islam on the Day of Resurrection, it will not benefit them. They will all go to Hell, despite the fact that they will go there as believers!' " To confirm this view he interpreted the Qur'anic verse: "And we did not create **jinn** and men except to worship" [Q.51:56] with the gloss of Ibn 'Abbas that this means "except to profess God's oneness," that is, except that both **jinn** and men attest to the oneness of God. True monotheism is to believe in the Unseen, but unbelievers only attest to God's Uniqueness and Unicity when faced with the punishment of Resurrection Day. The fate of both believers and unbelievers confirms the truth of Ibn ʿAbbas' gloss that by worship the Qurʾanic verse means 'to profess God's oneness'."

After that he remarked: "You should imagine everyone whom you see as better than yourself, even though someone may be obedient and someone else disobedient, since it might be that the obedience of the former is the last of his acts of obedience while the sinfulness of the latter is the last of his sinful acts." In this vein he told a story about Khwaja Hasan al-Basri—may God illumine his grave. "He used to say: 'I imagine everyone whom I see to be better than myself. But one day I met my own retribution, and this is how it came to pass. I saw an Ethiopian sitting by the edge of the river. There was a bottle next to him and every moment he was enjoying himself by drinking from that bottle. There was also a woman seated near him. The thought crossed my mind: 'At least I am better than **him.**' Just as I was thinking this, a boat began to sink in the river. Seven people were in that boat, and all seven began to drown. The Ethiopian immediately plunged into the river. He rescued six people. Then, turning to me, he said: 'O Hasan, you pull out the remaining one.' " "I stood there stupefied," remarked Khwaja Hasan. "After that he said to me, 'In this bottle is water, and this woman seated next to me is my mother. It is to test you that I was sitting here. It appears that you see only the outer man.' "

Conversation next turned to RECITING THE QURʾAN. "One must recite the Qurʾan with deliberate cadence (**tartil**) and also with rhythmic repetition (**tardid**)." One of those present asked: "What is rhythmic repetition (**tardid**)?" "**Tardid,**" he explained, "occurs when the verse that has been recited arouses such a taste for God and sensibility to His Presence that it must be repeated. Once," he recalled, "the Prophet—may peace be upon him—wished to recite a selection from the Qurʾan. But the very opening words, 'In the name of God, All Mercy, the Merciful' induced such a state in his blessed heart that he repeated those words twenty times!' "

After that he enumerated the EIGHT LEVELS OF PREPAREDNESS FOR RECITING THE QURʾAN, but he only explained five in detail. The first is that at the time of reciting the Qurʾan the heart of the reciter becomes attached only to God. If that is not possible, then the meaning of what he is reciting should pervade his heart, and if that, too, is not possible, then at the moment of reciting the Qurʾan, the experience of God's Majesty and Awe should pervade his heart." One of those present interjected: "Does not the third level of preparedness imply the same attachment to God as the first level?" "No," he replied. "In the first the reciter's heart is filled with God's essence, while in the third it is moved only by these two attributes. As for the fourth level," he continued, "this occurs at the time of reciting the Qur'an when the reciter feels overcome with humility and repeatedly asks himself: 'How am I worthy of this benefit? How did I merit such a high station of honor?' And if even that level is not attainable, then at the least he recollects that God Himself has promised to reward those who recite the Qur'an and, therefore, he will be rewarded for each moment that he recites the Qur'an."

At this point I interjected, "On every occasion that I recite the Qur'an, more of its meaning unfolds for me than I had ever before understood. During recitation, if my mind is distracted by some thought or my heart moved by some desire, I catch myself and ask: 'What is this thought? What is this desire?' And I keep asking myself these questions till my heart becomes clear in its focus. And at that same instant I chance upon a verse which counters that desire or else I recall a verse which solves the difficulty that had been vexing my heart." The master—may God remember him with favor—after he had heard me out, commented: "This is a fine practice; you should continue to pursue it." Praise be to God, Lord of the universe!

## II. Assembly 24

Wednesday, the 2nd of Rabi' al-akhir, A.H. 711 (18 August 1311)

I obtained the good fortune of kissing his feet. Conversation turned to RENOUNCING WORLDLINESS. He observed that real wisdom consists of abstaining from involvement in the world, that is, avoidance of worldliness. To illustrate this point, he drew attention to the case of a man making out his will. "If he declares, 'I will bequeath one third of my property, after my death, to the wisest of persons,' how will they determine who is the wisest? Real wisdom is this, that the bequester leave all his property to one who has already left the world!" One of those present interjected. "But how can someone who has already left the world be persuaded to accept such wealth?" "The issue is expenditure," replied the master. "How do you determine the venue of expenditure appropriate to this meaning? Worldliness," he continued, "does not consist of gold or silver or possessions or the like, rather, as a saint has observed (in

Arabic), 'Your stomach is your world!' If you eat less, you are among those who have renounced worldliness. If you eat to your full, you are not among them."

In this connection he began to speak about SATAN. "Satan has said: 'He who is sated when he says his prayers, I embrace him. Now when such a sated one has finished praying, can you imagine the extent to which my control over him increases? But from the hungry man when he sleeps I flee. Now when that hungry one awakes and says his prayers, can you imagine how terrified I become on account of him?' "

Then the master continued to speak about SATAN AND HIS POWER OF TEMPTATION AND HIS CONTROL OVER THE SONS OF ADAM. He specifically warned about Khannas, Satan's son. "Ceasely he has tried to penetrate the heart of Adam's offspring. Only when humankind is absorbed in remembering God can Khannas be deflected from his goal." Then he referred to Maulana ʿAla ad-din Tirmidhi and his account of Khannas in **Nawadir al-usul** (*Strange Anecdotes about First Principles*). "After Adam—upon whom be peace—descended from heaven into this world, Eve was one day sitting by herself. Iblis came and brought Khannas with him. To Eve he said: 'This is my son. Take care of him.' Then he left. When Adam returned he saw Khannas. 'Who is this?' he asked Eve. 'Iblis brought him,' replied Eve. 'He told me: "This is my son; take care of him." ' 'Why did you accept him?' rejoined Adam. 'This is my enemy.' Then Adam—on whom be peace—cut Khannas up into four pieces and cast him upon mountaintops. When Adam—peace be on him—left, Iblis came back and asked Eve, 'Where is Khannas?' 'Adam cut him up into four pieces and cast him on the mountaintops,' she replied. Hearing this, Iblis shouted: 'O Khannas!' Khannas immediately appeared and in his original form! When Iblis departed, Adam—upon whom be peace—came back. He saw Khannas standing there. 'What's this?' he asked. Eve told him what had happened. Adam then killed this Khannas and, having burned him, scattered his ashes in a river. Then he left and as soon as he was gone, Iblis returned, enquiring about Khannas. Eve told him what had transpired. Iblis again shouted: 'O Khannas!' and again Khannas at once reappeared. Iblis departed just as Adam was returning. Adam saw Khannas, this time in the form of a sheep. He learned from Eve what had happened, and resolved to kill Khannas yet again. This time, since he was in the form of a sheep, he cooked and ate him. Soon thereafter Iblis returned and shouted: 'O Khannas!' Khannas answered from the heart of

Adam: 'At your service! At your service!' 'Stay there!' commanded Iblis. 'That was my design from the beginning.' "

### II. Assembly 25
Wednesday, the 15th of Jumada al-ula, A.H. 711 (29 September 1311)

I had the good fortune of kissing his feet. He spoke about DIVINATION BY THE QUR'AN. I asked: "Is there any scriptural authority for this practice?" "Yes, there is," he replied. "It is authorized by a Tradition." Then he went on to explain how one should attempt to take an omen from the Qur'an using only the right hand, never the left.

In this connection he began to tell the story of Shaykh Badr ad-din Ghaznavi—may God be merciful to him. "He said: 'When I came from Ghazna to Lahore, I found Lahore at that time to be both prosperous and cultured. After I had been there for some while, I resolved to take a trip. I couldn't decide whether to go to Delhi or to return to Ghazna. I kept wavering between these two options for some time, even though I was inclined to go to Ghazna. After all, my mother, father, close relatives, and friends—all were there, while I had no one but a son-in-law in Delhi. In short, I resolved to seek an omen from the Qur'an. I went to see a saintly person. When I opened the Qur'an with the intention to visit Ghazna, the verse that was revealed spoke of punishment. When I looked again with the intention of visiting Delhi, the verse spoke only of heaven and described its delights. Though my heart was inclined to Ghazna, because of the decree from this omen I proceeded to Delhi. When I arrived in the city, I learned that my son-in-law had been imprisoned. I went to the royal court to learn what had befallen him. I saw him just as he was leaving the court. He had a cloth in his hand, and wrapped in that cloth were many silver coins. When he saw me, he embraced me with great joy. He took me to his home and set that heap of silver before me. I was thrilled that there was so much of it. It was then that I heard the report from Ghazna: The Mongols had reached that city and martyred my mother, father, and all my close relatives."

At that point I interjected: "After he came here did not Shaykh Badr ad-din Ghaznavi receive the honor of being enrolled as a disciple of Shaykh Qutb ad-din Bakhtiyar Kaki—may God sanctify his dear secret?" "Yes, he did," replied the master.

Then he began to speak about SHAYKH AL-ISLAM FARID AD-DIN—may God sanctify his dear and blessed secret. "His was a different kind of work. Removing himself from the company of people, he preferred the isolation of uncultivated regions. He settled in Ajodhan. He opted for the bread of dervishes and other things that were available in that region. He was content, for instance, to have rough wood for his tooth brush. Despite his longing for solitude, there was no limit to the number of people who were forever visiting him. The door to his hospice was never closed except for half of the night—more or less, that is to say, it was continuously open. Silver and food and blessings due to the kindness of the Almighty Creator—all were distributed from there to all comers. Yet no one came to the Shaykh for material assistance since he himself possessed nothing. What a marvelous power! What a splendid life! To none of the sons of Adam had such grace previously been available. If someone came into his presence for the first time and someone else who had been an acquaintance for some years also came, he would pay equal attention to each, and of kindness and concern he would give them equal measure."

After that the master noted: "I knew Badr ad-din Ishaq—may God have mercy on him. He used to say. 'I am his trusted servant. Whatever he wanted he told me and every work that he assigned to me, whether it was in public or in private, he would phrase his request the same way. At no time did he tell me one thing in private and then command me to do something else in public. In other words, his outer and inner self reflected one light, and that is among the marvels of God's creation!' "

### II. Assembly 26

Tuesday, the 12th of Jumada al-akhira, A.H. 711 (26 October 1311)

I obtained the benefit of kissing his feet. He spoke about **SURAT AL-FATIHA.** It was often recited for the satisfaction of many needs. He instructed: "Everyone who faces an important decision or a difficult task, should begin by reciting **Surat al-Fatiha** as follows: First he should recite **Bismillah ar-rahman ar-rahim,** eliding the **mim** of **rahim** with the **lam** of **al-hamdu lillah.** So he should say: **Bismillah ar-rahman ar-rahimil-hamdu lillah.** And when he has finished saying that, he should repeat three times: **ar-rahman ar-rahim,** and when he has finished reciting the whole **sura,** he should say **amin** three times. May it be that God Almighty will bring that important matter to a successful conclusion."

About REMEMBERING THE **FATIHA,** he went on to say: "There are ten articles of faith in the Qur'an. Of these ten eight are already set forth in the **Fatiha.** What are these ten articles of faith? They are: God's essence, His attributes, His actions, remembering the world to come, dedicating oneself to God and trusting to His mercy, remembering the saints and, also, one's enemies, fighting the unbelievers, and observing the divine statutes. Of these ten eight are to be found in **Surat al-Fatiha.** 'Praise be to God' is His essence; 'Lord of the worlds,' His actions; 'All Mercy and Merciful,' His attributes; 'King of Judgment Day,' remembering the world to come; 'You we worship' is dedicating oneself to God; and 'On You do we call for help' is trusting to His mercy; 'Guide us to the straight path, the path of those whom you've favored' is remembering the saints, while 'Those with whom You are not mad and who've not gone astray' is remembering one's enemies. Hence of the articles of faith to be found in the Qur'an eight are already set forth in **Surat al-Fatiha.** Only warring with the unbelievers and observing the divine statutes are not contained therein."

Then he alluded to the Imam, the Proof of Islam, Muhammad al-Ghazzali—may God have mercy on him. "He spoke the truth," observed the master, "when he noted in **Ihya 'Ulum ad-Din** (*Reviving the Sciences of Faith*), that 'fasting is one half of patience, and patience is one half of faith.' " After that he asked: "What does it mean to say that fasting is one half of patience?" Then, addressing the truth of patience, he asked: "What is patience? Patience is the dominance of the urge to seek God over the urges to satisfy one's own desire." Then he explained that there were two dispositions that spur desire: anger and passion. And since fasting curbs passion, we find confirmation of the dictum: "Fasting is half of patience." Concerning the other half of the dictum, that "patience is half of faith," he noted that faith also has two aspects: beliefs and actions, and it is for this reason that al-Ghazzali said: "Patience is half of faith" [since it is the basis for all virtuous actions].[60]

Conversation turned to **'AWARIF AL-MA'ARIF** (*INSIGHTS FROM MEN OF DISCERNMENT*) BY SHAYKH SHIHAB AD-DIN SUHRAWARDI—may God sanctify his lofty secret. The master recounted that he had studied five chapters of the **'Awarif** with the Great Shaykh Farid ad-din—may God sanctify his lofty secret. "How can I reiterate what he explained from those five chapters? None other could have offered such insights. How many times, due to the taste for God which his commentary evoked, did those present wish to expire then and there! They would have welcomed such a death as propitious. It also happened," he noted, "that on the day they brought him a copy of **'Awarif** a son was born to him. He named that son Shihab ad-din."

The master then began to speak about THE DISCOURSE THAT ONE HEARS FROM SAINTLY AND GRACE-FILLED PERSONS, and how such discourse evokes a pleasure that none other can match. For when you hear the same discourse from someone else it does not evoke the taste for God. Who can match the person who speaks from a station in which he has been touched by the light of divine intuition?

In this connection he told the following story. "There was a virtuous man full of race. He was the prayer leader in a mosque. After prayer he would discourse on some of the dicta and spiritual states of saints. His words would bring comfort to those who heard him speak. Among those who came to hear him was a certain blind man; he, too, found solace in the prayer leader's words. One day the prayer leader was absent and the **muezzin,** whose job was to call the faithful to prayer, took the prayer leader's place. He also began to narrate stories of the saints and their spiritual states, stories of the same sort that the worshipers used to hear from the prayer leader. When the blind man heard the discourse of the **muezzin,** he asked: 'Who is this who is reporting the dicta of the saints and telling stories about them?' 'Today the prayer leader is absent,' they told him. 'The **muezzin** is substituting for him and telling his stories.' 'Humph!' retorted the blind man, 'I don't want to hear such lofty words from every ne'er do well!' " As he was finishing this story, the master—may God remember him with favor—became teary-eyed. "He who does not have refined conduct cannot evoke the taste for God." And then some verses from Shaykh Saʿdi graced his blessed lips:

Who else but I can try to talk of loving You?
Since others have no basis, their words do not ring true.

## II. Assembly 27

Tuesday, the 18th of Rajab, A.H. 711 (30 November 1311)

I obtained the good fortune of kissing his feet. The night before I had had a dream which I related to the master. This was the dream. "The time for morning prayer was approaching. Intent on performing the prayer, I was doing my ablutions. There was little time left, and so I was hastening to finish my ablutions. I knew that there was a congregational mosque in the vicinity. I went as fast as I could to reach it in time for the morning prayer. Even as I rushed along, I felt the sun begin to rise. I feared that I would not reach the mosque in time to join the congregational prayer. I raised my hand toward the sun and exclaimed: 'Out of respect for the spiritual purity of my master, do not rise!' Having said this, even though I was still asleep, I felt an exhilaration in my spiritual state. I woke up, only to discover that morning was still a long way off!"

The master—may God remember him with favor—when he had heard me out, became tearful. He then related the following story. "There was a district magistrate named Muhammad Nishapuri. He was a precious person and firm in his commitment to the saints. I heard from him about an experience he once had while traveling in Gujarat. In those days Hindus controlled that country. Along the way I encountered one or two strangers and I had no weapon with me. Then I saw this Hindu brandishing a sword in his hand. I became fearful. Before long that sword-wielding Hindu advanced toward me. When he came near I said: 'O Shaykh, be present.' The Hindu immediately dropped his sword. 'Protect me!' he implored. I was astonished. Why was he asking me for protection? Again he cried out: 'Protect me!' 'You are safeguarded,' I replied. After that I gave him back his sword. He went his way, I went on mine." When he had completed this story, the master—may God remember him with favor—remarked: "Imagine! What did that Hindu see? What was it that appeared before him?"

### II. Assembly 28
Tuesday, the 2nd of the month of Shaʿban in the blessed community, A.H. 711 (14 December 1311)

I obtained the good fortune of kissing his feet. The topic was FEEDING OTHERS. "Dervishhood," he remarked, "consists of this: Every visitor should first be greeted with 'Peace!' then he should be served food, and then and only then should one engage in story telling and conversation." After this on his blessed tongue came the proverb (in Arabic):

"Begin with the peace, then food, then conversation."

### II. Assembly 29
Monday, 22nd of Shaʿban, A.H. 711 (3 January 1312)

I had the honor of kissing his feet. Food was brought out and people began to eat. The master—may God remember him with favor—recalled: "A saint used to say: 'People who eat food in front of me I find their food in my own throat, that is, it is as if I am eating that food!' "

Then one of those present interjected: "In the same vein it has been reported that once in the presence of Shaykh Abu Sa'id Abu'l-Khayr—may God have mercy upon him!—a powerful leather maker was beating an animal. Shaykh Abu Sacid said: 'Ah!' with such pathos that it seemed as though he had been the one beaten. A skeptic was present. 'Such a condition is impossible!' he protested. Shaykh Abu Sa'id disrobed and the signs of that leather belt appeared on his blessed back!" After that the teller of this story turned to the master—may God remember him with favor—and said: "This story, like the one you told, implies that a person can feel someone else's condition, but I don't understand how such an empathy works." In response on the blessed tongue of the master—may God remember him with favor—came this explanation: "When the spirit becomes powerful and is perfected, it attracts the heart and the heart, too, when it becomes powerful and perfected, attracts the body. Then, due to this union of all three, whatever happens to the heart, leaves its outward mark on the body."

At this point I interjected: "Is it a similar kind of experience that transpired on the Ascent (**mi'raj**) of the Prophet Muhammad—peace be upon him?" "Yes, it was," replied the master.

After that he remarked that a saint once said: "I don't know whether on the Night of the Ascent, They raised the Prophet—blessing and peace be upon him—to the realm where the Throne, the Chair, Heaven, and Hell were located and he saw Them there, or whether They brought all these to the place where the Prophet—peace be upon him—was." The master observed: "If indeed They brought all these to the place where the Prophet—peace and salutation be upon him—was, then in such an instance his status—peace be upon him—proved to be still higher!"

Then he spoke about PERSONS WHO DO NOT MAKE SPIRITUAL ALLEGIANCES IN THE PROPER MANNER. Some, for instance, make allegiance to one Shaykh and then join themselves to another, while still others seek to become disciples at the tombs of Shaykhs. I submitted that there are some people who visit the tombs of Shaykhs, shaving their heads and claiming to become disciples. "Is such allegiance correct?" I asked the master. "No," he replied. And in this connection he told a story. "Shaykh al-Islam Farid ad-din—may God sanctify his lofty secret—had a son. He was his eldest son. He went to the tomb of Shaykh al-Islam Qutb ad-din Bakhtiyar—may God sanctify his lofty secret—and shaved his head. They reported the matter to Shaykh Farid ad-din—may God illumine his grave. He remarked:

'Shaykh Qutb ad-din—may God increase his reward—was my spiritual guide and master, but this form of allegiance is not correct. Discipleship and allegiance require that you grasp the hand of a Shaykh.' And God knows best."

## II. Assembly 30
Wednesday, the 21st of Shawwal, A.H. 711 (1 March 1312)

I obtained the benefit of kissing his feet. The subject turned to DREAMS. "Formerly there was a Turk named Tiklish," recounted the master. "He was a man of God. One night God Almighty appeared to him in a dream. In the morning he went and reported his dream to Shaykh Najib ad-din Mutawakkil—may God have mercy on him. But first he made the Shaykh take an ironclad oath that he would tell no one else what he (Tiklish) was about to report, as long as he was still alive. Shaykh Najib ad-din accepted his stipulation and took the oath. After that Tiklish confided in him: 'Last night I saw God Almighty in a dream' and he went on to recount the spiritual sites and inner lights of that experience. Later, Shaykh Najib ad-din Mutawakkil—may God have mercy on him—told how that Tiklish lived for another forty years after he had had that dream. 'I, adhering to the oath that I had sworn, told no one about what he had reported to me. At the moment that his death seemed imminent, I was at his bedside. When he saw me, he asked: "Do you remember that dream that I had and then recounted to you?" "Yes, I do," I replied, "but what is your spiritual state at present?" "This very moment," said Tiklish, "I am leaving the world immersed in the same spiritual state that I experienced then." ' "

The master then began to speak about THE SPIRITUAL STATES OF SHAYKH NAJIB AD-DIN MUTAWAKKIL AND HIS ENCOMIA OF THE GREAT SHAYKH FARID AD-DIN—may God be merciful to both of them. "There was a Turk in Delhi," recalled the master. "Having built a mosque, he made Shaykh Najib ad-din the **imam** or prayer leader of that mosque, and he also provided a house for him and his family. That Turk later arranged a marriage for one of his daughters, and in making preparations for the wedding, he expended more than one lac of **jitals.**[61]

"Subsequently Shaykh Najib ad-din—may God have mercy on him —remarked to that Turk: 'The sign of a complete believer is that he has greater affection for God than for his own children. Now that you have expended more than one lac of **jitals** on behalf of your daughter, you should expend twice as much on behalf of God.' The Turk took umbrage at this remark. He withdrew Shaykh Najib ad-din's appointment as **imam,** and also evicted him from his house. Shaykh Najib ad-din left Delhi and returned to Ajodhan. Coming before Shaykh al-Islam Farid ad-din—may God sanctify his lofty secret—he related to him what had happened. The Shaykh replied: 'God the Almighty the Exalted has promised us: "We do not abrogate a verse of Ours or cause it to be forgotten, unless we bring another like it or better" (Q.2:106). That is to say, we do not abrogate any verse of the Qur'an without sending a better in its stead. And so we should not concern ourselves with this matter.'

"That Turk who dismissed Shaykh Najib ad-din was named Aitmar, and on the blessed tongue of Shaykh Farid ad-din came this prediction: 'If this Aitmar goes, God the Almighty the Exalted will raise up an Aitkar to replace him.' In that time a great king named Aitkar became the ruler in those parts [i.e., in the vicinity of Ajodhan]: Not only did he show great respect for the Shaykh and his noble family but he also rendered many services to them."

The master then began to speak about Shaykh Badr ad-din Ghaznavi—may God have mercy on him. "Nizam ad-din Kharitdar built a hospice for him. But no sooner had Shaykh Badr ad-din occupied the hospice than Nizam ad-din ceased to provide for its maintenance. He renounced even minimal observance of Sufi principles. Not long after Shaykh Badr ad-din had been installed in that hospice they began to investigate the accounts of Nizam ad-din Kharitdar and discovered irregularities. Shaykh Badr ad-din appealed to Shaykh al-Islam Farid ad-din—may God sanctify his lofty secret, and told him something like this: 'A man has built a hospice for me, and now a cloud of anxiety hangs over his head, and on this account I, too, feel anxious.' Shaykh Farid ad-din sent this reply: 'Whoever does not follow the conduct and custom of our spiritual masters will end up like this. In short, since our spiritual ancestors did not follow this practice of building hospices, he who opts to build a hospice will experience what you are now experiencing.' "

Then he spoke briefly about THE SPIRITUALITY OF SHAYKH QUTB AD-DIN BAKHTIYAR—may God sanctify his lofty secret. Toward the end of his life he memorized the Qur'an, and after he had memorized it, he died—God have mercy on him.

Conversation turned to THE DEATH OF SAINTS. Someone present told the story of how a particular saint had died. "So-and-so expired while slowly repeating the name of God the Almighty, the Exalted." The master—may God sanctify his lofty secret—became tearful as he recited the following quatrain:

I have come to Your street in a rush, in a rush.
My cheeks with my tears are all awash, all awash.
To be at one with you how I try, how I try.
As I invoke Your name let me die, let me die.

II. Assembly 31

Friday, the 28th of Dhu'l-Qa'da, A.H. 711 (6 April 1312)

I obtained the benefit of kissing his feet in the house which faces the Friday Congregational mosque of Kilogarhi. Before the time of Friday prayer conversation focused on THE WORLD OF SUFISM. Mention was made of those men who truly immerse themselves in remembering God, and the contrast between them and those who, just because they engage in research and study, want others to consider them as men of God.

In this connection the master told a story about a very bright student named Sharaf ad-din. "One day this Sharaf ad-din came into the presence of the Great Shaykh Farid ad-din—may God sanctify his lofty secret. The Shaykh asked him: 'How do you fare in your studies?' 'For the moment I have forgotten all about them!' was his reply. The Shaykh was unhappy with what he said. After he left, the Shaykh turned to those present and remarked: 'This man thinks he has the power to fly!' "

As he concluded telling this story, the master—may God remember him with favor—became teary-eyed. "There was once a spiritual master," he recalled. "One of his sons, named Muhammad, became extremely learned and was highly accomplished. He then resolved to pursue the path of Sufism. Coming to his father, he said: 'I want to become a dervish.' 'Fine,' said his father. 'First go and spend forty days and nights in ascetical devotion (**chilla**).' That son went and observed a **chilla.** When he had passed his fortieth night in prayer and solitude, he came back to his father. His father proceeded to ask him questions about what he had studied. The son answered all of them. 'Alas, Muhammad,' said his father, 'your **chilla** seems to have been useless. Go and spend another forty days and nights in ascetical devotion.' He went and did as he had been told. After the fortieth in prayer and solitude, he came back to his father. The father again asked him some questions. This time he began to stumble here and there in the answers that he gave. 'Go and perform one more **chilla,**' exhorted his father. When he had completed his third consecutive period of secluded immersion in prayer and meditation for forty days, he returned to his father. The father again put some questions to me, but this time he had become so immersed in God that he could give no reply!"

Conversation turned briefly to the topic of DREAMS AND THEIR INTERPRETATION. "The Prophet of God—peace be upon him," remarked the master, "once told about a dream that he had had. 'In it,' he reported, 'I saw all my companions and each one was wearing a cloak. One had a cloak that came down only to his chest, another to the navel, still another to the knees. But when I saw 'Umar, he was wearing a cloak that was dragging on the ground.' His companions asked him: 'O Prophet of God, how do you interpret this dream?' 'It is like this,' he replied, 'the length of each cloak is determined by the degree of one's faith!' "

The master then told a story about IBN SIRIN—may God have mercy on him. "How true were his interpretations!" exclaimed the master. "Once a man came to him and said: 'Last night I had a dream in which I saw a quince (**safarjal**).' 'You will be taking a trip,' said Ibn Sirin. 'Why do you say that?' asked the man. 'Because the first part of **safarjal** is **safar** (trip)!' Another man came and said: 'Last night I saw a lily (**susan**) in my dreams.' 'Alas, something bad will happen to you,' said Ibn Sirin. 'Why do you say that?' asked the man. 'Because the first part of **susan** is **su** (evil)!' "

After that he noted that Muhammad Ghazzali—may God reward him well—had reported in **Ihya ʿulum ad-din** that there were TWO DREAM INTERPRETATIONS FROM IBN SIRIN that rank among the wonders of the world. One of them went like this: "Once a man came to see Ibn Sirin in the month of Ramadan. 'Last night,' he reported, 'I saw in my dreams that I was carrying a signet ring in my hand and that it was blocking both the mouths of men and the wombs of women!' 'Are you not a **muezzin,** that is, do you not call the faithful to prayer?' asked Ibn Sirin. 'Yes, I do,' replied the man. 'Then,' said Ibn Sirin, 'why do you make the call to prayer at unseemly times?' Another man came to see Ibn Sirin and said: 'Last night in my dream I saw oil being extracted from grape seeds and then I was putting it back into the grapes!' Ibn Sirin advised him: 'The woman who is in your house—go and make a thorough search; you will discover that she is your mother!' The man returned home. He questioned his wife intensely and when he had completed his interrogation, lo and behold, he found out that she was indeed his mother!"

Then conversation shifted to AFFLICTION FROM TUMORS AND BOILS. The master counseled: "Everyone who, during afternoon prayers, recites **Surat al-Buruj** (Q.85) may it be that God Almighty will give him relief from tumors, and since boils fall under the same category, recourse to that **surat** might also provide relief from boils." He further noted that "everyone who included in the afternoon prayers a recitation of **Surat al-Nazi'at** (Q.79), God the Almighty the Exalted would assure that he remain in his grave only for the duration of one prayer cycle." Then his eyes filled with tears. "How," he asked, "is it possible that one will not remain in the grave?" "That comes to pass," he replied (answering his own question), "because the spirit becomes perfected, and when the spirit attains perfection it draws the body into itself!"

## II. Assembly 32
### Friday, 5th of Dhul-Hijja, A.H. 711 (13 April 1312)

I obtained the good fortune of kissing his feet before the congregational prayer in the house located opposite the Kilogarhi mosque. He told a story about RENOUNCING WORLDLINESS. "Once the Prophet—peace be upon him—declared: 'The dervish is given this choice, either you opt to have the world and all that is in it or the hereafter and all that has been prepared for you.' The dervish replied: 'I choose the hereafter and all that has been prepared for me there.' When he had completed the story, the Commander of the Faithful Abu Bakr Siddiq—may God be pleased with him—began to weep. 'What's the matter with you?' asked the other Companions. Replied Abu Bakr: 'When the Prophet—peace be upon him—said that the dervish was asked to choose between this world and the next, that dervish to whom he was referring was himself!' " The master—may God remember him with favor—when he arrived at this point explained: 'Shaykh al-Islam Farid ad-din—may God sanctify his lofty secret—used to speak similar words, saying 'a dervish had to experience this or do that,' until I also realized that the dervish to whom he was referring was himself."

Then, with reference to RENOUNCING WORLDLINESS, he remarked: "There was a saint among saints. Once he approached a river and, casting his prayer mat on the water, began to pray. 'O God,' he exclaimed, 'Khizr has committed a heinous sin. Make him repent of it!'

In the midst of his prayer, Khizr appeared. 'O saintly one,' he called out, 'what is the heinous sin I have committed that you are now asking me to repent of?' Replied the saint: 'You made a tree sprout up in the desert and sat in its shade and took rest, and yet you claim that you did this for God's sake! Repent at once!' Then that saint, concerning what was meant by leaving the world, said to Khizr—peace be upon him: 'Be as I am!' 'How are you and what do you do?' rejoined Khizr. 'I,' explained the saint, 'I am such that if they offered me the entire world and said, "Accept; there will be no punishment for you if you do, but if you do not accept, you will be sent to hell"—I am such that I would accept hell and reject the world.' 'Why do you say such a thing?' asked Khizr—peace be upon him. 'Because,' replied the saint, 'the world is detested by God and anything that God has declared to be His enemy—I'd rather go to hell than accept such a thing!' "

II. Assembly 33
Wednesday, the 23rd of Muharram, A.H. 712 (31 May 1312)

I obtained the benefit of kissing his feet. That day I presented him with my book, **Mukh al-Ma'ani** (*The Essence of Meaning*). He was pleased and gave me his blessing. The same day I renewed my allegiance and, taking the cap off his blessed head, he put it on the head of this unworthy servant. Praise be to God for that generosity! At the moment that he placed the cap on my head with his blessed hand, he recited the following couplet:

If each day out of love for You I begin anew
To do my work. How well I begin! How well I do!

With respect to the book that I presented him he remarked: "Of the books that the Shaykhs had written **Ruh al-Arwah** (*Soul of Souls*) offered much comfort. It was a fine book. Qazi Hamid ad-din Nagauri —may God have mercy on him—had memorized that book, and often used to quote it from the pulpit. Of the books that former masters had written, **Qut al-Qulub** (*Food for the Hearts*) was a fine book in Arabic, just as **Ruh al-Arwah** was in Persian." I interjected: "The letters of 'Ain al-Quzat Hamadani, even though they have not been completely preserved, are also a fine book, are they not?" "Yes," he said, "they are. 'Ain al-Quzat wrote them in a state of inspiration appropriate to the spiritual moment he experienced." After that on his blessed tongue came the remark that "ʿAin al-Quzat was only twenty-five years old at the time that they burned him. His work is a remarkable testament to the power of youth. So immersed was he in God, so attached to the Almighty! What a marvelous work is that book of his!"

After that the master noted that ʿAin al-Quzat had written about his own father that although he was a judge, he accepted bribes and ate forbidden food, that is, lived off of illegally earned money. He wrote many things like this. "What was his point in writing like this?" I interjected. "He also praised his father as an inspired person," rejoined the master. "The point of ʿAin al-Quzat's writing in this way was to indicate that the manifold blessings of the Almighty the Creator were not dependent on the performance of prayers, devotions, and good works. God inspired whomever he willed and chose whomever he favored as the vehicle of miraculous deeds." At this point someone asked: "Was Shaykh Ahmad Ghazzali the spiritual master of ʿAin al-Quzat?" "No, he was not," replied the master, "for in his letters he mentions Shaykh Ahmad Ghazzali and also his own spiritual master. He often refers to himself and to his Shaykh, and if Shaykh Ahmad Ghazzali has been his spiritual master, he would have made explicit reference to him as his Shaykh."

After that he spoke about ʿAIN AL-QUZAT'S CHILDHOOD AND HIS SPIRITUAL PROWESS. "When ʿAin al-Quzat was but a child, Shaykh Ahmad Ghazzali saw him playing with some other children. After some time he came to ʿAin al-Quzat's parents inquiring about his whereabouts. His parents hid him, telling Shaykh Ahmad that he had died. Shaykh Ahmad was not deceived. 'You are lying,' he told them, 'for how can he die without receiving those blessings that have been destined for him?' After that the master remarked: 'ʿAin ad-Quzat had been accused of cavorting with young boys, and it was on that account that his parents had hidden him from Shaykh Ahmad Ghazzali.'

"Shaykh Burhan ad-din—God grant him peace—was present and asked: 'Did they not say that ʿAin al-Quzat was crazed with an affection for young boys?' 'No,' answered the master, 'he was not, but he wanted to invite blame (**malam**) and so he allowed himself to be accused, but in fact, he was the model of purity and chastity, as is indicated by the story of the butcher's son. He had been accused of cavorting with a certain butcher's son. The father of that boy was told about the accusation and he began to vilify the Shaykh to every passerby. One evening, when his son was in the company of ʿAin al-Quzat, his father came to investigate the situation firsthand. He hid in a side room near the room where ʿAin al-Quzat was with his son. He began to espy them through a peephole. He saw the Shaykh performing his prayers, and when he finished his prayers he would begin to exhort and instruct that butcher's son. After every two prostrations of prayer, he would begin anew to exhort and instruct that lad. The whole night till dawn passed like this: The Shaykh would perform two prostrations of prayer and at their conclusion try to edify the spiritual disposition of that butcher's son. When morning dawned, the boy's father entered the room and fell at the Shaykh's feet. Both he and his son became disciples of ʿAin al-Quzat.' "Finally this pronouncement came from the blessed lips of the master: "Not everyone can arrive at such a spiritual depth. Only one possessed of a powerful essence, pure and chaste in his outlook, can do what ʿAin al-Quzat did."

After that he offered a personal reflection. "Once I came into the presence of the Great Shaykh in Ajodhan. A yogi entered. I asked him: 'Which path do you follow? What is the basis of your spiritual discipline?' He replied: 'In our science it has been set forth as follows: In the soul of man there are two worlds. One is the higher world, the other is the lower world. From the forehead to the navel is the higher world, from the navel to the feet is the lower world. The practical guideline is this: In the higher world sincerity, purity, high morals, and good conduct prevail, but in the lower world watchfulness must be exercised to ensure purity and chastity.' " The master—may God remember him with favor—added: "His explanation pleased me greatly."

Brief mention was made of RENOUNCING WORLDLINESS. Observed the master: "Even if someone spends his days in fasting, stays awake at night, and makes the pilgrimage to Mecca and Medina, the basis of his spiritual discipline must still be that he banishes from his heart friendliness with the world." After that he concluded: "Anyone who claims friendship with God while love of the world continues to dominate his heart, his claim is false; he is a liar!"

## II. Assembly 34

Friday, the 22nd of Rabiʿ al-awwal, A.H. 712 (28 July 1312)

I obtained the benefit of kissing his feet. Conversation turned to the SAINTLINESS OF KHWAJA ʿUTHMAN HARABADI—may God have mercy on him. "After he had abstained from the company of others for a long time, he again became sociable. A command from the Unseen World reached him: 'Invite people to seek God, but on this condition, that you yourself bear a thousand afflictions!' After that he set out to show others the Path. One came and slapped him on the neck, another came and did likewise. He counted each assault, making a knot as blow after blow rained on him. When the total reached a thousand, a voice from on high commanded: 'Now ascend the pulpit and invite the people to the Path!' 'My God,' he cried out, 'I lack knowledge and I'm far from perfect. How can I invite people to the Path?' The command came: 'You ascend the pulpit. We will provide the rest.' "

He next began speaking about DESISTING FROM THE COMPANY OF OTHER PEOPLE. "Shaykh Ahmad ibn Hanbal—may God have mercy on him—abstained from mixing with other people for many years, and even when he reentered human society, he remained silent. He did not speak to anyone. When some time had passed in this fashion, a confidant came to him and asked: 'When you are in the company of other people, why do you not speak?' 'What should I say?' he asked. 'Should I speak about the creation or the Creator? The creation cannot be contained in speech, and it is unseemly to speak of the Creator.' Shaykh Ahmad ibn Hanbal was also heard reciting the following quatrain about the benefit of two friends' meeting alone:

Till I be with you at the Prophet's call,
May you and I be set apart from all.
No sun I wish to rise with you, for then
Its shade on me, but not on you, would fall."

The master made mention of a group of ascetics who fasted and also went on journeys. Because they intend to awe people, they are mere hypocrites. About them the following judgment came on his blessed lips:

If your fasting makes you fat,
Better to eat your fill than that!

II. Assembly 35
Tuesday, 26 Rabi' al-awwal, A.H. 712 (1 August 1312)

I obtained the honor of kissing his feet. Conversation turned to THE DISCOURSE OF THE DERVISHES AND THE BEAUTY OF THEIR SPEECH. In this connection the first thing that he said was: "The masters of the Way have declared that divine mercy alights on three occasions—(1) at the time of a musical assembly (**sama'**), (2) at the time of eating food with the intent (of keeping fit) to obey God's will, and (3) at the time of discourse among dervishes when they clarify (to one another their inner thoughts)."

After that on his blessed tongue came (the following anecdote): "I once came into the presence of the master himself, Shaykh al-Islam Farid ad-din—may God sanctify his noble secret—at a time when six or seven dervishes had just arrived. All of them were young and beautiful. Perhaps they were related to the family of the masters of Chisht—may God bless all of them. They requested the master: 'We have been discoursing with one another. Would you please ask some friend of God to hear our discourse?' The Shaykh turned to me and said, 'You go and listen to their discourse.' And he ordered Badr ad-din Ishaq to go also. In short, one of them began to discourse with the others, displaying the utmost kindness and deference. 'That day you said such and such and I asked such and such a question. Then you said such and such yet I still did not know (what you meant) nor did I understand (the point) and I may have even given the wrong reply.' That friend of his began to respond with the same self-effacing tone. 'You said such and such. It was I who had erred. You had been right.' In short, they continued to speak things like this in the same manner until I and Badr ad-din Ishaq were reduced to tears by their humility and restraint. I said to myself, 'These are divine messengers sent to teach us how discourse (between dervishes) should take place!' "Afterward on the master's blessed tongue came this pronouncement: "You must control the jugular vein, that is, you must not show the effect of anger or intemperance (in discourse)."

After this there was much discussion of patience and forbearance. He said: "Everyone who bears injury is better than he who can scarcely repress anger, for one must not be bent on retaliation." These two lines of poetry came on his blessed tongue:

May God befriend all those who are my foes,
May all who hurt me gain increased repose.

After that he added another couplet:

May all who in my path place thorns from spite
Lead lives that flower like a thornless rose.

Then he remarked; "If someone puts a thorn [in your path] and you put a thorn [in his], there are thorns everywhere!" And he concluded: "It is like this among men, that you are straight with those who are straight with you, and crooked to those who are crooked. But among dervishes, it is like this, that you are straight with those who are straight with you, and with the crooked, you are also straight!"

### II. Assembly 36
### Wednesday, 7th of Rajab, A.H. 712 (10 November 1312)

I obtained the honor of kissing his feet. Discourse turned to AFFECTION AMONG MEN OF FAITH. He observed: "There are two kinds of brotherhood, one is biological, the other is spiritual. Of these the spiritual brotherhood is stronger because if two brothers related by blood are one a believer, the other an infidel, the inheritance of the believing brother cannot pass to the unbelieving brother. Hence I find this a weak (bond of) brotherhood. By contrast, spiritual brotherhood is strong because the tie that binds together two men of faith persists in this world and also in the next."

In this context he recited the following verse from the Holy Qur'an: "Among those who are friends on Judgment Day some of them will become enemies to others, except for the pious" (Q.43:67). He commented that "friends whose friendship is based on their mutual corruption, tomorrow will find themselves enemies of one another." Then on his blessed tongue came this couplet:

> These so-called friends of yours are not friends but deadly foes,
> Who claim tavern and garden as places of repose.

### II. Assembly 37
### Sunday, 25th of Rajab, A.H. 712 (26 November 1312)

I had the honor of kissing his feet. The subject of conversation turned to SUPEREROGATORY PRAYER. He said: "The Prophet Muhammad—peace be upon him—used to perform such prayer in three ways. One way depended on the appropriate time, another on just cause, and a third depended on neither time nor cause. I will begin with the prayer that depends on the appropriate time. Imam Muhammad Ghazzali—may God grant him a just reward—mentioned in **Ihya 'Ulum ad-Din** that the supererogatory prayer linked to time is oft repeated because it is the kind of prayer that may be said once a day or once a week or once a month or even once a year. An example of the kind of supererogatory prayer that is said every day is the eighth prayer. That is to say, after the five daily canonical prayers, the sixth prayer is the late morning prayer (**chasht**), the seventh is the twenty genuflections that come after evening prayer, while the eighth prayer (**tahajjud**) can be performed throughout the day and night. As for the weekly prayer that should be said every week, it is a prayer that is begun on Sunday, then continued on Monday until it is completed on Saturday. Such is a weekly prayer, while the monthly prayer is one that occurs every month, such as the prayer of twenty prostrations that the Prophet—peace be upon him—offered every month at the appearance of the new moon. This is an example of a monthly prayer. As for yearly prayer there are four: the two prayers of **ʿid** (**id-i saghir** and **id-i kabir**), the prayer of rest (**tarawih**), and the prayer on the eve of the fourteenth of Shaʿban (**shab-i barat**). These are all prayers that depend on the appropriate time.

As for prayers that depend on just cause, they are of two sorts. One is the prayer beseeching rain (**istiqsa'**); every time that there is lack of rain one should offer this prayer. The other is the prayer of the solar and lunar eclipse (**kusuf wa-khusuf**). Every time that the sun and the moon go into eclipse one should offer this prayer. Both these prayers depend on just cause, while the prayers that relate to neither time nor cause are laudatory prayers and also the greeting "Peace (be upon you)."

Conversation then turned to the question: CAN SUPEREROGATORY PRAYERS BE SAID AT THE TIME OF CONGREGATIONAL PRAYER? He replied: "They have been said (on such occasions), and some of the Masters of the Way have said them." Then he added: "It was the eve of the fourteenth of Shaʿban, and the Shaykh of Islam Shaykh Farid ad-din—may God sanctify his lofty secret—asked me to say the prayer appropriate to the occasion and to lead the congregational prayer. I did as he requested."

Then the topic turned to PRAYERS THAT ARE SAID FOR ONE'S SELF-PROTECTION. He said: "Every time that one must go out of his house he should make two prostrations before departing, so that whatever affliction may befall him on the way God Almighty will save him from it. In these two prostrations there is much benefit. When a man reenters his home he should offer two more prostrations so that whatever affliction may befall him in the house God Almighty will save him from it, too, for in these two prostrations also there is much benefit and security." After this he said: "If someone should not offer these two prostrations at the time of departing and reentering his house, he should recite the Throne Verse (Q.2:255). And if he does not recite the Throne

Verse, then he should recite four times: 'Glory be to God and Praise be to God. There is no god but God. God is great. There is no protection nor power save with God the Sublime, the Almighty.' And if one should enter a mosque at a moment not appropriate for canonical prayer and therefore can not pray as one should, then one ought to recite this same set of ascriptions four times. The desired result will be achieved."

II. Assembly 38
Saturday, 13th of Shawwal, A.H. 712 (11 February 1313)

I had the honor of kissing his feet. Khwaja Nur, who was privileged to be related to him, was present. He was seated near him, reading the **Mashariq al-Anwar.** The Khwaja was discussing that book and conversation focused on the Tradition that if saliva or phlegm came into the mouth during prayer and one wished to expectorate, it is NOT PERMISSIBLE TO SPIT IN THE DIRECTION OF THE KA'BA NOR TOWARD THE RIGHT, which is the direction of divine sovereignty. Rather, it is permissible to spit slowly toward the left foot, with the least possible movement. This much will not forfeit the value of prayer.

In this connection the master observed: "The believer is never defiled, for, as Tradition testifies, one day the Prophet—peace be upon him—chanced upon Abu Huraira. The Prophet—peace be upon him—used to jest with him. He raised his hand to shake hands with Abu Huraira. Abu Huraira withdrew his own hand, and the Prophet—peace be upon him—asked: 'Why do you withdraw your hand?' He said: 'O messenger of God, I have just this hour come from sleeping with my wife and I have not yet washed. How can I grasp the hand of a pure person such as you?' The Prophet—peace be upon him—said: 'The believer is never dirty. He may be ritually unclean but he is never dirty, so that even if someone drinks the water which remains after a ritually impure person has drunk from it, there is nothing to fear.' "

In the same connection he noted: "If a woman were to come before a man in the form of Satan, that is, if Satan himself were to appear before a man in the form of a woman and the man were to be attracted to her, that man must go at once and make love to his wife so that that temptation may be repelled from him. This is among the benefits of a married man!"

After Khwaja Nur had heard these morals (**fawa'id**), he got up to leave. The master—may God remember him with favor—told those present about Nur: "You have had among you this dear one. He is a fine person." After Nur had departed, the master spoke at length about his purity. He said: "Every Thursday evening he would recite the whole of the Qur'an. He is dedicated to knowledge. He has learned much and done much that is commendable. He has no traffic with anyone, no attachment of friendship, no feeling of enmity. He is so upright that one day I asked him: 'What is the purpose of your acts of obedience and perpetual devotions?' He said: 'My purpose is to lead a life like yours!' " The master—may God remember him with favor—remarked: "Who could have taught him such a reply?" In other words, Khwaja Nur's terse reply was itself an indication of the divine favor he enjoyed.

After this, conversation turned to the fact that WHOEVER IS QUESTIONED IT IS BETTER TO QUESTION HIM ABOUT HIS OWN PROFESSION, that is, about circumstances that he knows first-hand. In this regard he told the following story: "There was a scholar named Ziya ad-din. He taught at the base of the minaret of the congregational mosque in Delhi. He told me: 'I went to visit Shaykh Farid ad-din —may God bless his lofty secret—and I knew nothing about jurisprudence or grammar or other sciences. I had learned only the science of disputation. It came to my mind: "If the Shaykh asks me about jurisprudence or grammar or other sciences, what will I say?" I had no sooner greeted the Shaykh and sat down than he looked at me and asked, "What is the meaning of the technical term 'examination of the object of dispute' (**tanqih-i manat**)?" I was relieved. I began to clarify that term, explaining both the negative and the positive connotations of its meaning.' " The master—may God remember him with favor—said: "What perfect intuition had the Shaykh that he asked him not only about his profession but also about his particular discipline. Praise be to God the Lord of the universe!"

This fascicule of morals (**fawa'id**) covers three years. Others that will be heard and understood hopefully also will be written down and transcribed, if God Almighty wills.

# Fascicle III (Hereafter III)

In the name of God full of Compassion, ever Compassionate.

These signs (**isharat**) of the divine secrets are proclamations (**basharat**) of the infinite lights that have been heard from the mouth of the pearl scatterer, the tongue of the gem disperser, the true master, the seal of interpreters, the king of Sufi Shaykhs throughout the world, the Nizam of Truth, of Law, of Religion—may God extend the benefits of his breath(s). Praise be to God for that.

May this collection Hasan has presumed to make
Be centered by the pure holiness of his Shaykh!

## III. Assembly 1
Monday, 27 of Dhu'l-Qa'da, A.H. 712 (26 March 1313)

I had the benefit of kissing his feet. He talked about THE GENERATIONS OF MUSLIMS. "The Prophet—peace be upon him," he observed, "once said, 'After me, from my community (**umma**), there will be five generations. Each generation will live for forty years. The first generation will be marked by knowledge and witness, the second, by righteousness and piety, the third, by continuity and compassion, the fourth, by discontinuity and disaffection, while the fifth will cause tumult and uproar (**harj wal-marj**).' "

The master explained: "The first generation were the noble companions of the Prophet. The second were the followers of Islam. After them came the generation of continuity and compassion. Continuity means that even though the world seemed to favor them, they and others shared the worldly benefits they enjoyed. To others they appeared as easy-going and lazy since if one among them clung to something, the second would let him have it. This they call continuity with the (outlook of the) preceding generations. As for compassion it means that if the whole world had come into their possession and they shared dominion with no one, they would still expend what they had in the way of God.

"After them came the fourth generation of discontinuity and disaffection. Discontinuity means that if the world came into their possession, and they had to share it, quarreling and jealousy would erupt. Disaffection means that if the world came into the possession of a few, they would expend it completely on themselves, turning their back on others and sharing with no one. After them came the fifth generation that produced tumult and uproar. Tumult and uproar mean that people would fight tooth and nail and kill one another. The duration of all five generations was 200 years."

Then the master observed: "After these 200 years, if someone gave birth to a puppy, that was better than giving birth to a human child." Tears began to fill the master's eyes. "The Prophet was speaking about only the first 200 years after his death. If this was the case after 200 years, what can we say about the time in which we live?"

Conversation next turned to IMMERSING ONESELF IN GOD. That is true work and everything else not related to it is but an impediment to that blessing. The master noted: "Once concerning those books that I had read and studied, a doubt arose within me and I said to myself, 'What has become of me (from all that reading)?' " In this connection he told the following story: "Shaykh Abu Saʿid Abu'l-Khayr—may God have mercy on him—when he had reached a perfect spiritual state took all the books that he had read and put them in a corner. Others say that he washed them." The master paused: "Washing is not correct, but he did keep them in a particular place until one day he wanted to study something from one of those books. A voice from the Unseen declared: 'O Abu Saʿid, let us annul our pact, for you are immersing yourself in something else!' " The master, when he reached this point in the story, began to cry and these two lines of poetry came upon his blessed tongue:

For you, O shadow of hatred, how can there be space
In that place where nought but thought of the Friend dominates?

That is to say, in a circumstance where even books on the Shaykhs, not to mention tomes on jurisprudence and legal statutes, become a veil, how can one make room for things other than them?

## III. Assembly 2
### Wednesday, 12 of Dhu'l-Hijja, A.H. 712 (10 April 1313)

I had the honor of kissing his feet. A group was visiting the master —may God remember him with favor. Since there was not enough covered space, some of them had to sit in the sun. The master instructed others: "You sit closer to one another so that these others sitting in the sun may find a space; even I am burning from heat." In this connection he told the following story: "There was a saint in Badaun. They called him Shaykh Shahi Muy Tab—may God have mercy upon him. Once his friends took him out for a stroll and prepared a rice-milk mixture (**shir birinj**). When they served the food, Shaykh Muy Tab said: 'Someone has tampered with this food.' Before that moment two persons from the company of his friends had eaten some of the dish, and this is a grave infraction among dervishes. In short, when Khwaja Shahi said, 'Why is it that before the food was served among friends someone has eaten something from it?' they replied: 'The milk had boiled over from the pot and spilled down. We took that which had spilled. Now what were we to do? Should we have wasted it? There was no recourse but to eat it.' Shaykh Shahi retorted: 'No, that eating was an error. You should let it spill down and be wasted.' In short, that infraction was not forgiven. They were sent off to a shed. The sun was shining. They were standing in the sun, so much so that sweat began to pour out of them. Khwaja Shahi then exclaimed, 'Send for a barber!' They asked: 'Why do want a barber?' he said: 'That he may drain from me as much blood as is flowing from my friends.' " The master—may God remember him with favor—when he reached this point in the story exulted: "Well done! See how much love he had, and what an eye for fairness!"

Also, in connection with THE SAINTLINESS OF SHAYKH MUY TAB, he told another story. "Once Shaykh Nizam ad-din Abu'l-Muayyad was beset with an affliction. He sent for this Shahi Muy Tab, and asked him: 'Focus your attention (himma) till I recuperate from this affliction.' Khwaja Shahi tried to excuse himself, saying, 'You are an eminent person. How can you make a request like this of me, a mere man of the streets? How can you speak to me about a matter of such importance?' Shaykh Nizam ad-din would not accept his excuse. He replied, 'But of course, I have asked you and you must focus your attention so that I may find health.' Shaykh Shahi countered: 'Okay, but you must invite two friends of mine. One is named Sharaf, he is an upright man. The other is a tailor.' In short, both were invited, and Khwaja Shahi told them: 'Shaykh Nizam ad-din has commandeered me to do this particular work. Now you must assist me. I will care for the Shaykh from his head to his chest, and one of you must care for his lower parts from the chest to one foot, the other from his chest to the other foot.' In short, all three of them immersed themselves in this work, and Shaykh Nizam ad-din Muayyad recuperated from his affliction."

Also, in connection with THE MIRACLES OF SHAYKH SHAHI MUY TAB, the master told another story. "Many times he used to say,

'Whoever faces a difficulty after my death, tell him to visit my grave for a period of three days, and if after three days that work has not been accomplished, he should continue for four days, and if after four days, his importunity has not been removed, he should return for a fifth day and dismantle my grave brick by brick!' " Briefly he commented on THE INFALLIBILITY OF PROPHETS AND SAINTS. "The prophets are infallible," he observed, "and near to them are God's beggars, the saints, but prophets are intrinsically infallible, while saints must acquire infallibility."

## III. Assembly 3
Friday, the 22nd of Dhu'l-Hijja, A.H. 712 (20 April 1313)

I had the good fortune of kissing his feet. A visitor arrived and asked the master to recite **Surat al-Fatiha** in order that he might memorize the Qur'an. The master—may God remember him with favor—asked: "How much of the Qur'an have you already memorized?" "One-third," replied the man. "Keep memorizing more little by little," advised the master, "and be sure to repeat what you have memorized from the preceding day."

After that he told a story. "One night Shaykh Badr ad-din Ghaznavi—may God have mercy on him—appeared to me in a dream. I, too, asked him to recite **Surat al-Fatiha** on my behalf in order that I might memorize the Qur'an. He recited it, as I had requested. The next day I went to see a dear friend, and telling him about my dream, I asked him to recite **Surat al-Fatiha** on my behalf. 'If you recite it in wakefulness, as Shaykh Badr ad-din had done while I was asleep, perhaps I will succeed in memorizing the Qur'an on account of your recitation.' That saintly person recited **Surat al-Fatiha,** as I had requested, and then he counseled me: 'Everyone who each night before going to sleep recites these two verses will succeed in memorizing the Qur'an and also retain what he has memorized. The two Qur'anic verses are these:

> Your God is one God. There is no god but He, full of compassion, ever compassionate.
>
> Lo! In the creation of the heavens and the earth, and the distinction of night from day, and the ships which sail upon the sea with what is of use to humankind, and the water which God sends down from the sky to revive the earth after its

death, and the dispersion of beasts therein, and the ordinance of winds, together with the subjugation of the clouds, between heaven and earth—surely these are signs to people who discern. (Q.2:163–164)"

Conversation turned to THE ALMIGHTY—MAY HIS NAME BE EXALTED! He told a story in this regard. "Once the Prophet—peace be upon him—wished to meet the companions of the cave (also known as the sleepers of the cave, from Q.18). But the command had gone forth: 'You will not see them in this world; you must wait till Judgment Day. But if you want them to be brought into your faith, that can take place now.' After that the Prophet—peace be upon him—brought forth a carpet, and he asked four persons to each hold a corner of that carpet. These four were: Abu Bakr Siddiq, ʿUmar Khattab, ʿAli ibn Abi Talib, and Abu Dhar Ghaffar—may God be pleased with all of them. The Prophet—peace be upon him—then invoked the same wind that the Prophet Sulaiman—peace be upon him—used to invoke for great undertakings. The wind came. The Prophet—peace be upon him—then commanded the wind to bear that carpet, along with his four companions, to the cave where the seven sleepers were. It carried the carpet and the four companions to the entrance of that very cave. The four companions called out to the seven sleepers: 'Peace be upon you.' Because God Almighty had revived the seven sleepers, they replied: 'And on you also be peace.' The four companions then instructed the seven sleepers in the faith of the Prophet Muhammad—peace be upon him—and they accepted. Praise be to God, the Lord of the universe." After reiterating this story, the master—may God remember him with favor—asked: "Is there anything not within the power of Almighty God?"

### III. Assembly 4

Monday, the 1st of the month of Safar—may God grant it to conclude with favor and success, A.H. 713 (28 May 1313)

I obtained the benefit of kissing his feet. Conversation turned to SUPEREROGATORY PRAYERS AND INVOCATIONS. The master remarked: "One night I saw Shaykh al-Islam Farid ad-di—may God sanctify his lofty secret—in a dream. He said to me: 'Every day you must pray the following prayer a hundred times: **There is no god but God. He is Unique. He has no partner. To Him be dominion. To Him be**

**praise. For He has power over everything.'** When I awoke, I took it upon myself to repeat this prayer. 'Let me be firm in this resolve,' I kept telling myself. Then I saw that it had been written in the books of the Sufi masters that everyone who each day recites this prayer one hundred times will be free of concerns and will lead a happy life. And I realized that this had been the intention of my master." Also concerning the merit of this prayer, the master—may God remember him with favor—remarked: "It is recorded in Tradition that everyone who after each canonical prayer recites this prayer ten times, it will be as though he has released a thousand slaves!"

After that he observed: "One other time my master appeared to me in my sleep. He commanded me to recite **Surat al-Naba** (Q.78) five times each day, after evening prayer. When I awoke I began to implement this command, and again it occurred to me that in this directive, too, there must be lodged a blessing. I consulted Qur'anic commentaries and found there the statement that whoever after evening prayer each day recites **Surat al-Naba** five times will become the captive of God, and he will be known as 'God's captive.' Whenever someone falls in love, they remark that so-and-so has become the captive of so-and-so. In the same sense, the commentators use this phrase to indicate that whoever recites **Surat al-Naba** in the prescribed manner will become a captive of the love of God!"

Having communicated these two morals, the master instructed those present: "You, too, should persist in this practice."

### III. Assembly 5
Monday, the 2nd of the month of Safar, A.H. 713 (29 May 1313)

I had the good fortune of kissing his hand. One of those present remarked: "Some persons, when speaking about you, have ascended certain pulpits and gone to certain places and proceeded to say such unseemly things that we can not repeat them here!" The master—may God remember him with favor—replied: "I pardon them all. What sort of place would it be were men to be constantly engaged in hatred and slander of others! Everyone who speaks ill of me I pardon him. You also must pardon slanderers and not harbor any enmity toward them."

After that he spoke about a certain Chaju of Ind(ra)pat. "Continuously he would speak ill of me and wish me ill. Speaking ill of others is one thing; wishing them ill is something else, still worse. In short, the third day after he died, I went to his grave and offered prayers on his behalf. 'O God,' I prayed, 'whatever bad thing he said about me or bad thought he harbored of me, I forgive him. Would You please not punish him on my account?' " In this connection he said: "If there be trouble between two persons, one of them should seize the initiative and cleanse himself of ill thoughts toward the other. When his inner self is emptied of enmity, inevitably that trouble between him and the other will lessen." Finally the master exclaimed: "Why should one be vexed by these slanderous assaults? They have often said that the property of Sufis is claimable, even shedding their blood is permissible. When such are the boundaries of the Law, why bother to speak ill of someone who is a Sufi, or harbor enmity against him?"

In the meantime a person arrived and reported: "Right now in such-and-such a place your friends are gathering together for a musical assembly and they have musical instruments with them." The master—may God remember him with favor—was not pleased to hear this news. "I have forbidden them to play flutes and to use other forbidden instruments. Whatever they have done is not right." And he kept emphasizing this point, to such an extent that he finally declared: "If an **imam** offers prayers, and in the group offering prayers behind him ladies happen to be present, and if the **imam** happens to make a mistake, one of the men ought to say out loud: 'Glory be to God!' But if it is a woman who observes the error, how will she communicate it to the **imam?** She will not say 'Glory be to God!' because her voice should not be heard during prayers. Instead she would clap her hands, but not palm upon palm because that might seem lighthearted or frivolous. Rather, you would strike the back of one hand upon the palm of the other. In short, if proper conduct in worship requires going to such lengths to avoid the appearance of levity, then in musical gatherings the preferred approach is to avoid any such actions, that is, one should be vigilant in preventing both clapping and the use of musical instruments." Then he concluded: "If someone once lapses in performing a certain virtuous practice, may he slip and all within the bounds of the Law, for if he slips and falls outside the Law, what recourse remains?"

After that he said: "The great spiritual masters have attended musical assemblies and they are supporters of this activity. For that person who has a taste for God and has experienced the pain of separation from Him, hearing one line of poetry can create in him an overwhelming sense of pathos, whether or not instruments are used. But as for the person who has never experienced the taste for God, even if countless reciters appear before him and play every kind of musical instrument, what use will they be since he is not among the people of pain, that is, he is not among those who experience the pain of separation from God? Hence one should note that this activity is connected with pain not with musical instruments or anything else!" Later he remarked: "How can one experience awareness of God every day? If during the day one auspicious moment occurs, then all the moments of separation during that day recede into the shadow of that single memorable moment, and similarly, if in a crowd there appears one person who has a taste for God and enjoys His favor, all other persons recede into the shadow of that one person, even as they benefit from his protection!"

After this he observed: "In days gone by there was a judge in Ajodhan who was always picking a quarrel with Shaykh al-Islam Farid ad-din—may God sanctify his lofty secret. One day, in a pique of anger, he went to Multan and, appearing before a religious notable there, he exclaimed: 'Where is it permitted that someone may sit in a mosque, listen to musical performances, and from time to time even begin to dance?' They replied: 'Of whom do you speak? Be specific. Tell us who does such things.' 'It is Shaykh al-Islam Farid ad-din—may God sanctify his lofty secret.' 'Oh,' they demurred, 'about him we can say nothing.'

After that the master—may God remember him with favor—remarked: "Every time that I heard a musical performance, each attribute that I heard the reciter depict—I swear by the cloak of my Shaykh—I attributed all of them, all those virtues and all those attributes, to the Shaykh. Once, while he was still alive, I was in an assembly where the reciter delivered the following couplet:

> Stroll not so gracefully as this, lest
> From the evil eye you're made distressed.

I was at once reminded of the pleasing virtues and laudable qualities of the Shaykh. His perfect saintliness, his extraordinary piety, his surpassing grace—all overwhelmed me to such an extent that I cannot describe the mood they evoked. The reciter wanted to move on and recite other verses, but I had him repeat again and again these two lines." The master—may God remember him with favor—when he came to this point began to weep. "Not long afterward," he remarked, "the Shaykh departed this world."

Continuing on this same line of thought, he began to speak of ATTRIBUTION AND INTERPRETATION. He told a story. "On the Day of Resurrection a Sufi will be asked: 'Did you not listen to musical performances during your lifetime?' 'Yes, I did,' he will reply. 'And every line that you heard,' They will ask, 'did you attribute the qualities depicted to Us?' 'Yes, I did,' he will reply. 'But those qualities are transient (**hadith**),' will be the rejoinder, 'while the divine essence is permanent (**qadim**). How then can transient qualities be attributed to what is permanent?' 'O God,' the Sufi will lament, 'it was out of the extremity of my love for You that I made this attribution.' " After completing this dialogue, the master—may God remember him with favor—became misty-eyed. "Look!" he exclaimed, "if They find such fault with someone who is immersed in love of God, what will They say to others?"

Conversation turned briefly to THE MIRACLES OF THE PROPHET—peace be upon him. They were such that even animals and inanimate objects obeyed him. In this connection he told still another story: "The Prophet—peace be upon him—when he was commissioned to prophesy, sent Maʿadh ibn Jabal toward Yemen, instructing him that there was a spring there known as ʿAin az-Zuʿaf, sometimes also known as ʿAin adh-dhuʿaf. In short, that spring had a special quality: Whoever drank but a drop from it died on the spot. The master of the world—peace be upon him—commanded Maʿadh: 'When you reach there, tell that spring: "I (Muhammad) have been commissioned to prophesy." ' When Maʿadh reached that spring, he delivered the command of Muhammad—peace be upon him—telling the spring about the manifestation of his prophecy. That spring at once believed in the apostleship of the Apostle—peace be upon him—and afterward that fearsome quality that had set it apart from other springs was never again detected."

Conversation turned next to THE GREATEST NAME. The master remarked: "Ibrahim Adham—may God have mercy upon him—was once asked: 'Do you know the Greatest Name? Tell us which it is.' 'Yes, I do know it, and I will tell you about it,' he replied. 'First, you should cleanse your stomach of unlawful food, then you should empty your heart of love of this world, and after that by whatever name you call upon God **that** is the Greatest Name!' "

In the meantime they brought out food. As they added salt to it, the master—may God remember him with favor—observed: "One must begin with salt but one should never moisten the finger before picking it up. If, however, one tries to pick up salt without moistening the finger, one gets nothing. Hence one must remember to join the forefinger to the thumb in picking up salt." At this point I intervened, thanking the master for the moral he was teaching us. "Praise be to God!" I exclaimed. "The truth of salt has renewed our loyalty to you [i.e., we understand that the metaphor of finger and thumb refers to us and to you, and that salt represents the knowledge and love of God]." The master—may God remember him with favor—smiled and remarked: "Well said!" Maulana Muhyi ad-din Kashani—may God have mercy upon him—was present. "What a savory remark he has made!" observed the Maulana. "He is a savant in this regard," quipped the master—may God remember him with favor.

In a similar humorous vein the master noted: "Once someone came to Khwaja Shams al-Mulk—may God have mercy upon him—and asked him for something. The Khwaja gave a noncommittal reply. The questioner repeated his question. 'Why don't you simply go away,' replied Khwaja Shams al-Mulk. 'Because I want an answer.' 'But I've already given you an answer,' insisted the Khwaja Shams al-Mulk. 'I want a real answer.' 'Look,' quipped the Khwaja, 'could I possibly give you a more suitable answer than the one I've already given?' "

## III. Assembly 6
### Monday, 29th of Safar, A.H. 713 (25 June 1313)

I had the honor of kissing his hands. I told him: "I had come to see some relatives who lived near the master's hospice. Some friends had counseled that if a disciple goes near the abode of his spiritual master but does not intend to see him, he should not then go and call on him. I had said to myself: 'Though it may be the usual practice, I will not be at ease if I pass by this way and do not see my esteemed master. I will commit this one infraction of custom.' Having reflected on this in my heart, I came here now to pay my respects to you."

The master—may God remember him with favor—said: "You have done well." Then the following verses came on his blessed lips:

In the tavern's lane, where the common folk gather,
Come, sit, be at ease; who you are is no matter.

After that he observed: "Among spiritual masters there is a rule that before the sunrise prayer and also after the other prayers visitors are not admitted, but I have no such rule: Everytime that some one comes, I say, 'Welcome!' "

Conversation turned to PILGRIMS WHO, ON THEIR RETURN FROM ARABIA, SPEAK OF NOTHING BUT THE PIL-

GRIMAGE. They talk about it incessantly on every occasion. This is not proper. Then he remarked: "Somebody used to say: 'I have visited such-and-such a place, and I have seen such-and-such a holy person there. Another holy person said to him: 'Alas, sir, of what good has this been? Clearly no benefit has come from it;' that is to say, you are still the egotist you were before!"

He went on to comment about SERVICE TO OTHERS AND SEEKING THEIR SATISFACTION. "Everyone who serves is also served. Someone who does not serve, how can he be served by others?" Then this phrase in Arabic came onto his blessed lips: "Whoever serves is served."

He made a final brief comment about GOOD CONDUCT. "Someone once wrote a poem on ten traditions, five of which related to the head, five to the rest of the body. He concluded the poem with a beautiful couplet that goes like this:

Ten points in just two lines you've packed.
But these are words, while you should act!"

### III. Assembly 7
Wednesday, 19th of Jumada al-ula, A.H. 713 (12 September 1313)

I had the good fortune of kissing his feet, but at this time a local ruler had sent him the deed of ownership to two gardens and much land, along with the provisions and tools for their maintenance. The ruler had also made it clear that he was relinquishing all his own rights to both the gardens and the land. The master—may God remember him with favor—had not accepted that gift. Instead, he had lamented: "What have I to do with gardens and fields and land?" Then, smiling he added: "If I were to accept that gift, people might say of me: 'The Shaykh wants to stroll in his garden and strut about in his fields and on his land.' What kind of work would I be doing? What sort of environment is that for me?" And he became teary-eyed as he recollected: "None of our forefathers and none of our spiritual masters [in the Chishti lineage] has engaged in such activity."

Then he told an appropriate story. "At the time that Sultan Nasir ad-din—may God illumine his grave—was proceeding toward Multan he passed through Ajodhan. Sultan Ghiyas ad-din—may God illumine his grave—who at that time was still known as Ulugh Khan, came to visit Shaykh al-Islam Farid ad-din—may God sanctify his lofty secret. He offered some money and the ownership deeds for four villages to the Shaykh, the money being for the benefit of dervishes, the land for the Shaykh. Smiling, Shaykh al-Islam said: 'Give me the money. I will dispense it to the dervishes. But as for those land deeds, keep them. There are many who long for them. Give them away to such persons.' "

While he was telling this story, he also remembered a Tradition that suited the occasion. "The Prophet—peace be upon him—used to say: 'Whatever enters a house defiles it.' [That is to say, whatever one keeps defiles the space where it is kept.]" After that the master commented: "The Prophet—peace be upon him—spoke this Tradition in a specific context. It happened in the following manner. When he was visiting a certain house, he saw that they had brought two sticks into that house and made of them a yoke with which to till the ground. Having noticed this, he said: 'Whatever enters a house defiles it.' That is to say, these two sticks defiled the house [since one should not keep plowing instruments in a domicile]."

The master then thought of SHAYKH JALAL AD-DIN TABRIZI—may God sanctify his lofty secret. "He wrote a letter to Shaykh Baha ad-din Zakariya—may God have mercy upon him—in Arabic. I have seen a copy of that letter. In it he states: Whoever loves the thighs of women will never be happy. He also mentions 'tilling.' 'Tilling' refers to land cultivation, estates, and the like. I cannot remember the particular phrase in Arabic, but it meant something like: Whoever sets his heart on tilling, it is as if he has become either enslaved to worldliness, or else the slave of worldly people." I interjected, asking about the spiritual formation of Shaykh Jalal ad-din Tabrizi—may God illumine his grave. "Of whom was he the disciple?" "He was the disciple of Shaykh Sa'id Tabrizi—may God have mercy on both of them."

Conversation turned briefly to INVOCATORY PRAYERS. One of those present asked: "What does it mean, the Tradition which declares: 'He who persists in invocatory prayer is cursed, while he who desists from it is also cursed.' " "This Tradition," replied the master, "relates to the People of the Book. It happened in the following manner. They reported to the Prophet—peace be upon him—that a certain Jew or Magian was reciting many invocatory prayers. In technical language such prayer was called 'an ejaculatory prayer' (**tamkhitha**). The Prophet—peace be upon him—when he heard this said: 'He who persists in invocatory prayer is doomed,' and when they reported his response to the person of the Book, that fellow ceased to say invocatory prayers. The Prophet—peace be upon him—on hearing this, said: 'He who desists from invocatory prayers is also doomed.'

"Some say that this Tradition has a general applicability when interpreted as follows. If someone intentionally ceases to say invocatory prayers without valid cause, he becomes 'one who desists from invocatory prayer,' and with respect to such a person they say: 'He who desists from invocatory prayer is cursed,' but if someone is, for example, the leader of a group and if the vitality of his people depends on him and if, indeed, the collective interests of the Muslims hang on his commands, he should not busy himself in saying invocatory prayers, and were he to do so, then about such a person it would be said: 'He who persists in invocatory prayer is cursed.' "

At this point I interjected: "If someone is overwhelmed with work or has some other valid excuse for not saying invocatory prayers during the day but then says his invocatory prayers at night, what is his fate?" "That would be fine," replied the master. "If someone misses the daytime invocatory prayers, he should say them at night, and if he misses the evening invocatory prayers, he should say them during the day. Is not night the successor of day, and day the successor of night?"

After that he concluded: "There are three circumstances when it is permissible to desist from invocatory prayers without any other excuse: inclination toward what is forbidden, anger without provocation, or imminent calamity." And in this connection he told a story about Maulna ʾAziz Zahid—may God have mercy upon him. "One day the Maulana fell from his horse and broke his arm. 'What happened?' they asked him. 'Every day I recite **Surat al-Yasin**,' he replied, 'but today I did not recite it and took this tumble.' "

### III. Assembly 8

Wednesday, 4th of Jumada al-akhira, A.H. 713 (26 September 1313)

I obtained the benefit of kissing his feet. Conversation turned to POETRY, specifically, to discerning the connotations of **ghazals** and other forms of verse. The master observed: "Each individual must grasp the connotation of poems for himself. Consider the case of Shaykh al-Islam Farid ad-din—may God sanctify his lofty secret. Once the following verses came on his blessed lips:

O Nizami, what secrets are these, revealed from your heart?
His secret no one knows; bridle your tongue! bridle your tongue!

Throughout most of the day, right up till the time of evening prayer, he kept reciting this couplet. At the breaking of fast the same couplet remained on his blessed lips. It is reported that at dawn the following day he was still repeating this couplet, and each time he uttered it his countenance changed." After that the master—may God remember him with favor—asked: "What was going on in his mind? What could have caused him to say the same couplet over and over again?"

Then he began to speak about Shaykh Baha' ad-din Zakariya—may God have mercy upon him. "Once he was standing at the entrance to his room. As he grasped the door panel on either side, these two lines came again and again on his blessed lips:

O beauty, cast a glance once more on me,
For I've strayed not—may God my witness be!

After that, the master—may God remember him with favor—remarked: "What could he have been thinking? Nobody knows what the verse connoted for him, or what he derived from its constant repetition."

Conversation then turned to TRUST IN GOD. "One's reliance on God must be so complete," remarked the master, "that one never pays attention to others. Indeed," he added, "one's faith is never perfected till one regards all created beings as if they were mere camel dung!"

In this vein he then told a story about Ibrahim Khawass—may God have mercy upon him. "Once Ibrahim Khawass was on his way to the Ka'ba. A youth joined him. Ibrahim, staring at the youth, asked: 'Where are you going?' 'I am going to the Ka'ba,' he replied. 'But where are your provisions for the journey?' asked Ibrahim Khawass. 'God the Exalted and Sublime,' replied the youth, 'has sustained me without provisions till now. Can He not also direct me to Ka'ba without the wherewithal of a traveler?' In short, when Ibrahim Khawass reached the Ka'ba, the youth was already circumambulating the Black Stone. As their eyes met, the youth asked Ibrahim Khawass: 'O you of little faith, do you not now repent of what you told me on the journey?' "

Also in the same vein the master told another story. "There was a grave plunderer. He came into the presence of Khwaja Bayazid—may God have mercy upon him—and repented of what he had done. Khwaja Bayazid asked him: 'How many shrouds have you removed from corpses?' 'A thousand,' replied the grave plunderer. Bayazid asked him: 'Of the thousand how many did you find with their faces pointed toward the Kaʿba?' 'Only two,' replied the man. 'The others whom I saw were pointing away from the Kaʿba.' Those present asked Bayazid: 'What does this signify, that only two were facing the Kaʿba while the others were facing elsewhere?' 'Those two,' replied Bayazid, 'had total reliance on God. The others did not.' "

After that the master—may God remember him with favor—said: "Spiritual masters have specified FOUR KINDS OF SUSTENANCE: minimal sustenance, allotted sustenance, acquired sustenance, and promised sustenance. Minimal sustenance is that which one gets by way of food and drink that is necessary for survival. That is called minimal sustenance since God is its provide. 'And there is no creature moving on the earth but that its sustenance derives from God' (Q.11:6). Allotted sustenance is that which has been decreed for eternity, having been fixed on the preserved tablet, while acquired sustenance is that which has been saved up; it consists of money, clothes, and other goods. As for promised sustenance, it is that which God Almighty has vouchsafed for the righteous and the devout. 'And for whoever fears God, He prepares for him a relief [from distress and hardship], and He provides it for him from a source that he does not expect.' " (Q.65:3). After that he commented that trust related only to minimal sustenance, not to others, for what relevance can trust have when sustenance has been eternally allotted, or already acquired, nor can promised sustenance involve trust since whatever God has promised He will provide in due time. Trust, therefore, relates solely to minimal sustenance, that is, trust depends on being aware that the little that is needed to survive will certainly be provided.

## III. Assembly 9

Sunday, 29th of Jumada al-akhira, A.H. 713 (21 October 1313)

I obtained the good fortune of kissing his feet. Conversation focused on THE MERIT ACCRUING FROM CONGREGATIONAL PRAYER. Turning to me, he asked: "Do you always say prayer in congregation?" "There is a mosque near my home," I replied, "but in the place where we live, should we be absent, there is no one to look after papers and books, and so we perform congregational prayer at home." "You must perform congregational prayer," replied the master, "but it is better if you do it in a mosque."

After this he said: "Previously, in the times of former prophets, there was no place of worship except the mosque [i.e., a public place of worship], but in the time of our Prophet Muhammad—peace be upon him—every place became suitable for prayer. Also, with reference to ALMS, formerly one-quarter of one's property had to be given to charity, but in the time of our Prophet—peace be upon him—out of 200 **dirams** only 5 had to be expended for alms." Then he added: "About the person who gives 5 out of 200 **dirams** to charity, one does not say that he is a miser. However, even though one would not call him a miser, one would also not think of depicting him as a generous person! One never describes someone as generous unless he gives more than 5 of 200 **dirams** as alms." At this point I intervened and asked: "What is the meaning of the following Tradition: 'The generous person is beloved of God even if he be corrupt' "? "So they say," replied the master. One of those present remarked: "They include this Tradition in the Forty Traditions [made famous by an-Nawawi]." The master—may God remember him with favor—said: "Only that is authentic (**sahih**) which has been set forth in the Two Authentic Traditions (**sahihain**) [of Bukhari and Muslim]."

He next drew a distinction between the generous and the magnanimous person. "The generous person," he noted, "is he who gives something more than the minimum required for alms, while the magnanimous person gives much more. Of 200 **dirams,** for example, he might keep 5 and give away the rest." After that on his blessed lips came a story about Shaykh al-Islam Farid ad-din—may God sanctify his lofty secret. "He used to say that alms are of three kinds: alms of the Law, of the Path, and of Truth. Alms of the Law means that one gives 5 **dirams** of every 200. Alms of the Path means that one **keeps** but 5 **dirams** of every 200, while alms of Truth means that you expend all that you have and keep nothing!"

With reference to ALMS, he told a story about Khwaja Junayd Baghdadi—may God have mercy upon him. "To the religious scholars of his age he said: 'O wicked scholars, give alms of knowledge, that is, you vile scholars should give of your own knowledge as alms.' They asked him: 'What did you mean by such alms?' 'Simply this,' he replied, 'that of the 200 precepts they teach they should abide by 5 of them, and of the 200 Traditions they have studied they should implement the moral of at least 5 of them.' "

Then, with reference to Tradition, he began to discourse on THE VIRTUE OF MAULANA RAZI AD-DIN SAGHANI, the author of **Mashariq al-Anwar**—may God have mercy upon him. And he himself wrote about his book: 'Let this book be the proof of my worthiness before God!' And if it was ever difficult to ascertain the authenticity of a Tradition, the Prophet—peace be upon him—would appear to him in a dream, and confirm [or disconfirm] its authenticity."

After that he talked about the Maulana's life. "Maulana Razi ad-din came from Badaun and then settled in Kol, where he became assistant treasurer. The treasurer was a decent person, but one day he said something that caused Maulana Razi ad-din to smile. The treasurer then sent the Maulana an ink-pot, implying that if the Maulana thought he had erred, he wanted a written statement of his error. When the Maulana saw this, he got up, exclaiming, 'I will no longer work with such an ignoramus!'

"After he quit that job Maulana Razi ad-din was keen to pursue his studies. He began tutoring the son of the governor of Kol. For his labors he was paid 100 tankas, a sum which pleased him. From there he went on the pilgrimage and after visiting Baghdad, he returned to the vicinity of Delhi. In those days Delhi boasted of numerous great scholars. In all the sciences Maulana Razi ad-din was their equal, but in the science of Tradition he excelled; no one could match his knowledge of Tradition."

Then the master—may God remember him with favor—noted: "One Tradition, in particular, brought him great acclaim. It happened thus. At the point that he left Kol to perform the pilgrimage, he bought a pair of shoes for the journey. But he had gone no further than the first night's stopover when he realized that he could not complete the journey on foot. As this thought crossed his mind, he saw the son of the governor of Kol riding fast toward him, hoping to dissuade him from leaving. The boy drew nearer. The Maulana looked closely at him and noticed that he was riding a very fine horse. 'If only he were to give me this horse,' thought the Maulana to himself, 'I could proceed on my journey with ease.' Even while the governor's son was pleading with him to stay, this thought kept recurring in his mind. When at last the boy realized that the Maulana was resolved to leave, he sighed, 'Alas, this horse that I have been riding, please accept it as a parting gift.' The Maulana promptly mounted the horse and went riding off!

"Later, after he had gone on the pilgrimage, he returned by way of Baghdad. In Baghdad there was a great master of Tradition named Ibn-i Zuhri. A pulpit had been constructed for him. Ascending that pulpit, he would explain Tradition to the scholars who had come to hear him. The scholars would assemble themselves in concentric circles, those who were more knowledgeable sitting in the first circle, those less knowledgeable in a second circle, and others in still further circles. When everyone was properly seated, he would recite a Tradition and they would write down what he said.

"One day Maulana Razi ad-din came into this assembly, and took a seat in an outer circle. Ibn-i Zuhri was expounding a Tradition concerning the **muezzin,** or prayer caller, to the effect that whatever the **muezzin** said, the listener was to repeat exactly what he had said. The Tradition began as follows: 'When the **muezzin** poured out (Ar., **sakaba**).' **Sakaba** means 'pouring out water,' which is to say, when the words of the **muezzin** reach your ears you should repeat what he has said. As soon as Ibn-i Zuhri had cited this Tradition, Maulana Razi ad-din, from the place where he was sitting, said to the person sitting next to him: 'When the **muezzin** is silent (Ar., **sakata**),' meaning that when the **muezzin** has finished speaking and become silent, only then is it appropriate for you to repeat what he has said.' The first person to hear Maulana Razi ad-din's explanation passed it on to another, who passed it on to another, who passed it on to still others, until the comment reached the ears of Ibn-i Zuhri. 'Who is it who suggests this variant reading?' asked Ibn-i Zuhri. 'I did,' volunteered Maulana Razi ad-din. After that Ibn-i Zuhri said: 'Both readings are plausible. We will consult the appropriate books.' When the assembly concluded, they searched the books on Tradition. Although both readings were given, the preferred reading was 'When the **muezzin** is silent (**sakata**).'

"News of this exchange reached the Caliph. He summoned Maulana Razi ad-din. After bestowing honors on him, the Caliph asked the Maulana to teach all those present at his court something about Tradition.

"Eventually Maulana Razi ad-din returned from there to Delhi. Previously in Badaun he had had a teacher of high standing and saintly disposition. This teacher had a book on Tradition called **Mulakhkhas** (*Compendium*). Maulana Razi ad-din had requested that copy from him, but the teacher had not been disposed to lend it out. Now, when Maulana Razi ad-din, heaped with honors and distinction, reentered Delhi, he commented to someone: 'Once there was a teacher of mine who refused to lend me a copy of **Mulakhkhas.** Today a hundred persons like him would like to come and learn from me about Tradition!' Someone reported what he had said to his former teacher. 'Alas,' remarked the teacher, 'it appears that his pilgrimage has not been accepted, for had it been accepted, he would not have spoken in this vein!' "

The master—may God remember him with favor—when he had

narrated this remark, began to sob. His eyes flooded with tears as he reflected on the sincere faith of this saintly teacher from Badaun.

After that they brought out food. "You have prepared **tharid** (bread crumbs dipped in milk)," he observed. "Once there was a group of dervishes. They were sitting before Shaykh Baha' ad-din Zakariya—may God have mercy upon him. Food was served. The Shaykh began to eat from the same dish as others. But then he noticed one dervish making **tharid** and then eating it. 'Glory be to God,' exclaimed the Shaykh. 'In the midst of these dervishes there is one who knows how to eat food!' "

After that the master—may God remember him with favor—observed: "The Prophet—peace be upon him—once declared that **tharid** was as superior to other foods as he was to other prophets and 'A'isha to other women! And God knows best [whether the Prophet really said this]!"

III. Assembly 10
Sunday, 4th of Rajab, A.H. 713 (25 October 1313)

I obtained the good fortune of kissing his hand. Conversation turned to CONGREGATIONAL PRAYER. He spoke at length on this topic. "Even if there be but two people," he insisted, "they still must offer congregational prayer. Although two people do not constitute a congregation, they will nonetheless attain the reward of congregational prayer since they offered their prayer standing side by side."

He continued: "Once the Prophet—peace be upon him—wanted to offer congregational prayer, but no one was present except 'Abdallah ibn 'Abbas. The Prophet—peace be upon him—took him by the hand and made him stand next to him. When the Prophet—peace be upon him—finished saying the initial 'God is Great!' (**Allahu Akbar**), 'Abdallah retreated from his position and moved behind the Prophet—peace be upon him. The Prophet—peace be upon him—taking 'Abdallah by the hand, drew him back to his side, and then resumed his prayer. After the initial **Allahu Akbar,** 'Abdallah again retreated to a position behind the Prophet—peace be upon him. This kept happening till the Prophet—peace be upon him—exclaimed: 'Why do you insist on moving behind me?' 'How can I be so bold,' replied 'Abdallah ibn 'Abbas, 'that I might presume to stand and pray beside the Apostle of the Lord of the Universe?' The Prophet—peace be upon him—was pleased at 'Abdallah's sense of propriety. Invoking blessings on his behalf, he prayed: 'O God, deepen this man's knowledge of religion!' " After that the master

—may God remember him with favor—observed: "Among the companions of the Prophet, after the Commander of the Faithful ʿAli, ʿAbdallah ibn ʿAbbas was the most conversant in religious matters—may God be pleased with all of them."

In connection with this same ʿAbdallah, the master noted: "There are three ʿAbdallahs: ʿAbdallah ibn ʿAbbas, ʿAbdallah ibn Masʿud, and ʿAbdallah ibn ʿUmar." He then told a story about ʿAbdallah ibn Masʿud. "In his youth he had been a shepherd. Then one day the Prophet—peace and blessings be upon him—and Abu Bakr Siddiq—may God be pleased with him—went to a mountain pass where he was grazing his sheep. The Prophet—peace be upon him—approached ʿAbdallah, asking for some milk. 'I am only safeguarding this milk,' replied the shepherd; 'how can I give it away?' 'But this is the Prophet of God,' declared Abu Bakr Siddiq, 'and I am his friend. What would it matter if you milked the sheep and gave him some of it?' 'I have been entrusted with these sheep,' protested ʿAbdallah. 'No one has granted me the right to give away milk. How can I do it?' After that the Prophet—peace be upon him—said: 'Bring a sheep that has never been mated.' ʿAbdallah complied, bringing the Prophet a young female sheep. The Prophet—peace be upon him—put his blessed hand on the back of the sheep, and lo, milk appeared from the sheep, and they drank it. Then the Prophet, turning to ʿAbdallah ibn Masʿud, said: 'Come! Join the circle of my companions!'

"This ʿAbdallah ibn Masʿud," continued the master—may God remember him with favor, "was very short. The Prophet—peace be upon him—used to say of him: 'He is a little (shepherd's) purse of wisdom,' and it was from this nickname 'little purse of wisdom' that we know he was a short man. That small satchel," the master added, "that dervishes sew and call **kinf** (purse) should be called **kunaif** (little purse), because that is what the Prophet called ʿAbdallah ibn Masʿud: 'little purse of wisdom.' "

After that in this same connection, he told the story of a man named Raʾis: "He swore allegiance to Shaykh Qutb ad-din Bakhtiyar—may God sanctify his lofty secret. One night in a dream this Raʾis saw a dome and people were gathered around that dome and he saw a short man who kept entering and leaving that dome and the people would give him requests and he would go in and come out with an answer. This Raʾis said: 'I asked: "What is inside the dome? And this short man who keeps going in and out of the dome, who is he?" They replied: "Inside the dome is the Prophet of God—peace be upon him—and this man who comes out, brings in people's requests, then gives them the Prophet's reply—this man is ʿAbdallah ibn Masʿud." ' Raʾis continued: 'I went to ʿAbdallah ibn Masʿud (in my dream) and said: "Petition the Prophet—peace be upon him—that I wish to see him." ʿAbdallah ibn Masʿud went in and came out. "The Prophet of God says: 'You are not yet worthy to see me. But go, convey my greetings to Bakhtiyar Kaki and tell him: "The gift of invocations (**durud**) that you send me every evening did not arrive the last three evenings. There seems to be an obstacle." ' " '

"This Raʾis said: 'I woke up and immediately went to see Shaykh al-Islam Qutb ad-din Bakhtiyar—may God illumine his grave. I said: "The Prophet of God greets you." Shaykh Qutb ad-din—may God sanctify his lofty secret—when he heard that the Prophet sent greetings, stood up and asked: "What did the Prophet—blessings and peace be upon him—say?" I repeated what I had been told: "The gift that you send me every night has not arrived these last three nights. There seems to be an obstacle." Shaykh Qutb ad-din—may God sanctify his lofty secret—had just taken a bride. He summoned her, paid her the dowry which was her due, and then divorced her; for it happened that during the three nights after their wedding he had neglected to send that gift of invocations to the Prophet—peace be upon him.' "

After that the master—may God remember him with favor—noted that every evening Shaykh Qutb ad-din—may his reward be great—would offer three thousand invocations to the Prophet before going to sleep.

Concerning THE LOFTY SPIRITUAL STATUS OF SHAYKH QUTB AD-DIN—may God be very merciful to him—the master told this story. "Shaykh Baha ad-din Zakariya, together with Shaykh Jalal ad-din Tabrizi and Shaykh Qutb ad-din Bakhtiyar—may God be merciful to all of them—were once in Multan. An army of infidels had camped out at the foot of the minaret of Multan. The Governor of Multan was Qibacha. One night Shaykh Qutb ad-din—may God sanctify his lofty secret—handed an arrow to Qibacha. 'Shoot this arrow in the general direction of that infidel army,' he instructed Qibacha. Qibacha did as he was told. When daybreak came, not one of the infidels was to be seen; they had all fled!"

## III. Assembly 11

Wednesday, the 24th of Rajab, A.H. 713 (14 November 1313)

I had the good fortune to kiss his feet. [He then spoke in complex, grammatical terms about THE COMMENTARY **KASHSHAF** and the distinction which it and other Qur'an commentaries make between inflecting the word **hamd** 'praise' (the first word in the Holy Qur'an after the introductory phrase **bismillah ar-rahman ar-rahim,** discussed above) and the word which follows it **lillah** 'to God.' Commentators disagree on how to inflect **hamd** while they all concur on the inflection of **lillah.**]

The master, after describing these distinctions, observed: "I have drawn my own conclusions from this and here is what I have concluded: 'The **dal** of **hamd** resembles someone who has a spiritual master, for the spiritual master commands him to do this or that, that is, to be flexible, while the initial **lam** of **lillah** resembles someone who has no spiritual master; he remains exactly as he is, that is, inflexible and unchanging!' "

Conversation then turned to THE COMPILER OF THE **KASHSHAF** AND HIS BELIEFS. The master—may God remember him with favor—observed: "Despite the fact that he was extremely knowledgeable, his faith was null and void." Then he added: "There is unbelief. There is innovation. There is disobedience. Innovation is worse than disobedience, and unbelief is still worse, yet innovation borders on unbelief." [The implication is that Zamakhshari (d. 1144 A.D.), the famed compiler of the **Kashshaf,** despite his grammatical and rhetorical insights, was nonetheless prone to innovation and, therefore, guilty of unbelief.]

After that he told an anecdote, which he himself had heard from Maulana Sadr ad-din Qunyawi [or Kauli?]. "Once I chanced upon Maulana Najm al-Din Sunami," reported Maulana Sadr ad-din. 'What are you doing?' he asked me. 'I am studying Qur'an commentaries,' I replied. 'Which ones?' '**Kashshaf** and **Ijaz** and **'Umdah.**' 'Burn **Kashshaf** and **Ijaz,**' replied Maulana Najm al-Din, 'but keep on reading **'Umdah.**' This directive caused me anxiety," noted Maulana Sadr ad-din. 'Why do you speak in this manner?' I asked Maulana Najm al-Din. 'Because Shaykh Baha ad-din Zakariya—may God have mercy upon him—has said this very same thing,' was his reply. But this exchange continued to perplex me," confessed Maulana Sadr ad-din. "When evening came, I resorted to reading all three commentaries in front of a lamp. I placed **Ijaz** and **Kashshaf** below and **'Umdah** on top of the other two. Sleep overcame me. Suddenly a fire broke out. I woke up, only to find that **Kashshaf** and **Ijaz,** though underneath, had been burnt to a crisp, while **'Umdah** remained unscathed!"

The master then told another story. "Shaykh Sadr ad-din—may

God have mercy upon him—once wanted to study the grammatical text **Mufassal** (also written by Zamakhsahri). He asked his father's permission. Shaykh Baha ad-din Zakariya—may God have mercy upon him—replied. 'Be patient tonight. Wait till evening has passed.' That night Shaykh Sadr ad-din had a dream in which he saw a captive being dragged in chains. 'Who is this?' he asked. 'It is Zamakhshari, the compiler of **Mufassal**,' they replied. 'We are carting him off to Hell!' And God knows the truth!"

### III. Assembly 12
### Wednesday, the 7th of Shaʿban for the Favored Community, A.H. 713 (27 November 1313)

I obtained the good fortune of kissing his feet. One of those present told a story. "Once while on a journey I came to a spot that was said to be the grave of the prophet Hud—peace be upon him. It was a big grave—long and wide. The people who inhabited that region did not speak my language, nor did I speak theirs. I arrived there hungry, not having eaten for some days. They made some local preparation for me, a dairy dish with milk poured on top. So hungry was I that I devoured it." The master—may God remember him with favor—observed: "To be such a person in such a place with such a group of people is very difficult indeed."

The narrator of this story had also brought with him a carrot-based sweet dish. The master then told a story about this kind of sweet dish. He had himself heard this story from Maulana ʿAziz Zahid—may God have mercy upon him. "I and Maulana Burhan ad-din Kabuli, who later became the associate judge of Delhi, were fellow students," reported Maulana ʿAziz Zahid. Once Maulana Burhan ad-din came into possession of two gold **tankas** [equivalent in value to approximately 1,000 **dirams**]. 'Of these two **tankas**,' he said, 'I will expend one for a copy of the Qurʾan that I might became a person of substance, that is, that I might became prosperous and powerful.' And he did just that: He purchased a copy of the Qurʾan with one **tanka**. On that same day he happened to call on His Excellency Jamal ad-din Nishapuri, the Chief Magistrate of Delhi. They served food, including a carrot-based sweet dish. The Chief Magistrate placed that sweet dish before Maulana Burhan ad-din. 'How do you like it?' he asked. Replied Maulana Burhan ad-din: 'Students eat so much dry bread that they cannot gauge how a carrot-based sweet dish should taste!' The magistrate was very pleased with this remark. It made such an impression on him that he signaled his attendants to fetch twenty or thirty **tankas** and present them to the Maulana. Subsequently Maulana Burhan ad-din acquired much wealth and influence. He obtained a Delhi judgeship, along with other amenities. In short, his sincere intent produced appropriate effects!"

## III. Assembly 13

Friday, the last day of the blessed month of Ramadan,
A.H. 713 (18 January 1314)[62]

I had the benefit of kissing his feet. Conversation turned to JUSTICE AND TYRANNY. The master—may God remember him with favor—remarked: "Between God and man there are two kinds of relationship, between man and man, three kinds. The relationship of God to man is characterized by either justice or kindness. But the relationship of man to man can be marked by justice, kindness, or oppression. If people are just or kind to one another, God will be kind to them. But if people are oppressive or unjust with one another, God will judge them accordingly, and He will mete out the appropriate punishment, even if the offender be the prophet of his time!"

At this point I interjected: "Your reference to 'the prophet of his time' accords with what has been reported of the Prophet Muhammad—peace be upon him—namely, that he said: 'If tomorrow on the Day of Judgment God Almighty were to send me and my brother Jesus to Hell, that would be justice!' " "Yes," rejoined the master, "the whole universe is His domain. Whoever regulates what takes place in his own domain cannot be called unjust or oppressive. Oppression arises only when one intrudes into another's domain."

Then the master spoke on THE EXTREMITY OF THE ASHʿARITE VIEW CONCERNING DIVINE DETERMINATION. "The Ashʿarites," he explained, "reason that it is all right if God Almighty sends a believer to Hell and keeps him there forever, just as it is all right if He sends an unbeliever to Heaven and permits him to stay there indefinitely. In our tradition, however, such is not the case, for in the Holy Qurʾan God Almighty has declared: 'Are those equal, those who know and those who do not know?' (Q.39.9) and again, 'Say: Are the blind to be considered equal to those who see? Will you not recognize (the difference between them?)' (Q.7.50). That is to say, the ignorant are not the same as the wise, nor the blind like those who have sight.

Many other scriptural passages convey the same point. Now, out of His wisdom it is requisite that He send the believer to Paradise, the infidel to Hell, for He is wise and He acts in accordance with His wisdom. Consider a man of wealth. He chooses to expend all that he has, but if he went and pitched his entire wealth down a well, would that be wise?"

Then the master reflected on THE FATE OF THE BELIEVER. "If the believer leaves this world without repenting, there are three possible outcomes. It would be fitting if God Almighty, due to the blessing of that man's faith, forgave him, or if God Almighty, out of His own bounteous grace, forgave him, or it might be due to the intercession of some third party that He would forgive him. If, on the other hand, God Almighty sent him to Hell, he would be punished there in accordance with the degree of his sin, but then he would be transferred to Heaven. Because he had died a believer he would not remain in Hell forever."

### III. Assembly 14
Tuesday, 11th of Shawwal, A.H. 713 (29 January 1314)

I had the good fortune of kissing his feet. On that day I brought a slave of mine named Bashir. After informing the master that he performed his prayers regularly, I explained that this same slave had persistently asked me to be brought before the master, that he might receive the benefit of becoming a disciple. Since the generosity of the master—may God remember him with favor—knows no bounds, he agreed to this request. Turning to me, he asked: "Do you give this slave permission to take the oath of loyalty to me?" "Yes, I do," I replied. The master extended the hand of discipleship to Bashir, and giving him a hat, he commanded him to go and pray two cycles of prayer.

When the slave had left, the master told the following story. "Some time ago a dervish had come from Bihar. Wearing an elegant cloak, he alighted at the hospice of Shaykh ʿAli Sijzi—on whom may God be merciful and forgiving. He began begging everywhere from everyone. Shaykh ʿAli reproved him: 'When you are attired in such a garment, it is unseemly to go about begging. I will give you some money. Be satisfied with that amount. Use it to engage in trade, and when you become prosperous, see that other dervishes share in your prosperity.' Having said this, he gave the fine-clad dervish 500 **jitals.** The dervish took the money and began trading. After awhile he had earned thirty **tankas.** Through further trade, that thirty **tankas** became one hundred **tankas,** and with that hundred **tankas** he bought slaves. Shaykh ʿAli advised him: 'Take these slaves to Ghazni, where the potential for profit is still greater.' The dervish obeyed.

"Now among his slaves that dervish had one named Muʿtamid (lit., 'faithful,' 'reliable'). He invited that slave to become his disciple and the slave accepted. The dervish then shaved his head and donned him with a cap. 'This is the cap of Sayyid Ahmad,' declared the dervish, implying that he, too, belonged to the family of Sayyid Ahmad.

"In short, when they arrived in Ghazni, he sold the slaves for a great profit. Some people also wanted to buy the slave Muʿtamid. 'How can I sell him?' protested the dervish; 'he is my disciple.' But demand for that slave grew by leaps and bounds, till his price became four times that fetched by other slaves. The dervish had a change of heart and at last decided to sell Muʿtamid. As the buyers gathered around to determine who would be the lucky one allowed to buy that slave, Muʿtamid began to cry. 'Master,' he implored, turning to the dervish, 'that day that I became your disciple, you put a cap on my head and declared: "This is the cap of Sayyid Ahmad." Now you are about to sell me. Tomorrow, on the Day of Judgment, when they bring both of us before Sayyid Ahmad, what will happen?' The slave's words softened the heart of his master. Turning to the prospective buyers, he announced: 'As you are my witnesses, I am setting this slave free!' "

When the master—may God remember him with favor—had arrived at this point in the story, I also agreed to set free my slave. The master—may God remember him with favor—was very pleased. "You have done well. Indeed, you have done what is right!" Then, with the utmost kindness and compassion, he removed the hat from his blessed head and placed it on mine. Praise be to God, the Lord of the Universe!

### III. Assembly 15
Thursday, 27th of Shawwal, A.H. 713 (14 February 1314)

I had the benefit of kissing his feet. Conversation turned to EXPENDING ONE'S MONEY. The master stated: "Whenever the world is favorable to someone, he should expend his funds (on behalf of others), for it will not be a loss to him, and whenever the world turns its face away from someone, he should still expend his funds on others, for when he himself faces death, it is better for him to have given away his own funds (than to have left the task to others)."

Then he made a comment about SHAYKH NAJIB AD-DIN MU-

TAWAKKIL—may God have mercy upon him. "Shaykh Najib ad-din made the same point in the following [pithy lyric]:

> Whatever comes, give it away; there's no pain.
> And what does not come, don't fret; it brings no gain."

### III. Assembly 16
Friday, 11th of the blessed month of Dhu'l-Hijja,
A.H. 713 (29 March 1314)

I obtained the benefit of kissing his hand. Conversation focused on THE MEN OF GOD: Every morsel that they eat they EAT WITH THEIR FOCUS ON GOD. He recollected that Shaykh Shihab ad-din —may God sanctify his lofty secret—in **ʿAwarif al-Maʿarif** cited the example of a dervish who at every meal before taking a bite to eat would utter aloud: 'I take (this) in (the name of) God!' "

### III. Assembly 17
Monday, 21st of the blessed month of Dhu'l-Hijja, A.H. 713 (8 April 1314)

I obtained the benefit of kissing his feet. "Are you coming from the army compound or from the city?" he asked. "From the army compound," I replied, "for it is there that I have my home." "Do you ever go to the city?" "Once every ten to twelve days. Otherwise I stay in the army compound and say the congregational prayer at the Kilogarhi mosque." "That is the right thing to do," remarked the master, "since the air is better in the army compound than in the city, and the city is also filthy!"

In this vein he began to speak of DISTINCTIVE TIMES. "Some times," he noted, "are distinguished from others. The Festival Day, for instance, is set apart from other days as a day for general celebration. Similarly, there may be a place in which one can find comfort such as is available nowhere else. But a dervish should be the kind of person who has passed beyond considerations of time or place. He should not be uplifted by any joy or depressed by any sorrow. He should be the sort of person who has gone beyond the domain of this world, so much so that when he speaks, his heart remains focused on God: His tongue should be the instrument of his heart, his heart the instrument of God!"

Then the pearl-scattering tongue of the master declared: "I first heard about these guidelines for dervishes from Maulana ʿImad ad-din

Sunami. Once I had come to the royal reservoir (**hauz-i shamsi**). He had also come there. We sat together and discoursed on this topic. It was a wonderful time. About three or four years passed. We met again, but this time the Maulana showed none of that insight which had enlivened our earlier meeting." Concluded the master: "He had become engrossed in worldly concerns."

Then the master spoke about SHAYKH JALAL AD-DIN TABRIZI—may God sanctify his lofty secret. "Shaykh Jalal ad-din came to Delhi but then, after some time, left. As he was leaving, he observed: 'When I came into this city I was pure gold. Now I have turned to silver. What will I become next (if I remain here)?' "

Conversation shifted to **SAMAʿ**. I submitted: "I am bewildered in my devotional life. As for that obedience to prayer, ritual observance, and recitation of litanies that mark a true devotee, I am lacking. But when I listen to **samaʿ**, I am overcome with delight and I experience inner comfort, in the same way that when I am in the purifying presence of my master, I am released from selfish desires, worldly pursuits, and the claim of others upon me." "Are you free of such attachments this very moment?" asked the master. "Yes, I am," I replied.

"**Samaʿ** is of two kinds," he remarked. "One is invasive, the other is noninvasive. The former invades (the body). For instance, on hearing a voice or a line of poetry, one experiences great agitation. This is called invasive **samaʿ**, and it cannot be explained. As for noninvasive **samaʿ**, it happens like this: When one hears a verse in **samaʿ**, (one is drawn out of one's self). One links that verse to another realm, whether to God, or to one's spiritual master, or to some other realm that rules the heart." Praise be to God the Lord of the Universe!

And God knows the truth; this concludes Fascicle III.

## Fascicle IV (Hereafter IV)

In the name of God full of Compassion, ever Compassionate.

These lines from the pages of light (**nur**) and words from tablets of delight (**surur**) have been compiled from the perfect words and comprehensive signs of the munificent master, the sovereign of the domain of divine secrets, the unquestioned king of spiritual masters, the undisputed pole of the poles upholding the universe, the Nizam of Truth, of Guidance, and of Faith—may God favor the Muslims by lengthening his life. Amen.

These lines have been compiled from the beginning of the month of Muharram in the year A.H. 714.

I grasp my master's weighty words like that firm rope
Which, deep down into the abyss of pain, does reach.
Now, through the words of my Shaykh here gathered, may God
In His grace forgive Hasan's ev'ry deed and speech.[63]

### IV. Assembly 1
Wednesday, the 24th of Muharram, A.H. 714 (10 May 1314)

I had the benefit of kissing his feet. This day, as requested, I presented him with the first fascicle of **Morals for the Heart.** When he had reviewed it, he expressed his satisfaction. "You have written well," he observed, "and you write in a style suitable to dervishes. You have also chosen an apt title."

In this same connection he began talk about ABU HURAIRA—may God be pleased with him. "At the battle of Khaibar Abu Huraira professed faith in Islam, and even though the Prophet—peace be upon him—lived for only three years after that battle, Abu Huraira recorded so many Traditions during those three years that if one listed all the Traditions of all the Prophet's other companions, they would not equal the number of Traditions from Abu Huraira." Continued the master: "They asked him how it could happen that he had remembered so many Traditions in such a short period, while other companions, who had been with the Prophet far longer, did not remember very many Traditions. 'The Prophet—peace be upon him,' explained Abu Huraira, 'assigned every companion a specific task but I had the privilege of being in his personal service and so I remembered much more about him.' "

Then the master told an anecdote about Abu Huraira. "One day Abu Huraira—may God be pleased with him—was attending the Prophet—blessings and peace be upon him. 'O Prophet of God,' he complained, 'whatever I hear from your blessed tongue I memorize, yet there are some Traditions that I cannot recollect.' The Prophet—peace be upon him—remarked: 'When I begin to speak, spread out the fold of your garment. When I have finished speaking, slowly pull in that fold and then place your hand on your chest. If you do, you will recall all that you have heard from me.' "

After that he commented about OTHER COMPANIONS' TRANSMISSION OF TRADITIONS. "The Commander of the Faithful Abu Bakr Siddiq—may God be pleased with him—during his lifetime only recounted three or four Traditions, while ʿAbdallah ibn ʿAbbas transmitted less than ten. As for ʿAbdallah ibn Masʿud, even though he was a renowned religious scholar, he had only one Tradition to his credit. The day that he recounted this Tradition he was overcome with fear, so much so that his hairs stood on end and his shoulders shook as he uttered 'I heard from the Prophet of God.' When he had finished narrating the Tradition, he said: 'These are the words (of Muhammad) or their equivalent.' " On the blessed tongue of the master—may God remember him with favor—came this observation: "The reciters of Tradition, when they have finished their recitation, say 'These are the words (of Muhammad) or their equivalent,' and they do so because of what ʿAbdallah ibn Masʿud said."

Conversation then turned to THE COMPANIONS OF THE PROPHET—peace and blessings be upon them. "Among his companions," noted the master, "were the four righteous Caliphs and the three ʿAbdallahs (cited above)."

Then he alluded to THE COMMANDER OF THE FAITHFUL ʿALI—may God be pleased with him. "Once the Prophet—peace and salutations be upon him—extolled ʿAli when speaking with the other companions. 'The most judicious among you is ʿAli',' he said, 'and whoever is the most judicious must also be the most learned.' "

Next he spoke about the HARMONY that prevailed AMONG THE COMPANIONS. "A companion was once sitting in a group," he noted, "and someone sitting behind the person who was sitting behind him kept saying: 'I heard from the Prophet—peace be upon him—that he said that on such-and-such a day I was in such-and-such a place, along with Abu Bakr and ʿUmar.' The companion turned around to see who it was who was narrating this story. When he looked he recognized the

Commander of the Faithful ʿAli—may God be pleased with him. The purpose of telling this story," concluded the master, "was to explain the harmony that distinguished relations among the companions."

In stressing how considerate and fair-minded they were toward each other, he told a story about ʿUMAR. "Once ʿUmar said: 'O would that I were but a curl of hair on the chest of Abu Bakr'—may God be pleased with both of them!"

### IV. Assembly 2
### Sunday, 28th of Muharram, A.H. 714 (14 May 1314)

I had the benefit of kissing his hand. He began to talk about a dervish. "He was a dear person," remarked the master. "Everyone who distances himself from the contamination of the world is dear," he observed, "but whoever tries to be dear while also allowing himself to be contaminated by the world, he will not be dear for long!" A line of verse came on his blessed lips:

> Unless you be pure, His fire will never set you ablaze.

To which he added:

> Unless you be dust, His water will not become your waves.

Then conversation turned to the subject of what day of the month it was. It was either the twenty-eighth or the twenty-ninth of Ramadan. The master told a story about LAHORE. "Once in Lahore people cited the moon on the evening of the twenty-seventh or twenty-eighth of the month of Ramadan [marking the end of fasting and preparation for its sequel, the lesser festival of celebration]. But it happened in that particular year that for three continuous months prior to Ramadan the citizens of Lahore had not seen the new moon because at the end of each month cloud and mist had blocked their view. When three months had elapsed they at last did see the new moon [at the correct time, i.e., about three days ahead of when they expected to see it!], and then realized their error.

"This oversight," noted the master, "was among the ominous signs portending THE DESTRUCTION OF LAHORE. Another ominous sign was its traders. For in those days some traders had gone from Lahore to Gujarat. Gujarat was then ruled by Hindus. When they enquired from the Lahore traders about the price of their goods, the traders inflated the price of every item, so that what was worth ten dirams they quoted as twenty, and what was worth twenty they quoted as forty. In effect, they doubled the price of all the items that they were trading. Afterward, at the time of finalizing the sales, they lowered their prices, selling their goods for roughly half the figures they had originally quoted. The Hindus of that region were not used to such practices. When they sold goods they fixed a fair price and stuck to that price. Having seen how the Lahore traders did business, one of them asked: 'Where do you come from?' 'We are from Lahore,' was the reply. 'In your city is this how people conduct business?' 'Yes!' 'And your city still thrives?' 'Yes!' 'It cannot be,' retorted the Hindu, 'that a city which engages in such practices will thrive for long!' And it happened that as the Lahore traders were making their way home, they were informed en route that the Mongols had invaded their city and reduced it to rubble!"

## IV. Assembly 3

Tuesday, 12th of the month of Safar—may God conclude it with success —A.H. 714 (28 May 1314)

I had the good fortune of kissing his hand. He began to speak about those who perform miracles and claim divine inspiration. "There is no substance to their claims," he declared. Then on his blessed lips came this expression (in Arabic): " 'God Almighty has commanded His saints to conceal their miracles (**karamat**), just as He has commanded His prophets to demonstrate theirs (**muʿjizat**).' Since anyone who performs a miracle is disobeying God, what sort of work is this?" Then he added: "There are one hundred stages on the spiritual path. The seventeenth stage provides divine inspiration to perform miraculous acts. Now, if the traveler stops at this stage, how will he reach the other eighty-three?"

He next turned to the subject of SERVICE. He cited a Tradition of the Prophet: "The cupbearer who serves water to others should be the last to drink." Then he added: "With respect to food it should be the same rule, since it is not fitting to take food or drink before others if you are the host."

After that he spoke further about the DUTIES OF THE HOST. "It is incumbent on the host to wash his own hands before having the hands of his guests washed. He should first make sure that his own hands are clean. In other words, the rule for washing hands is the inverse of the rule for drinking and eating. In the former case, he should first wash his own hands and afterward have the hands of others washed. In the latter instance, he should provide water for others before taking something to drink himself. In this same connection," he noted, "they have asked whether the one who washes others' hands should remain standing or sit down. He should remain standing. Once," he recalled, "a person brought water to Shaykh Junayd—may God have mercy upon him—intending to wash his hands. But he sat down. Junayd immediately stood up. 'Why do you do that?' they asked. 'It is the rule,' replied Junayd, 'that you remain standing when washing others' hands, and so when he sat down I had to stand up!' "

After that he commented on IMAM SHAFI'I—may God have mercy upon him. "Once he was being hosted by a friend. That friend wrote down on a piece of paper the food that he wanted served and gave it to a maidservant. 'Prepare all the items that I have listed,' he instructed her and then left the house to attend to some other affairs. Imam Shafi'i asked the maidservant for that piece of paper and then noted on it the names of some other dishes that he wanted. When the maidservant read the list she prepared all the items that Imam Shafi'i had requested and, for good measure, made more of each of them than the other dishes. The master of the house returned. The meal was served. It was an abundance of food, much more than the master had ordered. On seeing this, he got up and going to the maid, confronted her: 'Why have you prepared such an excess?' The maid showed him the piece of paper. As soon as he realized that the added items were the notations of Imam Shafi'i, the master became very pleased, so pleased that he set free that maidservant, as well as all the other slaves of his household!"

The master then began to speak about HOSPITALITY and concern for conditions of hosting and serving food. "There was a dervish in Baghdad," he recalled, "who daily would serve 1,200 bowls of food and he would personally supervise their preparation and cooking. One day he called a meeting of his servants and asked: 'Did you not overlook someone while you were serving food?' 'No, we remembered everyone,' they replied. 'Think carefully,' insisted the Shaykh. 'No,' they rejoined, 'we have forgotten no one. At the time of serving food we provide it to everyone who comes to be fed.' But again the Shaykh remarked: 'Something has gone awry in this procedure.' 'O Shaykh,' implored the servants, 'what is the intent of your line of questioning?' 'For the past three days,' explained the Shaykh, 'you have given me no food. Everytime you forget me. Why don't you forget others?' Now it happened that during those three days at mealtime no one had brought food to the Shaykh. Since there were so many cooks, some of the cooks presumed that others had served the Shaykh and these others, in turn, had thought that still others must have served him. Everyone thought that someone else had taken care of the Shaykh, with the result that during those three days he had, indeed, been given nothing to eat. Yet it was only after three days had elapsed that the Shaykh at last reprimanded his servants!"

The master then told a further story about THE SWEETNESS AND BENEFIT OF WATER FROM THE ROYAL RESERVOIR (**hauz-i shamsi**). "Some people reported that in a dream after his death they had seen Sultan Shams ad-din (Iltetmish). They asked: 'How has God—may He be glorified and exalted—been treating you?' 'He has been merciful to me on account of this reservoir' was the reply. And God knows [the truth of whether such a dream dialogue actually transpired]."

IV. Assembly 4
Wednesday, 27th of Safar, A.H. 714 (12 May 1314)

I obtained the benefit of kissing his feet. The previous day I had consulted with the esteemed Nasir ad-din Mahmud—may God safeguard him—who is among the most faithful of the master's disciples.[64] I had consulted with him concerning the fact that the tomorrow would be Wednesday, the last day of the month of Safar. It is a day which many people consider to be inauspicious. "Come!" I said to him, "let us go to the master who can convert the inauspicious into the auspicious, so that every day becomes favorable."

When Wednesday arrived, we both called on the master and told him what we had discussed on the previous day. Smiling he said: "Yes, men consider this day to be ill-fated but they do not know what causes a particular day to be favored. This day is, in fact, highly auspicious, so much so that a child born today would become a saint."

The master then began to speak about PERSONS PRONE TO SUDDEN CHANGES IN MOOD. On his blessed lips came this observation: "Those who have a sensitive temperament are more likely to shift quickly." In this connection he quoted the following verse from Maulana Fakhr ad-din Razi:

Even half the smallest speck exceeds my desire,
For less than half that half is all that I require.
More subtle than water is my disposition:

Hurry, take hold of me, before I turn to fire.

He then spoke about THE MOOD SHIFT OF KINGS. "The Prophet once reported that God Almighty had said: 'The hearts of kings are in My hand.' In other words, as long as people maintain a proper relationship with God Almighty, He will dispose the hearts of their kings to be kindly to them, but when the people stray from God, He will turn the hearts of their kings against them." After that on his blessed lips came this pronouncement: "One must maintain one's focus on God, for everything that comes into being comes from Him."

In the same connection, he told a story about QIBACHA. "At the time when Qibacha held sway in Multan and Sultan Shams ad-din (Iltetmish) ruled Delhi, an enmity developed between them. Shaykh Baha ad-din Zakariya—may God be merciful to him—and the Qazi of Multan both wrote letters to Sultan Shams ad-din and both these letters found their way into the hand of Qibacha. Qibacha was furious. After having the Qazi killed, he summoned the Shaykh to his palace. The Shaykh proceeded to the royal court in the same way that he always visited there, without fear or awe! He sat down on the right hand of Qibacha as was his custom. Qibacha handed him the letter which he had written.

"Having examined it, the Shaykh declared, 'Yes, I wrote this letter; it is my handwriting.' 'Why did you write it?' asked Qibacha. 'Whatever I have written,' replied the Shaykh, 'I have written because it is true and I have also written it for the sake of Truth (i.e., God). As for you, do what you want. By yourself, what can you do? What rests in your hands?' Qibacha, when he heard this reply, pondered what to do. He ordered them to bring some food. It was his intent to trap the Shaykh, for it was not the Shaykh's custom to eat food in someone else's home. Qibacha reasoned that when the Shaykh refused to eat, that would be the pretext for punishing him. As soon as the food was served, everyone began eating. The Shaykh, after saying 'In the name of God full of Compassion, ever Compassionate,' also picked up some food and began to eat. When Qibacha saw this, his anger subsided. There was nothing he could do, and the Shaykh returned home safely."

There was a problem I had been pondering and that day I decided to broach it with the master. The problem was this: Which of two disciples is superior, that disciple who neglects the canonical prayers and says few invocations but feels much love for his master and is wholly reliant on him, or that other disciple who is faultlessly obedient, says innumerable invocations, and also goes on the hajj yet loves his master little and trusts him haltingly? "The one who loves his master and relies on him," replied the master. Then on his blessed lips came this pronouncement: "The disciple who loves and trusts in his master gains in one moment a spiritual benefit greater than that gained in all the obedient moments of that other disciple."

But then he reminded me about THE SUPERIORITY OF PROPHETS OVER SAINTS. "Some assert," he noted, "that saints are superior to prophets because prophets spend most of their time with people, but this assertion is false, for even though prophets are engaged with people, those few moments that they do spend with God are of more worth than all the spiritual moments of saints."

He told a further story about AN ISRAELITE ASCETIC. "This ascetic was seventy years old. He obeyed God—may He be glorified and exalted—but after seventy years he had a need. He asked God Almighty to meet that need. His need was not satisfied. He then retired to a secluded place and began to contend with his lower self: 'O self,' he exclaimed, 'for seventy years you have obeyed God—may He be glorified and exalted. Yet you were lacking in your profession of sincerity. If you had been fully sincere in your obedience, then that need would have been fulfilled.' While he was still contending with his lower self, the prophet of that time received a command: 'Go tell that ascetic: "Your single moment of rebuking your lower self is more precious to me than the seventy years of your obedience!" ' "

## IV. Assembly 5

Tuesday, 17th of the blessed month of Rabiʿ al-awwal,
A.H. 714 (1 July 1314)

I had the good fortune of kissing his hand. One of those present asked THE MEANING OF ʿ**URS.** "ʿ**URS,**" he replied, "may mean the celebration of a wedding, or it may mean the decamping of a caravan for the night."

Conversation then turned to THE SPIRITUAL STATURE OF THE SHAYKHS, THEIR SINCERITY AND THEIR ATTENTIVENESS, BOTH TO THE SECRET [OF THEIR RELATIONSHIP WITH GOD] AND ALSO TO CALLING ON GOD. In this connection he told a story about Shaykh Najib ad-din Mutawwakil—may God be merciful to him. "Once Shaykh Najib ad-din asked his Eminence Shaykh al-Islam Farid ad-din—may God sanctify his lofty secret: 'It is rumored that when you are praying, after you say "O

Lord!" you hear the reply: "I am present, my creature!" ' 'No, that is not true,' replied the Shaykh. 'Rumors are the mid-wives of facts' [i.e., what they produce are fictions, not facts].' Again Shaykh Najib ad-din asked: 'It is also rumored that the esteemed Khidr visits you.' 'No, that, too, is untrue,' replied the Shaykh. Shaykh Najib ad-din persisted: 'Some say that men of the Unseen call on you.' The Shaykh did not deny this statement but instead quipped: 'You, too [Najib ad-din], may be one of God's special deputies [i.e., those seventy persons of each generation to whom, it is said, the world owes its continued existence].' "

The master then began to speak about THE SPIRITUAL PROWESS OF SHAYKH FARID AD-DIN—may God illumine his grave—AND ALSO THE SPIRITUAL PROWESS OF HIS PIOUS MOTHER—may God be pleased with both of them and show them His mercy. "The piety of parents has a powerful influence on their children," he observed. "The mother of the Shaykh was a devout person. One night a thief broke into her home. Everyone was asleep. Only the Shaykh's mother was awake. She was engaged in her devotions to God. As soon as the thief entered, he became blind and could not find a door by which to leave. He cried out: 'If there be a man in this house, let him be as my father or brother. If there be a woman, let her be as my mother or sister. Whoever it may be, I know that it is due to her/his reverence for God that I have been blinded. Please pray for me that I may regain my sight. I repent of my sins. I swear that for the rest of my life I will never again commit a theft.' The Shaykh's mother prayed for that thief. Regaining his sight, he fled.

"At daybreak the Shaykh's mother told no one about what had transpired during the night. Early that morning a man was seen walking about with a jug of yogurt on his head, followed by the members of his household. 'What's the matter with you?' they asked. 'Last night,' he confessed, 'I broke into a home to rob it. A saintly woman was awake there. Due to her reverence I was blinded. I implored her to pray that I might regain my sight. I vowed that if my vision was restored I would forswear thievery. Now, this very hour, I come, and I bring my entire family with me, to embrace Islam and also to forswear thievery once and for all.' In short, due to the blessing of that woman, they all became Muslims and repented of their lives as thieves. Praise be to God, the Lord of the universe!"

After that conversation turned to THE SPIRITUAL PROWESS OF THE SHAYKH'S MOTHER. The master told the following story. "When Shaykh al-Islam Farid ad-din—may God sanctify his lofty secret—took up residence in Ajodhan, he requested his younger brother Shaykh Najib ad-din to accompany their mother from where she was living (in Kahtwal) to Ajodhan. Shaykh Najib ad-din complied, fetching his mother to bring her to Ajodhan. En route they stopped beneath a tree to rest. Both were thirsty, and Shaykh Najib ad-din went in search of water. On his return he did not find his mother where he had left her. He was aghast. He combed the entire vicinity, looking high and low, near and far. He expended every effort. He looked everywhere but still could not find her. No trace remained of his mother. Distraught, he returned to the great Shaykh—may God sanctify his lofty secret—and told him about what had happened. The Shaykh at once ordered them to prepare some food and offer alms [as was customary for a funeral].

"Some time later it happened that Shaykh Najib ad-din—may God have mercy upon him—was passing in that same area. When he came to the spot beneath the tree where he had stopped with his mother, the thought crossed his mind: 'If I comb this place, I may yet find some trace of my mother.' He began to search in the vicinity of that tree, and lo, he found some bones, some human bones. 'These must be the bones of my mother,' he said to himself. 'Probably a lion or some other beast attacked and killed her.' Collecting all the bones, he put them in a satchel. Then he returned to Shaykh Farid ad-din—may God sanctify his lofty secret—and told him what had happened. 'Bring that satchel to me,' requested the Shaykh. When they brought him the satchel and opened it, lo, they could not find a single bone." The master—may God remember him with favor—when he came to this point in the story, was overcome with tears. "This," he exclaimed, "is among the wonders of our age!"

The master then told a story about MEN FROM THE UNSEEN. "In the first stages [of my spiritual quest] I used to think from time to time that I would like to meet and discourse with them. Then I realized: 'What sort of desire is this? Far better is it to seek some useful end (**maslahati**)!' "

He next told a story about SHAYKH QUTB AD-DIN BAKHTIYAR—may God be exceedingly merciful to him. "In his youth he lived in Oush. On the outskirts of that city there was a dilapidated mosque, and in it was a minaret called 'Seven Minarets,' even though it was but one. The people there, when they wanted to pray for something, believed that if they ascended that minaret and offered a special prayer, they would meet the eminent Khidr. Even though they offered a single prayer, they would call it 'the Seven-fold Prayer'! There was also a two-cycle sequence of prayer which, if offered in the mosque, would cause the person praying to see Khizr.

"Now Shayh Qutb ad-din—may God sanctify his lofty secret—wanted to see Khizr. During one of the nights of Ramadan he went to that mosque. He offered the two-cycle sequence of prayer. He ascended that minaret and, after offering the appropriate prayer, came back down to the mosque. He waited some time. No one appeared. Disappointed, he left the mosque. No sooner had he stepped outside than he saw a man standing nearby. That man called out to Shaykh Qutb ad-din: 'What are you doing in this place at this time of night?' 'I came here,' replied the Shaykh, 'to meet the eminent Khizr. I said two cycles of prayer and I also recited the special prayer, but I never received the benefit [of seeing Khizr]. Now I'm going home.' 'What did you want Khizr to do?' asked the man. 'Khizr is a mere vagabond. Why would someone like you want to see him? Are you looking for worldly gain?' 'No.' 'Do you have to repay a debt?' 'No.' 'Then why do you seek Khizr?' persisted the man. 'In this city there is a man on whose door Khizr has knocked twelve times and still he has not met him!' As they were talking, a luminous stranger in splendid attire appeared. That man who had been talking with Shaykh Qutb ad-din approached the stranger with utmost respect and fell at his feet. Shaykh Qutb ad-din—may God favor his resting place—said: 'After that man got up, he retreated toward me while still facing the stranger. "This dervish," he declared, "does not seek to repay a debt nor to make a worldly gain. He simply wants to meet you." ' At that moment the call to prayer sounded, and from every direction dervishes and Sufis appeared. Forming a congregation, they uttered 'God is Great!' One of them came forward, led the prayers, and in the **tarawih** prayers[65] recited twelve sections of the Qur'an. 'It would have been better,' I thought to myself, 'had he recited still more of the Qur'an!' Then when prayers were done, they all scattered in different directions. 'I returned home,' concluded Shaykh Qutb ad-din. 'The next day, having made my ablutions well before dawn, I went to the same mosque and remained there till daybreak, but no one appeared!' "

## IV. Assembly 6

Friday, the 10th of Jumada al-awwal, A.H. 714 (22 August 1314)

I had the good fortune of kissing his hand. Conversation focused on FORBEARANCE AND GUARDING AGAINST ANGER. "There is the lower self and the heart," he explained. "Whoever gives vent to his lower self must be deflected by one motivated from the heart. That is to say, the lower self is the abode of anger, strife, and discord, while the heart nurtures peace, contentment, and gentleness. Hence, if someone displays the urges of his lower self, another must express the feelings of his heart, since the latter will overpower the former. Imagine if a person were to confront another's lower self with his own lower self! What limits would there be to the anger and strife that resulted?"

Then concerning the benefit of forbearance and compassion, the following verse came on his blessed lips:

> If, like straw, by every breeze you are beckoned,
> No mountain are you; less than straw you are reckoned.

### IV. Assembly 7

Thursday, 4th of Jumada al-akhira, A.H. 714 (15 September 1314)

I obtained the benefit of kissing his feet. He began to speak about THE ACCEPTANCE OF CHARITABLE OFFERINGS. I submitted that I had never sought anything from anyone and in my whole life had never crossed the threshold of relying on someone else, yet if another person, without any prompting on my part, were to offer me something, what should I do? "You must take it," replied the master. Then he told a story. "Once the Prophet—may peace be upon him—gave something to ʿUmar Khattab—may God be pleased with him. The Commander of the Faithful ʿUmar said: 'O Prophet of God, I already have something. Give this to another poor person among the impoverished Companions (**ahl-i suffa**)[66] or their like.' The Prophet—blessings and peace be upon him—said: 'Everything which is given to you unsolicited take and eat of it, then dispose of what is left over as alms.' And praise be to God, the Lord of the universe!"

### IV. Assembly 8

Saturday, 29th of the blessed month of Rajab, A.H. 714 (8 November 1314)

I had the honor of kissing his feet. During the preceding week my salary that had been in arrears was at last paid to me. The master—may God remember him with favor—already knew about my employment and also my recent salary payment. When I came to pay my respects to him, he remarked: "Having employment and persevering in one's work finally yields results!"

Then he added; "Kabir, the grandson of Shaykh al-Islam Farid ad-din, used to frequent the house of Malik Nizam al-Din Kotwal and work for him. But Nizam al-Din once became so upset with Kabir that he summarily dismissed him, saying, 'Leave and don't set foot in this house again!' Kabir departed, but did not feel constrained from returning. A confidant of Nizam al-Din then brought me six gold **tankas** on behalf of Kabir, but I did not accept them. I sent them back. Only when he saw his six gold **tankas** returned to him did Nizam al-Din then give them to Kabir." On his blessed lips came this observation: "Employment in any kind of work, no matter what it be, brings satisfaction."

He was then prompted to tell a story about my belated salary payment, a story the gist of which, thank God, I have remembered. This is the story. "There once was an Israelite ascetic. For years he had scrupulously obeyed God. Then one day a message came to the prophet of that time: 'Go tell that ascetic: "What do you gain from those discomforts caused by your strict observance? I have not created you but for chastisement!" ' As soon as the prophet had given this message to the ascetic, the ascetic got up and began to twirl around. 'Why,' asked the prophet, 'did this disclosure make you so happy that you've started dancing?' 'At least He has remembered me,' replied the ascetic. 'He has taken me into account; I have experienced His reckoning!

Though He speaks of killing me,
That **He** speaks is thrilling to me.' "

Then in connection with FORBEARANCE, he told a story about Shaykh al-Islam Farid ad-din—may God sanctify his lofty secret. It illustrated the Shaykh's forbearance, the effect of which was to undercut people who wished to harm him. On his blessed lips came this pronouncement: "He who kills kills, and the killer becomes known as a killer."

I interjected: "What is the meaning of this supplication: 'Assist me, O servants of God; may God have mercy on you!' " What I wanted to know was this: How can people ask for assistance from other than God? "Those who make this supplication," he replied, "mean by 'servants of God' sincere Muslims and it is right for them to make such a supplication. Saints also have made it, including," he noted, "Shaykh Najib ad-din Mutawakkil—may God have mercy upon him."

He then spoke about THE SPIRITUAL PROWESS OF SHAYKH NAJIB AD-DIN MUTAWAKKIL. "I have not found his equal in this city," he observed. "He does not know which day or which month it is, nor does he know what is the price for grain or meat! Nothing of such matters crosses his mind, so absorbed is he in his devotions to God—may God be exceedingly merciful to him."

He made one final comment about THE ABOVE PRAYER [SUPPLICATING GOD'S SERVANTS FOR ASSISTANCE]. "If a need arises, one should also recite **musabbiʿat-i ʿashr.**"[67] I asked: "Are these to be invoked only at a specified time?" "If an important matter arises," he replied, "whether it be spiritual or mundane, in order to resolve it, one might also recite **musabbiʿat-i ʿashr**ʾ, and by the grace of Almighty God, it might find a happy resolution."

IV. Assembly 9

Thursday, the 4th of the blessed month of Ramadan, A.H. 714 (12 December 1314)

I obtained the benefit of kissing his feet. He began to discuss **TARAWIH**[68] and that group of people who recite the entire Qurʾan during **tarawih** prayer. The master told the following story. "Once a dervish arrived at the hospice of Shaykh Junayd Baghdadi—may God sanctify his lofty secret—just as the new moon was due to appear that signaled the beginning of the blessed month of Ramadan. That dervish requested the Shaykh to permit him to lead the **tarawih** prayer. The Shaykh granted his request. Every evening thereafter he recited the entire Qurʾan. 'Each night,' said the Shaykh, 'take one loaf of bread and one jug of water to the cell of that dervish.' As the Shaykh had commanded, they took a loaf of bread and a jug of water to his cell every night. After he had recited the **tarawih** prayer for thirty evenings, the time of celebration (ʿ**id**) arrived, and the day after ʿ**id** the Shaykh bid that dervish farewell. He left. After his departure they searched his cell, and found all thirty loaves of bread untouched. Each night he had consumed one jug of water and nothing more!"

At the conclusion of this story the master commented about THE GREATEST IMAM ABU HANIFA KUFI—may God have mercy upon him. "In the month of Ramadan Abu Hanifa would recite the entire Qurʾan during those thirty evenings that he was performing the **tarawih** prayer. He would also complete one full recitation during the day, and another full recitation during the night. In all, during the month of Ramadan he recited the Qur'an sixty-one times—once during the **tarawih** prayer, thirty times during the day, and another thirty at night."

IV. Assembly 10
Tuesday, the 11th of the blessed month of Dhu'l-Hijja,
A.H. 714 (18 March 1315)

When there arrived the days of visitation at the heavenly seat of the master of this world, I was able to obtain the blessing of conversation with him. After I had garnered the benefit of kissing his feet, he turned to me and asked: "Friday was the day of celebration (**'id**). Did you compose something suitable for the occasion?" "Four or five days earlier," I replied, "there occurred the celebration of **nowroz** (the Persian New Year), and for that occasion I composed a poem in which I made mention of both **nowroz** and **'id.**" Then I recited that poem.

In this connection he told a story. "Once Shams Dabir brought to Shaykh al-Islam Farid ad-din—may God sanctify his lofty secret—a long poem that he had composed in praise of the Shaykh. He asked permission to recite it. The Shaykh—may God favor his resting place—assented. Standing upright, Shams Dabir recited that poem. When he had finished, the Shaykh—may God illumine his grave—told him to sit down. After he sat down, the Shaykh said: 'Recite it again.' Shams did. Then the Shaykh—may God sanctify his lofty secret—began to explain every line in that poem, and in some places he improved it, and in others he noted his appreciation. At this Shams became very happy." The master—may God remember him with favor—made an aside: "The Shaykhs seldom hear poetry that is specifically intended to praise them. Look at the perfect spiritual state of the Shaykh that he not only heard such poetry but viewed it favorably." "In short, when he had finished listening to Kabir, he asked: 'What do you want?' 'I am indigent,' pleaded Kabir, 'and I must provide for my aged mother.' 'Go fetch the alms of gratitude (**shukrana**),' ordered the Shaykh." At this point the master again interrupted his telling of the story. "In every instance," he observed, "where Shaykh al-Islam asked someone to fetch alms of gratitude, his affairs proceeded favorably." "Shams went and returned with some **jitals.** Now in those days **jitals** were a favored currency (equivalent in value to about ten **dirams**). Shams brought back five **jitals,** more or less. 'Distribute them,' commanded Shaykh al-Islam—may God sanctify his lofty secret." The master—may God remember him with favor—remarked: "I received four **dirams.** Finally the Shaykh recited the **Fatiha,** with the result that favors and fortunes began to flow to Shams. He became secretary (**dabir**) to the son of Sultan Ghiyas ad-din Tughluq. Despite the fact that his world prospered, when Shaykh al-Islam—may God sanctify his lofty secret—died, he did not look after the rights of his sons or retainers. Perhaps he did not know, nor did anyone inform him, about their condition."

The master then began to speak about THE BEAUTIFUL MANNER AND GRACIOUS TEMPERAMENT OF SHAMS DABIR. I interjected that he was a relative of mine. "Have you ever spent time together with him?" asked the master—may God remember him with favor. "Yes," I replied. "In the year that Sultan Ghiyas ad-din Tughluq attacked Lakhnauti, both he and I were in the advancing army. We traveled together on land and by boat." "In your spiritual observances were you also together?" asked the master. "Yes, we were." "Shams," continued the master, "had studied the **Lawa'ih** of Qazi Hamid ad-din Nagauri—may God have mercy upon him—in the company of the great Shaykh Farid ad-din—may God sanctify his lofty secret." He then told a further story about Shams. "Once I and Shams Dabir and Shaykh Jamal ad-din Hansawi—upon them both be God's mercy—were traveling together on our return from a visit to Shaykh al-Islam. We had gone several stages when we came to a crossroads that forked out in opposite directions. Shams wanted to go toward Sunam, Shaykh Jamal ad-din and I to Sirsi. As we were bidding him farewell, Shaykh Jamal ad-din turned toward Shams and recited this verse:

O old friend, take the straight path.

[Since "the straight path" is the goal for all Sufis,] this verse immediately spurred a keen taste for God in all of us—in Shams, in Shaykh Jamal ad-din, and in me."

## IV. Assembly 11
### Saturday, 29th of Dhu'l-Hijja, A.H. 714 (5 April 1315)

I obtained the benefit of kissing his feet. I was experiencing some anxiety that day, for I suspected that someone had spoken ill of me to the master. When I obtained the benefit of sitting with him, the first words that came to his blessed lips were these: "If someone speaks ill of someone else, the latter has the intelligence to discern and he knows this much, whether what has been said is true or false, and also what was the motive of the speaker." When I heard his counsel, I became very happy. I submitted: "The firm hope of your servants lies in this, that the master's intuition is the arbiter (**hakim**)[69] in all matters."

Conversation then turned to THE ABILITY OF SAINTS TO DISCLOSE MIRACLES. He told a story about Shaykh Saʿd ad-din Hamuya—upon whom be God's mercy. "He was a great saint, yet the ruler of that city had no confidence in the truth of his spiritual state. One day the ruler passed by the threshold of the Shaykh's hospice. He sent one of his retainers to deliver this message: 'Tell this Sufi lad to come out that I might cast an eye on him.' The retainer went in and delivered the ruler's message. The Shaykh took no heed of what he said; he was engrossed in his prayers. The retainer came out and reported what was going on. The ruler's anger subsided. He himself went into the Shaykh's hospice. When the Shaykh saw him enter, he got up and greeted the ruler cordially. The two sat down together in conversation.

"Nearby there was a small orchard. Shaykh Saʿd ad-din signaled his servants to fetch some apples. When they were brought in, the Shaykh cut up a few apples. He and the ruler began eating the pieces. There remained on that tray a big apple. It occurred to the ruler: 'If this Shaykh has spiritual insight and miraculous powers, he will take this apple and offer it to me.' No sooner had this thought crossed his mind than the Shaykh reached for that apple, and picking it up, he turned to the ruler. 'Once when I was traveling,' he recalled, 'I came to a certain city. I saw a huge crowd milling about in that city. A juggler was performing for them. That juggler had an ass, and he had covered the ass's eyes with a blindfold. He then produced a ring in his hand, and gave that ring to one of the onlookers. Turning to the crowd, he announced: "This ass will find out who has the ring." Then that blindfolded ass began to move through the crowd. He sniffed everyone till he arrived in front of the man who had the ring. Then he stood still and would not budge. The juggler came and took the ring from that man.' When he had finished telling this story to the ruler, Shaykh Saʿd ad-din Hamuya remarked: 'If a man claims that he has the ability to perform miracles, he is equivalent to that ass, but if he doesn't make that claim and doesn't perform any miracle, someone might suppose that he doesn't possess spiritual insight.' Having said this, he tossed the apple to that ruler!"

The master then related THE CIRCUMSTANCE OF SHAYKH SAʿD AD-DIN'S DEATH AND THE SPIRITUAL PROWESS OF SHAYKH SAYF AD-DIN BAKHARZI—may God be merciful to both of them. "One night," he began, "Shaykh Saʿd ad-din had a dream in which he was commanded to go and see Shaykh Sayf ad-din Bakharzi. When Shaykh Saʿd ad-din awoke, he left his home and spent the next three months traveling to the place where Shaykh Sayf ad-din lived. In the meantime Shaykh Sayf ad-din also had a dream in which he was told: 'We are sending Shaykh Saʿd ad-din to you.' In short, after Shaykh Saʿd ad-din had been traveling for three months, he arrived at a place where he was only three days' journey from the residence of Shaykh Sayf ad-din. He sent a messenger saying, 'I have spent three months traveling to see you. Now you please travel three days to receive me.' When this message reached Shaykh Sayf ad-din Bakharzi, he responded: 'This man is puffed up with pride; he will not see me.' " Then the master—may God remember him with favor—concluded: "Shaykh Saʿd ad-din became joined to God [i.e., he died] at that very spot without ever reaching Shaykh Sayf ad-din Bakharzi."

In this connection he told a story about SHAYKH BAHA AD-DIN ZAKARIYA—may God be merciful to him. "I heard from a disciple of his that one day on leaving his residence, Shaykh Baha ad-din exclaimed: 'Surely we belong to God and to Him we will return' (Q.2.156). 'Why did you cite this verse?' he was asked. 'At this very moment,' he rejoined, 'Shaykh Saʿd ad-din Hamuya has expired.' After sometime it was verified that Shaykh Saʿd ad-din had indeed died that very moment." Then the master—may God remember him with favor—noted: "Shaykh Saʿd ad-din Hamuya died, then three years later Shaykh Sayf ad-din Bakharzi died, and three years after him, Baha ad-din Zakariya, and finally three years later Shaykh Farid ad-din [also died]."[70]

## IV. Assembly 12

Thursday, the 11th of Muharram, A.H. 715 (17 April 1315)

I obtained the good fortune of kissing his feet. He began to speak about THE CHARACTERISTICS OF WORLDLINESS, raising the question: What sort of thing is worldly and what sort of thing is not worldly? He described four categories: "Something may be worldly both in form and essence, or it may not be worldly in either form or essence. Another may seem not to be worldly when, in fact, its essence is worldly. Finally, there could be something which, despite the appearance of being worldly, is in essence not worldly." About these categories he proceeded to give the following explanation: "That which is worldly in form and essence applies to whatever exceeds the minimal requirements for subsistence. Its opposite, that which is worldly in neither form nor essence, refers to acts of sincere obedience to God. In between these two are that which does not seem to be worldly but in essence is. That can be said of any act of obedience which is done only in the hope of personal gain. By contrast, that which seems to be worldly but is not applies to the performance of individual duties, for instance, meeting the needs of one's relatives: when one meets such needs only because it is one's duty, then their essence is not worldly even though their appearance is."[71]

### IV. Assembly 13
Saturday, the 5th of Safar—may God conclude it with favor and success —A.H. 715 (12 May 1315)

I obtained the benefit of kissing his feet. Conversation turned to INVOCATORY PRAYERS AND SUPPLICATIONS. He asked me: "Which invocations do you recite?" I replied: "Those which I have learned from the blessed tongue of the master. I recite them five times after every canonical prayer, along with the Qur'anic chapters that have also been recommended. After other prayers I recite five times **Surat an-Naba** and the other chapters specified in Prophetic Traditions. Twice a day I also perform **musabbiʿat-i ʿashr,** and I recite a hundred times the following profession of faith: 'There is no god but God. He is One. He has no partner. To Him belongs dominion, to Him glory, and He has power over everything.' "

The master then noted that there were ten other laudations that should be recited one hundred times each, a thousand times in all, and if one cannot recite each one hundred times, then one should at least recite them ten times apiece, to reach the sum total of one hundred. Of these ten laudations I remember eight fully. They are:

1. There is no god but God. He is One. He has no partner. To Him belongs dominion, to Him praise. He gives life and death. He is the Living who never dies, the Possessor of awe and mercy. Goodness rests in His hands, and He has power over everything.

2. Glory be to God. Praise be to God. There is no god but God. God is great. There is no power nor might, save that of God the Transcendent, the Supreme.

3. Glory and praise be to God. Glory to God the Transcendent, the Supreme. Praise is due Him, for from Him do I seek forgiveness and before Him do I repent.

4. I seek forgiveness from God. There is no god but He, the Living, the Eternal, and I ask Him to accept my repentance. I seek forgiveness from God for all the sins that I have committed, by deed or by neglect, consciously or unwittingly. Before Him do I repent.

5. Glory be to God, the King, the Most Holy, the Embodiment of all Holiness, our Lord, the Lord of the angels, and the Spirit.

6. O God, there is no censorship to what You give nor can anyone give what You have censored, nor can there be any alteration to what You have decreed. He who possesses power derives no profit, for power is Yours alone.

7. O God, forgive me and my parents and all believers, male and female, and all Muslims, male and female, both the living and the dead.

8. O God, bless Muhammad and the family of Muhammad. Blessings and peace and comfort be upon all the prophets and apostles.

The other two that I do not fully recall are:

9. I seek refuge in God the Omnipresent, the Omniscient, from cursed Satan, and I seek refuge in You from the tricks of all Satans, and I seek refuge in You especially when they are present.

10. In the name of God, the best of all names. In the name of God, the Lord of heaven and earth. In the name of God, through Whose name nothing in heaven or earth can do harm, for He is Omnipresent, Omniscient.

After prayer the master stated: "It was a happy moment when Shaykh al-Islam Farid ad-din—may God sanctify his lofty secret—ordered me to recite these ten laudations. 'I entrust to you treasures,' he said; 'be attentive in reciting these powerful laudations!' "

IV. Assembly 14
Monday, the 27th of Safar, A.H. 715 (2 June 1315)

I obtained the benefit of kissing his feet. He began to speak about LOVE AND REASON. "They are mutually exclusive," he declared. "The ʿ**ulama** are the partisans of reason, dervishes the partisans of love. The human intellect of the ʿ**ulama** dominates their sense of divine love, while attention to divine love among dervishes exceeds their use of the intellect. Prophets are equally strong in love and reason." To illustrate the dominance of love these verses came on his blessed lips:

The mind, which has no ear for love, make haste to block with cotton.
How else dare you hope to make, of the weaver's heart love's camel?

In this vein the master told a story about ʿAli Khokhri. "ʿAli Khokhri lived in Multan. He never trusted someone unless that person had experienced love or pain. Even if an individual was pious and devout, he would say: 'So-and-so is nothing. He doesn't have tears (**ishk**)!' The correct word never came on his tongue. He would invariably say **ishk** (tear) instead of ʿ**ishq** (love)." With respect to this word, the master recalled the statement of Yahya Maʿaz Razi—may God be merciful to him. "He used to say: 'One particle of love is better than the obedience of all humankind and also the entire angelic host!' " The master also recalled that Shaykh al-Islam Farid ad-din—may God sanctify his lofty secret—many times would say to those who came to visit him: 'May Almighty God give you pain!' People would be surprised. 'What sort of supplication is this?' they would ask themselves. Now it is evident," concluded the master, "what he meant by that supplication [for unless you experience the pain of separation from God, you cannot experience an intense love for Him]."

He then told a further story about Shaykh Jalal ad-din Tabrizi—may God be merciful to him. "One day during the time that he was visiting Badaun, he was seated on the threshold of his temporary residence. A yogurt vendor, carrying a pot of yogurt on his head, passed by. The vendor came from the wilderness area near Badaun called Kathir.

Many highway robbers lived there, and the yogurt vendor was one of them. When he caught sight of the blessed countenance of Shaykh Jalal ad-din Tabrizi, from the first glance he felt a change overcome him. After fixing his gaze on the Shaykh, the vendor said to himself: 'In the religion of Muhammad—on whom be peace—there are such men as these.' Immediately he embraced Islam, and the Shaykh named him ʿAli. After he had become a Muslim, ʿAli returned home and brought back with him one **lac** (i.e., 100,000) of **jitals,** which he presented to the Shaykh. The Shaykh accepted his gift, but told him: 'You keep these silver coins with you. When I want, I will tell you to disburse them.' Soon thereafter the Shaykh began to give away this silver. He ordered ʿAli to give one person a hundred **dirams,** another fifty, to some more, to others less. But the least amount that he gave anyone was five **dirams;** he never commanded ʿAli to disburse less than five **dirams.** Finally, there came a time when all that silver had been expended except for a single **diram.** ʿAli said: 'It crossed my mind that I had no more than one **diram,** and the least that the Shaykh had asked me to disburse was five **dirams.** If he commands me to give someone more than I have, what will I do?' As he was pondering that thought, a petitioner came and asked for money. Turning to me, the Shaykh said: 'Give him one **diram**!' "

Also in praise of Shaykh Jalal ad-din Tabrizi—may God have mercy upon him—he told another story. "When he resolved to leave Badaun and travel to Lakhnauti, this ʿAli followed after him. The Shaykh ordered him to go back to Badaun. 'To whom would I go back?' entreated ʿAli. 'Whom do I have but you? Who else do I know?' When they had gone a bit further, the Shaykh repeated his command: 'Go back!' Again ʿAli entreated him: 'You are my master and my guide. Without you what can I do here?' 'Go back,' ordered the Shaykh, 'I place this city under your protection.' "

Conversation then turned to THE CONDITION OF ZEALOTS. Explained the master: "They are persons who perform many acts of obedience but in their hearts remain preoccupied with other than God. There are four kinds of men," he continued. "Some are outwardly adorned with virtue but are inwardly corrupt. Some are outwardly corrupt but inwardly they remain adorned with virtue. Some are thoroughly corrupt, both within and without, while still others are perfectly adorned, their inner and outer states reflecting each other." Then he elaborated: "That group which is outwardly adorned but inwardly corrupt are the zealots, those who perform many acts of obedience while their hearts remain engrossed in the world. That group which is inwardly adorned though appearing to be corrupt are the spiritual crazies (**majanin,** s. **majnun**): Though outwardly they lack all material provisions, they remain inwardly preoccupied with God. Those who are thoroughly corrupt, both within and without, are the common people, while those who are perfectly adorned are the Sufi Shaykhs."

IV. Assembly 15
Thursday, the 22nd of Rabiʿ al-awwal, A.H. 715 (26 June 1315)

I obtained the benefit of kissing his feet. Observed the master: "On the path of God, no matter how one dresses, THE OUTCOME SHOULD REFLECT A SINCERE PURSUIT [of spiritual goals]." In this connection he told the story of a dervish who became fond of a ruler's daughter and she of him. "They fell in love with each other, and the ruler's daughter sent a note to the dervish. 'You are a dervish-type man,' she declared, 'and so it is very difficult for me to find a way to be united with you. Yet there is one way. If you pursue it, let us hope that I will reach you. This is the way. You make yourself out to be a pious person, frequent a mosque, and busy yourself in acts of obedience and devotion till your fame becomes widespread. When you have become renowned for your asceticism and abstinence, I will ask my father's permission to come and visit you, that I might be blessed through seeing you!' That dervish followed the instructions she set out. He frequented a mosque. And he immersed himself in obedience and seclusion. Yet once he experienced the taste of obedience, it engulfed his heart. Mention of him flowed from everyone's lips. The daughter of the ruler then asked her father's permission to go and visit him. He granted her permission. When she arrived at the mosque, though he was the same dervish and she the same beauty, the ruler's daughter could detect no sign of interest in him. At last she exclaimed: 'Was it not I who taught you this stratagem? How can it be that now you pay no attention to me?' The more she spoke in this vein the more the dervish asked: 'Who are you? How do I know you? Why should I recognize you?' In this way he turned aside from her and remained immersed in God." When the master reached this point in the story, he began to choke with tears. "Look," he declared, "someone who has experienced such taste for God, how can he show attention to another?"

In a similar vein he told this story. "In the days of his youth Shaykh ʿAbdallah Mubarak fell in love with a young woman. One night he went to her house and stood beneath a window in the wall nearest her room.

And that woman put her head out the window. They began to converse. Throughout the night they remained totally absorbed in their conversation. They were still telling each other stories when the call for dawn prayer was broadcast. ʿAbdallah reckoned that it was the call for late evening prayer. When he came to his senses, he saw that dawn had appeared. At that moment he heard a piercing voice: 'O ʿAbdallah, for love of a woman, from nightfall to daybreak you have remained awake. During no evening have you been so attentive for the love of God!' ʿAbdallah, on hearing these words, repented on the spot and became fully immersed in God, and this rebuke was the cause of his repentance."

In the interim food was served. A person came and, after greeting the master, sat down. In this connection the master—may God remember him with favor—told a further story. "Shaykh Abu'l-Qasim Nasrabadi who was the guide of Shaykh Abu Saʿid ibn Abi'l-Khayr—may God be merciful to both of them—was busy eating food with some friends when Imam al-Haramain, the teacher of Imam Muhammad Ghazzali—mercy be upon him—arrived. He greeted the Shaykh and the others but neither Shaykh Abu'l-Qasim nor his friends reciprocated his greeting. After they had done eating Imam al-Haramain asked: 'When I arrived and greeted you, no one answered me. Why was that?' Shaykh Abu'l-Qasim replied: 'It is customary that whenever someone comes into a group and that group is eating food, the new arrival should not offer a greeting but should quietly sit down and after the food has been consumed and hands have been washed, then that person should get up and greet the group.' 'Where did you learn such a custom?' asked Imam al-Haramain. 'Was it the product of your reason or was it transmitted by tradition?' 'It came from my reason,' rejoined Abu'l-Qasim, 'because food is consumed to have the power to obey God. Hence that person who is engaged in eating with such an intention in mind is performing the essential act of obedience. And if someone is performing an act of obedience, for instance, saying prayers, how can he respond to the greeting of peace?' "

One of those present asked: "If a Hindu says the profession of faith and calls upon God in His incomparable Unicity and on the Prophet as God's Messenger yet remains silent in the company of Muslims, what will be his fate?" The master—may God remember him with favor—replied: "His affair is with God. God will decree what to do, whether to pardon or to punish." In the same vein he remarked, "Some Hindus acknowledge the truth of Islam yet do not become Muslims!"

He then told the story of Abu Talib. When he fell sick, the Prophet —upon whom be peace—approached him, saying, "Once at least attest to the incomparable Unicity of God, whether outwardly on your tongue, or silently with a sincere heart, so that I might testify before God: 'O God, he died a believer!' " However much the Prophet tried to convince Abu Talib, his words left no impression. Abu Talib died an unbeliever. The Commander of the Faithful ʿAli—may God be pleased with him—brought the news of Abu Talib's death to the Prophet—peace be upon him. "Your errant uncle is dead," he declared. The Prophet then ordered them to wash his corpse, wrap it in a shroud, dig a grave without (the customary) niche, and place him in the grave from above (rather than from the side). In other words, he was not buried according to Muslim burial rites."

### IV. Assembly 16
Monday, 9th of Jumada al-ula, A.H. 715 (11 August 1315)

I obtained the benefit of kissing his feet. He told a story about those who levied EXCESSIVE TAXES FOR CULTIVATION. "There used to be a village on the outskirts of Lahore. A dervish who lived in that village made his living by cultivating his own land. No one had ever demanded anything from him till a deputy tax collector was appointed. He began to demand a share of the dervish's produce. 'Look how many years you have cultivated land without paying any share of your produce, despite the abundance of your grain. Either pay your overdue taxes or perform a miracle.'

" 'What sort of miracle do you expect?' asked the dervish. 'I am a poor man.' 'I will certainly not excuse you,' insisted the tax collector. 'Either hand over the produce due from years past or perform a miracle.' The dervish was perplexed. He thought to himself for awhile and then turning to the tax collector, he said, 'Tell me what miracle you wish to see me perform!' Since there was a river near the village, the tax collector told him: 'Walk on the river, if indeed you can perform a miracle!' The dervish set foot on the river and walked across it as if he had been walking on land! On reaching the other side, he asked for a boat to bring him back. 'Why do you not return the same way you came?' they asked him. 'One should not pander the lower self,' replied the dervish. 'Otherwise it might think: "At last I've become something!" ' "

The master then began to talk about SERVING FOOD and offered reflections on the different forms of hospitality that are available.

"There is a Tradition," he noted, that 'whoever visits a living person and does not taste something from him it is as if he visited a corpse!' " He then told a story about Shaykh Baha ad-din Zakariya—may God have mercy upon him. "He did not share the attitude reflected in this Tradition. People who came to visit him would leave without having been offered anything to eat. Someone asked him: 'There is this Tradition of the Prophet, to wit, "whoever visits a living person and does not taste something from him it is as if he visited a corpse." '

" 'Yes, I know,' replied the Shaykh. 'Why then do you not follow this Tradition?' asked the questioner. 'People do not know the true intent of this Tradition,' explained Shaykh Baha ad-din Zakariya. 'There are two kinds of people: the common and the elite. I have nothing to do with the common folk. But when the elite visit me, I speak to them about God, the Prophet, norms of conduct, and the like, that they might benefit from my instruction.' "

In the same vein the following remark came on the blessed lips of the master—may God be pleased with him. "The companions of the Prophet—on whom be peace—whenever they visited him, would always eat something before leaving—whether a piece of bread or a date or some other thing. Until they had had a bite to eat, they would not leave."

Then he noted about Shaykh Badr ad-din Ghaznavi—may God have mercy upon him: "He followed the practice that if he could not offer food to his visitors, he would at least offer them water."

The master had a further recollection of Shaykh Baha ad-din Zakariya—may God have mercy upon him. He told this story. "There was a precious person named ʿAbdallah Rumi. He came to call on Shaykh Baha ad-din Zakariya—may God have mercy upon him, and reported: 'I was once in the presence of Shaykh Shihab ad-din Suhrawardi—may God sanctify his lofty secret—and I performed **samaʿ** for him.' 'Since Shaykh Shihab ad-din listened to **samaʿ**,' replied Shaykh Baha ad-din, 'Zakariya also must hear it.' He then had this ʿAbdallah stay with him till evening. In the evening he told his attendants: 'Put ʿAbdallah and one of his friends in a cell, but only one; there should be no third person. Put these two and no more in a cell.' 'They did as they were told,' said ʿAbdallah. 'They put me and one of my friends in a cell. As the evening advanced and the late night prayer was said and the Shaykh finished his invocatory prayers, he came into the cell. We were alone—the two of us and the Shaykh and no one else. The Shaykh sat down and immersed himself in saying invocations. He also recited half a section of the Qur'an. Then he locked the door to the cell and told me: "Say something!" I began to perform **sama'**. After some time an agitation and a movement appeared in the Shaykh. Getting up, he extinguished the lamp. The cell became dark and I kept performing **sama'** in the dark. I only knew what I could feel, and whenever the Shaykh would come near, his skirt would just become visible, so that I knew that it was he who had become agitated and was moving. But since the cell was dark I did not know whether he was moving in beat with the music or not. In short, when the **sama'** was over, the Shaykh opened the door and returned to his own place. I and my friend remained in the cell. They gave us no food to eat or water to drink. Evening passed. Morning came. At daybreak a servant appeared and, giving us a fine garment and twenty **tankas,** said: "These are from the Shaykh. Take them and leave." ' "

After narrating this story, the master—may God remember him with favor—said: "That same 'Abdallah came to Shaykh al-Islam Farid ad-din—may God sanctify his lofty secret—and told him this story. After awhile this 'Abdallah wanted to return to Multan. He came to Shaykh al-Islam Farid ad-din—may God illumine his grave—and submitted: 'I want to go to Multan. The road is very dangerous. Please pray that I may reach Multan safely.' The Shaykh replied: 'From here to that place is such-and-such a distance. There is a reservoir. Up to it is my territory. You will reach the reservoir safely. From there to Multan is under the protection of Shaykh Baha ad-din—may God have mercy on him.' This 'Abdallah added: 'After hearing this message from the Shaykh, I went as far as that reservoir. It is said that highway robbers lie in wait there to fall upon passers by. Remembering the presence of the Shaykh, I proceeded without fear, and God Almighty kept those robbers at bay. They lost their way while I reached the reservoir safely. On arriving there, I made my ablutions and said two cycles of prayer. Then I brought to mind the presence of Shaykh Baha ad-din and I said: "I have passed safely through the territory of Shaykh Farid ad-din—may God sanctify his lofty secret. From here to Multan is your territory, as you know. [Please protect me!]" I then ventured forth from that reservoir and, without incident, I arrived safely in Multan. When I went to call on Shaykh Baha ad-din—may God sanctify his lofty secret—I was wearing a black garment. When the Shaykh saw this garment he became upset.

"What sort of garment is this?" he demanded. "This is the dress of the devil" and other such things he kept on saying. I became ashamed and distressed. "What does it matter if I wear such a garment?" I retorted. "There are men who have gold and silver and worldly possessions and even treasures and I don't criticize them. If I wear this garment, why should it draw any comment?" When the Shaykh saw that I had totally lost my composure, he turned toward me and said: "Why are you ranting on and on? Instead, recall your passage from that reservoir. Was there any shortcoming in Zakariya's protection of you?" ' "

IV. Assembly 17

Wednesday, 16th of Jumada al-ʿakhira, A.H. 715 (17 September 1315)

I obtained the benefit of kissing his feet. Conversation turned to ANGER AND DESIRE. The master observed: "Just as random desire is unlawful, so is random anger." Then he added: "If someone gets angry at someone else, and the latter shows patience and forbearance, is it not his patience, rather than the anger of the other, which will be praised as something beautiful?"

He then spoke about HOW TO GIVE ADVICE. "If someone advises someone else, he must not give his advice in public, for that would bring disgrace to the other. When criticism and advice are required, one should offer them in private rather than in public."

On this point he told a story about Qazi Abu Yusuf—may God have mercy on him. "Once the Qazi was sitting and dictating some lessons on Tradition to friends. He was wearing the Sufi hat on his head. It was a white rather than a black hat, and instead of sitting flat on the head, it was pointed and conical. While he was in the midst of dictating, someone entered and asked: 'Did the Prophet—on whom be peace—wear his hat like this on his head?' 'Yes, he did," replied Qazi Abu Yusuf. The questioner persisted: 'Did he wear a white or a black hat?' 'White,' replied the Qazi. Still the questioner persisted: 'The Prophet—on whom be peace—did he wear a flat hat or one that was pointed and conical?' 'A flat hat,' replied the Qazi. 'But you are wearing a black, pointed hat,' rejoined the questioner. 'Since on two scores you are violating the Tradition of the Prophet, how can you be trusted to dictate lessons from Tradition?' Qazi Abu Yusuf was overcome with shame and humiliation. To his inquisitor he replied: 'You have rebuked me for one of two reasons: Either you spoke for the sake of truth, or you spoke out of spite. If you spoke for the sake of truth, why did you choose to speak before my friends, since you gain no reward for making such a critique in public? And if you spoke out of spite, to shame and humiliate me, woe be unto you, woe be unto you, woe be unto you!' "

### IV. Assembly 18
### Wednesday, 7th of Rajab, A.H. 715 (7 October 1315)

I had the benefit of kissing his feet. He began to speak about REPENTANCE. "Repentance is of three kinds: past, present, and future," he explained. "Repentance of the present means repenting and feeling regret for whatever wrong one has done. Repentance of the past means being reconciled with one's enemies. If someone, for instance, takes ten **dirams** from another and then says, 'I'm sorry, I'm sorry,' that is not genuine repentance. Genuine repentance consists of giving back the ten **dirams** and admitting that one has done a wrong. That is genuine repentance. And if someone speaks ill of another, he should go, offer apologies, ask pardon of that person, and be reconciled with him. And if that person who was spoken ill of died [before reconciliation was possible], what to do? One should act as if he were still alive and had been spoken ill of. In other words, one should say such good things about him, even after his death, that he will be well remembered. And what to do if one kills a person who dies without heir? One should free a slave. That is to say, you cannot bring the dead to life and so instead you should free a slave. In freeing a slave, it is as if one has brought a dead person back to life. And what to do if one commits adultery with another's wife or with another's slavegirl? There is no provision [in the law] that one should go and apologize to the husband or owner. What to do then? Go and seek forgiveness from God!"

In this same vein he spoke about a wine drinker who decides to repent. "What should he do? He should give soft drinks and cool water to the people of God! For every act of penance should be consonant with the sin that was committed.

"The second kind of repentance," he continued, "pertains to past sins. That is what has just been described. As for the third kind of repentance, that pertains to the future. One makes the resolve never to sin again, never again to commit such sins as one previously committed." On this point he told a story about the time when he professed allegiance to Shaykh al-Islam Farid ad-din—may God sanctify his lofty secret—and also repented of his former misdeeds. "Several times on his blessed lips came the remark: 'One should be reconciled with one's enemies,' and he kept stressing that 'one must make restitution to those who have a claim on you.'

"Then I recalled that I owed twenty **jitals** to a certain man and also that I had borrowed a book from another and had lost it. As the great Shaykh—may God illumine his grave—continued to speak about reconciliation with one's enemies, I realized that he was indeed the channel for disclosing the world of secrets. I resolved to return to Delhi in order to settle my accounts with these two men. On reaching Delhi from Ajodhan, I first went to see the man to whom I owed twenty **jitals.** He was a cloth merchant from whom I had purchased a robe. At no time did I manage to save twenty **jitals,** that I might repay him. It was difficult for me to make a living. Some days I would earn five **jitals,** other days ten **jitals.** As soon as I managed to save ten **jitals,** I went to the house of that cloth merchant and called up to him. He came out of his house to meet me. I told him: 'I owe you twenty **jitals,** but I do not have the means to pay you the full amount at one time. I have brought you these ten **jitals.** Take them. I will bring the other ten shortly, if God Almighty wills.' When he had heard me out, the man remarked: 'Fine. You have come from the Shaykh.' Then taking the ten **jitals,** he told me: 'I forgive you the ten remaining **jitals**!' Next I went to see the man whose book I had borrowed. When I met him, he did not recognize me. 'Who are you?' he asked. 'O sir,' I replied, 'I am the person who took a book on loan from you and lost it. Now I will see to making another copy of the book like the one you lent me, and I will bring it to you.' When he had heard my pledge, this man replied: 'Fine. You show the influence of the place from which you came. I forgive you that book!' "

Then the master expanded on THE MORALS RELATED TO FORGIVENESS. "When someone sins, he confronts his sinfulness and turns his back on God. But when he repents and seeks forgiveness, he must turn his back on sinfulness and confront God." He concluded: "Whoever repents must first experience an overwhelming taste for obedience, and whoever relapses into sinfulness—we seek refuge in God from that!—it is because he has not yet acquired a taste for obedience."

The master then spoke about EXPENDING MONEY ON OTHERS. "The Commander of the Faithful ʿAli—may God be pleased with him—used to say: 'It is better for someone to expend one **diram** on a friend than ten **dirams** on beggars, and it is better for him to expend ten **dirams** on friends than one hundred **dirams** on beggars, and if he expends one hundred **dirams** on friends, that is equivalent to freeing a slave.' And God knows best [whether 'Ali actually said this.]"

IV. Assembly 19
Wednesday, 27th of Sha'ban, A.H. 715 (26 November 1315)

I had the good fortune of kissing his feet. He began to talk about RELATIONS WITH PEOPLE, WHETHER THEY WERE GOOD OR BAD. "During the time in which we live," he observed, "if someone is not called 'bad,' that amounts to saying that he is good." Then he added: "If a person does not find fault with others or speak ill of them—even though he be a bad person, one should call him good rather than bad." To make this point on his blessed lips came the following verse:

If you have faults but find none, then you're good.
If bad but speak no ill, then too you're good.

"If someone is bad," he continued, "and he calls God's people bad, what limits are there to badness?" He then turned toward me and asked, "Do you still live in the military compound?" "Yes, I do," I replied. "There's no comfort now in the city, nor has there ever been," he remarked. In this connection he told a story. "Long ago I had resolved not to stay in the city. One day I came to the edge of the reservoir known as Qatlagh Khan Reservoir. I was memorizing the Qur'an in those days, and I saw a dervish absorbed in God. Approaching him, I asked: 'Do you live in the city?' 'Yes, I do,' he replied. 'Do you live here by choice?' 'No!' That dervish then began to tell me a story. 'Once I saw a precious dervish. He was living outside the Kamal gate in an enclosure on the bank of the canal that ran near that gate. It was a vast area and in that enclosure martyrs were buried. Addressing me, that dervish said: "If you wish to keep your faith intact, leave this city." I resolved then and there that I would quit this city but obstacles kept cropping up. Now, twenty-five years later, I still have the same resolve yet I have not left the city.' " The master—may God remember him with favor—said: "When I heard what this dervish was saying, I resolved to myself that I would not stay in this city. I pondered many places and for a time considered the town of Patyala, for in those days the Turk lived there. (By Turk he meant Amir Khusrau—may God keep him from sin!)[72] But then I thought about Basnala, which was a clean and tidy place, and finally I went to Basnala. I stayed there for three days, but during those three days I could find no place to rent or to buy on mortgage or to purchase outright. During those three days I was always someone's guest. When I returned from there, I continued to ponder this matter, till one day I went to the Rani Reservoir located in the Jasrat Garden. I made supplications to God the Almighty and Exalted. It was an auspicious time. 'O God,' I prayed, 'I must leave this city. I will not choose the place to live; the place that You choose, there will I go to live.' A voice spoke: GHIYASPUR. I had never seen Ghiyaspur; I did not even know where it was. Having heard this voice, I went to see a friend. My friend had a chamberlain whose last name was Nishapuri. When I called on him, my friend said: 'My chamberlain has gone to Ghiyaspur.' 'It must be the same Ghiyaspur,' I said to myself.

"In short, I went to Ghiyaspur and in those days that place was not so inhabited. It was a neglected spot, with few people living there. I went and took up residence there. But then [some time later] Kaiqubad moved to Kilokhiri and people began to crowd into Ghiyaspur. Kings, princes, and many others, a great throng of people flocked to Ghiyaspur. 'I must leave this place, too,' I said to myself. While I was still entertaining this thought, an eminent person who had been my friend died in the city. I resolved to go and pay my respects to him during the ceremony marking three days after a person's demise. I made this resolve even though I did not want to return to the city. That same day, during one of the daily prayers, a handsome and slender youth appeared—and God knows whether he was among the Men of the Unseen or who he was. As soon as he arrived, he delivered this poem:

That day that you became the moon you did not know
That to behold you throngs and throngs would forward press.
Today, when the hearts of all are trapped by your tress,
To remain in seclusion is worse than useless."

The master—may God remember him with favor—said: "He spoke some other words, to the effect that I should stay in this place, and then he declared: 'At the outset you should not try to become famous.[73] But if you happen to gain fame, then it should not happen that tomorrow on the Day of Resurrection you will be embarrassed before the Prophet —upon whom be peace.' Having said this, he asked me: 'What power, what gain is there in retreating from people and immersing yourself in God?' " The master—may God remember him with favor—said: "When he had finished speaking, I offered him some food but he did not eat. Then I told him that I intended to continue residing in that place. As soon as I had made clear my intention, he took some food and left. I never saw him again."

IV. Assembly 20
Monday, 10th of the blessed month of Ramadan,
A.H. 715 (8 December 1315)

I obtained the good fortune of kissing his feet. He began talking about the MERIT OF **SURAT AL-IKHLAS.** On his blessed lips came this pronouncement. The Prophet—upon whom be peace—said: "**Surat al-Ikhlas** is equivalent to one-third of the Qur'an." In this regard he noted that "whoever recites the whole of the Qur'an should recite **Surat al-Ikhlas** three times at the end. The wisdom of this practice [relates to the preceding Tradition]: If you should miss some portion of the Qur'an in your recitation, the three times that you recite **Surat al-Ikhlas** are equivalent to having recited the entire Qur'an!"

He continued to speak about RECITING THE QUR'AN. "After finishing its recitation, people often recite **Surat al-Fatiha** and portions of **Surat al-Baqara.** Why do they do this? Because the Prophet—upon whom be peace—was once asked: 'Who is the best of people?' He replied: **'Al-hal al-murtihal.' Al-hal** means someone who stops at a resting place while on a journey, and **al-murtihal** means someone who keeps on traveling. By this expression the Prophet was indicating that whoever recites the Qur'an, when he finishes, becomes like someone who stops at a resting place, and when he resumes his recitation, he becomes like someone who keeps on traveling. Hence the best of people are those who, having finished their recitation of the entire Qur'an, immediately begin to recite it again. Such are the people whom the Prophet—upon whom be peace—had in mind when he said: **al-hal al-murtahil.**"

Conversation then turned to this: Some pray THE FUNERAL PRAYER FOR THE ABSENT [person who has died]. Is that proper? The master—may God remember him with favor—remarked: "That is a correct practice. The Prophet—upon whom be peace—said such a prayer for Najashi, who had died in an unknown place. And Imam Shafi'i also indicated that this was an acceptable practice. And even if only a limb of the deceased has been recovered—whether a hand or a foot or a mere finger—it is acceptable to say the funeral prayer over that limb."

With reference to this prayer he told a story about Shaykh Jalal ad-din Tabrizi—may God sanctify his lofty secret. "When Shaykh

Najm al-Din Sughra, who was then Shaykh al-Islam of Delhi, reproached Shaykh Jalal ad-din Tabrizi, he created such a controversy that Shaykh Jalal ad-din was compelled to leave Hindustan. When Shaykh Jalal ad-din—may God illumine his grave—reached Badaun, he was sitting one day on the bank of the river Soth. Suddenly he got up and began to make his ablutions. He announced to the bystanders: 'Come, let us offer the funeral prayer for the Shaykh al-Islam of Delhi since he has just expired.' And it occurred exactly as had been indicated by the blessed words of Shaykh Jalal ad-din—may God shower him with abundant mercy. After they had finished saying the funeral prayer, Shaykh Jalal ad-din turned to those present and said: 'If the Shaykh al-Islam of Delhi can expel me from his city, then my Shaykh can expel him from this world!' "

Conversation next shifted to that group of AWESTRUCK DEVOTEES who are so immersed in God Almighty that they pay no heed to any aspect of God's creation. One of those present told a story. "Once I reached a certain place where I saw seven or eight such persons. They had their gaze fixed on the sky and they remained awestruck day after day, except at the times for canonical prayer. But after saying their prayers, they would again become awestruck." "Yes," rejoined the master—may God remember him with favor—"the prophets are sinless while saints must be protected. They are just as you have described them to be: However much they may be awestruck, they never miss their obligatory prayers."

Then, with reference to the condition of being awestruck, he told the story about THE DEATH OF SHAYKH QUTB AD-DIN BAKHITYAR OUSHI—may God sanctify his lofty secret. "At the time of his death he had been awestruck for four nights and days. It happened in this way. There was an assembly of **sama'** in the hospice of Shaykh 'Ali Sanjari—may God have mercy upon him. Shaykh al-Islam the Pole (**qutb**) of the world His Eminence Qutb ad-din Bakhtiyar Oushi—may God sanctify his lofty secret—was present. They report that the singer recited a poem and when he reached the couplet:

All those by the knife of submission killed<br>
Each moment from God with new life are filled,

Shaykh al-Islam the Pole of the world his Eminence Qutb ad-din Bakhtiyar Oushi—may God illumine his grave—was overwhelmed. Leaving the assembly, he returned home. He remained stupefied and awestruck. He kept asking for them to recite the same couplet. As soon as it was recited, he again became awestruck. When the time for canonical prayer arrived, he would perform his prayer and then they would repeat the same couplet, with the result that a condition of awe and ecstasy would continue to overwhelm him. For four nights and days he continued in this spiritual state. On the fifth night he expired.

"Shaykh Badr ad-din Ghaznawi—may God have mercy upon him—reports: 'I was present that night when the death of the Pole of the world was imminent. I became drowsy and fell asleep. In my sleep I dreamt that I saw Shaykh al-Islam the Pole of the world his Eminence Qutb ad-din—may God sanctify his lofty secret. He had arisen from this place where he was, and he continued to go higher and higher. Turning to me, he said: "Look, the friends of God never die." When I awoke, I saw that the Shaykh had already journeyed to the Abode of Permanence—may God have mercy on all his saints.' "

## IV. Assembly 21

Monday, 15th of the month of Shawwal, A.H. 715 (12 January 1316)

I obtained the benefit of kissing his feet. Conversation focused on THE DESIRE OF PEOPLE FOR THE COMPANY OF SAINTS. "When it was the time of summer heat," recalled the master, "I had already been in the city for some days, and at the time of Friday prayer I went to the congregational mosque. People pressed about me so tightly that when I had come out of the mosque, I retreated to a side niche. A passerby remarked: 'Have people been annoying you?' 'Yes, they have,' I replied. 'My father-in-law,' said the passerby, 'was a disciple of Shaykh al-Islam his Eminence Shaykh Farid ad-din—may God sanctify his lofty secret. When Shaykh Farid ad-din arrived in Delhi [after the death of Shaykh Qutb ad-din], he would set out early for the mosque at the time of the Friday congregational prayer, hoping that the press of people would be less. But as soon as he left his house he would be faced with crowds of well-wishers. They would rush forward to kiss his hand. So many of them were there that they formed circles. He would no sooner emerge from one circle than he would be engulfed by another circle. This scene kept recurring till he became annoyed. At this point my father-in-law [who was his disciple] interjected: "This is a blessing from God; why should you be annoyed?" ' "

In the same vein he told another story. "At the time when Sultan Nasir ad-din was marching toward Uchch and Multan, he stopped en route in Ajodhan. A group of his soldiers went to pay their respects to

Shaykh Farid ad-din. The way to his hospice became blocked. A sleeve belonging to the Shaykh's garment was hung from a balcony overlooking the main street. People rushed forward to kiss and touch and take a piece of it. The sleeve was reduced to shreds. When the Shaykh was going to the mosque, he instructed his disciples: 'Make circles around me so that people can't press close to me. I will greet them from afar and then leave.' The disciples did as they were instructed, but an old domestic servant came and slipped through the circle upon circle of disciples surrounding Shaykh Farid ad-din. He threw himself at Shaykh Farid's feet and, grasping those blessed feet, he began to pull them toward himself so that he might kiss them. The Shaykh became very upset. 'O Shaykh Farid, do you feel annoyed? Give thanks to God Almighty, for what better blessing could He have bestowed on you?' As soon as the servant had spoken these words, the Shaykh began to weep. Then he embraced that servant and repeatedly asked his pardon."

The master spoke briefly about THE NECESSITY OF HAVING A WARM HEART AND A LIVELY COMPASSION FOR PEOPLE. "The Prophet—on whom be peace—had said with reference to Abu Bakr Siddiq—may God be pleased with him: 'Surely Abu Bakr is empathetic.' And they call someone empathetic who is quick to cry and easily moved to tears."

Concerning GOOD-NATUREDNESS AND HUMILITY [and their opposite], the master told this story. "During the period of ignorance [before he embraced Islam] ʿAmr ibn ʿAs used to ridicule the Prophet—upon whom be peace. When the Prophet—upon whom be peace—came to hear of this, he prayed: 'O God, Ibn ʿAs has ridiculed me, and I am no poet. I beseech You to ridicule him on my behalf!' " The master—may God remember him with favor—added: "God Almighty did cause ʿAmr ibn ʿAs to be ridiculed as a fraud. A fraud is someone who practices deceit, and ʿAmr ibn ʿAs is remembered for his fraudulence and deceit. Even though he did in time embrace Islam, yet this ridicule of him as a fraud will remain till the Day of Resurrection. Indeed, accusing someone of fraudulence and deceit is as much a slur as attributing gentleness, good naturedness, and humility to him would be a mark of praise."

### IV. Assembly 22
### Monday, 27th of Dhuʾl-Qaʿda, A.H. 715 (22 February 1316)

I had the honor of kissing his feet. A dear person who had been delegated to visit the master arrived, offering apologies: Someone had asked him to intercede before the master and he had delayed fulfilling that request. As soon as that delegate had offered his apology and asked for forgiveness, the master—may God remember him with favor—pardoned him, and on his blessed tongue came this pronouncement: "Although there is cause to be upset, I am not upset and I have forgiven this man." Then he observed: "When someone pledges allegiance to a Shaykh and becomes his disciple, that is called arbitration (**tahkim**). That is, he forswears his own authority and accepts the authority of his Shaykh as arbiter (**hakim**) in all that concerns him. Hence whatever the Shaykh says and the disciple ignores goes against the principle of arbitration." Then the master repeated [what he had said earlier]: "Even though there are grounds for distress [in what this delegate had done], I have forgiven him." At this point I interjected. "The Shaykh, due to his extraordinary generosity, may forgive the error of a disciple, but how would God Almighty regard that sin and would He also pardon the sinner?" Replied the master: "Since the Shaykh pardons only by permission of God, it is God Who in reality pardons."

Then he added: "Whatever the Shaykh commands his disciple to do he must do it. We have heard of instances where the Shaykh commands something [that seems to be] unlawful, and the disciple hesitates, not knowing whether to do it or not." He then explained this dilemma. "In every instance the Shaykh must be conversant with the precepts of the Law, the Path, and the Truth. Since the Shaykh is fully competent, even if he commands something on which there exists a difference of legal opinions—that is, according to some it is lawful, while according to others, it is not—the disciple must do what the Shaykh has commanded. Since the Shaykh must have reached his decision on the basis of a sound judgment, even though there may be disagreements about what is the correct action, the disciple must carry out the command of his Shaykh."

On this same subject he declared: "If a person asked someone else to intercede and the latter did not comply, one might deduce that he did not have the time or that he had not understood the request. One might also consider that the error or sin lay with the person who made the request, and this might be the case [with the delegate who earlier arrived]."

He then gave an illustration of such a circumstance. "There was an official in Ajodhan who had been vexed by the governor of that region. That official came to Shaykh al-Islam Farid ad-din—may God sanctify his lofty secret—and requested his intercession. The Shaykh sent greetings to the governor and reported the official's complaint. But the governor remained engrossed in his own affairs. The Shaykh then told the official: 'I have sent a message to the governor, but he has given no response. Perhaps the request came at an inopportune time or perhaps someone earlier came to you interceding on behalf of another and you did not hear him!' Even as the Shaykh was speaking, that governor arrived and offered his apologies. The Shaykh forgave him."

In the same vein he told a story about FORGIVENESS AND DECIDING WHETHER OR NOT A MAJOR SIN HAS BEEN COMMITTED. "Shaykh al-Islam Farid ad-din—may God sanctify his lofty secret—had a grandson named Muhammad, who was also affectionately known as Mamman. They reported to the Shaykh that he had been drinking wine. Shortly thereafter, he appeared before the Shaykh. 'Muhammad Mamman,' asked the Shaykh, 'Is it true what people report, that you have been drinking wine?' 'No, it is not,' replied the lad. 'I do not drink wine. They are lying.' 'It will be as you say,' concurred the Shaykh. 'They are spreading a false report.' In sum, he was pleased with what the lad told him and accepted his explanation."

After that he narrated a further story about THE GIVING OF COMMANDS BY SHAYKHS AND THEIR ACCEPTANCE BY DISCIPLES. "There was an old woman who used to frequent the hospice of Shaykh Abu Sa'id ibn Abi'l-Khayr—may God have mercy upon him—and several times she swept the courtyard of the Shaykh's hospice. 'What is the purpose of your service?' the Shaykh asked her. 'Tell me, that I may grant your wish.' Replied the old woman: 'I have a purpose. When the time comes I will tell you what it is.' The old woman kept performing her customary service till one day a handsome young man came to the Shaykh [seeking to be enrolled as his disciple]. Coming to the Shaykh, the old woman stood before him and announced: 'Now is the time for me to disclose my request.' 'Speak,' replied the Shaykh. 'Say what you want.' 'Tell this young man that he must marry me!' The Shaykh thought to himself: 'This woman is old and ugly, this man young and handsome. What is going on here?' To ponder this matter the Shaykh went into seclusion. For three days and nights he took no food to eat or water to drink. After three days and nights he summoned that youth and that old woman before him. Turning to the young man, he said: 'Take this old woman to be your bride.' The young man eagerly obeyed. Then that old woman demanded: 'May the Shaykh also command that I be married in all the splendor that is customary for brides.' The Shaykh acceded to her request, and they prepared a sumptuous wedding feast, a feast with double the customary provisions. The old woman had one more request: 'May the Shaykh please command the young man to lift me off the ground and carry me with his own hand on the bridal canopy.' 'Do as she requested,' the Shaykh commanded the young man. No sooner had he lifted her from the ground than she made still another request of the Shaykh: 'Since this young man has lifted me from the ground in the presence of the Shaykh, may the Shaykh please command him never to drop me on the ground [that is, may he be faithful to me and never forsake me]!' The Shaykh so ordered and that young man consented." Such was the story that the master told in order to emphasize how disciples must comply with the commands of their Shaykhs.

He then told a further story about Shaykh al-Islam Farid ad-din—may God sanctify his lofty secret. "I was about twelve years old. I was engaged in reciting a paean of praise to the Prophet Muhammad. A man whom some called Abu Bakr Kharrat, others Abu Bakr Qawwal, came to visit my teacher. He had just returned from Multan and related how he had performed **sama**ʿ before Shaykh Baha ad-din Zakariya—may God remember him with mercy. 'Once I recited this poem in his presence:

Each morning and, again, each evening
My eyes, due to love of you, keep weeping.
My liver, bitten by the snake of desire,
No doctor nor charmer has the means of curing.

Two other lines I could not remember. The Shaykh remembered them:

For none but he who enflames me with desire
Can, if he chooses, quench that raging fire.

In Persian the last two couplets might be translated as:

My liver's been pinched by a serpent's deadly bite,
Which no spell, however potent, can hope to right.
Only that one whose love distracts and destroys me
Can cast a healing spell; who but he knows my plight?' "

After that he began to depict the virtues of Shaykh Baha ad-din Zakariya—may God have mercy upon him." So busy was everyone [in Multan] in remembering God, performing prayers, and reciting invocations that even the slavegirls, while grinding corn, would chant God's name. Many such things he reported but they did not affect my heart. But then he described how he went from Multan to Ajodhan where he saw such and such a king. In short, when he began to depict the virtues of Shaykh al-Islam his Eminence Shaykh Farid ad-din—may God sanctify his lofty secret, a love and sincere desire took root in my heart, so much so that I began to repeat his name ten times after every prayer. My love for him reached such proportions that all my friends heard me speak about him, and if they asked me something and they wanted me to swear by it, they would say 'Swear by the name of Shaykh Farid ad-din.'

In short, when I resolved to go to Delhi, a dear old man named ʿAwad accompanied me. Along the way, if we came to a place where he feared that lions or robbers might be lurking, he would cry out 'O master, be present!' or 'O our master, we are proceeding under your protection!' 'Who is the master to whom you are calling out?' I asked. 'His Eminence Shaykh Farid ad-din—may God illumine his grave'."

Added the master—may God remember him with favor: "Another desire and taste for meeting him took root in my heart. On this journey we were accompanied by a second man, Maulana Husayn Khandan. When we came into the outskirts of Delhi, as if by divine decree, he stopped at the house of Shaykh Najib ad-din Mutawakkil [the younger brother of Shaykh Farid ad-din]—may God have mercy upon him. The purpose of this story is to indicate that when God Almighty decides to reveal that benefit of discipleship, the means appropriate to its attainment will appear."

He then told a further story about SHAYKH FARID AD-DIN—may God sanctify his lofty secret—AND HIS INCLINATION FOR SAMAʿ. "Once he wished to listen to **samaʿ**, but no reciter was present. He then directed Badr ad-din Ishaq—may God grant him mercy and be pleased with him: 'Go, fetch the letter that Qazi Hamid ad-din Nagauri—may God have mercy upon him—has written.' Badr ad-din left and, fetching the satchel that contained letters and notes, he brought it to the Shaykh. He reached into the satchel. The very first letter that he selected was the one from Qazi Hamid ad-din. He brought it to the Shaykh. 'Stand up and read,' ordered the Shaykh. Badr ad-din stood up and began to read from that letter. It began as follows: 'This humble, weak and worthless beggar Muhammad ʿAta, who is the servant of the dervishes and from head to toe is but dust under their feet.' The Shaykh had heard but this much when a spiritual state and a taste for God became manifest in him." After that the master recalled this quatrain which was also in that same letter:

Where's the mind to grasp Your sovereignty?
Where's the soul to mirror Your majesty?
Beauty's face, I know, You could unveil
But where are eyes to behold Your beauty?

The master—may God remember him with favor—also said with reference to this letter: "Once Shaykh Badr ad-din Ghaznawi—may God have mercy upon him—wrote a letter to the Shaykh in which he, too, included a poem that he had composed." The master—may God remember him with favor—then recited some verses from this poem. I remember the following:

Farid has been, for faith and the faithful, a mighty friend.
That he spend his life bestowing wonders has been my prayer.
But how I wish that my own heart could have been more composed,
For I'd have laid before him pearls of praise, layer upon layer.

Conversation then turned to THE MEETING OF SHAYKH QUTB AD-DIN AND SHAYKH JALAL AD-DIN. "It happened that Shaykh Qutb ad-din Bakhtiyar Oushi had invited Shaykh Jalal ad-din Tabrizi—may God have mercy upon both of them—to be his house guest. The Shaykh's house was located on the outskirts of the Katheir district. In order to receive his guest, Shaykh Qutb ad-din had left his house, and instead of proceeding on the main street, he had taken the narrow bylanes. Shaykh Jalal ad-din, coming to the house of Shaykh Qutb ad-din, also did not choose the main street but instead took the same narrow bylanes as his host. Each chanced upon the other." The master told a further anecdote about another meeting of these two saints. It took place by the public bath which is adjacent to the mosque of Malik ʿIzz ad-din Bakhtiyar. May God be abundantly merciful to both of them!

## IV. Assembly 23
Monday, 11th of the blessed month of Dhu'l-Hijja,
A.H. 715 (7 March 1316)

I obtained the good fortune of kissing his feet. Since the days of celebration after the Great Festival had arrived,[74] I went to visit the master of humankind, that I might obtain the honor of clasping his hands. I had no sooner come into his presence than he asked me about the Festival prayer. Rains had been heavy this year; there had even been some hailstone. Many people had not been able to attend the public prayer.[75] I, too, did not go. When the master—may God remember him with favor—asked about the Festival prayer of this year, I told him that I had not attended. "Yes," he remarked, "many people did not attend." Then he added: "I, too, completed but one cycle of prayer. During the second cycle it began to rain [and I had to discontinue my prayer]. When the prayer observance was over, there remained only the preacher. The caller to prayer, along with every one else, had left." At this point I interjected: "If due to obstacles prayer is not possible at the conclusion of this (the Great) Festival, is it permissible to congregate for public prayer the next day?" "Yes, it is," he replied. "if prayer is not possible immediately after this Festival one can congregate for prayer the day after, or even two days after the designated time. But for the Lesser Festival (which takes place at the end of the Ramadan fast), if public prayer is not immediately possible, it cannot be postponed till a later date." Then on his blessed lips came this remark: "It occurred to me in thinking about this Festival that since the rains were so heavy that people could not pray on the customary day, we could have assembled to pray the day after, but since some people had already begun to assemble and the preacher had begun the prayer, it had to be continued." After that he observed: "THE PRAYER ASKING FOR RAIN, which is offered daily, is to ensure the welfare of that day. Similarly, it is offered every Friday to ensure the welfare of that week, and it is offered on the Festival day(s) to ensure the welfare of the entire year." I asked: "Is the prayer asking for rain offered on the Greater or Lesser Festival Day?" "On every festival day that occurs it is offered," he replied.

### IV. Assembly 24

Saturday, 11th of the month of Muharram, A.H. 716 (5 April 1316)

I had the good fortune of kissing his hand. That day I brought with me a young child who was among my relatives. I said to the master: "I am sending this child to school to learn to read the Qur'an. I wanted to first bring him into your esteemed presence that due to the blessing of your beneficent look and saintly soul God Almighty might make the Qur'an accessible to him." The master offered a prayer for the child's welfare, and then taking the child's writing slate in his blessed hand, he wrote on it (in Arabic): "In the name of God full of Compassion, ever Compassionate. Make it easy and do not make it difficult. **Alif, ba, ta, tha, ja** [the initial letters of the Arabic alphabet]." Then, with his own blessed tongue, he instructed the child how to pronounce these letters.

Consonant with this moment he told the following story. "It has been reported in a Tradition (of the Prophet) that there is a group of people who will be dragged into heaven in chains!" Then he added: "There are three interpretations [about the identity of this group]. One interpretation suggests that this group of people are children who have been compelled to learn. Even though they proceed with difficulty, they are led bound into the mosque. Gradually they progress from learning letters to learning the meaning of words, and from the surface meaning of words into their deeper meanings, and so their lot improves. Another interpretation proposes that that group consists of slaves who are being dragged in chains from the Abode of War into the Abode of Peace [i.e., they are high-minded men who never converted to Islam during their lifetime]." Then the master's eyes began to fill with tears. "The third group," he related, "are those who tomorrow on the Day of Resurrection testify 'We have believed; we have been sincere.' They are a group of the lovers of God whom He has directed to enter Paradise. Yet they protest: 'We did not beseech You for the sake of Heaven or for fear of Hell. We called on You only out of love for You." The command resounds: 'So you did, but the promise of seeing Me and being united with Me is fulfilled in Heaven. Enter there that you may obtain what you were promised.' Still, they do not budge. Then the nearby angels are commanded to bind their necks with chains of light and drag them into heaven! Praise be to God, the Lord of the universe!"

## IV. Assembly 25

Tuesday, 3rd of the month of Safar—may God conclude it with favor and success—A.H. 716 (27 April 1316)

I obtained the benefit of kissing his feet. He began to talk about CONTENTMENT AND SHOWING MODERATION IN PURSUIT OF WORLDLY GOALS. "Maulana Hafiz ad-din," he recalled, "is the author of numerous books, including **Kafi** and **Shafi'**. In them he has described how a dog is trained to hunt. When it has been taken hunting three times and caught its prey each time, it is called a 'trained dog.' The cheeta also is taught to hunt but they put a cheeta on the trail of prey and only when they come near the prey do they prod the cheeta. It then pounces and at once seizes the prey, unlike the dog, which is given free reign and runs hither and yon in search of the prey.

"In short, that eminent scholar has written that man ought to emulate some traits of the cheeta. He should not run after his daily provisions as does the dog. Only if something comes before him should he grasp it. Also, like the cheeta, when he is hunting prey, he should sit down once he has got it and not continue to run about wildly. Further, man should note that if the cheeta is slow afoot, they bring a dog and, heeling it opposite the cheeta, they prod it with a stick till the cheeta becomes frightened. Similarly, man must take note of others, to observe what they are doing and to be on guard against any improper actions."

### IV. Assembly 26
### Saturday, 20th of Rabiʿ al-awwal, A.H. 716 (12 June 1316)

I obtained the good fortune of kissing his feet. That day in the public audience hall [adjacent to the hospice], they had apprehended a man wielding a knife. And God knows who he was and what he was about. After servants had seized him and told the master—may God remember him with favor—what had happened, the master did not allow them to remove that man or hassle him. He summoned the intruder before him. "Swear by God," he told him, "that you will harm no Muslim." The man swore that he would not. The master—may God remember him with favor—then set him free and gave him some spending money. When I came to meet the master on that same day, they informed me about what had transpired.

Appropriate to the occasion the master then told the following story. "One day Shaykh al-Islam Farid ad-din—may God sanctify his lofty secret—had just finished saying his morning prayer. Still engrossed in God, his head remained prostrate on the ground. For a long time, as often happened, he remained like that, absorbed in God, his head prostrate on the ground. But because it was winter they had brought a garment and spread it over his blessed body. No attendants remained. Just I and he and no one else. Suddenly someone entered and in a loud voice shouted 'Peace!' The Shaykh was jolted from his meditative mood. But with his head still prostrate on the ground and the garment covering him, he asked: 'Who is here?' I spoke up and said: 'I am!' 'The man who just entered,' said the Shaykh, 'is a Turk of medium stature with a sallow complexion.' I looked at the man. He was exactly as the Shaykh described him. I said: 'Yes, he is.' 'Does he have a chain around his waist?' I looked at him, and saw that he did. 'Yes, he has,' I replied. 'And does he also have something in his ears?' I looked and saw that he did. 'Yes, he has an earring,' I replied. And every time I looked at him and then responded to the Shaykh, the man became more and more uneasy. After I had said 'Yes, he has an earring,' the Shaykh replied: 'Tell him to go away lest he become disgraced.' When I looked back toward the man, he had already taken to his heels and disappeared."

In this same assembly the master told the following anecdote. "There was a man in Ghaznin named Maulana Husam ad-din. He was the grandson of Shams al-ʿarifin—may God have mercy on him—and the disciple of Khwaja Ajall Shirazi—may God sanctify his blessed secret. One day this Maulana Husam ad-din and another disciple came and stood before Khwaja Ajall Shirazi. The Khwaja looked at them and then looked at the sky and then looked again at them. On his blessed lips came this pronouncement: 'Just now the robe of martyrdom has been sewn for one of the two of you [i.e. one of you will soon die a martyr's death].' When they left the presence of Khwaja Ajall Shirazi, they asked each other: 'How do we know which of the two of us will have this good fortune?' The Maulana was a preacher. Not long after meeting with Khwaja Ajall Shirazi he preached a sermon and, as he was descending from the pulpit, people flocked to kiss his hand. Suddenly an assailant lunged forward and, brandishing a knife, martyred the Maulana. They carried him to his home. He had a breath of life left in him. He used it to despatch an attendant to his master. 'Go tell him,' he gasped, 'that it was I who received that robe!' "

## IV. Assembly 27
### Saturday, 27th of Rabiʿ al-awwal, A.H. 716 (19 June 1316)

I obtained the good fortune of kissing his hand. He spoke about THE BLESSING THAT DERIVES FROM MEMORIZING THE QUR'AN. "There was a man in Badaun," recalled the master, "who had memorized all seven of the variant methods for reciting the Qur'an. A paradigm of virtue and a master of miracles, he was nonetheless indentured to a Hindu. His name was Shadi Muqri. Among his miracles was that whoever recited one page of the Qur'an before him God Almighty would make the whole of the Qur'an accessible to that person. I, too, recited one section of the Qur'an before Shadi Muqri, and through that blessing I succeeded in memorizing the entire Qur'an.

"It happened that one of Shadi Muqri's teachers lived in Lahore. His name was Khwajai Muqri and he was a saintly giant. Once when a visitor from Lahore came to Badaun, Muqri asked him: 'How is my teacher's health?' Though the teacher had died long ago, the visitor did not tell Shadi Muqri about his demise. Instead, the visitor told him that his teacher was in fine health. But then he began to narrate the conditions that prevailed in Lahore. He described how there had been heavy rains, washing away many houses. A fire also had raged out of control, burning down several more houses. By the time he had finished describing these catastrophes, Shadi Muqri remarked: 'Perhaps my teacher also perished.' 'Yes,' admitted the visitor, 'a long time ago he was joined to the mercy of God.' And God knows best [what actually happened]."

### IV. Assembly 28
Sunday, 20th of Rabiʿ al-ʿakhir, A.H. 716 (12 July 1316)

I obtained the good fortune of kissing his feet. He discussed a group of INDIFFERENT BELIEVERS, to wit, those who make the canonical pilgrimage but on their return immerse themselves in worldly concerns. I submitted: "I would be surprised if any group attached to the master would journey in that direction (i.e., to Mecca)." At the time that I was speaking, my friend Malih was with me. Continuing to address the master, I said: "Broken-hearted though I be, I once heard from my friend Malih a phrase that has made a lasting impression on me. The phrase that Malih told me was this: 'Someone goes on the pilgrimage who has not found a spiritual guide.' " When the master—may God remember him with favor—heard this phrase, his eyes filled with tears. On his blessed tongue came this line of poetry:

That way to the Kaʿba leads, this one to the Friend!

Then he remarked that after the death of Shaykh al-Islam Farid ad-din—may God sanctify his lofty secret—he had had a strong urge to make the canonical pilgrimage. "I said to myself: 'First I will go to Ajodhan to visit the tomb of the Shaykh.' In short, when I had paid my respects to Shaykh al-Islam, I achieved my purpose. Nothing more remained [to be done]. Another time, the same desire [to make the pilgrimage] arose. Again, I visited the tomb of Shaykh al-Islam and fulfilled my goal."

### IV. Assembly 29
Sunday, 11th of Jumada al-ula, A.H. 716 (1 August 1316)

I obtained the benefit of kissing his feet. He told a STORY ABOUT THE PROPHET MUHAMMAD. "One night the Prophet—on whom be peace—saw in his dream a well and a bucket above that well. It was the sort of well known as **qalib,** that is, they drilled until water appeared but then they did not build a structure of stone or wood around that spot. This is what is known as a **qalib** well. A well around which a container wall is built and then maintained, that is called a **tawa** or **tawiya** well. In short, the Prophet—upon whom be peace—saw a **qalib** well in his dream with a bucket above it. Taking that bucket, he drew some water and then retired. Next he saw Abu Bakr Siddiq—may God be pleased with him. He came and drew two or three buckets. Twice the Prophet saw Abu Bakr do this. Then he saw ʿUmar Khattab —may God be pleased with him. He came and drew ten to twelve buckets, and it was a big bucket that he used. It is called a **gharb** bucket because it can draw out a lot of water and can also be used to irrigate a large plot of land." The master—may God remember him with favor—added: "The point of this story is to focus on the function of the well. One drills a well to get water, whether or not one builds a container wall, whether or not one maintains that wall. The function of the well is simply to provide water. Likewise, in every work there must be one principal goal and one must pursue that goal."

In the interim one of those present conveyed greetings from a disciple named Muhammad Gwaliyori. The master—may God remember him with favor—said: "Yes, I remember him. He is a dear man. He once asked me: 'Which is better, celibacy or marriage?' I told him: 'To be celibate is a matter of courage while to get married is to do what is permitted. If someone is so immersed in God that he gives no thought to marriage, and remains unaware of what it entails because every moment his eyes, his tongue, and his limbs are protected (**mahfuz**),[76] then he should remain celibate. But if someone cannot be so immersed and if he continues to ponder the prospect of marriage, then he ought to get married. The heart of the matter is intention (**niyya**). When one intends to be immersed in God, that intention affects one's limbs, but when one's inner being has another coloration, that also affects the limbs.' "

The master then continued to speak about the life of this Muhammad Gwaliyori, noting that he lived a long life. Then he recalled the death date of Shams ad-din Iltetmish. On the blessed lips of the master came this verse:

> When six hundred and thirty-three years from the **hijra** had passed
> Then the Lord of the World Shams ad-din ʿAlamgir breathed his last.

Conversation then turned to NORMS OF CONDUCT FOR DISCIPLES. "When disciples bid farewell to their master, they should not return unless an urgent matter arises or they are coming home from a trip." In this connection the master told the following story. "A disciple named ʿAli Makki once bid farewell to Shaykh al-Islam Farid ad-din—may God sanctify his lofty secret. After bidding the Shaykh farewell, he went to the outskirts of Ajodhan to meet his travel companions, but they delayed their departure. And so he returned to the Shaykh. 'Yesterday you said goodbye,' recalled the Shaykh, 'why do you return today?' 'It is because my companions have lingered that I am returning.' 'Good day!' retorted the Shaykh curtly. When evening came, he again left and joined the caravan in preparation. But for a second day his travel companions lingered. Again ʿAli returned to the Shaykh. 'Why did you come back today?' queried the Shaykh. ʿAli immediately rejoined that his travel companions continued to linger, and so he had come back once again to call on the Shaykh. Turning to an attendant, the Shaykh asked for two loaves of bread. As soon as he was brought the two loaves of bread, he gave them to ʿAli and dispatched him. ʿAli left, never to return and see the Shaykh again."

The master then spoke for awhile about this ʿALI MAKKI. "He was a good man, replete with spiritual qualities. Often he used to say, 'Would that God would grant me a place to die which is not in my native city nor in a place where I intend to die, that is, may You grant me to die in a place that no one has made known or indicated to me.' " Then the master—may God remember him with favor—remarked: "This ʿAli was going toward Badaun and along the way experienced some affliction. After he had passed Bachlana, his affliction became still more intense, and before he could reach Badaun, he died, just on its outskirts, and was buried there."

And about this same ʿAli Makki, he told a further story. "I heard him recount the following incident. 'Once I was visiting Kirman, and there was a Qazi of Kirman who one day held a musical assembly to which he invited all the notables, officials, and scholars of the city. A dervish of mean disposition came uninvited. He had heard that there would be a musical assembly in the Qazi's house, and going there, he sat in a corner. When the **samaʿ** began, the dervish was overcome with a spiritual mood and stood up to dance. The Qazi, as chief of the assembly, was upset. He wanted either the chief of the assembly or some other notable to be the first to get up. Why did this dervish have to be the first to rise [and dance]? He slapped that dervish and told him to sit down. The dervish, overcome with shame, immediately sat down. Gradually the **sama‘** became more intense. The Qazi rose. No sooner had he gotten up than the dervish slapped him and told him to sit down. The way that the dervish gave this command struck terror in the heart of the Qazi and in the hearts of all those present. The Qazi sat down in his place. In short, when the **sama‘** at last ended, people dispersed. The dervish, too, left. The Qazi alone remained seated in his place. No matter how hard he tried to get up he could not. For a period of seven years he remained in that spot! After seven years had elapsed, that dervish returned. He knew what sort of deed he had done. On entering, he saw the Qazi, by now grown feeble and haggard. The dervish came and stood in front of him. "Get up!" he ordered the Qazi. The Qazi did not move. A second time he shouted: "Get up!" The Qazi remained seated. A third time the dervish exclaimed: "Too bad! Sit like that, and die like that!" Having spoken, he left. The Qazi motioned to him, and people went running to bring him back. But he was nowhere to be found, and the Qazi died in that condition!' "

## IV. Assembly 30

Wednesday, 28th of Jumada al-ula, A.H. 716 (18 August 1316)

I had the good fortune of kissing his feet. "Where did you perform the congregational prayer last Friday?" he asked. "In the Kilokhiri mosque," I replied. "But that day I did not trouble your Eminence [by visiting you] because of the droves of common people [who descended on you]." "I have often said," rejoined the master, "that special friends who call on me in the hospice do not need to trouble me by joining the crowds of visitors [in the assembly hall]."

Then he began to speak of THE PRECAUTIONS WHICH DISCIPLES SHOULD TAKE NOT TO TROUBLE THEIR MASTER. "Maulana Burhan ad-din Nasafi—may God be merciful to him—was a scholar with a perfected disposition. Whenever someone would come to study with him, he would say: 'Before you can learn from me, you must first fulfill three conditions. (1) Eat one meal only. Whatever food pleases you, eat no more than one portion of it till your studies [for the day] are completed. (2) Do not be absent. If you miss even one day of class, the next day I will not admit you to the lecture. (3) When you pass by me in public, greet me with the peace; do not try to kiss my hand or foot or show other gestures of respect.' "

After he had finished speaking of the Maulana, the master—may

God remember him with favor—noted: "People who come to see me touch their head to the ground. When they came to visit Shaykh al-Islam Farid ad-din and Shaykh Qutb ad-din—may God sanctify both their lofty secrets—neither Shaykh prevented their visitors [from making that gesture of respect], and so I also do not prevent them." I then submitted: "Those who come before you and touch their heads to the ground obtain an added benefit: They subdue their lower selves since the master is a creature of God Most High, and it is from God that he acquires his spiritual stature, not from the disciple's submission."

The master—may God remember him with favor—then told the following story. "In days gone by the descendant of an eminent person came to see me. He had just returned from a journey to Syria and Turkey. After he had come in and sat down, Wahid ad-din Qureishi called on me, and as was the custom of servants, he paid obeisance by touching his head to the ground. The much-traveled visitor let out a cry and berated him, saying, 'Do not prostrate yourself. It is not permitted.' He was so quarrelsome that I did not want to respond to his charges. But when he continued to harangue Wahid ad-din, I at last said this much: 'Listen! Do not insist on the correctness of your viewpoint. Every act that has been deemed obligatory, even when it ceases to be obligatory, still remains commendable. Among pre-Islamic nations fasting during the bright days and the **ʿashura** days[77] was obligatory but with the coming of the Prophet—upon whom be peace—the fast of Ramadan became obligatory, replacing the obligation to fast during the bright days and the **ʿashura** days. Yet fasting during those days still remained commendable. As to prostration, among pre-Islamic nations it was commendable. For instance, a subject prostrated when approaching the ruler or a student when approaching his teacher. Members of religious communities also prostrated before their prophets. During the lifetime of the Prophet—upon whom be peace—prostration ceased to be obligatory [though it remained commendable]. Even if it ceased to be commendable, it would be permissible. In other words, were it no longer commended, it would still be permitted. How then can you eliminate or prohibit what is permitted? Please tell me, what sort of work is it to deny that such changes in the Law take place?' Having said this much, I fell silent. He could give no reply."

The master—may God remember him with favor—after he had narrated this anecdote, added: "I regret having said even this much. Had he been a dispirited person, it would not have been fitting for me to talk like this. There are two things about my response to him that I regret. First, why did I feel compelled to speak to him in this manner? Second, since he was a traveler [just returned from a trip], why did I not present him with something? It would have been nice to give him, for instance, a cloak or some silver money. I regret both these oversights."

Then, about THE IMPORTANCE OF GIVING SOMETHING, he quoted Shaykh al-Islam Farid ad-din—may God sanctify his lofty secret. "He used to say: 'Whenever someone comes calling on another, the host must see that his caller leaves with something in hand.' "

Consonant with this moral, he told a further story. "Once an old man came calling on Shaykh al-Islam Farid ad-in—may God sanctify his lofty secret. He said: 'When I once called on Shaykh Qutb ad-din—may God favor his resting place—I saw you there.' The Shaykh did not recognize him. But after the man informed him further, he did remember who he was. And that old man had brought a young lad with him, who happened to be his son. As they talked on and on, that lad began to become discourteous and even rude to Shaykh Farid ad-din. The conversation seemed endless." The master—may God remember him with favor—remarked: "I and Maulana Shihab ad-din, the Shaykh's son, were seated outside. When the atmosphere became charged, we went in, and that lad kept on speaking rudely. At last Maulana Shihab ad-din stepped forward and slapped the lad. He became ashamed that Maulana Shihab ad-din had made a fool of him. I then grabbed him by the hand, but as I did, the great Shaykh—may God sanctify his lofty secret—intervened. 'Make restitution,' he instructed his son. Maulana Shihab ad-din swiftly produced some money, and giving some silver to the father as well as the son, he made them both very happy and they departed.

"Now, it was the habit of the great Shaykh that every evening after eating some food he would summon me and Maulana Rukn ad-din. Maulana Shihab ad-din would also sometimes be present and sometimes not. He would then query us about the news and events of that day. 'What transpired today?' he would ask. 'What kind of a day was it?' And so on that particular day after eating some food he summoned me and Maulana Rukn ad-din and asked us about the day's events. We talked about the encounter with the old man and the crude talk of his son and the response of Maulana Shihab ad-din. The great Shaykh laughed!" Then the master—may God remember him with favor—said: "I asked him: 'When the quarrel broke out between that lad and Maulana Shihab ad-din, did I act correctly in taking that lad by the hand?' Again laughing, the Shaykh replied: 'You did well, very well indeed!' "

### IV. Assembly 31
### Wednesday, 24th of the blessed month of Rajab, A.H. 716 (12 October 1316)

I obtained the benefit of kissing his feet. Since my previous visit I scalded my toe and it had become very painful. For some time I had not had the good fortune to visit the master, but now as I came before him, I told him about my condition. "Is it a boil or some other affliction?" he asked. "No, it is not a boil," I replied. "One of my toes has become swollen and the pain is intense." "Have you ever had boils?" he asked. "Yes, I have," I replied, "but it is five years now since I had my last boil. It happened that once when I had this affliction I came to visit the master and told him the nature of my illness. On his blessed lips came the directive: 'The remedy for tumors is to recite **Surat al-buruj** (Q.85) during the customary afternoon prayer, and since tumors are like boils, one may hope that recourse to that surah will ward them off also.'[78] Since that time I have recited **Surat al-Buruj** during afternoon prayer and I have never been afflicted with boils!"

Then I submitted: "I have also heard from the blessed tongue of the master that during afternoon prayer one ought to recite five other **surahs: Surat al-Zilzal** (Q.99) and the four **surahs** that follow it (Q.100, 101, 102, and 103)." The master then reiterated THE IMPORTANCE OF **SURAT AL-ʿASR** (Q.103). "During the afternoon prayer one should recite it ten times, four times in the first prayer cycle, three times in the second, twice in the third, and once in the fourth."

Next he asked: "Do you say the Friday prayer in a congregational mosque?" "Yes, I do," I replied, "and the present prayer leader is a very sincere person who is attached to the master. He is an upright young man." "Has he shaved his head?" asked the master. "No," I replied, "he has not." "It would be better for him to shave," advised the master, "since in doing ablutions it is difficult to be circumspect; a person whose hair is unshaved may remain in a state of ritual uncleanness. By contrast, someone who has been totally shaved may perform his ablutions without lingering doubts."

After that he began to speak about THE BENEFITS OF BEING SHAVED. "There are three things," he observed, "that men say one must do for oneself and that one cannot instruct others to do. The first is shaving. One has to shave oneself and cannot instruct another. That is to say, its benefits pertain to that individual and to him alone. The second is drinking before eating, while the third is rubbing oil on the soles of one's feet. Or so men say," added the master, "but I say that one should **not** act in this way. Rather, you should behave in such a way that whatever you find to be of personal benefit for yourself you also direct others to do."

In this connection he told the following story. "There was an Arab who used to preface his prayers with the invocation: 'O God, have mercy on me, have mercy on Muhammad and do not show mercy to anyone but us!' When this was reported to the Prophet—peace be upon him—he told that Arab: 'You should expand your boundaries!' "

After that the master—may God remember him with favor—explained. "If someone in the desert wants to build a house, he demarcates a place. He takes some stones and arranges them in such a manner as to indicate: 'This area is reserved for my house.' Hence the Prophet—peace be upon him—informed that Arab through this analogy that the mercy of God Almighty is expansive. Why then should someone pray: 'O God, forgive me and forgive Muhammad but do not forgive anyone else'? You are erecting boundaries that restrict and confine. Instead," concluded the master repeating the Prophet's dictum, "you should expand your boundaries."

## IV. Assembly 32
### Saturday, 10th of Ramadan, A.H. 716 (26 November 1316)

I had the good fortune of kissing his feet. When I arrived the master—may God remember him with favor—was sitting in the shade, out of the sunlight. On his blessed lips came this utterance: "The Prophet—peace be upon him—once told ʿA'isha—may God be pleased with her: 'Do not sit directly in the sun lest it dry up the moisture of your skin.' "

Then he spoke about SHAMS DABIR.[79] "Have you ever seen Shams Dabir?" he asked me. "Yes," I replied, "he is a close relative of mine." "He is a fine man," observed the master. "He read the **Lawa'ih** of Qazi Hamid ad-din Nagauri[80] with Shaykh al-Islam Farid ad-din—may God sanctify his lofty secret."

Then the master spoke about SHAMS DABIR AND SHAYKH AL-ISLAM FARID AD-DIN. "After the Great Shaykh had taken breakfast, he would busy himself with God and he would remain immersed in his devotions till the time of evening prayer. From breakfast to evening prayer is the span of an entire day. In this interval Shams Dabir would prepare some food and he would request two or three of his friends to join him. Together they would break fast and then wait till it was time for the Shaykh to break his fast. I also used to join them. Such was the way Shams Dabir comported himself in his early years," noted the master, "but when he became prosperous, he forsook this practice." After that on his blessed tongue came the pronouncement: "Look what happens when one accedes to worldliness!"

Conversation turned to **TARAWIH** PRAYERS. "Do you say these prayers at home or in the mosque?" he asked me. "At home," I replied, "but the prayer leader of the mosque is a virtuous man." "Yes," noted the master, "once, in the congregational mosque, he completed a full recitation of the Qur'an during **tarawih** prayer." "Every evening," I added, "that prayer leader, whose name is Sharaf ad-din, recites a portion (one-thirtieth) of the Qur'an." The master—may God remember him with favor—remarked: "Indeed he does. One evening I said prayers behind him. Even though there had been heavy rains that evening and the streets were full of mud, I still went to say my prayers. With such care did that man recite the prayers that he seemed to pronounce each letter as correctly as it is possible to pronounce it." In this connection the master began to talk about a scholar from Sunam. "His name was Maulana Dawlatyar. He, too, would recite prayers so eloquently that no one could succeed in reciting as he did."

Then he spoke about THE ELOQUENCE OF SHAYKH FARID AD-DIN. "I read six portions (or one-fifth) of the Qur'an with the Great Shaykh—may God sanctify his lofty secret. I also read three books with him—one I heard him read and two I read together with him. One day I asked if I could recite the Qur'an before him. 'Recite,' he replied. From then on every Friday, after the noon congregational prayer till the time of later afternoon prayers, as often as possible, I would recite some of the Qur'an before the Shaykh, and in this way I finished reciting six portions of the Qur'an before him. When I first began to recite, he told me: 'Recite **al hamdu lillah** (praise be to God).' I began to recite and continued till I reached (the end of **Surat al-Fatiha**):

**wala dalin** (and not among those who have gone astray). 'Say the **dad** (in **dalin**) as I say it' commanded the Great Shaykh. I tried and tried, but however much I wanted to say it as he said it, I could not. So articulate, so eloquent was the Shaykh," remarked the master, "that no one could succeed in pronouncing the **dad** as he did. Similarly," he added, "the special **dad** which was bequeathed to the Prophet—peace be upon him—was unavailable to others. They used to call the Prophet—peace be upon him—the apostle of **dad**," noted the master, who then pronounced the dictum: " 'O apostle of **dad**, he to whom was revealed the **dad**!' " And God knows best!

### IV. Assembly 33
### Thursday, the 15th of the blessed month of Ramadan, A.H. 716 (1 December 1316)

I obtained the benefit of kissing his feet. Conversation turned to **TARAWIH** PRAYER. "**Tarawih** is a Tradition," observed the master, "and to finish a cycle of Qur'an recitation in **tarawih** is also a Tradition, whether it takes one evening or three evenings. Then the master repeated what he had said: "**Tarawih** is a Tradition, just as congregational prayer is a Tradition and one complete recitation of the Qur'an in **tarawih** is a Tradition." "Is this a Tradition of the Prophet—peace be upon him," I asked, "or is it a Tradition of the Companions—may God be pleased with all of them?" "It is a Tradition of the Companions," he replied. "The Prophet—peace be upon him—commended the recitation in three nights and also the recitation in one night but the regularization of this Tradition (during the month of Ramadan) was made by 'Umar Khattab—may God be pleased with him—during the Caliphal period."

One of those present asked: "Is a Tradition of the Caliphs also called a Tradition?" "In our juridical practice, yes," replied the master, "but in the practice of Imam Shafi'i Tradition is restricted to what the Prophet—peace and blessings be upon him—did."

He then told a story about the Greatest Imam Abu Hanifa Kufi—may God have mercy upon him. "In the blessed month of Ramadan he used to complete sixty-one cycles of Qur'an recitation—one during **tarawih** prayer, thirty during the day, and another thirty at night."[81]

After that the master remarked: "For forty years he would say the dawn prayer with the ablution of the evening prayer [i.e., he never rendered himself ritually impure through a nocturnal discharge]." Then on his blessed tongue came the observation: "How many religious specialists and scholars are there whose names and whereabouts are unknown! The fame which Abu Hanifa attained was due solely to his exemplary conduct. His behavior reflected his inner, spiritual life, a match not easily achieved. When did Shibli and Junayd live? [No one knows precisely but] men do know that tomorrow and the day after tomorrow will pass. They will be remembered only for (the) exemplary conduct (of men who live then). And God knows the truth!"

## IV. Assembly 34
### Sunday, 9th of Shawwal, A.H. 717 (15 December 1317)

I obtained the benefit of kissing his feet. He asked: "Have you been recording what you have heard from me?" "Yes, I have been," I replied. On his blessed tongue came the observation: "How amazing that you remember all this!" I submitted: "I wrote down whatever I remembered, and whatever I did not remember or whatever did not seem quite right I left blank till I heard it a second time, and then I would record your words. For example, in the previous assembly you recalled that the Prophet—peace be upon him—had told ʿA'isha: 'Do not sit directly in the sun lest it dry up the moisture of your skin!' I had it in mind to ask: 'What sort of Tradition is this?' " On his pearl-scattering tongue came the reply: "I never saw this Tradition in a book, but I did hear it from Maulana ʿAla ad-din Usuli: Not only was he my teacher in Badaun but he was also a saintly person who had attained a perfect spiritual state."

The master then began to describe THE VIRTUES OF MAULANA ʿALA AD-DIN. "He was a very saintly man even though he never clasped the hand of someone in discipleship, for in his view you should not become bound to another unless that person was a Shaykh with a perfected spiritual state. Yet it happened," continued the master, "that once when this Maulana ʿAla ad-din was but a child he was passing through the streets of Badaun and chanced upon Shaykh Jalal ad-din Tabrizi—may God have mercy upon him. Shaykh Jalal ad-din was sitting on the porch of a house. As soon as his eye fell on the lad, he summoned him and gave him the cloak off his own back." Observed the master—may God remember him with favor: "All the good qualities and laudable traits of Maulana ʿAla ad-din were due to the blessing of that cloak!"

Then he told the following story. "This Maulana ʿAla ad-din had an old servant who was newly indentured. Near Badaun was a shady grove named Kathir. This servant came from that place. One day he began to cry. Maulana ʿAla ad-din asked: 'Why do you cry?' He said, 'I have a son, but now I am separated from him.' Rejoined the Maulana: 'If I take you to the reservoir that is about two miles outside the city, on the road to Kathir, do you know the way from there to your home?' 'I know it,' replied the servant. In the morning the Maulana took him from the house and, leaving him at the reservoir, went away." When he reached this point in the story the master—may God remember him with favor—became teary-eyed. "The externalist scholars will never grasp this meaning, yet," added the master, "one can understand what the Maulana was trying to do."

He then spoke briefly about the Maulana's knowledge and his deep insight into problem solving. "The Maulana used to say: 'If there be a complex issue or a question for which you seek an answer yet it is so difficult that you find yourself saying: "My mind will not be at ease till I get to the bottom of this problem,' then you should look somewhere else for its solution!' " The master—may God remember him with favor—commented: "What wisdom is there in this remark!"

To illustrate what he meant, the master told the following story. "Once this Maulana ʿAla ad-din brought two copies of the same text to class. He kept one copy and gave me the other. Sometimes he would recite and I would follow. At other times I would recite and he would follow. We proceeded in this fashion till we reached a verse that did not scan properly nor was its meaning clear. We spent much time pondering that verse. We could find no solution to the problem it posed. In the meantime a man named Malik Yar arrived. Maulana ʿAla ad-din said: 'I will ask him what is the correct reading of this verse.' Then he recited the verse to Malik Yar. Malik Yar proceeded to recite it back to him—rhymed and with a meaning that we immediately grasped!

"Afterward, Maulana ʿAla ad-din said to me: 'Malik Yar intuited that meaning through the mystery of spiritual taste (**dhawq**).' Although I already knew about sensory taste, on that day I learned about spiritual taste!"

Then the master remarked: "This Malik Yar could not read a single word, yet God Almighty had granted him insight as a boon! Once he had been offered the position of prayer leader at the congregational mosque of Badaun. Some questioned whether or not he was qualified for such a prestigious post. Everyone had his own view on this matter. When reports of the controversy reached Maulana ʿAla ad-din, he retorted: 'If they were to offer Malik Yar the position of prayer leader at the congregational mosque of Baghdad, [it would be beneath him; indeed] it would demean his high spiritual stature!' " And God knows best!

### IV. Assembly 35
### Wednesday, 26th of Shawwal, A.H. 717 (1 January 1318)

I obtained the good fortune of kissing his feet. Conversation turned to CHARITY, CHIVALRY, AND PREEMPTION. "There is charity, there is chivalry, and then there is preemption," he explained. "Charity is giving something to a person in need, while chivalry is giving something to a friend, whether it be a cloak or a gift or some such thing, and the friend whom you have so honored gives you something equivalent in return. This is called chivalry. But preemption is not charity nor is it chivalry. Preemption occurs when you deflect a possible injury that someone may do you, either in speech or deed. For instance, there may be someone who, if you do not give him something, he may say something bad or take some rash action, and you therefore give him something to protect yourself. This is called preemption, and the Prophet—peace be upon him—understood all three terms. Consider 'those whose hearts need to be reconciled' (Ar., **muallifat al-qulub:** Q.9.60). In the early period of Islam the Prophet gave something to 'those whose hearts need to be reconciled,' but when Islam became powerful he no longer gave this kind of gift."

In those days there was a call to war. I asked the master: "How can one carry a copy of the Holy Qur'an into battle, since it is so difficult to preserve it intact?" "You must carry it nonetheless," he replied. Then on his blessed lips came this observation: "When Islam was still in its infancy, the Prophet—peace be upon him—would not carry the Qur'an into battle. He feared that his army might be defeated and the Qur'an fall into the hands of unbelievers. But when Islam grew strong and its army vast, then Muslim warriors would carry the Qur'an into battle." "But it is still difficult to find a proper place for the Qur'an in an army tent," I protested. "One must rest it near one's head," replied the master.

He then told a story about SULTAN MAHMUD (of Ghazna). "They saw Sultan Mahmud in a dream after his death. They asked him: 'How has Almighty God treated you?' 'One night I was in the house [of a friend],' he replied, 'and there was a copy of the Holy Qur'an in a niche [in my room, and not on its proper stand]." I said to myself: 'How can I sleep with the Qur'an here [on this perilous perch]?' Then I said to myself: 'I will ask them to remove the Qur'an from here,' but then I thought further: 'How can I have peace of mind if I ask them to remove the Qur'an from my room?' In short, I remained seated upright and awake throughout the entire night, and after my death they rewarded me on account of the respect that I had shown to that copy of the Holy Qur'an!"

I submitted another request to the master. "When a man enters the army it occurs to him that he should make provision for the possibility of his death. In his will should he direct his retainers to bury him in the very place where he dies? Otherwise, it seems tasteless in the extreme to have his corpse conveyed to a faraway place." "Yes," replied the master, "it is fitting that a person should be buried in the place where he died. If someone is worried about the safety of his gravesite and elects to have his corpse returned to where he came from, that is not good. Since earth is the domain of God the Almighty and Exalted, how can there be any question of safety? Were earth the domain of another, then it would be fitting to want to extricate oneself from there. But as for that man who leaves home in army service and goes far away, there is nothing better for him than to be buried in the very place where he dies." Then he added: "Whoever travels a long, long way from his family, if he should die and be buried in that faraway land, then the same distance between his home and his gravesite will be allotted him as space in heaven!"

Conversation next turned to GOOD KINGS AND UPRIGHT RULERS. Recounted the master: "There was a monarch who was the model of piety, a true mediator of divine secrets. One day he sat in a reflective mood. His wife was seated beside him on a throne. After looking at the courtyard, he turned and looked skyward, focusing his eyes on the sky for a long while. After that he turned and scanned his courtyard again. Then he turned his gaze up once more and stared at the sky for a long, long time. Finally he turned to look at his wife and broke down crying. 'What's the matter?' she asked. 'First you look at the sky for a long time, then at the courtyard, then back to the sky, and then at me and begin to cry. What's the matter?' 'Withdraw your question,' replied the monarch. 'It's not a subject fit to be discussed.' But his wife kept insisting: 'Tell me the answer. Tell me the answer.' 'Okay,' agreed the monarch, 'since you press me, I'll tell you.' Then he spoke what was on his mind. 'Know and make no mistake about it, this very hour my glance fell on the Preserved Tablet. There I saw that my name had been erased from the ledger of the living. Hence I know that the moment of my death is near. I looked again to see who would be in my place. I saw an Ethiopian who is in this courtyard. He will assume my place, and you will fall into his embrace. This is what I saw!' His wife, when she heard him out, exclaimed; 'Now what do you imagine? What do you propose to do?' 'I? What can I do?' replied the monarch. 'Whatever God Almighty has decreed will come to pass. I am content with His judgment.'

"The monarch then summoned that Ethiopian from his courtyard and, giving him the very cloak he was wearing, he made him his heir. He then put that Ethiopian in charge of an army unit, nominating him to a certain rank with a complement of notables under his command. The Ethiopian accepted the monarch's order. He completed the task assigned him by vanquishing the enemy army. From the battlefield, with booty in hand, he came to pay homage to the monarch. The day after his return the monarch died. Because that Ethiopian was flush with victory's laurels, he had won the good will of the inhabitants of that kingdom. Upon the monarch's death, the kingdom passed to the Ethiopian, and the wife too fell into his arms."

He then told a brief story about PHILOSOPHERS. "Farabi was a philosopher," he noted. "One day he came into the assembly of the Caliph dressed in a short cloak and simple clothes, for he was of Turkish origin. Farabi began to play his cymbal and to sing. Now there were three kinds of music, according to this philosopher. One made people laugh, another made them cry, and a third put them to sleep or rendered them unconscious. In short, when Farabi began to play the cymbal, at first the whole assembly erupted in laughter. Then when he began to sing, they all fell to crying, "Ah! Ah!" Then when he kept on singing, they all became unconscious. Writing these words on the wall, he left:

> Farabi did indeed appear here, but then he disappeared.

When the members of the assembly regained consciousness and read what he had written, they said to themselves: 'This Farabi was indeed a philosopher; alas we did not recognize him as such!' "

In this same vein the master told the story of the philosopher who came to visit the Caliph and misled him into thinking that planetary movement was voluntary, a view that contradicts orthodox Muslim teaching. Now it happened that Shaykh Shihab ad-din Suhrawardi—may God have mercy upon him—was alive at this time. When the Shaykh learned that the philosopher had inclined the Caliph to that [false] doctrine, Shaykh Shihab ad-din paid a visit on the Caliph (and we have told the story of his visit in an earlier assembly).[82] In short, the Shaykh, by performing a miracle, was able to expose that dangerous allurement: To the philosopher as well as the Caliph he made appear that angel who causes the planets to move at the command of Almighty God.

In short, the master—may God remember him with favor—was in the middle of (re)telling this story when someone arrived and announced: "Tonight in my home a baby boy has been born." The master—may God remember him with favor—said: "Name him ʾUmar and give him the surname of Shihab ad-din: Since I have just been recollecting Shaykh Shihab ad-din, he should be given the Shaykh's name and surname!" One of those present said: "This child whom you name ʾUmar, whenever you call him by that name, take care not to ridicule or belittle him." In the same connection the master—may God remember him with favor—commented: "Shaykh Najib ad-din Mutawakkil—may God have mercy upon him—had two sons. He named one Muhammad, the other Ahmad. Sometimes Shaykh Najib ad-din Mutawakkil would become irritated with them, and in a fit of anger he would call out to them: 'O master Muhammad, why did you do that? O master Ahmad, why did you do that?' Imagine: Even though he had been overcome with anger, he would address them in this polite fashion, saying 'O master Muhammad, O master Ahmad!' "

Then in connection with GIVING NAMES, he observed: "The Prophet—peace be upon him—frequently changed names. If someone had been given a vile name, he would give him a good name. Once a man came to the Prophet, and the Prophet—peace be upon him—asked: 'What is your name?' '**ʿAsi** (sinner),' he replied. The Prophet—peace be upon him—said: 'I name you **mutiʿ** (obedient).' Another time a man came to the Prophet, and the Prophet—peace be upon him—asked him: 'What is your name?' '**Mudtajiʿ**,' replied the man. And they call someone by this name who lies down on the ground. The Prophet—peace and blessings be upon him—said: 'I name you **Munbaʿith.**' And they call someone by this name who lifts himself off the ground and gets up. Once a woman came to the Prophet and the Prophet—peace be upon him—asked her: 'What is your name?' She replied: '**Shaʿb ad-dala** (person led astray).' The Prophet—peace be upon him—said: 'I name you **Shaʿb al-huda** (rightly guided person).' Another time the Prophet—peace be upon him—named a man **Jamal** (beauty). And it happened thus. He was a very powerful man. Once when people were going from one place to another, they happened to pass by him. One came and gave him an ablution vessel, which he then sent to another house. Someone else brought him a cloak, another something else. All these gifts he accepted in a humble manner. Hence the Prophet—peace be upon him—named him **Jamal** (beauty)."

He then spoke about THOSE WHO BECOME ESTRANGED FROM THEIR SPIRITUAL MASTERS. "Many persons, having pledged allegiance to a **pir**, become estranged from him. Their disposition does not remain the same after that." To illustrate the point he told the story of a saint who used to say: "Whoever comes to me and, after pledging to be my disciple, leaves, it is as if there is a barrier blocking me from him. He no longer has that disposition that he had as my disciple."

In the same vein he told the story of a saint who used to say: "If They have chosen me to be your spiritual master, have They then closed the inner door of your home, wherein lies your soul, together with your faith, or have They made it appear to you as some miracle that touches only the outer door?" The master—may God remember him with favor—explained this [difficult] declaration. "The door which leads into [the courtyard of] a home they call 'the inner door,' while the door which leads out [onto the street] they call 'the outer door.' The saint was saying something like this: 'If They have chosen me to be your spiritual master, are They saying that They have sealed your soul, together with your faith, behind this inner door, or are They saying instead that They have sealed it behind the outer door where it is still visible? I am saying that they have sealed it behind this door, which is the inner door, together with your faith, for who knows where the outer door leads? Either your faith is safe with me or it is not!' "

After that the master noted: "It is not only in the present age that men are prone to change their minds. It also happened in former times. When the Prophet—peace be upon him—died, thousands of Muslims became apostates. They sent a message to Abu Bakr Siddiq—may God be pleased with him—saying: 'If you will excuse us from paying the alms tax, we will remain Muslims.' Abu Bakr—may God be pleased with him—consulted with his friends. Some of them advised: 'If the Caliph accedes to their demands and excuses them from the alms tax so that they do not forsake Islam, that would be in the community interest.' After they had spoken, Abu Bakr—may God be pleased with him—drew his sword and exclaimed: 'That is a divine duty. Whoever is of sound mind and can mount a camel and gives less than God requires, I will make war against him with this sword.' They reported what he had said to the Commander of the Faithful ʿAli—may God be pleased with him. 'The Caliph acted wisely,' commented ʿAli. 'If he had excused them from the alms tax, when someone else became Caliph, they would say: "Please excuse us from prayer." By this process all the statutes of Islam would become null and void.' "

After that the master—may God remember him with favor—said: "Once Shaykh al-Islam Farid ad-din—may God sanctify his lofty secret—said: 'There was a person who professed allegiance to me and after he left my presence, for some time his disposition remained the same. But then it changed. There was another who went far away from my presence and he stayed away for a long, long time. Although his disposition remained the same and for an extended period did not change, eventually it, too, changed.' Then the Shaykh looked toward the place of prayer while motioning to me. 'This man who has remained attached to me,' he announced, 'has the same disposition and has not changed one whit.' " The master—may God remember him with favor—when he came to this point in the story, began to cry. With tears in his eyes, he made this blessed declaration: "Till today I remain constant in my love for the Shaykh. Nay, my love for him increases more and more!" And praise be to God, the Lord of the universe!

### IV. Assembly 36
Tuesday, 10th of Dhu'l-Qa'da, A.H. 716 (14 January 1318)

I obtained the good fortune of kissing his hand. He began to talk about KHWAJA SHAHI MUY TAB—may God have mercy upon him—who was from Badaun. He recalled that Qazi Hamid ad-din Naguari—may God have mercy upon him—used to call him "the Sovereign of Inner Light" (**Shahi raushan-i zamir**). "When Shahi Muy Tab was at last given the cloak [signifying that he had completed his discipleship under a Sufi master]," said the master, "he sent someone to Shaykh Mahmud Muina Duz with the message: 'We have done such-and-such today, and we have also donned Shahi Muy Tab with the emblematic cloak. Is this action pleasing to you?' Shaykh Mahmud Muina Duz replied: 'Whatever you do is always pleasing and always fine.' "

Then he began talking about KHWAJA ABU BAKR MUY TAB, the brother of Shahi Muy Tab—may God have mercy upon him. "Maulana Siraj ad-din Hafiz Badauni, who was a special disciple of his, reported that one evening Khwaja Abu Bakr was exhausted. He renewed his ablution and after performing two cycles of prayer, he expired." On the blessed lips of the master—may God remember him with favor—came this pronouncement (in Arabic): "As you live so will you die!"[83]

Conversation then turned to SHAYKH AHMAD NAHRAWANI.

"He was a saintly person," declared the master. "Shaykh Baha ad-din Zakariya—may God have mercy upon him—had good words to say about very few people yet about Shaykh Ahmad Nahrawani he declared: 'If you could weigh the preoccupation with God of Ahmad Nahrwani it would be equivalent to that of ten other Sufis!' Whenever Shaykh Ahmad Nahrwani would enter the congregational mosque, his friends would accompany him and he would enter with this multitude. There was another dervish named Shaykh ʿAli Shurida. Every time that Shaykh Ahmad Nahrwani went to the mosque he would block his way, saying 'Don't enter the mosque with this crowd.' One day Shaykh Ahmad Nahrwani was going to the mosque with his friends when they came upon a man being pummeled by another. Forming a circle around him, Shaykh Ahmad and his friends prevented this man from being further beaten. In the meantime Shaykh ʿAli Shurida arrived. On seeing him, Shaykh Ahmad Nahrwani said: 'It is to do works such as these that I leave home in the company of friends.' "

Conversation turned to the question: WHOSE DISCIPLE WAS AHMAD NAHRWANI? Remarked the master: "God alone knows whose disciple he was. Some have said that he had been blessed by Faqih Madhu, the same Faqih Madhu who was the prayer leader at the congregational mosque of Ajmer. One day Shaykh Ahmad was singing a Hindi song, for in his youth he had a fine voice and used to sing beautiful Hindi tunes. When Faqih Madhu heard of this, he berated Shaykh Ahmad: 'With a voice such as yours, what a shame to waste it on Hindi melodies! Memorize the Qurʾan instead!' Shaykh Ahmad then committed the Qurʾan to memory; he also became a Muslim. Yes," recalled the master—may God remember him with favor—"Shaykh Ahmad Nahrwani was also present in that musical assembly where Shaykh Qutb ad-din Bakhtiyar Kaki—may God sanctify his lofty secret—expired." (And the story of the death of Shaykh Qutb ad-din has been narrated in the preceding pages.)

Conversation next turned to the DERVISHES OF BADAON. "In Badaon," recalled the master, "there was a dervish named ʿAziz Bashir. He left Badaon for Delhi, intending to enter the service of Maulana Nasih ad-din, the grandson of Qazi Hamid ad-din Nagauri—may God have mercy upon him. He hoped to earn a cloak (emblematic of discipleship) from Maulana Nasih ad-din. Toward this end he organized an expedition of dervishes to the Royal Reservoir, for everyone knew about the sweet quality of its water. Yet that 'Aziz Bashir who sought a cloak, on seeing Hauzi Sultan, exclaimed: 'What a paltry pond! The small reservoir in Badaon is better than this reservoir!' Khwaja Muhammad Karim was present in the group. When he heard this comment he advised Maulana Nasih ad-din: 'Do not confer a cloak on someone who has made such a foolish remark!' And Maulana Nasih ad-din followed his advice; he did not give that dervish from Badaon a cloak of discipleship."

He then told a further story about SHAHI MUY TAB. "A light appeared to him in Badaon. And all the people flocked to see him; everywhere he went a crowd followed behind him. Now that Shahay was a man with dark lips. At that time there was a dervish named Mahmud Najashi [i.e, someone from Ethiopia]. When he saw Khwaja Shahi with that crowd around him, he exclaimed: 'O you who are dark as though well warmed, [know that] you will indeed be scorched!' And it came to pass that Khwaja Shahi did die in the bloom of youth—may God have mercy upon him!"

The master then began to talk about KHWAJA 'AZIZ, the chief police officer of Badaon. "He was a fine man, a disciple of dervishes, himself attached to Shaykh Diya ad-din of Badaon. From time to time he would remember (other) dervishes and, summoning them to an audience, he would arrange a special event on their behalf." There was in Badaon a youth who had recently converted to Islam. He related to the master the following incident: "One day I was proceeding toward the public gardens of Badaon. This noble officer was seated underneath a tree and had set up a table. When he saw me from afar, he shouted: 'Hello! Come here!' I was afraid; I did not want to disturb him. Yet I did approach him. And he treated me with extreme deference, seating me next to himself. After eating some food, I got up and left."

Maulana Siraj ad-din Hafiz Badaoni—may God Almighty grant him peace—was present. He interrupted the master, asking: "The dictum 'He who has no Shaykh then Satan is his Shaykh'—is that a Prophetic Tradition?" "No," replied the master—may God remember him with favor—"that is a dictum of the Sufi masters." Maulana Siraj ad-din then asked: "The dictum 'He who does not see a successful person will not himself succeed'—is that a Prophetic Tradition?" Replied the master: "They are both dicta of the Sufi masters."

Then he spoke about that dervish who, when he saw someone who was attached to a master, would say: "He does not sit in anyone's scales." "Does that mean such a man is unbalanced?" I asked. "No," replied the master. "It means that whoever is attached to a spiritual master knows that on Judgment Day his deeds will be placed in the scales of his master. Hence of SOMEONE WHO IS NOT THE DISCIPLE OF ANOTHER, they say: 'He DOES NOT SIT IN ANYONE'S SCALES!'—that is to say, he does not have a spiritual master." And praise be to God, the Lord of the Universe!

The conversation next turned briefly to THE SUPPRESSION OF MIRACLES. Commented the master: "To perform miracles is not a commendable work for saints. Rather a Muslim should be a helpless beggar seeking only Truth." In this connection he told a story about KHWAJA ABU'L-HASAN NURI—may God have mercy upon him. "Once he was sitting on the bank of the Tigris River. Seeing a fisherman, he asked him: 'Throw your net into the river, and catch a fish. If I am a true saint (**sahib-i wilayat**), you will catch a fish that will weigh exactly two and a half **mans,** no more, no less!' The fisherman cast his net into the river and caught a fish and, on weighing it, he found that it weighed exactly two and a half **mans,** no more, no less! When Shaykh Junayd—may God sanctify his lofty secret—was told about this, he remarked: 'Alas, it would have been better had there been a black snake in the net, to bite Abu'l-Hasan and kill him.' 'Why do you say this?' they asked. 'If a snake had bitten him and he had died,' replied Junayd, 'he would have been acclaimed a martyr, but since he is still alive, who knows what will be the outcome of his work?' "

Then in the same vein the master told a further story. "There was a dervish who, if anyone had stomach pain, would tell the person: 'Go eat tripe and you'll be cured.' If a person came to him with a headache, he would say: 'Go eat the choicest rice dish, and you'll be cured.' And whatever he said came to pass. But Shaykh ʿAli Shurida told him: 'Desist from this, or perish!' And soon that dervish was afflicted with a terrible pain. Coming to him, Shaykh ʿAli Shurida said: 'Did I not tell you: "Desist from this, or perish"? 'I did wrong,' confessed that dervish, 'now please pray for my recovery!' But Shaykh ʿAli Shurida did not pray, and he died from that affliction!"

## IV. Assembly 37

Tuesday, 11th of Dhu'l-Hijja, A.H. 717 (14 February 1318)

I obtained the good fortune of kissing his hand. When I was honored to enter his presence, many people had already arrived, and more and more food was being brought in. On this occasion, by way of jest, the master told the following story. "They asked a dervish: 'Among God's Holy Words (the Qur'an), which verse do you keep close at hand?' He replied: 'Its (heaven's) perpetual food (**akluha daimun**) (Q.25:13).' Then he explained its benefit. 'There is **akala** and **akl.** There is **akalahu** and **akluhu.**' Then he clarified the meaning of these four words. '**Akala** is the root, to eat, while **akl** is what they eat. **Akalahu** means "he ate it once,' and **akluhu** means "one morsel." ' "

Into this assembly came a dear fellow. With him he brought his young son and a writing board. Addressing the master, he said: "This is my young son. Would you please write on this board with your blessed pen, so that one day, due to this blessing, God Almighty might grant him the ability to memorize the Qur'an?" The master—may God remember him with favor—took that board in his hand and wrote on it these words: In the name of God full of Compassion, ever Compassionate, **alib, ba, ta, tha, jim, ha, kha** [the first six letters of the Arabic alphabet]. Then he said: "Everyone who writes something on behalf of some work, if the pen writes easily and flows, there will be no difficulty. That benefit will be quickly achieved. But if the pen moves with difficulty and the writing is tentative, then that work will face obstacles and delay." Then he added: "These are rationalizations. Whatever comes from here that comes from (true) instinct, its realization will be permitted!"

Finally the master told a story about a dervish from Gujarat, a dervish who, in turn, had told him a story. This was the story. "I happened upon a mad dervish in Gujarat. United with God, he was the mediator of divine secrets. I and that mad dervish occupied the same home; we even slept in the same room. Once I went to a reservoir that is well known, a reservoir in which no one is allowed to set foot. I was well known to the custodians of that reservoir, however, so they let me perform my ablutions there. Some women, hoping to fill their pitchers, came to that reservoir but were not allowed to use it, that is, until an old woman approached me and asked if I would fill her pitcher for her. I did, and returned it to her. Then another old woman came with the same request, and I complied for her too. Then another and another and another came, until I had fetched and filled and returned five pitchers of water to these women. In short, after I departed there I went back to my room. That mad dervish was still asleep. Soon after my return the time for prayer came, and as he was still sleeping, I made the call to prayer in a loud voice. That mad saint bolted awake. Turning to me, he exclaimed: 'What sort of racket is this? True work is to fetch and fill and return the waterpitchers of women!' And praise be to God the Lord of the universe!"

### IV. Assembly 38

Thursday, 12th of the month of Sha'ban, A.H. 717 (20 October 1317)

I obtained the benefit of kissing the master's feet after an absence of eight months. This absence was due to army maneuvers that took me to Deogiri (in the Deccan). When I had the good fortune to kiss his feet on this particular Thursday, he addressed me with great compassion and solicitude. He asked about the severity of the long journey, showing sympathy as well as concern. Malih, who was an old and trusted servant, had suffered some discomfort on the trip. Seeking relief, he had accompanied me to kiss the master's feet. The master enquired about the circumstances of his illness. "It was due to his (Malih's) illness," I replied, "that we halted on the return journey." "You did well," said the master, "for a friend, when he accompanies someone who falls ill and whose illness becomes known, should immediately pay attention to him and take care of his needs."

In this connection the master told the following story of IBRAHIM KHAWASS—may God have mercy upon him. "Ibrahim Khawass was perpetually on the move. He would not stay in any city longer than four days. Wherever he went, after less than four days he would travel on to another place. He spent his whole life in this way, till once he met a young man who asked to accompany him. Replied Ibrahim Khawass: 'You cannot keep pace with me. Sometimes I'm in this city, then in that city. Sometimes I have no provisions; at other times, I do. You could not accompany me.' But that youth stood firm by his request. 'Certainly I could keep abreast of you,' he replied, 'as long as I expended the necessary effort.' At last Ibrahim consented to his request.

"In short, Ibrahim Khawass, keeping to his resolve, traveled from city to city. Wherever he went he would stay there for less than four days, till at least he arrived at a place where that youth fell ill. Khwaja Ibrahim—may God have mercy upon him—due to the lad's illness, remained three months in that place. Then one day that lad wanted some bread and water, and he communicated his desire to Ibrahim. Ibrahim had a donkey, a donkey on which he rode around from place to place. He had no other material goods except that donkey, so he sold that donkey to provide for the needs of the lad. After some time had elapsed, the lad began to feel better. Khwaja Ibrahim Khawass—may God have mercy upon him—desired to travel again. The youth asked him: 'That donkey of yours, let me ride on it, so that I may accompany you.' Ibrahim was then compelled to tell him what had happened. 'I sold that donkey,' he confessed, 'to provide you bread and water.' In short, they set out from there, and Ibrahim Khawass transported that lad on his back for three days."

The master—may God remember him with favor—told this story to illustrate EXEMPLARY CONDUCT TOWARD ONE'S TRAVEL COMPANIONS. When he had finished talking about Shaykh Ibrahim, he recounted the story of his own affliction. I had heard this unfortunate news in the army, to the effect that someone had perpetrated MAGIC AGAINST THE MASTER. I enquired about how this had happened. "For two months," he explained, "I had a pain, a pain so intense that they summoned a man skilled in countering the effects of magic. That man came and searched around the house and neighborhood. From time to time he would take a sample of dirt from the ground and it exuded an aroma; the aroma seemed to come from the middle of the earth. Wherever he began to dig, signs of magic appeared. Then I began to experience a bit of relief. At that the man remarked: 'I have such powers of exorcism that if asked, I can conjure up the name of the one who perpetrates this magic.' On hearing his disclosure, I said: 'Take care not to prevent him from saying what he says until you first inform him that I forgive him. I forgive him no matter what he has done!' "

On this occasion I asked: "Did they not also perpetrate magic against Shaykh Farid ad-din—may God sanctify his lofty secret?" "Yes," he said. "He repelled that magic, and then they apprehended the group who had perpetrated it. The governor of Ajodhan and other officials arrayed that group before Shaykh al-Islam Farid ad-din—may God sanctify his lofty secret. They asked him: 'What do you order us to do to this group?' 'Pardon them all,' he replied. 'Set them free!' "

In this connection the master told the following story. "They perpetrated magic against the Prophet—peace be upon him. The two prophylactic chapters (Q.113–114) were revealed to counter the women who blow on knots (Q.113). The Commander of the Faithful ʿAli came before the Prophet and announced: 'If you give the order, I will strangle the women who perpetrated this magic.' The Prophet—peace be upon him—said: 'As soon as Almighty God restored my health, I forgave those women." Then he told a related story about THE MURDER OF ʿUMAR KHATTAB—may God be pleased with him. "It was on Friday," he recalled, "when ʿUmar had mounted the pulpit and was in the midst of delivering the Friday sermon. 'Take note,' he told his listeners, 'my death is imminent.' He knew this on account of his miraculous powers. 'In a dream I saw a bird approach me,' he explained, 'and that bird pecked me twice with its beak. Now a bird in one's dream signifies the angel of death. Due to this sign I am informing you that my death is imminent.' And the next week ʿUmar did attain martyrdom. (It happened like this.) A disaffected slave named Ibn Lulu struck him with a sword in the mosque. As soon as the Commander of the Faithful ʿUmar—may God be pleased with him—fell, the servant fled, slaying nine other persons before finally killing himself. The Commander of the Faithful ʾUmar—may God be pleased with him—said: 'Praise be to God that he killed himself, so that they did not have to kill him on my account!' "

The master then told the story about THE MURDER OF ʿALI—may he be graced with God's bounty. ʿAbd ar-Rahman (Ibn) Muljam killed him, and it happened in this manner. He approached ʿAli from behind with a concealed weapon, while ʿAli was unarmed. They had arrived at a river bank, and ʿAli was looking for a ford to cross over the river. They were standing on the edge of the river opposite a graveyard. Facing the graveyard, the Commander of the Faithful ʿAli—may he be graced with God's bounty—called out a name, and seventy persons by that name called back from their graves! Again, the Commander of the Faithful ʿAli called out: 'O so-and-so, son of so-and-so,' and seven more voices answered! Once more the Commander of the Faithful ʿAli called out: 'O so-and-so, son of so-and-so, son of so-and-so,' and this time one person responded. The Commander of the Faithful ʿAli—may he be graced with God's bounty—then asked him: 'Where is the ford across the river?' Replied the voice: 'In front of where you are standing!' The Commander of the Faithful ʿAli—may he be graced with God's bounty—approached the water and crossed over. ʿAbd ar-Rahman Muljam heard what was said and also crossed over the river behind ʿAli. Once on the other side he asked ʿAli: 'Since you knew the names of all these men and also the names of their fathers, how did you not know where the ford in the river was?' The Commander of the Faithful ʿAli—may he be graced with God's bounty—replied: 'I knew but I did not want to disclose my spiritual state to you!' In short, the Commander of the Faithful ʿAli said his prayers. ʿAbd ar-Rahman then raised his sword to slay him, and as the Commander of the Faithful ʿAli was expiring, he exclaimed: 'I have triumphed by the Lord of the KaʿBa!' These were the last words of the Commander of the Faithful ʿAli—may God be pleased with him."

I interjected: "Was ʿAbd ar-Rahman Muljam a Muslim?" "Yes," replied the master. "He was a Muslim inclined to the party of Muʿawiya." "How did he come to be a partisan of Muʿawiya?" I asked. "Muʿawiya was a Muslim," explained the master. "He was among the Prophet's companions, and he was also a brother-in-law of the Prophet —peace be upon him—since he had a sister named Umm Habiba who was married to the Prophet—blessings and peace be upon him.

After he had finished recounting this story, since it was the first time after eight months I had been in his presence and since other officers of the army had also come to see him, he spoke at length about estrangement and separation. "Once," he recalled, "I had submitted a request in writing to Shaykh al-Islam Farid ad-din—may God sanctify his lofty secret. I included in it the following quatrain:

Since by all your creature I'm known to be,
Men's gaze reserves a special place for me.
Nought but your grace could grant such favor,
For who am I to warrant their scrutiny?

When I next came to visit the Shaykh, he remarked about the above quatrain: 'I have committed it to memory, and peace be upon you!' "

## IV. Assembly 39

Monday, the 3rd evening of Shaʿban, A.H. 717 (11 October 1317)

I obtained the benefit of kissing his feet. One of the master's disciples from Deogiri had sent back about three **jatils**. "Present this to the master of the world, and also convey my greetings," he had asked me. Complying with his request, I presented those three **jatils** to the master and told him the circumstances in which they had been entrusted to me. The master—may God remember him with favor—took those three **jatils** in his blessed hand and set them in front of him. Then he told the following story about SHAYKH SHIHAB AD-DIN SUHRAWARDI. "Once on returning from the pilgrimage he was greeted by the people of Baghdad. Everyone who came to see him offered him some lavish gift, whether in cash or kind. Among them was an old woman. She reached into the hem of her tattered garment and taking out one **diram** set it before the Shaykh. Shaykh Shihab ad-din took that one **diram** and placing it above the other gifts, he said to the assembled company: 'Come, take what you need from among these offerings!' Everyone got up and helped themselves to money and other fine things. Shaykh Jalal ad-din Tabrizi—may God grant him a fine reward—was present. Shaykh Shihab ad-din gestured to him, saying: 'You too come and choose something.' Shaykh Jalal came forward and took that **diram** that the old woman had presented to the Shaykh. On seeing this, Shaykh Shihab ad-din remarked: 'You have taken everything with this [i.e., the spiritual worth of that coin matched the sum total of all the other donations!].' "

At this point I interjected: "Shaykh Jalal ad-din Tabrizi was a disciple of Shaykh Shihab ad-din, was he not?" "No," replied the master, "he was the disciple of Shaykh Abu Sa'id Tabrizi. When his master was concealed (with God, i.e., he died), he attached himself to Shaykh Shihab ad-din Suhrawardi, and he performed for his Shaykh services such as no other disciple or devotee could do. For instance, every year Shaykh Shihab ad-din would leave Baghdad to perform the pilgrimage. But when he became old and infirm, the food prepared for him on the journey did not please him: Because he was old he did not like to eat cold food. Hence Shaykh Jalal ad-din Tabrizi devised a way to carry both a hearth and a pot on his head and to keep the hearth warm without burning his head. Whenever the Shaykh wanted to eat, he would then serve him hot food!"

The master next began to speak of THE SPIRITUAL GREATNESS OF SHAYKH ABU SA'ID TABRIZI—may God have mercy upon him. "He was the spiritual master of Shaykh Jalal ad-din and a great saint," said the master. "He excelled in rejecting worldliness, to such an extent that much of the time he went hungry. He never took anything from anyone. There was once a period of three days when no food was to be found in his hospice. He and his disciples subsisted by sharing some barley and watermelon seeds at the time of breaking fast. Their condition was reported to the governor of the city. 'They will not accept anything from me,' observed the governor. 'Take some money, give it to the Shaykh's servant, and tell him to tell the saint: "A small sum has come for us to expend," and don't tell him the source.' The governor's retainer went to the Shaykh's servant and, giving him some money, related the governor's message: 'Protect the collective good, expend what is needed, and don't tell the Shaykh where it came from.' In short, when they had taken the silver and expended it for food, the Shaykh did not experience that appetite and satisfaction that comes from obedience (to one's spiritual discipline). Summoning the servant, he asked: 'The food which you brought last night, from where did you obtain it?' The servant could not conceal the truth from him; he disclosed the circumstances of that gift. 'That person who brought the silver,' enquired the Shaykh, 'how did he enter and where did he set foot?' The very ground on which he had set foot they dug up and removed. That servant, along with the silver, was also cast out of the Shaykh's hospice."

In this way did the master recount the intensity of Shaykh Abu Saʿid's commitment to renouncing worldliness. "Shaykh Shihab addin," he went on to say, "also received many offerings but he, too, expended them all. At the time that the Shaykh was about to die, his son ʿUmad had reached the age of thirty. He did not have the spiritual temperament of his father. Approaching the Shaykh's servant, he asked for the key to his father's storeroom. The servant in distress pleaded: "What kind of a request is this at such a moment?" The Shaykh was on his deathbed, yet they informed him about his son's request. "Give him the key," ordered the Shaykh. The son took the key and opening his father's storeroom, he found less than six **dinars,** and even these six were expended on the Shaykh (for his funeral)!"

### IV. Assembly 40
Thursday, 4th of the blessed month of Ramadan
in the favored community, A.H. 717 (10 November 1317)

I received the good fortune of kissing his feet. A scholar came, and the master—may God remember him with favor—inquired about his well-being. "I make my living," he replied, "by constantly visiting the palace; it provides me with bread and comfort." When he departed, the master—may God remember him with favor—recited this couplet:

Poetry, when it speaks from the heart, is best.
Once begging begins, it is nought but a jest.

Then he began to speak about POETRY. "Poetry," he observed, "is a subtle matter, but when poets write paeans and ascribe them to everyone, it becomes distasteful in the extreme. The same applies to knowledge: When it is pursued for its own sake, it is a noble endeavor, but when used to gain money and peddled from door to door, it loses all respectability."

A disciple of the master's arrived and brought a Hindu friend with him. He introduced him by saying, "This is my brother." When he had greeted both of them, the master—may God remember him with favor—asked that disciple: "And does this brother of yours have any inclination toward Islam?" "It is to this end," replied the disciple, "that I have brought him to the master, that by the blessing of your gaze he might become a Muslim." The master—may God remember him with favor—became teary-eyed. "You can talk to this people as much as you want," he observed, "and no one's heart will be changed, but if you find THE COMPANY OF A RIGHTEOUS PERSON, then it may be hoped that by the blessing of his company the other will become a Muslim."

Then he told the following story. "During the Caliphate of ʿUmar Khattab—may God be pleased with him—Iraq was invaded and the king of Iraq captured. They brought him before ʿUmar. 'If you become a Muslim, I will reinstate you as the king of Iraq.' 'I am not going to embrace Islam,' retorted the king. 'Either Islam or the sword,' intoned ʿUmar. 'If you do not accept Islam, I will kill you.' 'Then kill me,' replied the king, 'for I am not going to embrace Islam.' ʿUmar ordered them to bring the sword and the executioner. Now that great king was very clever and very wise. When he saw the situation before him, he turned to ʿUmar and said: 'I am thirsty; ask them to bring me some water.' ʿUmar gave the command and they brought him water in a glass tumbler. 'I will not drink water from this vessel,' said the king. 'Since he is a king,' declared ʿUmar, 'bring him water in a gold and silver tumbler.' They complied, but still he would not drink. 'Bring me water in an earthen vessel,' he demanded. They filled an earthen vessel with water and gave it to him. Turning to ʿUmar, he said: 'Promise me that you will not kill me till I finish drinking this water.' 'I promise,' said ʿUmar. The king then dashed the earthen vessel to the ground, breaking it and spilling out the water. To ʿUmar he said: 'I have not drunk this water, and you promised that you would not kill me till I finished drinking it. Now you must spare my life.' ʿUmar—may God be pleased with him—was impressed with the king's ingenuity. He agreed to spare his life. He then entrusted him to the company of a friend who was the model of piety. After the king had been brought to the house of that friend and spent some time there, the company of this righteous Muslim made an impact on him. He sent a message to ʿUmar, saying, 'Summon me to your presence that I might profess faith in Islam.' ʿUmar summoned him, and professing faith in Islam, that king became a Muslim. After he had embraced Islam, ʿUmar—may God be pleased with him—said: 'I bequeath to you the kingdom of Iraq.' 'I have no interest in kingship,' replied the former king. 'Give me instead but one desolate village from the kingdom of Iraq that I may earn my income from its produce. That will suffice.' ʿUmar agreed. 'But remember,' declared the former king, 'it must be a desolate village so that I may cultivate its lands and make it prosper.' ʿUmar sent some delegates to Iraq but they searched the entire province without finding a single desolate village. On hearing this, ʿUmar announced to the former king: 'In the whole of Iraq my men found not even one desolate village.' Remarked the former king: 'It was for just this reason that I made such a request: I have surrendered to you an Iraq so prosperous that no desolate village can be found in it. If any part of Iraq now becomes desolate, it is you who will have to account for it on Judgment Day.' "

The master—may God remember him with favor—when he came to this point in the story, began to cry. He praised the ingenuity and wisdom of that Iraqi king. And then in connection with SINCERITY AND HONESTY AMONG MUSLIMS, he told the following story. "There was a Jew who lived in the neighborhood of Khwaja Bayazid Bistami—may God sanctify his lofty secret. When Khwaja Bayazid died, they said to that Jew: 'Why did you not become a Muslim?' 'If Islam is what Bayazid professed,' he replied, 'then I cannot attain it, but if it is this that you profess, then of such an Islam I would be ashamed!' "

## IV. Assembly 41

Saturday, 27th of the month of Ramadan, A.H. 717 (3 December 1317)

I obtained the benefit of kissing his feet. Malih, who was an old servant of mine, brought a number of his daughters to see the master. One of them had been recently married. Now the master—may God remember him with favor—knew that this Malih had four marriageable daughters. On seeing them, he asked: "What is this?" "One of his daughters has just been married," I replied. Turning toward Malih, the master—may God remember him with favor—remarked: "Everyone who has one daughter enjoys a barrier against Hell, and you have four!" Then on his blessed tongue came the Arabic dictum: "The father of daughters is well endowed." In the same connection he told a story about blessed Khizr. "When Khizr killed that lad and blessed Moses complained, 'Why did you kill an innocent person?' blessed Khizr, due to the perfection of his spiritual state, gave him a satisfactory explanation. In short, the father of that lad, after his son had been killed, was blessed by Almighty God with the birth of a daughter, and that daughter produced seven sons, each of them a paragon of saintliness!"[84]

Then the master asked me: "Where do you perform **tarawih** prayers?" "I perform them at home," I replied, "(when) a prayer leader is present." "What does he recite from the Qur'an?" asked the master. "**Surat al-Fatiha** and **Surat al-Ikhlas** (Q.1 and 112)," I replied. "Good," he rejoined, noting that Shaykh al-Islam Farid ad-din—may God sanctify his lofty secret—used to have the same Qur'anic chapters recited during **tarawih** prayers. "When the Shaykh grew old," recalled the master, "he would still say the compulsory prayers standing, but the rest he would perform seated."

Then the master recalled a great saint who used to say: "If I eat one morsel and go to sleep, it is better than eating my fill and staying awake all night." He observed that the great Shaykh used to break fast rather than maintain a continuous fast, unless he became ill or feverish or required bloodletting and then, of course, he would fast continuously. He next spoke about SHAYKH BAHA AD-DIN ZAKARIYA—may God have mercy upon him. "He would seldom fast, yet he performed numerous acts of obedience and devotion." The following verse from the Qur'an came on his blessed lips: "Eat of good things and do righteous deeds (Q.51)." And he added: "This verse was fulfilled in the case of Shaykh Baha ad-din!"

## IV. Assembly 42

Saturday, 24th of the month of Shawwal, A.H. 717 (30 December 1317)

I obtained the benefit of kissing his feet. Conversation turned to LOVE OF CHILDREN. "The Prophet—peace be upon him—had a great affection for children, and liked to frolic with them. "Once," he noted, "the Prophet—peace be upon him—saw Imam Hasan in a group of children. Coming near, he put one hand under his chin, the other behind his head and 'kissed his face.' " "They tell a story," I interjected, "about how the Prophet used to play the role of a camel for Hasan and Husayn." "Yes," he rejoined, "this is a famous and well-documented story." On his blessed tongue came this Tradition: "Indeed, here is the camel. (I am) your camel!"

Then he told the following story about the Commander of the Faithful 'Umar—may God be pleased with him. "During his Caliphate, he appointed a friend to a high administrative post and had a document drawn up in his name. While the ceremony was taking place, and after he had already presented him the document, the Commander of the Faithful ʿUmar—may God be pleased with him—took one of his children onto his knee and began playing with him affectionately. That friend looked askance at ʿUmar and said: 'I have ten sons. Not one do I cuddle or cajole like this!' Replied ʿUmar: 'That document of appointment that I just gave you, give it back to me.' The friend gave it back. ʿUmar—may God be pleased with him—then tore that document into shreds, saying 'How can someone who does not care for children show concern for adults?' " And God knows best!

### IV. Assembly 43
### Wednesday, 5th of the month of Dhuʾl-Hijja, A.H. 717 (8 February 1318)

I obtained the benefit of kissing his feet. A newcomer arrived. "From where did you come?" asked the master—may God remember him with favor. "I came from the caliphal capital (**dar al-khilafat**)" replied the man, "from the army headquarters located on the palace grounds." Since that place was called 'the caliphal capital,' he had said: "I come from 'the caliphal capital.' " With reference to this name the master began to speak of THE NAMING OF BAGHDAD. "At first Baghdad was called the city of Mansur, since Mansur was the name of the Caliph during whose reign it had been built." After that he noted: "Baghdad was also called the city of Islam [before acquiring its present name, 'the caliphal capital']."

Next the master spoke about THE SAINTS OF GOD AND THEIR UNSTINTING LOVE. "Tomorrow on the Day of Judgment," he observed, "Maʿruf Karkhi—may God have mercy upon him—will be among those assembled before the divine tribunal. Maʿruf will appear as an out-of-control inebriate. Others will be horrified. 'Who is this?' they will ask. A voice will declare: 'This man has been inebriated with love of us. He is Maʿruf Karkhi.' Then they will command Maʿruf Karkhi: 'Enter Heaven!' 'No,' he will reply, 'I did not worship You to gain the bliss of Heaven.' Then they will command the angels: 'Bind him in chains of light,' and they will lead him bound into Heaven!"

One of those present asked: "Almighty God is the epitome of Exaltation and Purity, while the sons of Adam occupy the lowest rung (in the cosmos). How can there be any relationship of love or nearness (between them)?" The master—may God remember him with favor—said:

"On this matter reason cannot speak, inquiry will not succeed." "A related poem just came to mind," I interjected. "It begins like this:

About love Abu Hanifa never taught."

And the master—may God remember him with favor—added the second verse:

"Nor did Shafi'i ever give it a thought."

### IV. Assembly 44

Saturday, the 18th of the month of Rabi' al-awwal, A.H. 718 (20 May 1318)

I obtained the benefit of kissing his feet. Conversation turned to the MERIT OF EXERCISING RESTRAINT. "There was a saint," recalled the master. "He was the paragon of forbearance and restraint. 'Where did you acquire this grace?' he was asked. Replied that saint: 'I acquired it from my teacher. His name was 'Asim (lit., the sinless); he had also mastered the art of Qur'anic recitation.' 'Tell us something about his qualities of restraint,' they asked that saint. 'Once,' he replied, "'Asim went into the desert, far from civilized life. He encountered a fool who began to talk foolishly, and to utter impertinences to him. 'Asim kept quiet. He did not respond to that man's provocations. As he was returning to the city, that fool still kept pestering him. When at last they came into the company of others 'Asim turned to that man and announced: 'Noble sir, we have returned. Here are many of my friends and acquaintances. They should not hear you speak so foully of me, lest they begin to feel contempt for you!' "

Then that saint told a further story about his teacher's ability to exercise restraint. "Once I was sitting in his presence, and he was conducting a class. We were reading some texts, from which he would deduce the morals and we would note them down. 'Asim himself was wearing a cloak that clung to his back and extended down to his knees. The cloak never moved as he offered us instruction. During the class someone arrived and reported: 'They have killed your son.' 'Who killed him?' he asked. 'Your nephews. An argument flared up between them and your son was killed.' 'Asim said: 'Go! Have so-and-so perform the funeral prayer and in such-and-such a place bury him.' Having said this, he turned to his students and said: 'Resume reading what you were reading.' The saint added: 'I did not detect any change in his facial expression. Not the slightest change was evident. Even that cloak that he was wearing did not ripple nor was there any other sign of distress; he remained fully engaged in the task of teaching that class!' "

Then the master—may God remember him with favor—said: "Among the Companions of the Prophet, Abu Bakr Siddiq—may God be pleased with him—was especially noted for exercising restraint. Once a vile person began to berate him, dwelling with special emphasis on one of his 'faults.' 'Noble sir,' rejoined Abu Bakr, 'I have so many faults that it makes easy your task of bringing them to the attention of others!' "

After the master—may God remember him with favor—had finished this story, it was time for those present to leave. I interjected: "If it happens that a disciple comes to see his master less and less, but remembers him more and more at home, what does this signify?" "It is better," replied the master, "for someone to be absent from his master and remember him than to be present with him all day yet not be touched by his love." Then this verse came to his blessed lips:

Better out than in, if out while you are in!"

Next he spoke about Shaykh al-Islam Farid ad-din—may God sanctify his lofty secret. "Shaykh Farid," he recalled, "was admitted into the presence of his spiritual master Shaykh Qutb ad-din—may God illumine his grave—after only two weeks, even though Shaykh Badr ad-din Ghaznawi and other dear disciples had also been waiting to see him. At the time of Shaykh Qutb ad-din's death," he continued, "there was a saint who had hoped to succeed him, and wanted to occupy his place. That was Shaykh Badr ad-din Ghaznawi. But in that musical assembly where Shaykh Qutb ad-din was at the point of expiring, he declared: 'Give this cloak, this staff, and these shoes to Shaykh Farid ad-din.' The master—may God remember him with favor—said: 'I have seen that cloak; it was a double-pleated, stitched-up cloak.' In short, on the night that Shaykh Qutb ad-din expired, Shaykh Farid ad-din was in Hansi—may God have mercy on both of them. The next day he set out from Hansi. Four days later he arrived in Delhi. Qadi Hamid ad-din Nagauri—may God have mercy upon him—was still alive. He presented that cloak to Shaykh Farid ad-din—may God reward him well. The Shaykh performed two cycles of prayer, and then putting on that cloak, he went to the house that Shaykh Qutb ad-din had occupied. He had only been there three days—seven days according to another report—when he returned to Hansi. And the cause of his sudden departure was as follows.

While the Shaykh was living in Shaykh Qutb ad-din's house—may God have mercy on both of them—a man from Hansi named Sarhanga came to see him. He came to the house two or three times, and each time the doorman would not admit him. One day, as the Shaykh was leaving the house, Sarhanga came and, falling at his feet, began to sob. 'Why are you crying?' asked the Shaykh. 'Because,' replied Sarhanga, 'while you were in Hansi, I could see you easily, but now when I come to see you it is very difficult.' That same day the Shaykh said to his friends: 'I am going to return to Hansi.' 'But your Shaykh has ordered you to stay here,' counseled those who were present, 'how can you go elsewhere?' Replied the Shaykh: 'The blessing that my Shaykh bestowed on me will remain the same, whether I stay in the city (of Delhi) or return to the wilds (of the Punjab)!' "

## IV. Assembly 45
### Saturday, 3rd of Rabiʿ al-akhir, A.H. 717 (15 June 1317)

I had the honor of kissing his hand. Conversation focused on THE BEAUTY OF THE DISCIPLES' BELIEF IN, AND REGARD FOR, THEIR SPIRITUAL MASTER. In this connection he told the story about a grandson of Qazi Hamid ad-din Nagauri—may God have mercy upon him—named Sharaf ad-din." Sharaf ad-din wished to become a disciple of Shaykh al-Islam Farid ad-din—may God sanctify his lofty secret. With this intention he departed Nagaur. Now it happened that he had an expensive female slave, worth 100 **tankas,** more or less. That slave asked her master: 'When you go to the Shaykh and become his disciple, also indicate my indenture to him, and take this turban wrapped around my head and give it to him as a token of my submission.' In short, after Maulana Sharaf a-din met with the Shaykh and had obtained the honor of becoming his disciple, he said: 'I have a household slave. Bowing her head to the ground, she asked me: "Please take this turban that I am giving you and present it to the Shaykh." On the blessed lips of Shaykh al-Islam Farid ad-din—may God sanctify his lofty secret—came these words: 'May God Almighty set her free!' When Maulana Sharaf ad-din heard this pronouncement, he got up, thinking to himself: 'Since these words come from the blessed Shaykh, they must be true; she will be set free. But this is an expensive slave, and I can't afford to set her free. I will sell her, and it may be that the buyer will set her free.' No sooner had he entertained this thought than a further thought crossed his mind: 'If this slave is set free in another house, that person will obtain the reward, so why don't I set her free?' Resolving to free her, he came before the Shaykh and announced: 'I have set her free!' "

### IV. Assembly 46

Sunday, 18th of the month of Rabiʿ al-akhir, A.H. 718 (19 June 1318)

I obtained the benefit of kissing his hand. Conversation turned to LOVE AND LOATHING OF WORLDLINESS. On his blessed tongue came this remark: "There are three types of people. One type consists of those who love worldliness, are constantly engaged by it and in quest of its rewards. They are numerous. A second type are those who, while they detest worldliness, constantly censure it and are preoccupied with resisting its allure. The third type are those who neither befriend nor detest worldliness. They discuss neither loving nor loathing worldliness. This group is better than the other two."

After that he told the story of a man who came to Rabiʿa and, once seated, began talking on and on about worldliness. Rabiʿa finally told him: "Don't come back again. You must be attracted to worldliness, since you spend so much time discussing it!"

In this connection, about RENOUNCING WORLDLINESS, he told the story of a dervish who lived near Kaithal and Kahram. His name was Sufi Badhni. "He was adamant about leaving worldliness," observed the master, "to such an extent that he would not even wear a cloak." I interjected: "Did he never clasp the hand of someone?" "No," replied the master, adding: "If he had taken a master, he would had to wear 'a woman's veil,' that is, a cloak. For this reason we know that he had no spiritual master. He prayed much," continued the master, "and he used to say: 'Though heaven is supposed to be a place of bliss, what a pity that there's no room there for prayer!' " I interjected at this point: "If a spiritual master is worldly-minded, can he nonetheless direct his disciples to eschew love of worldliness?" The master—may God remember him with favor—answered: "If he claims to eschew it, his words will have no effect, for there is the message of deeds as well as the message of words. Counsel and guidance come through the message of deeds. When there is no message of deeds, the message of words is ineffectual."

He then told a short story about Shaykh Shihab ad-din Suhrawardi —may God have mercy upon him. "Shaykh Shihab ad-din once found a handkerchief from his master. He kept it in his possession and received many blessings on that account, till once he had a dream in which he dreamt that that handkerchief had fallen near his feet and that he, unawares, had stepped on it! When he awoke, he was beset with constant trembling and severe distress, so much so that he cried out: 'I hope that tomorrow on the Day of Judgment I will not experience grief and sorrow due to that crime!' "

In this vein he told the following story: "Once I obtained from Shaykh al-Islam Farid ad-din—may God sanctify his lofty secret—a cloak, a cloak of the cut peculiar to the Chishti order. I still have that cloak with me. In short, when I departed Ajodhan for Delhi, I took that cloak with me. Traveling with a companion, I reached a place where there was a dangerous fork in the road, due to heavy rains. I and that friend paused. We were standing beneath a tree, when some Hindus of the sort we fear approached. I began to focus on that cloak that I had with me. I said to myself: 'This cloak that the Shaykh has given me these Hindus cannot take from me.' Then a further thought crossed my mind. 'If they did take it, I would remain in the wilderness and never return to the city.' An hour or so passed like this. One by one those Hindus drifted off, one in one direction, another in another direction. They all scattered and departed without saying a word to us. And we returned safely home!"

The Shaykh then spoke briefly about AMASSING AND DISPENSING WITH WORLDLY GOODS. "One ought not to to harbor worldly goods," he warned, "except the minimum that is necessary, such as the cloak that resembles a woman's veil. That and nothing more should one keep. All else that one obtains should be dispensed with rather than hoarded." Then on his blessed lips came this verse:

> Gold is there only for giving, my son.
> For keeping, a stone will do just as good.

In this connection he remembered the following lines from Khaqani that conveyed the same meaning:

> When a man will not give up his self-obsession,
> Look at all his vaunted treasure and say: "It's mine!"

In the interim he asked someone for a toothpick and told the following story about TOOTHPICKS. "There was a scholar named Nur Turk. He had departed India to go on the pilgrimage, and had remained in Mecca. Having built a house there, he would sit in front of his door and announce: 'Whoever wants to enter my house but has no toothpick I forbid him to enter my house!' "

Then he began speaking of THE EXCELLENT MORAL QUALITIES OF DERVISHES. "Shaykh Abu Saʿid Abu'l-Khayr—may God have mercy upon him—and Bu ʿAli Sina used to meet and talk with one another. No sooner had they become separated than Bu ʿAli approached a Sufi attached to the Shaykh and said: 'Since I have just returned from having been with the Shaykh, whatever he says about me, please write and tell me.' Once Bu ʿAli had left, however, Shaykh Abu Saʿid—may God have mercy upon him—made no mention of him, either good or bad. Since that Sufi heard no mention of Bu ʿAli, one day he asked the Shaykh: 'What sort of man is Bu ʿAli?' Replied the Shaykh: 'He is a philosopher, a doctor, and knows a great deal yet he does not have excellent moral qualities.' The Sufi wrote to Bu ʿAli what he had heard. Bu ʿAli then penned a note to the Shaykh, and in it he protested: 'I have written so many books about excellent moral qualities. How can the Shaykh say: "So-and-so does not have excellent moral qualities?' " The Shaykh smiled and quipped: 'I did not say that Bu ʿAli doesn't **know** about excellent moral qualities, rather I said that he doesn't **have** such qualities!' "

He then began to tell a story about QAZI MINHAJ AD-DIN. "Every Monday I would go to hear him preach. One Monday while I was listening to his sermon, he began to recite the following quatrain:

> With your own lips you touch that moon-faced beauty's lip
> And also toy with her dishevelled tress's tip.
> It may be fun today, tomorrow not such fun
> When you become like tinder in hell's fiery grip."

The master—may God remember him with favor—said: "When I heard these verses, I was overcome with ecstasy, and not till an hour later did I regain my consciousness."

Then he began to speak of THE SPIRITUAL STATES OF QAZI MINHAJ AD-DIN. "He was a man consumed with a taste for God. Once they summoned him to the home of Shaykh Badr ad-din Ghaznawi. It was a Monday and he promised: 'After I have finished preaching, I will come to see you.' In short, when his sermon was over, he went to see Shaykh Badr ad-din. They convened a musical assembly there and he tore off both the turban and the cloak he was wearing, ripping both to pieces. Then they began to recite the verse of Shaykh Badr ad-din Ghaznawi composed in the rhyme 'set ablaze,' and on his blessed lips came these verses:

All gathered round as the mourner fixed on me his farewell gaze;
From my scorched soul a sigh escaped, setting the mourner ablaze!"

"It was on account of verses such as these," concluded the master, "that Qazi Minhaj ad-din used to call Shaykh Badr ad-din 'the red lion.' "

Then in connection with this meeting he began to recount the story of SHAYKH NIZAM AL-DIN ABU'L-MUAYYAD—may God have mercy upon him. "Did you yourself hear about him through meeting with him?" I asked. "Yes," he said, "even though I was still a youth and did not understand a lot of what I was told. One day I went to meet him and saw that he was about to enter the mosque. After first removing his shoes, he carried them with him into the mosque. I never saw anyone pray with such a pious mien. After completing two cycles of prayer with total composure, he ascended the pulpit. There was a Qur'an reciter named Qasim present there. He had a beautiful voice, and began to recite a Qur'anic verse. After that Shaykh Nizam al-Din Abu'l-Muayyad—may God have mercy upon him—began to speak: 'I have seen it written in my own father's hand,' and then he stopped without saying anything more. So moved were those present that they all began to weep. He then spoke these two verses:

Out of love for You to gaze on You my only thought,
Despite the chaos, the pain that on my soul be wrought.

As soon as he had said this, loud cries went up from the congregation. After that he repeated these verses two or three times, saying: 'O Muslims, I cannot remember the other two verses. What am I do?' He said these words with such pathos that all those present were moved. Qasim, the Qur'an reciter, finally remembered the other two verses:

My hapless heart weighed down with pain, to dust will be brought.
Yet my head light with love, above the grave must be sought.

The Shaykh then recited the complete quatrain and descended."[85]

Also in connection with the SAINTLINESS OF SHAYKH NIZAM AL-DIN ABU'L-MUAYYAD—may God have mercy upon him—he told the following story. "Once in a period of drought he was asked to pray for rain. He mounted the pulpit and offered the prayer for rain. Then turning his face skyward, he added: 'O God, if You do not send down rain, I will never again darken anyone's doorstep!' Having said this, he descended from the pulpit. Mercifully God Almighty sent down rains. Afterward, Sayyid Qutb ad-din—may God have mercy upon him—met him and spoke to him as follows: 'I have great esteem for you and I know that you communicate intimately with the Almighty, but still these words that you spoke, to the effect 'If You do not send down rain, I will never again darken anyone's doorstep,' if He had not sent down rains, what would you have done?' Shaykh Nizam al-Din Abu'l-Muayyad replied: 'I knew that He would send down rain.' 'How do you know?' retorted Sayyid Qutb ad-din. 'Once,' he said, 'I had a dispute with Sayyid Nur ad-din Mubarak about the tyranny or tolerance of Shams ad-din (Iltetmush). I said something that offended him. Later (after Sayyid Nur ad-din's death) when they asked me to pray for rain, I went to his grave and announced: 'They have asked me to pray for rain. You have taken offense at me. If you will be reconciled with me, I will go and pray for rain, but if you will not be reconciled with me, I cannot make this prayer.' From his grave came forth the voice: 'Go and offer that prayer!' "

## IV. Assembly 47
Wednesday, 5th of Jumada al-ula, A.H. 718 (5 July 1318)

I obtained the benefit of kissing his feet. Conversation focused on PRAYER. I asked: "After completing canonical prayer, what are the rules about changing the place where one prays?" "It is preferable to change one's place of prayer," he replied. "If the prayer leader does not change, that is abhorrent, but if the follower does not change, it is not abhorrent, though it is still better for him to change." Then he added: "When one changes place, one ought to move to the left, so as to keep the direction of prayer (**qibla**) to one's right."

## IV. Assembly 48
Thursday, the 13th of Jumada al-ula, A.H. 718 (13 July 1318)

I had the good fortune of kissing his feet. Conversation turned to PEOPLE WHO KISS THE HANDS OF DERVISHES AND SEEK THEIR BLESSING. "In every case," remarked the master, "those who kiss the hands of shaykhs and dervishes hope that thereby the hand of forgiveness will be extended to them."

Then he told a story about the LOWER SOUL OF DERVISHES. "Once one of the disciples of Shaykh Ajall Shirazi—may God have mercy upon him—came before the Shaykh. 'I have a neighbor,' he complained, 'who always stares at my house. Whatever I do to deflect him, he will not listen; he just continues to annoy me.' 'Does he know,' asked

Khwaja Ajall, 'that you are my disciple?' 'Yes, he knows that I am among the devotees of Your Eminence!' 'How is it then,' remarked the Khwaja, 'that at this very moment he is breaking his pearl necklace?' After the Khwaja had given just this much free rein to his lower soul, the disciple returned home. He saw that neighbor, staring at a broken pearl necklace! 'How did this happen?' he asked. 'The shoes I was wearing slipped,' replied the neighbor. 'I fell and look what happened!' "

The master then told a brief story about THE MEN OF GOD. "In former times," he recalled, "there were four men named Burhan who came to Delhi from the North [i.e., from beyond the Zagros mountains]. Of these four one was named Burhan Balkhi, a second Burhan Kashani, and I forget the full name of the other two Burhans. In short, there was complete accord between them. They ate and drank in the same place; they even studied in the same place. When the first of them came to Delhi, the Chief Judge of the city was Nasir Kashani. In a moot court he questioned Burhan Kashani. Now this Burhan was a small, slight man. When he began to explain a point, the students quipped: 'What will this minute person have to say?' But his knowledge was also minute, that is, he discerned the fine points of law. When Burhan Kashani got up to leave, he became known as Burhan Reza-ye ʿIrf, literally, he who is the proof of subtle wisdom.' In short, this Burhan was a noble man, and he eventually became one of the deputies (of the Unseen)."[86]

The master—may God remember him with favor—remarked: "I have seen this Burhan. Every day at dawn he would leave his house on foot, even though he owned more than ten horses, and he would be accompanied by no retainer, even though he had more than one hundred servants! He also had a son named Nur ad-din Muhammad. One day that son said to his father: 'Every day you leave the house and even though we have many enemies, no one accompanies you. If you were to take a retainer with you, he could watch over you, and also provide you with a jug of water. That would be better!' To his son's query Maulana Burhan ad-din replied: 'Baba Muhammad, if I left here and had to be accompanied by a servant, you would be the first I'd take, since you are my son!' "

### IV. Assembly 49
### Sunday, the 29th of the month of Jumada ʾl-akhira, A.H. 718 (28 August 1318)

I obtained the benefit of kissing his hand. Since the month of Rajab was approaching, I asked: "Khwaja Uways Qarani—may God be pleased with him—used to say a prayer on the third, fourth, and fifth of Rajab, and it occurred to me that every saint has a special prayer or supplication that he has heard from the Prophet or from the noble companions. How did Uways Qarani—may God be pleased with him—come to say those prayers as well as those selections from the Qur'an and particular devotions linked to him?" The master—may God remember him with favor—replied: "These are all due to inspiration."

After that he told the following story. "Previously when I came from Delhi to Ajodhan to visit the Shaykh I would recite these three lofty names: 'O Preserver! O Victor! O Succorer!' And I had heard this supplication from no one. In this way I would go to see the Shaykh, calling on God with these three names. Later, some time later, a dear friend gave me a written supplication, and this was the supplication: 'O Preserver! O Victor! O Succorer! O Sovereign of Judgment Day! To You do we pray! On You do we depend for succor!' " (adapted from Q.1).

Then he spoke briefly about the SPIRITUAL STATES OF THE SHAYKHS. I submitted that I had heard some dicta alleged to be from Khwaja Bayazid Bistami, and however I tried, I could not interpret or make sense of them. "What are these dicta?" asked the master. I replied: "It is said that he said: 'Muhammad, along with others, will be under my skirt on Judgment Day.' " The master—may God remember him with favor—said: "No, he did not say such a thing. Once," he explained, "Khwaja Bayazid did declare: 'Glory be to me! Such is the greatness of my worth!' But then toward the end of his life he repented of this remark, confessing: 'I did not speak aright. I was a Jew. This hour I have cut my pagan girdle. Joining the ranks of Muslims, I declare: "I testify that there is no god but God. He is alone, without partner. And I also testify that Muhammad is His servant and His apostle." ' "

Then he began to speak about THE SPIRITUAL STATES OF THE PROPHET—peace and blessings be upon him. "The spiritual states that appear in Shaykhs and men of God," he observed, "derive from those spiritual states that characterized the Prophet—peace and blessings be upon him. For instance, they report that one day the Prophet—peace be upon him—entered a garden in which there was a well. The Prophet—peace be upon him—came and sat on the edge of that well. Dangling his feet over its side, he became immersed in God. To Abu Musa Ashʿari who accompanied him, he gave the order: 'Don't let anyone enter here within my permission!' Soon Abu Bakr Siddiq—may God be pleased with him—came. Abu Musa Ashʿari approached the

Prophet—peace be upon him—and announced the arrival of Abu Bakr. 'Invite him in,' responded the Prophet—peace be upon him, 'and greet him warmly.' Abu Musa went and admitted Abu Bakr. As he entered, Abu Bakr sat on the right of the Prophet—peace be upon him—and also dangled his feet down the the side of that well. After, ʿUmar Khattab—may God be pleased with him—also appeared, and Abu Musa gave word of his arrival. The Prophet—blessing and peace be upon him—also invited him to enter with good cheer. ʿUmar came and sat on the left of the Prophet—peace be upon him—dangling his feet like the others. After that ʿUthman—may God be pleased with him—also arrived. He, too, was ushered in, and after pondering for a while, ʿUthman—may God be pleased with him—sat opposite the Prophet—peace be upon him—before also dangling his feet over the side of that well. Still later, the Commander of the Faithful ʿAli—may God view him kindly—arrived, and having been granted permission to enter, sat down in the same manner as the others. Then the Prophet—peace be upon him—announced: 'Just as we are all now at one place, so at death we will all be together at one place, just as we will be again at the Resurrection.' "

When the master had finished relating this story, he began to speak about POVERTY AND THE CLOAK. "On the night of the ascent," he observed, "the Prophet—peace be upon him—obtained a cloak, and that has been called 'the cloak of poverty.' After that he summoned the companions and told them: 'I have been given a cloak, with the directive: "Give that cloak to whomever you will but first ask something of your friends. No matter how they answer you and whatever they tell you, give them that cloak, for I already know what they will say!" ' After that he turned to Abu Bakr and said: 'If I give you this cloak what will you do?' Replied Abu Bakr: 'I will be righteous and obedient, zealous but generous.' After that he asked ʿUmar: 'What will you do with this cloak?' 'I will be just and show fairness,' replied ʿUmar. Then of ʿUthman he asked the same question: 'What will you do with this cloak?' 'I will be liberal and generous as well as zealous,' he replied. And finally to ʿAli he put the question: 'What will you do if I give you this cloak?' 'I will wrap myself in it,' replied ʿAli, 'and I will also wrap in its folds the sins of God's servants!' The Prophet—peace be upon him—said: 'I give all of you this cloak, just as I was commanded to give it, on this one condition: "No matter what they answer, give them this cloak!" ' "

Then he began to speak about THE VIRTUES OF THE COMMANDER OF THE FAITHFUL ʿALI—may God be pleased with him—noting, in particular, his fair-mindedness and generosity. "He was once missing a coat of armor," noted the master, "and one day he saw a Jew carrying that same coat of armor. Seizing him, he said: 'This is my coat of armor.' Replied the Jew: 'Claim it, support your claim, and only then take it from me!' Now in those days the Commander of the Faithful ʿAli—may God be pleased with him—was also the Caliph. "Since I am the Caliph,' said ʿAli, 'how can I also be the claimant laying claim to this coat of armor?' 'Let us go to Sharih,' he proposed to the Jew, 'and let him settle this claim.' This they did. At the time Sharih was an administrative assistant to ʿAli, and when they came before him to set forth the claim about that coat of armor, Sharih turned toward the Commander of the Faithful ʿAli and said: 'Although you are the Caliph, nonetheless at this moment, by the authority delegated to me, I will become the final arbiter. Since you are bringing the claim, come and stand side-by-side with this Jew.' The Commander of the Faithful ʿAli did as he was commanded. Standing next to that Jew, he said: 'This is my coat of armor, and it has come into the hands of this Jew unlawfully.' 'Support your contention,' said Sharih. 'What do you want?' asked ʿAli. 'Bring witnesses,' said Sharih. The Commander of the Faithful ʿAli brought Hasan and Qanbar as witnesses. 'But Hasan is your son and Qanbar your slave,' protested Sharih. 'I will not admit them as witnesses.' Rejoined the Commander of the Faithful ʿAli: 'I have no other witness.' Then, turning to the Jew, Sharih said: 'Take the coat of armor and go in peace. With these two witnesses, he cannot lay claim to ownership.' Upon observing this procedure, the Jew was overcome with amazement. He said to himself: 'So the religion of Muhammad is this kind of religion?' On the spot he embraced Islam and surrendered that coat of armor to the Commander of the Faithful ʿAli. 'This belongs to you by law; it has come into my hands unlawfully.' But the Commander of the Faithful ʿAli insisted that he keep that coat of armor, and gave him a fine stallion as well!"

Into this same assembly came one of the master's disciples. He announced: "A son has been born in the house of your servant." The master—may God remember him with favor—asked: "What name did you give him?" "I gave him no name (**khair nam**)," said the servant, "so that I might ask the master what name to give him!" Replied the master—may God remember him with favor—"Since you said: 'I gave him no name (**khair nam**), let that be his name,' " that is, let him be named Khair (which also means "happy" or "good")!

In this connection he told a story about Khwaja Khair Nassaj—may God have mercy upon him. "Once when he had gone outside the city, a kidnapper seized him. 'Be my slave,' he ordered, and Khair Nassaj did not argue with him, acquiescing in this new role. For some time he remained in the house of that man. Now since that man had a garden, he made Khair the caretaker of that garden. A while later, coming into his garden, he ordered Khwaja Khair Nassaj: 'Fetch me a sweet pomegranate.' Khwaja Khair Nassaj brought him a pomegranate and handed it to him. On tasting it, the man found it to be bitter. 'I wanted a sweet pomegranate from you,' he complained. Khwaja Nassaj went and fetched him a second pomegranate. That pomegranate also turned out to be bitter. Scoffed the owner of the garden: 'I asked you for a sweet pomegranate; how is it that you brought me a bitter one?' Replied Khwaja Khair Nassaj: 'How am I to know the difference between a sweet and a bitter pomegranate?' Retorted the man: 'It has been some time now since I appointed you caretaker of this garden, how could you not know the difference between a sweet and a bitter pomegranate?' 'Well,' explained Khwaja Khair Nassaj, 'you did appoint me caretaker of this garden, but since I am an honest man, I did not taste or eat your pomegranates, so how could I know the difference?' When the owner of the garden heard this explanation, he set him free. Previously Khwaja Khair Nassaj had had a different name, but that man was named Khair, and since he had freed Khwaja Khair Nassaj, Khwaja Khair Nassaj said: 'Let my name be the same as that man's!' "

## IV. Assembly 50

Saturday, 20th of the month of Rajab, A.H. 718 (27 September 1318)

I obtained the benefit of kissing his feet. I had a Tradition in mind, and I wanted to to confirm its veracity. This was the Tradition: "Visit intermittently and increase (the bonds of) love!" "Is this a Tradition of the Prophet—blessings and peace be upon him?" I asked. "Yes," he replied. "This Tradition has been transmitted by Abu Huraira—may God be pleased with him. The occasion for its pronouncement was as follows. Abu Huraira was always in attendance on the Prophet. Then the Prophet—blessings and peace be upon him—told Abu Huraira: 'Visit intermittently.' " The master—may God remember him with favor—explained: "You see when someone comes one day but does not come the next day, they call that 'intermittent visitation.' Hence the Prophet—blessings and peace be upon him—told Abu Huraira: 'Visit intermittently, that is, come one day but do not come the next (to increase the bonds of love)!' "

Conversation next turned to SAINTLINESS [i.e., the challenge of being saintly] IN THE MIDST OF FAMILY AND OTHER PEOPLE. "There are three kinds of PATIENCE," observed the master. "The first is 'patience apart from them,' then there is 'patience with them,' and finally there is 'patience before the fire.' " Then he clarified what he meant. "The first requires patience from women. If someone basically does not make an effort in that direction and has no inclination for such work, this patience is the best. Hence it is called 'patience apart from them!' But if that is not feasible and a man desires a wife as well as children, then he must be patient with the trials and tribulations that ensue. That is called 'patience with them.' And then, if God forbid, one bypasses both these kinds of patience and falls into sin [e.g., by pursuing young boys], then there is 'patience before the fire (of hell).' Hence we find three levels of patience. The first is patience apart from them, the second patience with them, and the third, patience before the fire."

IV. Assembly 51

Tuesday, 13th of the month of Shaʿban, A.H. 718 (10 October 1318)

I had the good fortune of kissing his hand. He began to talk about MAULANA NUR TURK. "Some of the Delhi religious scholars used to deride his religious views," I interjected. "But," rejoined the master, "none except he was purer than rain water!" I submitted: "In the historical chronicle **Tabaqat-i Nasiri,** I have seen it written that he called the religious scholars impostors and backsliders." "He was angered and outraged at them," explained the master. "And why? Because he saw how contaminated they had become. And they, for their part, concocted slurs about him." "Who are the impostors and backsliders?" I asked. "An impostor," he replied, "is one who renounces allegiance to Islam after having first pledged to uphold it. A backslider, on the other hand, belongs to that sect of Muslims who abandon themselves to divine mercy. Actually," he went on, "there are two kinds of backsliders. One are special backsliders, the other are ordinary backsliders. The special are those who rely totally on divine mercy, while the ordinary allow for belief in punishment even while favoring belief in divine mercy."

After that he told the following story about MAULANA NUR TURK. "He was renowned for the power of his speech, even though he professed allegiance to no one. Whatever he said, he said on the basis of insight and a striving for truth. He had a servant named Naddaf and every day Naddaf would give him one **diram,** and he would subsist on that one **diram.** When he went to Mecca," continued the master, "he decided to live there. A man from this region later made the pilgrimage and, bringing two **mans** of rice, presented them to Maulana Nur Turk. The latter at once accepted them and offered up a prayer of thanks. Now in earlier times when Maulana Nur Turk still lived in India, Sultan Razia had once sent him a sum of gold, wrapped in a bundle. The Maulana rejected that gold. Taking a wooden stick, he pummeled that bundle, saying 'What is this? Take it away from me!' In short, when that man from India brought him two **mans** of rice in Mecca and he readily accepted them, that man thought to himself: 'This is the same saint who in Delhi rejected a big amount of gold but now accepts a little amount of rice!' Maulana Nur Turk turned to him: 'O noble sir!' he exclaimed, 'do not compare Mecca with Delhi! In those days I was young. What do I still retain of that power and discipline? Now that I've become old some little bits of grain seem precious!' "

"Once," continued the master, "this saint arrived in Hansi and began to preach there. I heard Shaykh al-Islam Farid ad-din—may God sanctify his lofty secret—say: 'I used to attend many of his sermons. No sooner had he arrived in Hansi and begun preaching than I went to hear him. I had a dirty and tattered cloak, and he and I had never met. Yet at the moment that I entered the mosque his glance fell on me and he exclaimed: "O Muslims, the weigher of words has arrived." After that he began to praise me with paeans such as were never addressed to any king!' "

The master next told a story about the WRITING AND GIVING OF AMULETS. "Once," he recalled, "Shaykh Farid ad-din—may God sanctify his lofty secret—asked Shaykh al-Islam Qutb ad-din Bakhtiyar—may God illumine his grave: 'People approach me asking for amulets. What should I do? Should I write and give them?' 'This work,' replied Shaykh Qutb ad-din, 'rests neither in your hands nor in mine. The amulet is God's name; write and give them God's word!' " After that the master—may God remember him with favor—said: "Many times it occurred to me that at an opportune moment I should ask Shaykh Farid ad-din for permission to write amulets. Then once Badr ad-din Ishaq, who used to assist in writing amulets, was not present. Many people had come hoping to obtain amulets. The Shaykh motioned to me: 'Write!' And I began to write amulets. It was a huge crowd. I wrote and wrote but was still overwhelmed by further requests. At one point, turning to me, the Shaykh asked: 'Are you growing weary?' 'The spiritual boon of the master is present [and sustains me],' I replied. After that he declared: 'I authorize you to write and give amulets on your own initiative!' And then he added: 'Something touched by the hands of saints produces an effect!' "

IV. Assembly 52

Monday, 11th of the month of Ramadan, A.H. 718 (6 November 1318)

I obtained the benefit of kissing his hand. Everyone who came to see the Shaykh, by way of greeting him, would bring something. Yet on this occasion a person came and brought nothing. As he was leaving, the master—may God remember him with favor—said: "Give him something!" And then he added: "Shaykh al-Islam Farid ad-din—may God sanctify his lofty secret—used to say: 'Everyone who comes to see me brings something. But whenever a poor person comes, bringing nothing, it is I who must give him something!' "

"The companions used to come and visit the Prophet," observed the master, "because they sought knowledge and practical guidelines. When they left his presence, they would transmit his dicta, that is, they would provide guidance and morals (**fawa'id**) for others. Once they had dispersed, they would not return to the Prophet (the same day), even if they later found themselves with nothing to eat. In this connection," continued the master, "the Commander of the Faithful ʿAli—may God be pleased with him—once remarked in a sermon: 'I can never remember the Prophet—peace be upon him—keeping anything for himself till evening. From morning till mid-afternoon, whatever came to him he gave away, and from mid-afternoon till evening, whatever else came to him he also gave that away!' "

At this point I asked: "What are GENEROUS DONATIONS, and what are the conditions for offering them?" Replied the master: "Everything which is given without a specific intent or to comply with God's laws, that is a generous donation. Even if one donates knowingly, it can still be deemed a generous donation, but that which is given to satisfy a divine mandate, even if one gave the whole world, it would not be considered 'generous.' " Then the master recalled how Shaykh Abu Saʿid Abu'l-Khayr—may God have mercy upon him—had a very generous disposition. "A person once came into the Shaykh's presence and recited this Tradition: 'There is no legal benefit in generous giving!' to which Shaykh Abu Saʿid replied: 'Nor is there anything generous about legal benefits!' "

Conversation next turned to SPIRITUAL AMBITION. "There

are different ambitions," observed the master. "There was once a saint who had both a son and a slave. A sense of high-mindedness had become apparent in the slave. The saint summoned both his son and his slave before him. First he asked his son: 'What is your ambition?' 'My ambition,' replied the son 'is as follows: to acquire many houses and many slaves.' Then he asked the slave: 'And what is your ambition?' Replied the slave: 'My ambition is to free every person enslaved as I am, and also to treat free persons with the same consideration I show for slaves!' The ambition of one," continued the master, "was to seek the world, the ambition of the other was to not have the world revolve around him. Of the two kinds of ambition the second is better. Is it not the case that if one enjoys worldly success, one says 'Hello! Welcome!' yet if one does not enjoy such success, one still says 'Hello! Welcome!' Similarly," he went on, "someone who says: 'I do not need worldly success' is no different from one who says: 'I need it': It is futile to deny or to seek worldly success. What is essential is to be content with doing God's will. If worldly success comes, one should be generous. If it does not come, one should be patient. Only in this way can one be content."

At this moment he turned toward me and asked: "Do you give ALMS FOR THE END OF RAMADAN FESTIVAL?" "By way of clarification," I submitted, "can you tell me if it is incumbent on me to give such alms?" Replied he: "If you have yet to satisfy your basic needs and must still expend funds for clothing, horses, and other such essentials, then it is not incumbent, but whatever surplus funds you have you must give." "And if I don't have surplus funds?" I asked. Without answering me directly, he observed: "At this moment I have an abundance, but when I didn't possess even a single coin, I would borrow in order to contribute to the Ramadan festival alms. As soon as I heard the Tradition: 'Divine acceptance of the Ramadan fast is conditional on the giving of festival alms,' I began to give these alms." Bowing my head to the ground, I submitted: "My eyes have been opened; I, too, will contribute to the Ramadan festival alms." Added the master: "Don't give only your own alms; also give on behalf of your servants and your dependents!"

In the same assembly I addressed the master as follows: "While in Deogir (in the Deccan), Malih, who was the oldest of my servants, bought a young female slave for five **tankas.** When the army decamped to return to the capital city (Delhi), the parents of that young slave appeared before Malih. Overcome with distress, they shed tears of pathos as they offered him ten **tankas,** saying: 'Take these for the return of our daughter.' I was so moved by their plight that I took ten **tankas** from my own pocket and giving them to Malih, I said: 'You bought this young girl for five **tankas,** now sell her to me for ten.' He did as I asked and I then returned the daughter to her parents and also gave back the ten **tankas** they had offered for her purchase price. What I seek, above all else, is the master's reaction to my intervention." The master—may God remember him with favor—began to cry. "You have done well!" he exclaimed. "In buying this slave and returning her to her parents," I remarked, "I was trying to act as Maulana ʿAla ad-din Usuli—may God have mercy upon him—acted in that story which I heard from your Eminence." The master—may God remember him with favor—said: "Indeed this is how it happened. Maulana ʿAla ad-din had an old servant, but the servant had been newly endentured in Badaun. One morning, on waking up, the Maulana saw the servant crying while kneading dough. 'Why are you crying?' asked the Maulana. 'I am crying,' he replied, 'because I have a son in the vicinity of Kathir and now I am separated from him.' The Maulana asked: 'If I took you near the prayer ground, could you find your way home from there?' 'Yes,' replied the Maulana, 'I know my way home from there.' Maulana ʿAla ad-din took some bread and gave it to that man. Accompanying him to the road that leads to Kathir, the Maulana then left him."

As the master finished telling this story, a scholar who was present recalled the time when the Prophet—peace be upon him—took the daughter of Hatim Tai prisoner. So fervently did that daughter praise her father that the Prophet—peace be upon him—after listening to her, set the woman free.

Finally the master—may God remember him with favor—observed: "Each obedience that you perform, whether financially, physically, or morally, as long as you perform it with a pure motivation, it may be that one of your deeds will be accepted, and once it has been accepted, all your other works will then fall under its shadow. For," he continued, "there are many keys to the lock of happiness. One cannot know in advance which key will fit that lock. Hence one must try all the keys so that if the first doesn't fit, try another and another and another till at last one works!"

### IV. Assembly 53
Saturday, the 23rd of the month of Ramadan, A.H. 718 (18 November 1318)

I obtained the good fortune of kissing his hand. Conversation turned to MAINTAINING RITUAL PURITY. "Maintaining ritual purity," he observed, "depends on putting your heart at ease. Some count correctly, others mistake, the proper steps to take, yet purity cannot be calculated!" Then he remarked that Maulana ʿAla ad-din Usuli —may God have mercy upon him—used to say: "This matter depends not on place but on time. It is irrelevant to calculate steps. What is relevant is to deem suitable (for prayer) that time when your heart is at ease."

Conversation then turned to this: If someone has a continuous flow of menstrual blood or a prolonged hemorrhage or some other health problem, what is to be done? "Once," remarked the master, "a woman came to the Prophet—peace be upon him—and described her condition, namely, that she had a continuous flow of blood. 'What is my remedy?' she asked. The Prophet—peace be upon him—said: 'Perform ablution at each time of prayer, even if blood flows on the prayer mat!' "

He then spoke briefly about PRAYER AND THE SPIRITUAL AWARENESS THAT ONE OUGHT TO HAVE DURING PRAYER. I submitted: "I have heard that Shaykh al-Islam Farid ad-din —may God sanctify his lofty secret—often would prostrate himself in the place where he sat, even outside the times of proscribed prayer." Then the master observed: "Once in the cell where the great Shaykh secluded himself, I happened to espy him. I saw that he would stand up and then prostrate himself, uttering each time this verse:

> I wish always to live in longing for You.
> May I become dust, dwelling under Your feet.
> My goal freed of both worlds is only You.
> I die for You, just as I live for You."[87]

Then he told the story of SHAYKH FARID AD-DIN'S DEATH. "The evening of the fifth of the month of Muharram he became very ill. In the company of others he said the final evening prayer, then fell unconscious. After awhile he regained consciousness, asking: 'Did I say the final evening prayer?' 'Yes, you did,' they all replied. 'I better say it once again,' he murmured, 'for who knows what will happen?' Then he became unconscious for still longer, but once again regained consciousness. 'Did I say the final evening prayer?' he asked. 'You have already said it twice,' they replied. 'Then I better say it once again,' he murmured, 'for who knows what will happen?' Then, saying the evening prayer a third time, he became joined to the mercy of God (i.e., he died)—may God sanctify his lofty secret!"

### IV. Assembly 54

Sunday, 13th of the month of Dhu'l-Qa'da, A.H. 718 (6 January 1319)

I obtained the benefit of kissing his feet. Conversation turned to THOSE EMPLOYED AS SERVANTS OF OTHERS. On his blessed lips came this statement: "One should be less preoccupied with servile chores than with attaining peace of mind."

Then he told the following story. "In former days there was a man named Hamid. In his youth he lived in Delhi as the servant of Tughril, that same Tughril who late in life had himself crowned as king in Lukhnauti. In short, this Farid became the servant of that Tughril, and he remained in his service till one day, as he was waiting on Tughril, a form appeared to him. 'O Hamid,' it asked, 'why are you waiting on this man?' Having spoken, it disappeared. Hamid was puzzled about who this could be. Then a second time, as he was waiting on Tughril, again that form appeared and asked: 'O master Hamid, why are you waiting on this man?' Hamid remained perplexed. Then he saw this form a third time, and again it asked: 'O master Hamid, why are waiting on this man?' But this time Hamid rejoined: 'Why should I not wait on him, since I am his servant, he my master. I receive wages from him; why should I not wait on him?' Replied the form: 'You are wise, while he is ignorant. You are free, but he remains enslaved. You are righteous, he is corrupt.' Having spoken, it disappeared. When Hamid understood what the form had said, he went to the king and announced: 'If I owe you some service or have unpaid debts, tell me; for I will no longer be your servant.' 'What nonsense are you speaking?' retorted the king. 'You must be mad.' But Khwaja Hamid stood firm. 'No, I will no longer serve you. I have been blessed with contentment.' "[88]

When the master—may God remember him with favor—came to this point in the story, I interjected: "That form that appeared to Hamid was surely one of the men of the Unseen?" "No," replied the master. "Whenever a man cleans his inner self of defilements, he will see many things of this sort. A myriad of such qualities exist in each of us, but on account of despicable deeds they remain occluded. Only when the inner self becomes completely translucent can a person recognize the many, many wonders within himself." And then on his blessed lips came this verse:

That musk-pod you seek will deep inside you remain
For your fate is such that no scent of it you'll gain.

Then he spoke further about that KHWAJA HAMID. "When he left the service of that king, he entered the service of Shaykh al-Islam Farid ad-din—may God sanctify his lofty secret—and became his disciple. I used to see him. He had become a truly pious person. From time to time he would preach. In spiritual discipline, as in ritual observance, he was unswerving. So advanced did he become that Shaykh al-Islam Farid ad-din—may God sanctify his lofty secret—told him: 'Go to Indrapat and settle there, for now you have become like a star, but a star blocked by the moon cannot radiate its light! Go, settle in Indrapat!' As soon as he heard the Shaykh's command, Khwaja Hamid complied. But that very night seven of his friends resolved to go on the pilgrimage. This Hamid came and, standing in the courtyard of Shaykh Farid ad-din's hospice, he declared: 'I am standing in this courtyard to make a request. Your eminence has commanded me: "Go, settle in Indrapat!" I have already seen much of Indrapat and Kilokihri. My friends are now going on the pilgrimage. Will your Eminence permit me to accompany them and also perform the pilgrimage?' 'Go!' replied the Shaykh. In short, he accompanied them on the pilgrimage and received the benefit of that journey, but on his return he was joined to the mercy of God (i.e., he died)!"

A youth came to renew his vow of obedience to the master. Even though he had been taunted by a neighbor, he had not responded in kind. On the blessed lips of the master came this couplet:

Of many a lion You make a gazelle.
From many a sickness You make a man well.

### IV. Assembly 55
Monday, the 21st of Dhu'l-Qa'da, A.H. 718 (14 January 1319)

I had the good fortune of kissing his hand. He began to talk of PERSISTENCE IN REPENTANCE AND FIRMNESS IN THE OATH (of loyalty to one's master). "Whoever grasps the hand of a Shaykh and pledges loyalty to him," observed the master, "has made a pact with God! He must remain firm in his commitment, for if he becomes distracted from his resolve, in such circumstances on whom or what can he depend?"

Then he told the story about HIS OWN PLEDGE OF LOYALTY AND ATTACHMENT to Shaykh al-Islam Farid ad-din—may God sanctify his lofty secret. "On leaving him, I journeyed till I reached a point where I became very thirsty. The air was hot, water far off. At this moment I arrived at a turn in the road where I saw an ʿAlawi (a descendant of the Prophet Muhammad). I knew this ʿAlawi, Sayyid ʿUmmad was his name. He was traveling on his own. As soon as I saw him, I asked: 'Is there a waterhole close by? I'm very thirsty.' He was carrying a waterjug. 'Be my guest!' he replied. 'Take this jug and drink of it.' But the contents of this jug, I could tell, were wine or hemp juice. 'I will never drink this,' I replied. That ʿAlawi persisted. 'In this vicinity there is no place for drinking water. I have brought this along in the absence of water. Beyond here, for a long way to come there is no water. If you don't drink this, you'll expire!' 'No, sir!' I replied. 'On the contrary, I would expire if I drank this water, for I have pledged allegiance, and bound myself by oath, to my Shaykh. I swore that I would never drink such as this!' Having declined his help, I departed, and not far down the road on which I was traveling I found a waterhole, praise be to God!"

After that he told the following story. "Khwaja Hamid Suwali was a disciple of Shaykh Muʿin ad-din and he also received the cloak emblematic of discipleship from Shaykh Qutb ad-din—may God have mercy on both of them. After repenting and receiving the cloak, Khwaja Hamid was approached by his friends and neighbors. 'Come!' they said. 'Let us go and have some fun!' Replied Khwaja Hamid: 'I will never indulge in such play!' They persisted. Again Khwaja Hamid declared: 'I will never indulge in such play!' They kept pestering and pestering him till finally he exclaimed: 'Go and find your own niche, for I have tied this band so tight around my waist that it will not be loosed, even on Judgment Day, even for the **houris** of heaven!' And God knows the truth!"

## IV. Assembly 56

Saturday, the 11th of the month of Dhu'l-Hijja, A.H. 718 (3 February 1319)

I obtained the good fortune of kissing his hand. I submitted: "I will not fast till the thirteenth of this month due to the Greater Feast [which extends from the eleventh to the thirteenth of Dhu'l-Hijja]. What is the period of fasting for the brightest days of the new moon (**ayyam-i biz**)?" "Till the sixteenth one should fast," he replied. And then he added: "Imam Shafiʿi—may God have mercy upon him—stated that one ought to fast continually for the fourteenth, fifteenth, and sixteenth days, in observance of the brightest days of the new moon. Especially in this month, due to the coincidence with the Greater Feast, one should keep fasting till the sixteenth."

In the interim food was served, including rice. I submitted: " 'The rice is from me'—is that a Tradition?" "Yes," replied the master. "It occurred in this way. Once the companions prepared some food. Everyone brought something. One said: 'The meat is from me.' Another said: 'The trimmings are from me.' Everyone spoke up in this manner and the Prophet—peace and blessings be upon him—said: 'The rice is from me.' "

IV. Assembly 57
Monday, the 20th of the month of Dhuʾl-Hijja, A.H. 718 (12 February 1319)

I had the good fortune of kissing his hand. They brought food and after it was consumed, they brought a bowl and waterpot. At that moment, with a smile on his face, the master remarked: "Among the Arabs when they bring a bowl and waterpot after food they call it Abuʾl-Ilyas, that is to say, the sign of exhausted hope, for after that no more food will be brought." Then by way of a joke he added: "In India the equivalent of Abuʾl-Ilyas is the betel-leaf, for after it no more food will be brought!" He went on to note: "Among the Arabs, there is no betel-leaf; for that reason, they call the bowl and waterpot Abuʾl-Ilyas." After a pause he concluded: "While they call the bowl and waterpot Abuʾl-Ilyas, they call salt Abuʾl-Fath [i.e., the father of victory, over hunger]."

IV. Assembly 58
Monday, the 27th of the month of Dhuʾl-Hijja, A.H. 718 (19 February 1319)

I had the honor of kissing his hand. He began to talk of FOOD, quoting a Tradition of the Prophet—blessings and peace be upon him—to the effect that "the food one eats should come from a devout person and the one to whom one distributes food should also be devout!" Then the master observed: "One can make every possible effort to eat the food of a devout person but as for restricting the distribution of food to those who are devout, that is very difficult. If, for example, ten guests come, how is the host to know who are the devout among them?" Then he added: "I have found another Tradition in the **Mashariq,**[89] and it is more hopeful. It goes as follows: 'Give food to everyone, to those you do not know as well as to those you do know, that is to say, to all comers known and unknown.' "

Then he told a story: "In Badaun there was a man who would fast throughout the day till evening prayer. Coming to the porch of his own home, he would sit down, and with servants standing at the front door, he would invite all passersby to come in and join him for the breaking of the fast!"

After that he told still another story, about blessed Abraham—peace and blessings be upon him. "He would only eat in the company of guests, till one day he found himself with only a polytheist as guest. Blessed Abraham, when he saw that he was alone (with the polytheist), did not give him anything to eat. Then a command came forth: 'O Abraham, how is it that we can confer life on him yet you cannot give him bread?' "

Then he told a further story. "Some time ago, after I had come to the city, a Sufi among the friends of Shaykh Baha ad-din—may God have mercy upon him—came to visit me. On that occasion Saʿid Qurayshi, ʿAli Khukhari, and other students were present. It was a propitious assembly, and food was served. All had a hearty appetite, that is, until a neighbor of mine, Sharaf Payada by name, also came and began eating. Now that Sharaf Payada was a hairdresser! As soon as he arrived and started to partake of the food, Saʿid Qurayshi and some others stopped eating. They found it difficult to eat in his presence. Soon thereafter Saʿid Qurayshi left the assembly." The master—may God remember him with favor—observed: "I was surprised. What could have caused them to stop eating? I asked: 'Why did they leave?' Others replied: 'Because this man who began to eat with them was a hairdresser.' " The master—may God remember him with favor—said: "I began to laugh. 'How did it happen that they couldn't eat with a hairdresser? What can excuse such an extreme display of contempt?' " At this point I interjected: "Recently I had seen Saʿid Qurayshi and even been in the same place with him. I had never known him to display again such an attitude, of the sort just described." "Yes," replied the master, "it was due to the ill-omen from that incident that misfortunes have befallen him!"

He next spoke briefly about the ASCENSION OF THE PROPHET. A dear one who was present asked: "How did the Ascension take place?" The master—may God remember him with favor—

replied: "From Mecca to Jerusalem was the Night Journey (Q.17:1), from Jerusalem to the first heaven was the Ascension, and from the first heaven to the place of 'two bows' length' (Q.53:7) was the Ascent." Then that dear one elaborated his question, asking: "Some claim that the Ascension was bodily, others that it was spiritual. How can it be both?" On the blessed tongue of the master—may God remember him with favor—came this verse:

> Imagine the best, ask not for details!

In matters of religion," he added, "one must have faith; one should not show excessive zeal in either asserting or exploring them." Then he recited the following two couplets in their entirety, adding that it was a beloved present that evening who had composed these verses in a moment of inspiration:

> He came to me, wrapped in the cloak of night,
> Approaching with steps of caution and fright.
> Then what happened, happened; to say more fails.
> Imagine the best, ask not for details.

### IV. Assembly 59

Monday, the 18th of the month of Muharram, A.H. 719 (11 March 1319)

I obtained the good fortune of kissing his hand. That day he had just returned from a visit to Badaon. He began to talk about THOSE SAINTS WHO LIE BURIED IN THE VICINITY OF BADAON. I submitted: "The sense of security evident in the army is no greater than the comfort that derives from the visit to these saints, such as the esteemed father of the master, Maulana ʿAla ad-din Usuli, Maulana Siraj ad-din Tirmidhi, Khwaja Shahay Muy Tab, Khwaja ʿAziz Kirki, Khwaja ʿAziz Kotwal, Khwaja Shadi Lukhnauti, and Qazi Jamal Multani." As I mentioned the names of these dear ones, the master—may God remember him with favor—began to well up with tears, and he echoed a refrain of commendation after each name. When the name of Qazi Jamal Multani was mentioned, he remarked: "Once in a dream this saint saw the Prophet—blessings and peace be upon him. The Prophet was passing through Badaon, and stopping at one place, he performed his ablutions there. As soon as the Maulana awoke, he went at once to that place. Finding the ground moist, he said: 'Dig my grave here.' And when he died, they did as he directed, burying him in that very spot!"

IV. Assembly 60

Tuesday, the 26th of the month of Muharram, A.H. 719 (19 March 1319)

I had the benefit of kissing his hand. Conversation turned to THE VIRTUE OF FASTING, in particular, to the Tradition: "For the faster there is a double delight, delight in the breaking of the fast, and delight in meeting the Everlasting King." The master then commented: "The delight of the faster in the breaking of the fast is not in food and drink but rather in the completion of the fast, that is to say, he experiences delight because he has completed the fast! 'Praise be to God that I have completed this,' he prays, 'and now I am hopeful of the blessing of seeing God!' " Continued the master: "Every act of obedience has a specific reward. Since the specific reward for the faster is the blessing of a vision of the Lord, every time that he successfully completes the fast he is filled with joy in anticipation of that blessing."

During this discussion mention was made of the Tradition: "The fast is for me, and I am the reward that comes with it!" One of those present remarked: "I have also heard a variant of this Tradition, namely, "the faster is for me, and so forth." The master—may God remember him with favor—smiled and quipped: "One should rather say: 'I am the reward for it,' but then he corrected himself, adding: 'The meaning of "with" in "reward with it" is the same as "for" in "reward for it" [i.e., the initial form of the Tradition is correct].' "

In connection with fasting he spoke also about **SABR.** "**Sabr** [which usually means patience] may also mean imprisonment," he explained. "The Prophet—blessings and peace be upon him—once said: 'Imprison him who imprisons another, and kill him who kills another!' This is a well-known Tradition," he observed, "and it occurred as follows. In the time of the Prophet—blessings and peace be upon him—a man drew a sword and came running after another man. The latter fled before his pursuer, but another man came and, intercepting him, held the pursued one till his assailant overtook them both and slew the 'imprisoned' man. When this was reported to the Prophet—blessings and peace be upon him—he made the pronouncement: 'Imprison him who caught that fleeing man then held him, and put to death him who slew that man.' From this pronouncement came the Tradition: 'Imprison him who imprisons another and kill him who kills another.' "

Finally, conversation turned to another Tradition. The Prophet—blessings and peace be upon him—often promised: "Whoever does such-and-such a work, tomorrow will be in the same place with me in heaven." In explaining this Tradition, the Prophet held together his index and middle fingers, adding: "Like these two!" The master—may God remember him with favor—explained: "This gesture does not merely signify that I and he will be in the same place just as these two fingers are side by side in the same place; it also signifies rank, that is to say, the same rank that I will attain will also be granted to him. Why? Because for [most of] humankind the middle finger is longer than the index finger yet in the case of the Prophet—blessings and peace be upon him—these two fingers were the same length!"

### IV. Assembly 61

Thursday, the 13th of the month of Safar—may God conclude it with favor and success—A.H. 719 (5 April 1319)

I obtained the good fortune of kissing his feet. He began talking about SINLESSNESS AND REPENTANCE. "The spiritual master of Herat (i.e., Shaykh ʿAbdallah ʿAnsari) used to say: 'Attention to this matter is important, whether one be sinless from the outset or repentant at the end!' "

Then he spoke further on the subject of REPENTANCE AND PIETY. "The pious," he observed, "is he who is never contaminated by impurity, while the penitent is he who has been contaminated but turns to God (for forgiveness). There has been much discussion of these dicta. Some say: 'The pious and the penitent are equivalent.' Others say: 'The penitent is more virtuous than the pious because after having tasted sin he has repented of it, for he who has tasted and then rejected is stronger than he who has never tasted at all.' But still others say: 'The pious is more virtuous than the penitent.' "

Which of these dicta is true? The master told the following story. "Once two men were having a lively discussion. One said: 'The pious is more virtuous than the penitent.' The other said: 'No, the penitent is more virtuous than the pious.' They talked on and on about this subject. Finally they both came before the prophet of that age, seeking his pronouncement. The prophet of that age said: 'I cannot make a pronouncement on my own. I will seek inspiration to see what command I receive from on high.' And this was the command that came to that prophet. 'Tell these two to go and spend the night under the same roof. When they leave that house in the morning, whomever they first chance to meet let them ask him for his pronouncement on this question.' Both men complied with the command. The next day as they came out of the house where they had been staying, a man approached. 'O sir,' they called out to him, 'we have this problem. Please solve it for us.' 'What is your problem?' he asked. 'We must know,' they explained, 'whether that one who has never once sinned is better than he who having sinned repents of his sin.' Replied that man: 'Dear sirs, I am a weaver, unversed in any field of knowledge. How could I possibly solve this problem? I only know this much: In weaving a garment I often break a piece of thread. That thread, once I have repaired it, becomes stronger than a thread which has never broken!' The two men then returned to the prophet of that age and told him what they had been told. Said the prophet: 'The same answer applies to you both!' "

He then told a brief story about WORLDLINESS AND HOW PEOPLE ARE DECEIVED BY IT. "Once," he recalled, "blessed Jesus—peace be upon him—saw a decrepit, old, black-faced woman. She was crying. 'Why are you crying?' asked Jesus. 'I am worldliness,' she replied. Blessed Jesus—peace be upon him—asked: 'How many husbands have you had?' 'Countless, countless,' she repeated. 'If it were possible to reckon them, I would tell you!' 'Of these husbands,' asked blessed Jesus—peace be upon him, 'have any divorced you?' 'Not one,' she replied. 'I have killed them all!' "

In this connection the master remarked: "A dervish is he who enjoys complete composure because he is safe from such calamities. The most difficult of the works of the dervish is to experience hardship throughout the night, yet that night during which he experiences hardship is the same night during which he experiences an ascent (**miʿraji**) to his Lord!"

He also spoke briefly about MEN OF WEALTH AND THEIR LOVE OF WEALTH. He told the following story: "Once a person came to see Shaykh al-Islam Farid ad-din—may God sanctify his lofty secret—and told him the story about a contemporary Shaykh who had extensive wealth. 'Despite the fact that he has so much wealth,' observed the visitor, 'this saint would say: "I have not been granted (divine) consent to expend my wealth!" Shaykh al-Islam Farid ad-din—may God sanctify his lofty secret—smiled as he listened to the visitor and then exclaimed: 'This is Baha, Baha (ad-din Zakariya)!' Then he added: 'If that Shaykh put me in charge of disbursement, in two or three days I would empty his treasury, yet I would not give away even one **diram** without (divine) consent!' "

He then told a brief story about HOW GOD IS THE GIVER. "Since God Almighty is the giver, who can prevent Him from giving (as He pleases)?" In this connection he told a story about Sultan Shams ad-din Iltetmish. "Sultan Shams ad-din had a polo ground built in Badaun. It was a polo ground with two entrances. He would go there to play polo. One day, as he was playing, he rode by one of the entrances and saw a bent-over old man. The man asked him for something but the Sultan gave him not a thing. Then, as he was riding by the other entrance, he saw a strapping young lad. Sultan Shams ad-din was carrying a purse. Reaching in, he took out some gold **tankas** and gave them to that youth. Then he remarked: 'To that old man who wanted something, I gave nothing. To that youth who wanted nothing, I gave something. If it was up to me I would have given something to that old man, but to whomever one gives God is the true giver. What can I do?' "

Then he told still another story about SULTAN SHAMS AD-DIN. "Once he came to Badaun," recalled the master, "and they brought him some mangoes. Now these mangoes were very sweet, and after he had eaten them, he asked: 'What do you call these?' 'These are called **anab**,' was the reply. But since **anab** in Turkish means something loathsome, Sultan Shams ad-din said: 'You must call these **naghzak** [which means in Turkish "something strange and wonderful"].' Ever since this term came on his lips, it has been the name used for mangoes!" Then the master remarked: "Sultan Shams ad-din came to know both Shaykh Shihab ad-din Suhrawardi and Shaykh Awhad Kirmani—may God have mercy upon both of them—and one of them said to him: 'One day you will become a king!' "

Then he related a brief story about FORSAKING WORLDLINESS. "There was a spiritual master who lived in Badaun," he recalled. "His name was Sufi Badhni. According to Islamic law, anyone who abstains from the minimum of food and water needed to keep the body fit, or who does not wear enough clothing at least to cover the private parts, such a person is committing a punishable offence, yet Sufi Badhni was a saint of such high repute that he was exempt from both restrictions!"

In the same connection, about forsaking worldliness, he told the following story about Shaykh al-Islam Farid ad-din—may God sanctify his lofty secret. "All the gold and other blessings that were showered upon him he expended, so much so that when he died it was difficult to prepare for his funeral or even to make a shroud. (As the poet has said:)

Just as Hallaj for his funeral shroud could save no cotton,
So this pauper on God's path has for his grave no tombstone.

Such was his poverty that there were not even bricks with which to build his tomb. At last they produced a door with a brick lintel, and they destroyed it in order to use those bricks for the Shaykh's tomb!"

### IV. Assembly 62
Sunday, 28th of the month of Rabiʿ al-awwal, A.H. 719 (19 May 1319)

I obtained the benefit of kissing his hand. He began to talk about KINGS WHO HAVE A KEEN DESIRE TO LISTEN TO POETRY. "Once," he recalled, "Sultan Shams ad-din was holding court when the poet Nasiri arrived and offered a poem in his praise that began:

O you, from fear of whose might strife itself seeks refuge,
Your sword exacts from infidels wealth and elephants huge.

The Sultan, while listening to this poem, was also busy with other matters, and Nasiri continued to recite some more verses. The Sultan at last turned his mind to poetry. Addressing Nasiri, he asked:

'O you, from fear of whose might strife itself seeks refuge,
Your sword exacts from infidels wealth and elephants huge—

Would you please recite the verses that came after this?' " Commented the master: "Look how sharp was his memory: even while occupied with other matters, he could still recall the opening verses of this poem!" He then went on to commend his sound faith. "Every night," recalled the master, "Sultan Shams ad-din would wake up and as soon as he woke up, he would perform his ablutions, offer two cycles of prayer, and then go back to sleep . . . without ever awakening others!"

### IV. Assembly 63
Wednesday, the 16th of the month of Rabiʿ al-akhir,
A.H. 719 (6 June 1319)

I obtained the benefit of kissing his feet. Conversation turned to FASTING AND BREAKFAST. "Someone approached Shaykh Jalal ad-din Tabrizi—may God have mercy upon him," recalled the master, "and asked him: 'If a man does not fast yet eats breakfast, what happens?'

Replied Shaykh Jalal ad-din: 'If a man eats not only breakfast but also lunch and dinner in order to obtain the power to obey God Almighty, then he is not sinning.' " In connection with this remark, I recalled the following Qur'anic verse: "Eat of the good things" (Q.23:51). The master—may God remember him with favor—remarked: "[Recite the full verse: 'Eat of good things and (also) do good works!' " Concerning "good things," I asked: "What did the companions of the cave mean when they spoke about 'the choicest of food' (Q.17:19)?" Replied he: "They wanted a food that they were disposed to like." Then on his blessed tongue came the further remark: "According to some what they meant by that food was rice! And God knows best!"

### IV. Assembly 64

Sunday, the 12th of the month of Jumada al-ula, A.H. 719 (1 July 1319)

I obtained the good fortune of kissing his feet. Conversation focused on THOSE SAINTS WHO ARE CONTINUOUSLY ABSORBED IN REMEMBERING GOD. "Once," recalled the master, "a person approached such a saint with this request: 'When you are beseeching God, if memory of me comes to mind, please offer a prayer on my behalf.' Replied that dervish: 'Woe to that time when memory of you comes to mind!' "

Then he told a story about KHWAJA ʿAZIZ KIRKI, who was buried in Badaun. He spoke at length about his saintliness. I interjected: "I have heard it said that he used to swallow birds live, and after some time emit them one by one alive from his throat, and then send them flying off!" Replied the master—may God remember him with favor—"I never saw him do that, though I heard that he had." Then he remarked: "I have also heard that during the winter he used to go into a warm oven at night and reappear in the morning!" Then he added: "Khwaja ʿAziz was a resident of Kirk. In his youth he bought a celestial turquoise bangle, of the kind that women wear on their wrists. Though he busied himself remembering God, the governor of Kirk was unhappy with him and had him imprisoned. After his arrest the governor was told: 'But this is a righteous young man, engrossed in remembering God.' The governor then ordered him released but when they told Khwaja ʿAziz, 'The governor has ordered your release, come out,' he replied, 'I will never leave here till I eject him from house and home.' In short, a severe calamity befell that governor, and only then did Khwaja ʿAziz leave his place of confinement!"

IV. Assembly 65

Thursday, the 23rd of the month of Jumada al-ula, A.H. 719 (12 July 1319)

I obtained the benefit of kissing his feet. Conversation turned to MAKING THE PILGRIMAGE AND CIRCUMAMBULATING THE KAʿBA. "There are those," lamented the master, "who having circumabulated the Kaʿba then return home and constantly recall that experience: In every place and on every occasion they never cease to talk of it. That is not good." One of those present remarked: "Sometimes in making the pilgrimage, whether due to lack of water or the inconvenience of stops, one neglects to say the prescribed prayers." The master —may God remember him with favor—then told this story. "There was a preacher from Lahore. He preached superb sermons, commanding the attention of his listeners and providing them with a sense of spiritual comfort. Then he went on the pilgrimage, and when he came back, there was no longer in his preaching that spiritual comfort and taste for God that had been evident before. 'Your words have lost that flavor they used to have,' he was told. 'Yes,' lamented the man, 'and I know the reason why. The reason is this: While making the pilgrimage, I twice missed saying the prescribed prayers at the prescribed times!' "

IV. Assembly 66

Tuesday, the 5th of the month of Jumada al-akhira, A.H. 719 (24 July 1319)

I obtained the benefit of kissing his hand. Conversation turned to RULES BETWEEN THE MASTER AND HIS DISCIPLE. In this regard he noted: "The master should never desire anything from his disciple." By way of illustration he told this story. "Once a disciple, coming to see his master, brought him some watermelon. The master did not accept it and gave it back. Someone asked: 'Why must a master reject an offering from his disciple?' Replied that master: 'Just as it is improper for a master to be dependent on his disciple in religious matters, so, too, in worldly affairs he should never be dependent on one who is his disciple!' "

Then he began to talk about THE PROSTRATION OF DISCIPLES WHEN THEY ENTER THE PRESENCE OF THEIR MASTER. The master—may God remember him with favor—lamented: "I wish that I could restrain people from doing this but because they prostrated before my Shaykh I cannot restrain them." At this point I interjected: "For those who are committed to the master and have become his disciples and have sworn an oath of allegiance, both their discipleship and their oath are expressions of affection and love for the master. And for those who have become lovers to place their head to the ground is but a natural gesture."

The master—may God remember him with favor—commented: "I heard from Shaykh al-Islam Farid ad-din—may God sanctify his lofty secret—that once Shaykh Abu Sa'id Abu'l-Khayr—may God have mercy upon him—was riding on a horse. A disciple approached him on foot, and kissed the Shaykh's knee. 'Lower,' ordered the Shaykh. The disciple then kissed his foot. 'Lower still,' ordered the Shaykh. The disciple then kissed the knee of the horse. 'Go lower still,' ordered the Shaykh. The disciple then kissed the horse's hoof! 'Go even lower!' commanded the Shaykh, whereupon the disciple kissed the ground. Then remarked the Shaykh: 'In commanding you to go lower and lower my purpose was not to have you kiss the ground, but rather [to indicate to you that] the lower you go the higher will be your spiritual rank!' "

Then he spoke about DERVISHES WHO WERE CONFIRMED AS SUCCESSORS TO SHAYKH AL-ISLAM FARID AD-DIN—may God sanctify his lofty secret. On his blessed tongue came this account: "One of these was a dervish named 'Arif. He had been sent to Siwistan and adjacent regions, with permission to enroll disciples. It happened that there was a ruler in the vicinity of Uchch and Multan, and he appointed this 'Arif to be mosque prayer leader or some equivalent position. In short, that king once sent Shaykh al-Islam Farid ad-din—may God sanctify his lofty secret—one hundred **tankas** through this 'Arif. Keeping fifty **tankas** for himself, 'Arif gave the other fifty to the Shaykh. Smiling, Shaykh Farid ad-din remarked: 'You have made this division on a brotherly basis [i.e., each receives half of the whole]!' That 'Arif became embarrassed. Immediately he handed over his fifty **tankas** to the Shaykh and, pleading for forgiveness, asked to renew his oath of loyalty as a disciple. The Shaykh gave him the hand of allegiance. He also had his head shaven. After that he remained so fully committed to serving the Shaykh that eventually the Shaykh once again gave him permission to enroll disciples and sent him toward Siwistan."

## IV. Assembly 67

Monday, 3rd of the month of Rajab, A.H. 719 (23 August 1319)

I had the benefit of kissing his hand. Conversation turned to CONCEIT AND SELF-DECEPTION, especially those who think they know something of their own accord. The master remarked: "'A'isha—

may God be pleased with her—was once asked: 'Who is a bad man?' Replied she: 'Anyone who thinks himself to be good!' " To explain further what was meant the master told the following story: "There was a poet named Farzuq. Once he and Hasan Basri—may God be pleased with him—were together with a group of friends. One of that group asked in a loud voice: 'Who is the best of men among us, and who is the worst?' Farzuq then turned to Khwaja Hasan Basri and asked: 'Did you understand what he said?' Replied Khwaja Hasan Basri: 'How can one know who is the best of men? Only God knows this.' 'O Khwaja, you are the best of men,' announced Farzuq, 'and I, I am the worst of men!' After Farzuq died they saw him in a dream. 'How goes it with you?' they asked. Replied Farzuq: 'When they brought me before the Throne of Judgment, I was overcome with fear. A decree was directed to me: "It is We who instructed you that very day when you claimed that you knew yourself to be the worst of men!" ' "

I had had a thought in mind and that day I voiced it to the master. What I had wondered was: A tomb, once it has been built, if it becomes defiled, should one then rebuild it? "No," replied the master. "Whatever has been defiled should not be refurbished. It is better to consign its contents to the mercy of Almighty God!"

Then he told a story about MEN WHO WISH TO BE BURIED AT THE FEET OF SAINTS AND SPIRITUAL MASTERS. "There was in Badaun," he recalled, "a saint by the name of Maulana Siraj ad-din Tirmidhi. He went on the pilgrimage to Mecca with the intent that if it be God's will, he would die and be buried there. After he had circumambulated the Kaʿba and been rewarded with that boon, he returned to live in Badaun. 'But,' he was asked, 'didn't you go there with the intention that when you die you would be buried in that very spot?' 'Yes, I did,' he replied, 'but one night in a dream I saw funeral prayers being performed from several directions and the corpses over whom the prayers were being said were being transported for burial in the vicinity of Mecca. At the same time, some of the corpses that had been buried in or near Mecca were disinterred and carried away from there! "What is going on?" I asked. Came the reply: "A group of those whom we have buried here, though they died in faraway places, by divine decree we were told to bring them here, while another group that is not worthy of this place, even though they died here, by divine decree we are taking elsewhere!" ' Maulana Siraj ad-din said: 'When I realized the import of this dream, I came back to Badaun because should I be worthy of that place, I will achieve my objective, if God Almighty wills!' "

And this completes the fourth fascicle of the book **Morals for the Heart,** by the help of God and with the favor of success that He alone confers.

Now that the lofty book of Hasan's done,
The joy that he feels is all the more keen,
This Tuesday, the second of Shawwal,
In the year seven hundred and nineteen.

From the time that I first began to record these words till today when I reached the conclusion, there has elapsed a full twelve years, and this sum of twelve years, having been forged in the crucible of Truth, has been transformed into the gold coin of twelve months in the eyes of present-day moneychangers. It is to be hoped that this gold coin will now become a seal stamped on the hearts [of readers], ensuring both the full value of true faith and its universal circulation, if God Almighty wills. And God alone knows the Truth!

## Fascicle V (Hereafter V)

In the name of God, full of Compassion, ever Compassionate.

Praise beyond limit and glory without measure to the Eternal Lord who out of the bounty of His Grace accepted the string of pearls knotted with the knots of Nizam, through the existence of the master of mercies and generosity, the source of the secrets of subtleties, the revealer of the treasures of truths, the prince of saints, the pole of the world, the master of spiritual masters and men of insight, the Nizam of Truth, of Law, and of Faith—may God bless the Muslims through prolonging his life.

From the community of the Seal of the Prophets,
None but he has been appointed the Seal of the Saints.[90]

The servant Hasan ʿAli Sijzi says that when divine Providence became consonant with the spiritual state of this weak being and eternal felicity aided the intuitive moments of this broken vessel, the inspiration of the Almighty so guided his thoughts that he collected the life-ennobling discourses of this great one. Before the present volume he completed another volume; it took twelve years to commit to writing and comprised four fascicles. Now he has begun this second volume. May God—the Blessed and Almighty—remember with favor the essence of kingship (which also expresses) the attributes of dominion and grant him the life span of Khidr so that from this spring, which is the source of life, both the elite and the common folk may drink. Let us hope that a draught from this life-giving cup which provides spiritual meaning will give solace—if God Almighty wills—to the one who speaks, to the one who listens, and to the one who writes.

### V. Assembly 1
Sunday, 21st Shaʿban, A.H. 719 (7 October 1319)

I received the fortune of kissing his feet. I was pondering a Tradition which I related to the master: "WHOEVER LOVES KNOWLEDGE AND THOSE WHO ATTAIN IT, HIS SINS ARE NOT WRITTEN (IN THE BOOK OF DEEDS)." I then commented that it seemed to be the intent of the Tradition that due to love of the **ʿulama,** the sin of such-and-such is not recorded. The master observed: "The proof of love is obedience, and whenever someone loves them (the ʿ**ulama**), he follows them every moment, and becomes far removed from impropriety. When such a thing happens, his sins cease to be recorded." Then he added: "As long as love of God remains in the outer sphere of the heart, there is the possibility of sin, but when love enters the core of the heart, the possibility of sin is removed.[91]

"Repentance and penance," he went on, "are most fitting in the period of youth, for in old age, what is there to do for which one should repent and become a penitent?" Then he recited the following couplet:

When you grow old, and to life's close progress,
When you regret how you have lacked success,

And added:

Then only, driven by gloom in excess,
Will you at last for God your love profess.

After this he observed: "God the Exalted will ask His slave about his youth, as it says in the Tradition: 'He will ask man about his youth.' "

At this point in the conversation a learned man arrived, and placing his head at the foot of the master—may God remember him with favor —he explained, "The reason I have come before you is to relate the following incident. I was in Afghanpur recently, by the edge of the water. When the time for evening prayer came, I gave myself to prayer. I saw your blessed face in the midst of prayer, and awe overcame me. I had never before met you, but at the sight of your blessed face, I began to confuse my prayer. I almost lost my composure. On completing the evening prayer, I said to myself, 'I must go and place myself in the service of the master of both worlds and attach myself to the band of his servants.' For this reason I have come into your service, to pledge my allegiance to you."

When the scholar finished telling his story, the master—may God remember him with favor—rejoined: "A certain man once left Delhi for Ajodhan, intending to repent before Shaykh al-Islam Farid ad-din. En route a wayward female singer joined him. Attaching herself to that man, she hoped to engage in an affair with him. But since he was sincere in his intent, he was not at all inclined to that adultress—until they reached a way-station on the road where it happened that they both had to proceed riding on one animal. That woman sat so close to that man that every barrier and obstacle between them was removed. In such a circumstance there appeared a bit of lust in the man's heart. He was on the verge of wanting to say something to her or to extend his hand toward her. At that moment he saw a man come and slap him on the face. 'You are going to such-and-such a saint,' he exclaimed, 'with the intention of repenting, so what is this?' That man immediately got the message and no longer looked toward his woman companion. When at last he came before Shaykh al-Islam Farid ad-din, the first words the Shaykh uttered to him were: 'That day God the Exalted kept a firm vigil over you!' "

Conversation next turned to THE PERFECT ELOQUENCE OF THE PROPHET—blessings and peace be upon him. There was a companion of the Prophet who had sold one of his sheep but then changed his mind. He came to the Prophet and explained to him what had happened. The Prophet told the people who had bought the sheep from him. "This man has changed his mind. Please return the sheep to him." That man's name was Naʿim. It was on that occasion that the Prophet exclaimed, "Naʿim, you hesitated, then bought back your sheep." [Shaykh Nizam ad-din then proceeds to explain how eloquent is this turn of phrase, since the Prophet sums up the whole episode in but four words, each of them identically shaped in Arabic calligraphy and distinguished from one another only by their diacritical markings.]

### V. Assembly 2
Thursday, 9th Ramadan, A.H. 710 (24 October 1319)

I was honored with kissing his hand. It was the winter season. He inquired about the tumultuous political conditions in the environs (of North India). He suggested that that VIGILANCE which is incumbent on these accursed ones (i.e., the political rulers) is NOT ADEQUATELY EXERCISED AT THIS TIME. To illustrate his point, he cited the fate of Sher Khan, the governor of Uchch and Multan, who had no reliance on the sanctity of the Shaykh of Islam, Farid ad-din—may God sanctify his secrets. About him Shaykh Farid ad-din had said:

What a pity that you know not who I am.
When someone tells you, more the pity for you!

After that he noted that when Shaykh Farid ad-din died, the same year the infidels (i.e., the Mongols) invaded that region (Uchch and Multan).

Conversation then turned to SHAYKH BAHA AD-DIN ZAKARIYA AND HIS SAINTLINESS. "There was once a scholar who had journeyed from Bukhara," observed Shaykh Nizam ad-din. "In search of knowledge he had come to see Shaykh Baha ad-din Zakariya—may God be merciful to him. As he approached, the Shaykh noted that he was wearing a turban, with a braid of hair draped down in back. "Why has he come burdened with two loads?" quipped the Shaykh, alluding to the turban and the braid of hair. On hearing this, the scholar at once asked to have his head shaved before the Shaykh (i.e., he wanted to become a disciple of the Shaykh). "What a powerful sense of intuition had Shaykh Baha ad-din Zakariya!" exclaimed the master.

In this connection he told a further story about UCHCH. "There was in Multan a devout man named Sulayman. When his fame reached Shaykh Baha ad-din Zakariya, the saint went to see him. 'Get up,' he ordered the man, 'and do two cycles of prayer that I may observe how you pray.' That man got up and did two cycles of prayer, but he did not set his feet in the prescribed manner: He left either too much or too little space between them. 'Keep this amount of space between your feet,' remonstrated the saint. 'No more, no less.' That man went back to praying. And again he failed to place his feet in the manner that the Shaykh had prescribed. Again, the saint instructed him. 'Set your feet like this~!' But the man could not comply. 'Go settle in Uchch,' commanded the Shaykh, and the man went and settled in Uchch."

Conversation next turned to THE DEATH OF SHAYKH BAHA AD-DIN ZAKARIYA—may God be merciful to him. "One day," said the master, "a disciple brought a letter, and gave it to Shaykh Sadr ad-din (his son and successor), saying, 'A man gave me this letter and said, "Take it to Shaykh Baha ad-din Zakariya.' " Shaykh Sadr ad-din, when he read the address of the letter, turned pale. He went and gave that letter to Shaykh Baha ad-din Zakariya. The Shaykh, on reading the letter, turned aside and uttered loud cries. That night Shaykh Baha ad-din Zakariya—may God have mercy upon him—died.

"What a glorious period it was," he exclaimed, "that period when these five saints were alive: Shaykh Abul-Gaith Yamani, Shaykh Sayf ad-din Bakharzi, Shaykh Saʿd ad-din Hamuya, Shaykh Baha ad-din Zakariya, and Shaykh al-Islam Farid ad-din—may God sanctify their lofty secrets!"

In this connection he told the following story about SHAYKH SAYF AD-DIN BAKHARZI. "It was his custom, after saying the evening prayer, to sleep for one-third of the night. When one-third of the night had passed, he would get up. The **imam** (prayer leader) and the **muezzin** (caller to prayer) would also be present. He would say the morning prayer and then would remain awake for the remainder of the night till daybreak. All his life he followed this practice."

"Did he listen to **sama'** (mystical music)?" I enquired. "Yes," replied the master, "but it was not his practice to arrange an assembly or to invite people to attend. Instead, he would sit down, tell a story, and listen to the story of others. When he came to his **waqt** (numinous moment), he would become happy and ask, 'Is there anyone here who has something to recite?' Then a **qawwal** (singer) would come forward and recite something. Such was the manner of his **sama'**."

After this the master spoke about THE CIRCUMSTANCES OF SHAYKH SAYF AD-DIN BAKHARZI'S DEATH. "There was a man in Bukhara," he said. "One night in a dream he saw that the lighted torch above the gateway to Bukhara was being carried away. When day broke, he came to see a saint, and told him what he had seen in his sleep. Replied the saint, 'That luminary from Bukhara, who is the vehicle of divine favor, he will leave Bukhara.' Shortly thereafter, Shaykh Sayf ad-din Bakharzi died."

And he told another story. "At that same time (some say) Shaykh Sayf ad-din saw his own master in a dream. The master said to him, 'I am seized with yearning. Come!' After this dream Shaykh Sayf ad-din engaged in **dhikr** (remembrance of God) throughout the following week. Every formula he used would mention 'separation' and 'farewell.' People were astonished that all his words alluded to separation. Then he offered an explanatory verse on the rhyme 'farewell':

Packed I am, my friends, and ready to start—Farewell!
How painful it has been to live apart—Farewell!

"When he had finished the verse, he looked out at the assembled group and said, 'O Muslims, note well and forget not that it was my master who told me in a dream, "Come!" I am going. Farewell!' "

Having said this, he descended from the dias on which he was seated and soon thereafter died—may God have mercy upon him. And God alone knows [which of these two stories is true]."

V. Assembly 3

Tuesday 27th Ramadan, A.H. 719 (11 November 1319)

I obtained the benefit of kissing the master's feet. Praise be to God! A dear one arrived and brought with him an esteemed visitor. They came into the presence of the Shaykh. "Who is that? Who has come?" asked Shaykh Nizam ad-din. It was explained to him who the visitor was, but the Shaykh did not recognize the person of whom they spoke. Afterward he said, "I know many people and when I see them, I recognize them, but I do not remember them by name."

In the same connection he told the following story, "One of the sons of Shaykh Farid ad-din was named Nizam ad-din. The Shaykh favored him over all his other sons. He was a soldier, and in the presence of the Shaykh he was very rude. Yet whatever he said, the Shaykh would take it with a smile and not be offended. Once that son went on a journey, and a few days later sent back his greetings through an intermediary. When the messenger came before the Shaykh, he said, 'Your excellency's son, Nizam ad-din, sends his greetings.' 'Who is that man?' asked the Shaykh. 'Your excellency's son, Nizam ad-din,' replied the man. Again the Shaykh asked, 'Whom are you talking about?' 'Your excellency's son, Nizam ad-din! Your son!' exclaimed the man. 'Oh, him,' rejoined the Shaykh. 'How is he? Is he well?' " On reaching this point in the narration, Shaykh Nizam ad-din remarked, "Just see how engrossed was the Shaykh in REMEMBERING GOD that only after so much exchange and explanation did he recall even his own son, his favorite son!"

In the same vein he went on to tell a story about SHAYKH BAHA AD-DIN ZAKARIYA. "Someone came into his presence, and conveyed greetings from someone else to the Shaykh. 'Who is this?' asked the Shaykh. The visitor explained but the Shaykh did not recognize who the person was. The visitor began to offer more and more detail but the Shaykh cut him off, saying, 'What is the need of so much explanation? Has he ever seen me?' 'Indeed,' replied the visitor. 'He is your slave, one of your disciples!' 'Enough said,' quipped the Shaykh, and fell silent."

After that, he told another story about Shaykh Baha ad-din Zakariya. "He used to say, 'If you give something to someone, you should GIVE IT WITH A FLOURISH.' He was exceedingly generous to the scholars who tutored his sons, and would pour silver into their laps."

He then narrated the following anecdote: "Once the governor of Multan needed some grain, and made a request of the Shaykh.[92] Shaykh Baha ad-din ordered one stack of grain to be sent to him. The governor sent a group of his subordinates to fetch the grain. In the middle of the grain they found a carafe full of silver coins. They reported what they had found to the governor. 'The Shaykh has provided us with grain, not this silver. It must be returned to him,' ordered the governor. When the

Shaykh was told about what had transpired, he sent this reply to the governor: 'Tell him that Zakariya knew about this; I intentionally gave you that silver along with the grain.' "

Conversation then turned to RENOUNCING THE WORLD. In this connection he told a story about Jesus—peace be upon our Prophet and also upon him! "Once Jesus came upon a sleeping man and in a loud voice commanded him to get up and worship God. 'I have already rendered unto God that devotion which is the best of devotions,' replied the man. 'What is that?' asked Jesus. 'I have renounced the world, together with (all) its inhabitants.' " And then the master added: "One whom God Almighty has blessed with little sustenance, from him the Almighty will be pleased with little action." And he continued: "Whoever departs this world and nothing remains after him, 'neither **diram** nor **dinar,**' in heaven there will be none richer than he. And God knows best."

### V. Assembly 4
### Saturday, 24th of Shawwal, A.H. 719 (8 December 1319)

I obtained the benefit of kissing his hand. Conversation turned to THE QUR'AN. "In a certain book," observed the master, "I have read two interpretations (of the Qur'an) that I have seldom seen in other books. One concerns the Qur'anic verse: 'And when you look, then will you see a blessed one and a great kingdom' (Q. 76:20). Changing **mulk** (kingdom) to **malik** (king), they read 'a great king' and interpret it as a reference to the Commander of the Faithful 'Ali—may God bestow kindness on him and grant him peace! The second concerns the verse: 'And has not a prophet arisen among you (**min anfusikum**)?' (Q. 9:128). By reading **anfasikum** instead of **anfusikum,** that is, taking the word to be the superlative of the adjective nafis (precious), the translation becomes: 'And has not a prophet arisen from the most esteemed of you?' "

The master then told a story to the effect that AN INVOCATORY PRAYER OR ACT OF OBEDIENCE WHICH A PIOUS PERSON NEGLECTS TO PERFORM WILL RESULT IN A CALAMITY FOR HIM. "Once a soldier came to see Shaykh Baha ad-din Zakariya—may God have mercy upon him. 'I saw last night in a dream' reported the man, 'that I had failed to say my prayers.' 'Your end is near,' replied the Shaykh. 'Devote yourself to repentance.' After the soldier got up and left, another Sufi from his own hospice entered. He reported having had the same dream. When he finished describing the content of his dream to Shaykh Baha ad-din Zakariya, the Shaykh was astounded. 'That other man was a soldier,' he thought to himself. 'Perhaps he will be killed in war. But this Sufi is at peace, and bears no sign of imminent calamity. What am I to tell him?' While he was pondering the mystery of these conversations, news reached the Shaykh that the soldier had indeed been killed and that the Sufi had missed saying his prayer with (pure) intent (i.e., he said the words but not as God's servant and hence, having lost their benefit, he would die)." When the master reached this point in his narration, tears welled up in his eyes. "Look," he exclaimed, "one moment's neglect of prayer (by the Sufi) is tantamount to death!"

Then the master began to discuss THE NECESSITY OF INVOCATORY PRAYERS. "No matter what the pretext for a pious person to undertake the recitation of such prayers, if on account of illness he should once fail to say his prayers, it will be recorded in the Book of Deeds that he has recited it. But as for those who do not recite an invocatory prayer but instead recite words of their own selection, the one who recites an invocatory prayer is better than such since his reason for missing the invocatory prayer (if he should miss it) is accepted, and the prayer itself recorded (as if it had been recited), but what will They record of him who does not have a fixed form of invocation?"

In this connection the master began to speak at great length about THE BENEFIT OF RECITING THE **MUSABBIʿAT-I ʿASHR** (a twice-a-day seven-fold invocation of ten prayers).[93] He noted that there was once a man who used to recite continuously the **musabbiʿat-i ʿashr.** One time when he was traveling, a band of robbers descended on him. They were about to kill him. All of a sudden, ten armed horsemen appeared. They saved him from the band of robbers. Now all ten of these armed horsemen were bareheaded. That man asked them: "Who are you, and why have you come in this manner?" They replied: "We are the **musabbiʿat-i ʿashr,** that is, those ten prayers which you recite sevenfold twice daily." "Then why do you come bareheaded?" asked the man. "Because at the beginning of each prayer you neglect to say, 'In the name of God full of Compassion, ever Compassionate!' "

At this point I interjected and asked the master, "Where is one supposed TO INVOKE GOD'S NAME?" "At the beginning of each Qurʾanic chapter," replied the master. Then he told the story of Qazi Kamal ad-din Jaʿfri, who had been the judge of Badaʾun. He did many pious works. Despite his involvement in legal and other duties, he was in the habit of reciting the Qurʾan frequently. But when he had grown quite old, he desisted from reciting the Qurʾan. "Why?" they asked him." He replied: "I have opted for the **musabbiʿat-i ʿashr** since it is the epitome of invocatory prayers."

After that, the master said that Ibrahim Tamimi, one of those favored few who had found union with God, once met Khizr in the vicinity of the Kaʿba. He asked a favor of Khizr. Khizr taught him the **masabbiʿat-i ʿashr,** saying, "I transmit it to you on the authority of God's messenger—blessings and peace be upon him!"

## V. Assembly 5

Wednesday, 28th of Shawwal, A.H. 719 (12 December 1319)

I obtained the benefit of kissing his feet. Discourse turned to this topic: "EVERY SORROW AND PAIN THAT BEFALLS A PERSON HE SHOULD KNOW, OR TRY TO KNOW ITS SOURCE," observed the master. "One's welfare depends on being aware of the cause of affliction. But whoever, at the height of bravado, entertains the whim that nothing odious will befall him, that man will be disappointed. We take refuge in God, that he may keep us from such a fate and far away from such thoughts."

Then the master told the story of a pious, elderly woman about whom Shaykh Farid ad-din—may God sanctify his lofty secret—had told him. She would say repeatedly: "If a thorn pricks my foot, I know from whence it comes."

And he added: "When they cast aspersions on ʿA'isha (Q. 24:11–20)—and that is a very long story—she afterward used to say in her invocatory prayers: 'O my God, I know the source of these slanders which have arisen against me. It is due to the fact that the Prophet—blessings and peace be upon him—was responding to the claim of Your love and had a very little bit of love left for me. It is on this account that I have been slandered.' "

And as the master was talking, a dear friend arrived, bringing with him some collyrium. This prompted the master to mention the following Tradition: "The Prophet used to say, 'THREE THINGS OF THIS WORLD HAVE I LOVED: PERFUME, WOMEN, AND A TOUCH OF COLLYRIUM IN PRAYER.' "[94] Then he commented: "By 'women,' the Prophet meant ʿA'isha, because of all his wives (after Khadija) he had a special preference for her, and 'by a touch of collyrium in prayer,' he meant Fatima the Pure (Khadija's daughter), for at that moment she was reciting her prayers." After that he added: "Some say that the Prophet meant 'prayer' not Fatima at prayer, but," he continued, "if he had meant prayer by this expression, then he would have mentioned it as the first of the three (things that he loved)."

He concluded: "The four righteous Caliphs—Abu Bakr Siddiq, 'Umar Khattab, 'Uthman, and 'Ali—may God be pleased with all of them—used to say following the custom of the Prophet: 'We also love these same three things.' But when Gabriel—upon whom be peace—came, he conveyed the following message from God Almighty: 'These three things also do I love: the penitent youth, the weeping eye, and the God-fearing heart.' "

Conversation next turned to this: SHOULD PEOPLE COME EMPTY-HANDED TO GREET THE SHAYKH, OR SHOULD THEY BRING HIM SOMETHING? WHICH IS BETTER? To address this issue, the master told the following story. "Someone brought a handknife to Shaykh Farid ad-din—may God sanctify his secret. The Shaykh gave the knife back to that man, saying, 'You are bringing me a knife. Bring me instead a needle. The knife is an instrument for cutting, the needle for sewing.' "

He then began to talk about PEOPLE WHO FIND FAULT WITH ONE ANOTHER. "If someone claims that fault lies with another," observed the master, "he first ought to ascertain if that fault really exists or not within himself. If that fault does exist in himself, would he not then be ashamed to draw attention to its existence in someone else? Now if a person is free of a fault which he detects in another person, then he should give thanks to Almighty God for having preserved him from that fault; he should not accuse another of having that fault."

Conversation turned to LISTENING TO MUSIC (**sama'**). One of the persons present said: "Hasn't it been decreed at this time that in the presence of his eminence **sama'** is permissible whenever he must hear it?" The master replied: "Something that is forbidden cannot become permissible by anyone's decree. Likewise, something that is permissible cannot become forbidden by anyone's decree. We have entered into a controversial topic. For example, Imam Shafi'i—may God have mercy on him—issued a decree permitting **sama'** with the use of the cymbal and tamborine, contrary to (what has been decreed by) our **'ulama.** Concerning this controversy at present, whatever the judge decrees will be upheld (as the definitive statement on **sama'**).

One of those present said, "In these very days some dervishes of your circle are participating in a group where people dance while playing on lutes and wind instruments." The master—may God remember him with favor—rejoined: "They are not acting right. What is forbidden by law is not acceptable." Afterward one person said, "When that group came out of that place, they were asked, 'What did you do? (For in that assembly there were wind instruments.) Why did you listen to **sama**ʿ? Why did you dance?' They replied: 'We were so immersed in **sama**ʿ that we didn't know whether or not there were wind instruments there.' " When the master—may God remember with favor—heard this reply, he said, "This answer is not satisfactory. That declaration will be included on the record of their misdeeds."

In the meantime I submitted, "The author of **Mirsad al-ʿIbad** (The Path of God's Bondsmen) has written in this connection the following couplet:

"**Sama**ʿ is forbidden, in my opinion," you say.
Fine then, to you forbidden let it stay.[95]

The master—may God remember him with favor—said, "Yes, indeed!" and then repeated the full quatrain:

You seek the world: may it your needs repay.
Go seize its rotting carcass as your prey.
"Samaʿ is forbidden, in my opinion," you say.
Fine then, to you forbidden let it stay.

I submitted: "If the scholars investigate **sama**ʿ and declare it prohibited, they are entitled to do so, but as for he who donned the robe of poverty, how can he be denied **sama**ʿ, and even if it is prohibited to him, all he can do is not listen to it but he should not be hostile to others (who listen to it), for hostility is **not** a quality of dervishes." The master—may God remember him with favor—smiled and in this connection told the following story. "There were some ʿ**ulama** present and they were not saying anything. Then one ignoramus made an uproar by telling the following story. 'Once a student was leading the prayer and a group of ʿ**ulama** and others were praying behind him. Included among them was a person of low breeding. The prayer consisted of four prostrations but the student **imam** forgot to perform a prescribed step, joining the third to the second prostration. When he realized this, he said to himself, "How am I to end this prayer?" And the ʿ**ulama** who were following him in prayer also were silent. But the lowly person kept reciting the phrase, "Glory be to God!" so many times that he voided his prayer. When the student **imam** said, "Peace!" at the end of the prayer, he turned to that lowly person and said, "O Khwaja, what happened to you? So many learned people were present here. How was it that they finished the prayer, remaining silent, while you voided yours by continuously repeating, "Glory be to God"?' "

At this point I interjected: "This group that denies **sama**ʿ I know full well their temperaments. Those who do not listen to **sama**ʿ say: 'We do not listen because it is forbidden.' I do not swear by it but I think I speak the truth when I say: 'Even if **sama**ʿ were permitted, they would not listen to it!' " Then the master—may God remember him with favor—smiled and said, "Yes, indeed, since they lack taste, how can they listen to it? For what reason would they listen? And God knows best."

V. Assembly 6

Monday, 10th of Dhu'l-Qaʿda, A.H. 719 (23 December 1319)

I obtained the benefit of kissing the master's hand. Conversation turned to THE QUESTION OF COMMUNAL SOLIDARITY: What should be done when one gets sick to the point where one can no longer perform the canonical prayers? In this connection he told the story of a saint who lived on the bank of a river. "An affliction befell him. Every time that he rose up due to some pressing need, he would afterward go to the water, cleanse himself, and perform two cycles of prayer, only to have his affliction again become intense. Twenty or thirty times he repeated this sequence: After tending to his need, he would go to the water, wash himself, and perform two cycles of prayer. He kept doing this till one night he experienced the need sixty times. Each time he would go to the water, wash himself, and perform two more cycles of prayer till finally he went to the water and surrendered his soul to God."

When the master—may God remember him with favor—came to this point in the story, his eyes began to well up with tears. "Look," he marveled, "look at what steadfastness this man showed in the work of obedience: Till his dying breath he did not waver from that norm of conduct."

"That man who experiences an affliction," continued the master, "obtains a beneficial sign, even though he may not recognize it as such." He then told the story of an Arab who came to the Prophet—peace be upon him—and embraced Islam. Soon after that he returned to the Prophet, exclaiming, "O, Prophet of God, I professed faith (in God and in you). Yet now I have suffered a loss of my property and at the same time an affliction is pressing my soul!" The Prophet—peace be upon him—replied: "When a believer experiences loss of property and sickness of soul, it is a sign that his faith is healthy."

The master—may God remember him well—noted: "Tomorrow on the Day of Resurrection, [it will be said] 'We believed and we were counted among the righteous.' How many ranks will there be for the poor [in heaven]? All creatures will plead, saying, 'Would that we while we were in the world had been poor!' And those who suffer illness, how many ranks will there be for them on the Day of Judgment? All mankind will say, 'Would that while we had been in the world we had been afflicted with pain!' And God knows [what actually will happen]!"

### V. Assembly 7
Tuesday, the 2nd of Dhu'l-Hijja, A.H. 719 (14 January 1320)

I obtained the blessing of kissing his hand. An itinerant dervish (**juwaliq**) was present. At the time of leaving he invoked the divine name and then departed. I asked: "What is THE BASIS FOR THE INVOCATION THAT DERVISHES MAKE?" The master—may God remember him with favor—replied: "After taking food, they invoke God's name, and that is by way of praising Him, that is, instead of offering thanks for God's bounty, they praise Him."

After that the master observed: "Once the Prophet—may peace be upon him—told his companions, 'I am hopeful that tomorrow on the Day of Judgment, one-quarter of you will be among the people of Paradise, and three-quarters of you will be close by.' In gratitude for this blessing they invoked God's name. Another time the Prophet said: 'A third of you will be counted among the people of Paradise, while two-thirds of you will attend the others.' Again the companions invoked God's name. Still another time the Prophet said, 'One half of you will be among the people of Paradise, while the other half will wait upon them.' Once more the campanions invoked God's name."

Then the master observed: "In these circumstances the invoking of God's name is an alternative to rendering praise unto Him. But there are some dervishes who on every occasion in every circumstance say, 'We invoke God's name; it is not a substitute [for some other formula].' "

After that I asked: "If Sufis offer a lengthy prayer of remembrance (**dhikr**), should they recite it slowly?" "It is better if they recite it slowly," he replied, then added, "The companions of the Prophet in reciting the Qur'an spoke so rapidly that no one knew what they were saying. At the appropriate point they would prostrate themselves. Only then was it known that they were reciting the Qur'an!"

### V. Assembly 8
Thursday, 26th of Dhu'l-Hijja, A.H. 719 (7 February 1320)

I obtained the benefit of kissing the master's hand. Conversation turned to THE GREETING FORMULA 'PEACE' AND THE APPROPRIATE RESPONSE TO IT. He noted that "When God Almighty created Adam, he commanded him: Say 'Peace' to the nearby angels and listen to their reply of 'Peace' so that among your descendants the greeting of 'Peace' and the reply of 'Peace' may be likewise!" Adam —peace be upon him—greeted the angels: 'Peace be upon you,' and the angels replied: 'And upon you be peace and the mercy of God and His blessings.' And this decree remains among the descendants of Adam till now."

After that he added: "If someone comes and greets you saying, 'Peace be upon you and the mercy of God and His blessings,' how should you reply? You should say, 'And on you also be peace and the mercy of God and His blessings.' "

Then he told a story about the companions of the Prophet. "Once they were seated and a person entered, greeting them with the formula: 'Peace be upon you and the mercy of God and His blessings.' One of those present gave the following greeting in reply: 'And on you also be peace and the mercy of God and His blessings and His **forgiveness.**' Ibn 'Abbas was present. He corrected that other companion, saying, 'This is not fitting. The reply should be from 'peace' to 'His blessings' and no more.' "

I then asked: "If a disciple is saying a supererogatory prayer and a saint arrives, should this disciple leave his prayer and pay respects to the saint?" "No," replied the master. "He should complete his prayer." "But," I persisted, "if someone is saying a supererogatory prayer for reward and attainment of happiness and in the midst of his prayer, his spiritual master (**pir**) arrives, will he not attain more happiness by kissing his master's feet, since it is the firm belief of the disciple that this benefit is one hundred times greater than that reward?" "No," replied the master, "the injunction of the Law is that you finish your prayers before turning to any other activity."

Then he told a story. "Once Shaykh Baha ad-din Zakariya—may God have mercy upon him—arrived at the bank of a river. He saw some of his disciples performing ablutions. When they saw the Shaykh, they came to pay their respects to him. Although they had finished but half their ablutions, all of them arose to greet him. Except one Sufi. He completed his ablutions and then came to the Shaykh to offer his respects. The Shaykh said: 'Among all of you this is the true dervish, he who first completed his ablutions and then came to pay his respects to me.' "

"But," I asked, "if someone leaves off doing a supererogatory prayer in order to pay his respects to his master, should one say that he has committed an act of unbelief?" "Yes," replied the master.

Then out of consideration for me on his blessed tongue came the following story about THE FIRMNESS OF FAITH A DISCIPLE SHOULD HAVE IN HIS MASTER. "Once the Shaykh of Islam Farid ad-din—may God sanctify his lofty secret—summoned Badr ad-din Ishaq. Badr ad-din was saying his prayers. In the midst of his prayers, he replied in a loud voice: 'Here I am!' "

After that he told another story. "Once the Prophet—peace be upon him—was eating food. He called out to one of his followers. That friend was at prayer. When he delayed coming, the Prophet asked, 'Why did you not come quickly?' 'I was at prayer,' he replied. The Prophet—peace be upon him—said: 'When the Prophet of God Almighty calls, you should answer immediately!' "

After that on the blessed lips of the master—may God remember him with favor—came the statement: "The command of the Shaykh is like the command of the Prophet—may God's blessings and peace be upon him."

Then he told a story about SHAYKH SHIBLI. "Once a man came to him and said, 'I wish to become your disciple.' Shibli replied: 'It is a precondition of becoming my disciple that you must comply with whatever I command.' The disciple replied: 'I will.' Shibli asked: 'How do you say the profession of faith?' The disciple said: 'There is no god but God; Muhammad is the apostle of God.' Shibli replied: 'Say it like this: 'There is no god but God; Shibli is the apostle of God.' The disciple immediately repeated what Shibli had said. After that Shibli—may God have mercy on him—said: 'No, Shibli is but a lowly attendant to that master. He is the apostle of God. I was merely trying to test the steadfastness of your loyalty to me.' "

He next told a story about CONGREGATIONAL PRAYER. "There is nothing to explain about missing the weekly congregational prayer," he began. "There is no excuse unless one is the servant of another or has become sick. As for someone who is able to go but does not go, a terrible thing will happen to his heart." "Should someone fail to go to Friday prayers once," continued the master, "a black dot will appear on his heart. If he fails to go twice, two black dots will appear; and if he fails to go three times, his whole heart will turn black. We take refuge in God from that!"

On this occasion he told a story about Sultan Giyas ad-din Balban, about his faithful attendance at Friday prayers, his strict observance of the five daily prayers, and his firm faith. Then he noted that once Balban was talking with the **qazi** who accompanied his army. "What holy night was last night?" he asked. "It is well known to you," replied the **qazi**, "Yes," said the Sultan. At this point I interjected, "But it must have been the Night of Power (the twenty-seventh of Ramadan)." "Of course," rejoined the master, "**that** was the holy night about which they were speaking. Each knew what was transpiring in the mind of the other."

## V. Assembly 9

Tuesday, the 2nd of Jumada al-'ula, A.H. 720 (10 June 1320)

I obtained the benefit of kissing his hand. Conversation turned to PRAYER—whether one should call upon God as full of Compassion, ever Compassionate at the beginning of every prayer cycle or at the beginning of each Qur'anic chapter. The Greatest Imam, that is, Abu Hanifa—may God be pleased with him—declared that at the beginning of every prayer cycle one should call upon God as full of Compassion, ever Compassionate. On this point he differed from other imams, with the result that some '**ulama** say it at the start of each prayer cycle, others only at the start of each Qur'anic chapter.

The master observed: "Sufyan Thauri and one other friend disputed with the Great Imam on this point. Once, when they were thrown into a crowd together, Sufyan Thauri and that other friend asked the Greatest Imam, 'When does the person at prayer call on God as full of Compassion, ever Compassionate—at the start of each prayer cycle or at the start of each Qur'anic chapter?' The intent of their query was to confront him: If he denied its appropriateness at a certain juncture, they would instantly recite the formula at the same juncture. In short, when they asked the Greatest Imam, 'What do you direct? Is the invocation to be made at the beginning of each new prayer cycle or at the beginning of each Qur'anic chapter?' due to the perfect knowledge that he had as the Greatest Imam and also due to his observance of propriety, Abu Hanifa replied: 'You should say it once.'

"See," concluded the master—may God remember him with favor, "how the Greatest Imam's intent was to confirm his decree: They could recite the formula where they wished, whether at the beginning of each prayer cycle or at the beginning of each Qur'anic chapter."

Conversation then turned to THE LOWER SELF OF THE SHAYKHS AND THEIR SUPPLICATIONS. In this connection he spoke about a friend among the friends of Shaykh al-Islam Farid ad-din —may God sanctify his lofty secret. "His name was Muhammad Shah Ghuri. He was a sincere, pious man. Once he approached the Shaykh in the throes of worry and despair. 'What is your problem?' asked the Shaykh. 'I have a brother,' he replied. 'He is very ill and I fear that he may even have expired this very hour while I am coming to see you. For that reason I have become upset, even distraught.' "Shaykh al-Islam Farid ad-din—may God sanctify his lofty secret—said: 'As you are this hour, I have been my whole life, but I have never disclosed my condition to anyone.' Then he told him: 'Go! Your brother will regain his health.' Muhammad Shah Ghuri arose from the Shaykh's presence and returning home, he found his brother sitting up and eating food. And God knows best [how this happened]."

### V. Assembly 10

Sunday, 17th of Jumada al-'ula, A.H. 720 (25 June 1320)

I obtained the benefit of kissing his feet. [Two anecdotes about the nature of **hadith** (Tradition) are followed by this story concerning THE RECITATION OF HADITH.] The master—may God remember him with favor—related that once Maulana Razi ad-din Nishapuri—may God have mercy on him—fell ill and his illness lasted for a long time. A scholar came to his bedside and sitting down recited this **hadith:** The Prophet—blessings and peace be upon him—said, "Pride is worse than adultery." Maulana Razi ad-din, though he was extremely sick, said to that scholar: "What effrontery is it that has led you to recite this **hadith** at a time like this, when there has been no mention of adultery, no mention of pride. Due to what effrontery have you chosen to recite it?" That scholar replied: "My intention was neither effrontery nor its opposite. I have heard that whoever comes to a sick person and recites before him a Tradition among the genuine Traditions of the Prophet—blessings and peace be upon him—that sick person will regain his health. And I chose to read this **hadith,** which is in common circulation and is known to be authentic, in order that you might be healed." Maulana Razi ad-din said nothing more, but soon thereafter he recovered from that illness.

Conversation next turned to SUBMISSION TO GOD'S WILL AND CONTENTMENT WITH ONE'S FATE. The master told the story about a dervish who was sitting down. A fly came and alighted on his nose. The dervish shooed the fly from his nose. Again the fly returned, and alighted once more on his nose. Again, the dervish shooed the fly away. Once more, the fly returned. The dervish declared: "O God, I want that fly not to sit on my nose. But if you want him to sit there, I surrender my will; whatever you wish I will do. After this I will not shoo that fly from my nose." By the time he had finished speaking the fly was no longer sitting on his nose. And God knows [how that happened]!

## V. Assembly 11

Saturday, 22nd of Jumada al-ʾula, A.H. 720 (30 June 1320)

I obtained the blessings of kissing his feet. Conversation turned to this subject: SOME PENITENT SINNER AFTER REPENTING MAY SIN AGAIN, BUT IF SOME BLESSING REMAINS THAT PERSON WILL RETURN TO THE STATE OF REPENTANCE. In this connection the master told the following story: "There was a female singer named Qamar. She was the epitome of charm and beauty. But toward the end of her life she repented and, having become a disciple of Shaykh Shihab ad-din ʿUmar Muhammad Suhrawardi—may God sanctify his lofty secret—left Baghdad to perform the pilgrimage of the Kaʿba, that is, the canonical pilgrimage. On her return journey she reached Hamadan. The governor of Hamadan had learned of her imminent arrival. He sent word to her through an intermediary, saying, 'Come, sing before me.' 'I have repented of this work,' replied that woman. 'I have made the pilgrimage to the Kaʿba. I no longer wish to engage in such work.'

"That governor persisted and paid no heed to what she had said.

That woman was at a loss as to what to do. She went to Shaykh Yusuf Hamadani, and explained the situation to him. 'What a pity!' he exclaimed. 'Go back to the place from which you came. I will busy myself in pondering your situation, and I will give you an answer in the morning.'

"When morning came, that woman returned to see the Shaykh. 'In the storehouse of destiny,' observed the Shaykh, 'there still remains one sin of yours.' The woman was at her wit's end. Some retainers of the governor were still following her. They went to the governor and returned, bringing with them a cymbal. They gave it to her. That woman started to play the cymbal and began to sing. She gave voice to a couplet which enthralled the whole assembly. At first the governor of Hamadan repented, and after him, everyone in the assembly. Praise be to God the Lord of the universe!"

V. Assembly 12
Tuesday, 16th of Rajab, A.H. 720 (22 August 1320)

I obtained the blessing of kissing the master's hand. Conversation turned to THE KNOWLEDGE AND PROBITY OF QAZI QUTB AD-DIN KASHANI—may God have mercy upon him. The master explained that he had been in Multan and had set up a **madrasa** there. Every day Shaykh Baha ad-din Zakariya—may God have mercy on him—would come there in the morning to say his prayers. Finally Maulana Qutb ad-din asked him: "Why is it that you come so far from your place every day to pray here in this place?" Shaykh Baha ad-din Zakariya replied: "I am acting in accordance with this **hadith:** 'Whoever prays in the company of a pious scholar, it is as though he is praying in the company of the Apostle of God.' "

After that the master—may God remember him with favor—commented: "I have heard it on good authority that one day Shaykh Baha ad-in Zakariya was in that place, but Qazi Qutb ad-din was leading the morning prayer and had already performed the first cycle of prayer before Shaykh Baha ad-din Zakariya arrived. Shaykh Baha ad-din joined in during the second cycle. When Qazi Qutb ad-din came to the profession of faith before he said the concluding 'peace,' Shaykh Baha ad-din Zakariya arose and finished his prayer. When he had completed his own prayer, Qazi Qutb ad-din asked Shaykh Baha ad-din: 'Why did you arise before the peace at the end of the prayer? You were not able to perform the final prostration.' Shaykh Baha ad-din replied: 'If someone learns through intuition that the prayer leader has made an error, it is appropriate for him to arise before the end of the prayer.' Qazi Qutb ad-din rejoined: 'Every intuition which is not in accord with the dictates of the Law, that is a heinous sin!' In short, they say that after that incident Shaykh Baha ad-din Zakariya was never again present at morning prayer in the **madrasa** of Qazi Qutb ad-din."

In the same connection they tell another story about Qazi Qutb ad-din. "Do you have no faith in dervishes?" he was asked. Replied the Qazi: "Those dervishes whom I used to see I do not now find other dervishes like them." Then he said: "Once I was in Kashgar. I had a small knife. Its cutting blade was broken. I took it to the bazaar and showed it to knife makers. I told them: 'Fix this knife so that it works as it used to work.' They all said that it could not be done; it would really be of limited use. That is to say, when you pull it out for some task and grasp it by the handle (trying to cut), it will prove to be ineffective. None of them could help me. All told me to go to a certain shop, where there was an old knife maker, highly skilled and renowned for his moral rectitude. 'Go, take this knife to him,' they said. 'Perhaps he can comply with your request.' "

Qazi Qutb ad-din continued: "I went to that shop. I saw an old man. I explained to him the condition of the knife. He gave the same answer that the other knife makers had given: 'It will be of limited use.' I replied: 'Please, I must have it restored to its original form.' The old man pondered for a moment, then he said to me: 'Close your eyes.' " "I did close my eyes," explained the Qazi, "but I peeked out from the corners of my eyes and saw that this old man raised the broken knife and, passing it near his beard, lifted his eyes toward heaven and slowly said something. Then he addressed me, 'Open your eyes.' I opened my eyes. He placed the knife in front of me. It was in exactly the same form that it had been when it was brand-new. It was absolutely perfect!"

They tell another story that when Qazi Qutb ad-din Kashani came to Delhi, he was once invited to the court of Sultan Shams ad-din (Iltetmish). He went. At that time the Sultan was sitting in that quarter of his palace reserved for amusement and relaxation. Sayyid Nur ad-din Mubarak—may God have mercy on him—was seated in front of the door to that quarter, and Qazi Fakhr al-A'imma was seated opposite him. Both were seated outside the quarter in which the Sultan was relaxing and amusing himself. When Qazi Qutb ad-din entered, they asked him, "Where would you like to sit?" He said: "At the hand of his Eminence." In short, when he approached the Sultan and greeted him, the Sultan arose, took the Qazi's hand and, leading him back inside the leisure quarter, seated the Qazi next to the royal dias.

Then there followed a story about SHAYKH JALAL AD-DIN TABRIZI—may God sanctify his lofty secret. When he reached Badaun, he stayed there for some time. One day he went to the house of the governor of Badaun, Qazi Kamal ad-din Jaʿfri. The servants sitting at the front door told him: "At this moment the Qazi is praying." The Shaykh smiled and asked: "Does the Qazi know how to offer prayer?" In short, when the Shaykh left, this remark was reported to the Qazi. The next day the Qazi paid a call on the Shaykh. He apologized [for not having received him the day before] and then asked: "Why did you ask whether or not I knew how to perform the canonical prayer? I have written several books on prayer and its requirements." The Shaykh replied: "Alas, the prayer of scholars (**ʿulama**) is one thing, the prayer of God's beggars (**fuqara**) is another thing." The Qazi asked: "Do they perform a different kind of bowing and a different kind of prostration or do they read the Qurʾan a different way?" The Shaykh replied: "In their prayer the scholars face the Kaʿba and then pray. If they cannot see the Kaʿba, they pray in the direction of the Kaʿba, and if they are in a place where even the direction of the Kaʿba is not known, they select the most likely direction that would orient them to the Kaʿba. The prayer orientation (**qibla**) of the scholars is not other than these three possibilities, whereas the beggars of God never offer prayer unless they see the Throne of God."

The Qazi, though this explanation annoyed him, said nothing. He returned from there to his own home. That night the Qazi had a dream in which he saw Shaykh Jalal ad-din Tabrizi—may God sanctify his lofty secret—with his prayer carpet spread before the Divine Throne, saying his prayers. The next day they both met in a gathering. Shaykh Jalal ad-din said: "O so-and-so, the work of scholars and their stage of vocational achievement is known. Their concern and nonconcern is limited to teaching, and they can only become a teacher or **qazi** or **sadr-i jahan.** Their stage of vocational achievement cannot be higher than this. But for the saints there are higher stages. The initial stage for saints is this which was manifest to the Qazi last night." On hearing this, Qazi Kamal ad-din arose, offered his full apology to the Shaykh, and placing his son Burhan ad-din at the feet of the Shaykh, asked that he might become the Shaykh's disciple and obtain the cap of discipleship from him.

## V. Assembly 13

Wednesday, the 14th of Rajab, A.H. 720 (20 August 1320)

I obtained the blessing of kissing the master's feet. Conversation turned to FORBEARANCE. The master observed: "The conduct of human beings with one another is of three kinds. The first kind is that whatever a person does neither benefits nor harms another. Such conduct replicates the order common in the mineral and plant world. The second kind is that whatever a person does brings only benefit to his fellow man, not harm. This is better. But the third kind is still better: that whatever a person does benefits another and even if someone harms him, he does not retaliate but exercises forbearance. This is the conduct of the righteous."

## V. Assembly 14

Monday, 17th of Shaʿban, A.H. 720 (22 September 1320)

I obtained the blessing of kissing the master's feet. Conversation focused on this query: WHICH ARE THE BEST [HUMAN] NAMES? On the blessed lips of the master came this directive: "The most beloved of names are servant of God and servant of the merciful." After this he added: "The most edifying of names is cultivator (**harith**)." Then he explained: "Cultivator is the most edifying of names because everyone who exists cultivates something, whether it be obedience or sin." After that he noted: "The most despicable of names are king and eternal because king can only refer to God the Almighty and He alone is Eternal."

## V. Assembly 15

Thursday, the 5th of Ramadan, A.H. 720 (9 October 1320)

I obtained the benefit of kissing his hand. Conversation turned to THE EFFECT OF COMPANY. The master remarked: "Once there was a scholar named Nasir. He came to see Shaykh al-Islam Farid ad-din—may God sanctify his lofty secret, but he was still attached to commercial pursuits. In short, after meeting the Shaykh, he was admitted as a disciple and, having professed the oath of allegiance, had his head shaved. One day a yogin came to the hospice. That scholar-turned-disciple queried the yogin. He sought to learn from him how one could make hair grow long!" The master continued: "When I heard that a stranger who had been granted the honor of professing allegiance to the Shaykh had asked a yogin how to make the hair of his head grow long, there arose a suspicion within me: 'Why would one who has made a profession of allegiance need to ask about growing long hair? Moreover, since the whole purpose of having one's hair cut is to remove pride, what would be the point of wanting long hair?'

"Subsequently, when some days had passed, Khwaja Wahid ad-din, who was a descendant of Shaykh Muʿin ad-din Sanjari, came to see the Shaykh. He sought to profess allegiance to him and to have his head shaved. Said Shaykh Farid ad-din: 'I have this spiritual bequest from your esteemed forefather. It is not proper for me to extend the hand of discipleship to you.' But Khwaja Wahid ad-din persisted and persisted: 'I want to become your disciple. I do! I do!' At long last the Shaykh extended his hand and commanded them to shave the new disciple's head. On that very day that Khwaja Wahid ad-din was shaved, Maulana Nasir ad-din also volunteered to have his head shaved in the same manner, and it was done."

Conversation next turned to PRAYERS FOR THE DEAD. "How," I asked, "should one write prayers and Qur'anic verses on tombs?" Replied the master: "One should not write them there nor should one write them on coffin shrouds."

## V. Assembly 16
### Wednesday, 18th of Shawwal, A.H. 720 (21 November 1320)

I obtained the benefit of kissing his feet. Conversation turned to THE SPIRITUAL PROWESS OF MAULANA BURHAN AD-DIN BALKHI—may God have mercy on him. The master remarked that Maulana Burhan ad-din Balkhi told the following story: "I was a youth, about five or six years old, when Maulana Burhan ad-din Marghiyani, the author of *Hidayat,* passed my father on the road. My father greeted him and then proceeded in another direction, leaving me standing alone. When the carriage of Maulana Burhan ad-din Marghiyani approached, I came forward and greeted him. He looked intently at me and said, 'I see in this lad the light of learning.' On hearing this, I went to greet his driver and, as I did, from his blessed lips came these further words: 'To me God Almighty has revealed that this lad in his lifetime will become the scholar of his age.' "

Mawlana Burhan ad-din Balkhi added: "I was still walking beside his carriage. No sooner had I heard this second pronouncement than

Maulana Burhan ad-din Marghiyani added a third: 'God Almighty has revealed to me that this lad will be such a preeminent person that rulers will come to his door.' "

When the master—may God remember him with favor—had finished telling this story, from his blessed lips came the further comment: "Maulana Burhan ad-din Balkhi, in addition to his vast learning, was so refined in manners that he often remarked to his friends: 'On the Day of Judgment God Almighty will not ask me to repent of any grievous sin.' " Then the master—may God remember him with favor—paused and smiled: "Maulana Burhan ad-din, when he used to say, 'God Almighty will not ask me to repent of any sin,' would add, 'except one.' And his friends would say: 'Which is that?' '**Sama**ʿ,' he would reply. 'However much I heard it, I wanted to hear more, and even now I would like to listen to it, if it were available.' "

From this story conversation turned to **SAMA**ʿ. The master observed: "**Sama**ʿ was given legal sanction in this city by Qazi Hamid ad-din Nagauri—may God have mercy upon him. Qazi Minhaj ad-din (Jurjani), like Qazi Hamid ad-din Nagauri, was also a judge and also devoted of **sama**ʿ. It was through these two men that the practice of **sama**ʿ was regularized and maintained. And Qazi Hamid ad-din Nagauri, despite the fact that many debated him and bitterly opposed him, stood firm by his decision (to permit the practice of **sama**ʿ in Delhi). Once he was invited to a residence near Koshk-i Safid. Shaykh Qutb ad-din Bakhtiyar Kaki—may God sanctify his lofty secret—was also there, along with other saintly persons. It was reported to Maulana Rukn ad-din Samarqandi that there was going to be **sama**ʿ in that place. He was a fierce opponent of this practice. Leaving his own residence, together with servants and retainers, he proceeded to that other residence in order to prevent the occurrence of **sama**ʿ.

"Qazi Hamid ad-din Nagauri was apprised of this situation. He said to the proprietor of the house. 'Go, hide yourself somewhere. No matter how much they ask for you, don't show your face.' The proprietor did as he was told. After that Qazi Hamid ad-din quipped (to the others present), 'You may act in jest since they have acted in jest,' and they began to engage in **sama**ʿ. Maulana Rukn ad-din Samarqandi, when he arrived at the house with his retainers, asked: 'Where is the proprietor of the house?' They said: 'The proprietor of the house is not here. We do not know where he has gone.' Again he asked and persisted in his inquiry:

'Where is the proprietor of the house?' Time and again they answered: 'How do we know where the proprietor of the house has gone?' Since he could not see the owner of the house, the Mawlana left."

As he came to this point in the story, the master—may God remember him with favor—smiled and said, "Qazi Hamid ad-din Nagauri was well advised to have the owner of the house absent himself, for without the permission of its owner you should not enter any house. If Rukn ad-din Samarqandi had entered without such permission, he would have been called to account for his unlawful conduct."

Afterward the master commented: "Valiant men also contended with Qazi Hamid ad-din Nagauri on the issue of **sama**ʿ. Once Maulana Sharaf ad-din Bijri was ill. Qazi Hamid ad-din, due to the purity of heart which dervishes have, went to pay a sick call on Maulana Sharaf ad-din. They informed him: 'Qazi Hamid ad-din Nagauri—may God have mercy on him—has come to see you.' 'That man who has called God Beloved?' retorted the Maulana. 'May I never see his face!' In short, he did not give him leave to enter."

At this juncture I interrupted: "By this phrase 'Beloved' did he mean 'loved one'?" Replied the master: "On this matter there are many opinions. Men, to the extent that they know about it, have given numerous answers. But when one who is in the house of the Beloved says something about love, what can you say to that man?"

After that he said that once Qazi Hamid ad-din Nagauri and Qazi Kabir and Maulana Burhan ad-din Balkhi were all proceeding to the same place together. Qazi Hamid ad-din was on a scruffy little horse and they were riding sturdy large stallions. While they were en route, Maulana Kabir ad-din turned to Qazi Hamid ad-din and said, "Your mount is quite small!" Quipped Qazi Hamid ad-din, "Better small than big," that is, better is he than you whose name is "big" and than your horse whose size is "big"! The master—may God remember him with favor—paused and smiled: "Look what an answer he gave, so clever that no one could object."

After that he noted that when Qazi Hamid ad-din's views on **sama**ʿ became well known, many of his contemporaries wrote legal opinions against its practice. They publicized their replies (to his condolence of it), and all decreed that **sama**ʿ was forbidden. There was one jurist, a friend of Qazi Hamid ad-din Nagauri, who also wrote a negative opinion in response to Qazi Hamid ad-din's. News of what he wrote was reported to the Qazi. Soon afterward that friend came to see Qazi Hamid ad-din. The Qazi turned to him and said, "You also wrote a rejoinder to that decree of mine on **sama'**." The jurist became embarrassed. "Yes," he replied, "I did write such a rejoinder." At this point the master—may God remember him with favor—observed: "On that day Qazi Hamid ad-din spoke his mind forthrightly. To that jurist friend who had admitted, 'Yes, I did write against you,' Qazi Hamid ad-din said, 'All those other jurists who wrote rejoinders to my decree are, in my opinion, still fetuses in their mothers' wombs, but as for you, you are a newborn infant. Such a child!' "

After that he told a story about Qazi Hamid ad-din Nagauri—may God have mercy upon him—and Qazi Qutb ad-din Kashani. Recalled the master: "Qazi Qutb ad-din told me: 'I came to Delhi to meet Qazi Hamid ad-din Nagauri, but by the time I arrived there he had already died.' One day he asked to see the collected writings of Qazi Hamid ad-din, and he began to delve into the books that he had written on spiritual progress (**suluk**). After making a thorough perusal, Qazi Qutb ad-din turned to the scholars who had gathered around him and said: "What you have read is in these pages and what you have **not** read is also there. What I have read is in these pages, and what I have not read, that also is there.' "

### V. Assembly 17
Saturday, 27th of Shawwal, A.H. 720 (30 November 1320)

I received the benefit of kissing the master's hand. Conversation turned to THE SAINTS OF GOD, THEIR TRUTHFULNESS IN DEALING WITH OTHER PEOPLE, AND THE REWARDS OF SUCH CONDUCT. He noted: "In Nishapur there lived a saint named Abu'l-Ghiyas Qassab. Once the father of this Abu'l-Ghiyas was about to go on a journey. There were some goats in the house. He instructed Abu'l-Ghiyas: 'Slaughter these goats, sell their meat and keep the money till I return.' After some time his father came back. He saw a pile of bones in the house. 'What is this pile of bones?' he asked. Abu'l-Ghiyas said: 'The bones of the goats which you told me to slaughter and then to sell their meat. I have done as you instructed.' 'Why did you not sell the bones?' asked his father. 'The people came to buy meat from me. Why should I sell them the bones?' At this reply his father burst into laughter. 'Why did you do this? You have caused me to lose a great deal of money.' And he went on and on speaking in this vein. Finally Abu'l-

Ghiyas asked: 'What sum of money did you lose?' His father, after making some calculations, announced: 'You lost about 1,000 **dinars** (by what you did).' When he heard this, Abu'l-Ghiyas raised his hands in prayer and in that instant from the Unseen a purse full of gold came into his grasp. He placed it before his father. When they opened it, they found an amount equivalent to 20,000 **dinars**!"

When the master had finished telling this story, I asked: "Is Jalal a contemporary butcher?" "No," he replied, "Jalal is a butcher from former times." I recited the following verse:

> A butcher's son am I, and flaying is my trade.
> Beware! each one who enters my bazaar is flayed.

"Is this verse from Jalal the butcher?" I asked. "Yes," replied the master. And then he began to speak about A BUTCHER IN DELHI WHO WAS AMONG THE SAINTS OF GOD. "Numerous people obtained blessings from him. Qazi Fakhr ad-din Naqila, early in his life, used to come to see him often. Once that butcher asked, 'What do you want?' Replied (the future) Qazi Fakhr ad-din: 'I want to be Qazi.' 'Go,' replied the butcher, 'you will become Qazi.' " After this the master said: "There was another man who used to come to this Qazi. Once of him also the butcher asked, 'Is there something that you desire?' 'What I desire,' replied the man, 'is to become Chief Justice.' To that man also he said, 'Go! You will become Chief Justice.' And that man became Chief Justice.' " Then the master said, "Maulana Wajih ad-din Husam also came to see that butcher and to him was put the same question: 'What do you seek?' Maulana Wajih ad-din replied: 'I seek knowledge.' And knowledge was granted him. Still another man was acquainted with this butcher. One day the butcher asked of that man: 'And what do you want?' 'What I need,' replied the man, 'is to be bound by the love of God.' And that man is among those have attained union with God (**wasilan-i haqq**)." Then the master—may God remember him with favor—declared: "I too have seen that butcher."

### V. Assembly 18
### Tuesday, 22nd of Dhu'l-Qa'da, A.H. 720 (24 December 1320)

I obtained the blessing of kissing the master's feet. Conversation turned to THE 'ALAWIS (descendants of the Prophet Muhammad through 'Ali). I had had it in mind to ask the master something on this matter, and on that day I put my question to him: "I have heard from some of the ʿAlawis," I began, "that the Prophet of God—peace be upon him—wrote a letter in which he said, 'My descendants who come after me, if they wish, will cause a controversy among Muslims,' and they also report that Abu Bakr Siddiq and ʿUmar Khattab tore that letter up. Is this true?"

"No," replied the master. "This tradition is not to be found in any book. Moreover, noble qualities necessarily characterize descendants of the Prophet—blessings and peace be upon him, for from the family of the Prophet there has not come into existence anything which is unworthy of him, nor will there come any such thing in the future."

Then he told a story. "There was once an ʿAlavi of impeccable lineage in Samarqand. He was known as Sayyid Ajall, the author of the book *The Benefits of Hamadan.* It happened that he had a maidservant and from this maidservant a son was born into his house. He proved to be a son unlike any that had ever been, or has yet to be, born into an ʿAlavi family. Once when that lad was about five or six years of age, a water carrier came to the house, his skins full of water. Having poured out the water, he left the house and refilled his skin. This time, however, there was a small hole in his skin and some water began to seep out. Sayyid Ajall asked: 'What has happened to your water skin?' Replied the water carrier: 'When I had brought the first full skin into your house, your son took a small bow and arrow. He shot the arrow. It made a hole in the waterskin.'

"Sayyid Ajall, on hearing this story, went into his house, seized his maidservant, and, drawing his sword, he exclaimed: 'I will put one question to you. If you do not tell me the truth, I'll kill you. The question is this: Speak the truth—by whom did you conceive this son?' At first the maidservant concealed the truth, but at last out of fear she confessed: 'I conceived this son by such-and-such a slave.' Sayyid Ajall, when he heard this, went out and taking the two curled locks of that lad, he made them into one lock, indicating that he was no longer a **sayyid.** 'In short, whoever is from the family of the Prophet—peace be upon him—would not do the kind of thing that boy had done.' "

The master then told another story. "There was an ʿAlavi in Badaun," he noted. "Into his house was born a son but he was born on that day of the month which is under the sign of Scorpio. His parents reacted as people of common stock would have reacted: They were repelled by the child and took a dislike to them. They gave him to a sweeper. The sweeper took that child and reared him. It happened after four or five years that there appeared in that child such a light and beauty that someone came to his parents and reported: 'At least you should go and see how this child of yours is faring!' The mother and father, after they saw their child, took him back, instructed him in the Qur'an, and taught him knowledge and good manners.

"In short," observed the master, "I have seen that 'Alavi and in him was to be found the apogee of splendor and beauty. He became a scholar-teacher, steeped in learning. The preeminent scholars in Badaun studied under him. So polished were his manners, so lofty his virtues that whoever saw him knew for certain that he was a descendant of the Prophet Muhammad—peace be upon him."

He then began to speak about DERVISHES AND THEIR PREOCCUPATION WITH GOD. "I have heard from Badr a-din Ishaq," he related, "that a Sufi once came to visit Shaykh al-Islam Farid ad-din—may God sanctify his lofty secret. 'He was a fine dervish,' reported Badr ad-din Ishaq. 'Day and night he remained engrossed in the remembrance of God, so much so that his clothes had become filthy beyond description. One day I asked him: "Why do you not wash your clothes?" The dervish did not reply. After some days I asked him again: "Why do you not wash your clothes?" And this time he replied in a very sharp tone of voice. The dervish exclaimed: "Where do I have time to wash my garments? " He said this with such total pathos that Badr ad-din Ishaq remarked: "Everytime I recall the answer that dervish gave me and the utter pathos with which he said, 'Where is the time for me to wash my garments?' I am overcome with a sense of amazement." ' "

Conversation next turned to THE DISTINCTION BETWEEN TASTE AND DESIRE FOR DERVISHES, AND THE SENSE OF BEING OVERCOME WITH DESIRE WHICH TRAVELERS ON THE PATH EXPERIENCE. In this connection he told a story. "In Lahore there was a scholar renowned for his eloquence. One day he came to the Qazi of Lahore and said: 'I desire to go on pilgrimage to the Ka'ba. Give me permission that I may go.' The Qazi replied: 'Why do you want to go? At present your discourses and counsels are benefitting many people.' The scholar refrained from going. After another year had lapsed, he again approached the Qazi and again sought permission to go to Mecca. Again the Qazi advised him to stay, and again he convinced that scholar to remain in Lahore. The third year came, and the scholar approached the Qazi once more. 'I am overcome with desire to visit the Ka'ba. Please give me permission that I may go.' 'O master,' replied the Qazi, 'if you are overcome with desire to visit the Ka'ba, what need do you have to ask permission of me or to seek my consultation? You should simply go.' " Then upon the blessed lips of the master came these words. "In love there is no need of consultation."

### V. Assembly 19
### Sunday, 11th of Dhu'l-Hijja, A.H. 720 (12 January 1321)

I obtained the benefit of kissing the master's feet. Conversation turned to REVEALING MIRACULOUS POWERS. "Before this time," he observed, "there lived in the locale of Indrapat a virtuous, elderly woman named Bibi Fatima Sam. I had seen her. She was a fine woman. She had memorized many verses pertaining to every circumstance of life. I especially remember these two lines from her:

For love you search, while still for life you strain.
For both you search, but both you can't attain.

"Shaykh Najib ad-din Mutawwakil—may God have mercy on him—was very fond of this Bibi Fatima," remarked the master, "in the way that brothers are fond of their sisters. There were many evenings that Shaykh Najib ad-din used to spend fasting and on account of him the members of his family would also fast. Often when the evening had passed like this, on the morning of the next day Bibi Fatima would give a large disc of one **mani** or one half **mani** to someone and send it speedily to Shaykh Najib ad-din, saying, 'They have fasted through the evening; now let them eat.' Once when such a disc had been sent to him from Bibi Fatima, Shaykh Najib ad-din exclaimed about her goodness, 'O God, you made that woman as aware of my circumstance as the ruler of the city is unaware: Even were he to send some food with the hope of obtaining my blessing, he would remain unaware!' Then he would smile and ask, 'Where is that purity among rulers that they could become aware [of my spiritual state]?'

"Once I was in the presence of this Bibi Fatima," remarked the master. "She turned toward me and said, 'There is a man who has a daughter. If you want to marry that daughter, it would be a good match.'

I replied to her as follows. 'Once I was with Shaykh al-Islam Farid ad-din—may God sanctify his lofty secret—and a yogin was also present at that time. Discussion focussed on the fact that some children were born without any inclination for the spiritual life due to the fact that men did not know the proper time for sexual intercourse. At that point the yogin began to comment that there are twenty-nine or thirty days in each month. Every day has its special quality. For example, if a man makes love the first day of the month, such-and-such a child will be born; if on the second day, the offspring will be such-and-such, and he continued in this vein until he had given his estimate for every day of the month.

"When the yogin had finished speaking," said the master—may God remember him with favor—"I asked him to repeat what he had said about the influence of each day. As he detailed the qualities of each and every day, I memorized them, and then I said to that yogin, 'Listen carefully and note how well I have memorized what you said.' Shaykh Farid ad-in—may God sanctify his lofty secret—turned to me and said, 'Of these things about which you are inquiring there will never be an occasion for their use.' " The master—may God remember him with favor—concluded: "When I had finished telling this story to Bibi Fatima, she remarked, 'Now I know what is your condition (concerning marriage).' Then she added, 'Indeed, you are right not to seek marriage with that young woman. I also have spoken with you just to please her father.' "

### V. Assembly 20
Monday, 19th of Dhu'l-Hijja, A.H. 720 (20 January 1321)

I obtained the blessing of kissing his hand. In those days one of our adversaries had launched an attack on **sama'**, arguing for its prohibition in some unrepeatable language. An atmosphere of adversity prevailed. The master—may God remember him with favor—spoke these words: "God Almighty has declared His enmity to 'he [who] is extremely violent in quarreling' (Q.2:204), for 'he [who] is extremely violent in quarreling' refers to that one who uses abusive language in disputation."

He then spoke about THE BENEFIT OF **SAMA'**. In this connection he said: "Whenever certain conditions are met one can listen to **sama'**. Each of these must be right: the singer, what is sung, the listener, and also the musical instrument." He proceeded to elaborate the content of each category: "The one summoned to sing must be a man, a mature man. The singer cannot be a boy or a woman. Similarly, what is sung cannot be something lewd or ludicrous. As for the listener, it must be someone who listens to God and is filled with remembrance of Him. As for the instrument of music, one must use the harp or lute or viol or similar instruments. When these conditions have been observed, **sama`** becomes permissible."

Then he added: "**Sama`** is a voice. Why should rhythm be forbidden? And that which is spoken is a word. Why should the comprehension of its meaning be forbidden? **Sama`** is also movement of the heart. If that movement is due to remembering God, it is beneficial, but if the heart is full of corruption, then **sama`** is forbidden."

## V. Assembly 21
Sunday, 23rd of Muharram, A.H. 721 (22 February 1321)

I obtained the benefit of kissing his feet. Conversation turned to THE MORALITY OF DERVISHES AND THEIR DEALINGS WITH THOSE WHO HARBOR ILL WILL TOWARD THEM. "There was a king named Tarani," recalled the master, "but they killed him in an uprising. Shaykh Sayf ad-din Bakharzi—may God have mercy upon him—had a great affection for this Tarani. After his death, they made another man king. That newly installed king appointed a certain astrologer to a position of favor, and that astrologer harbored enmity toward Shaykh Sayf ad-din Bakharzi. When the astrologer had the opportunity to address the monarch, he said, 'The kingdom has been entrusted to you. Drive out Shaykh Sayf ad-din Bakharzi, for he is a master in toppling kingdoms.' The king accepted his advice. 'Go,' he commanded that astrologer, 'and by whatever means you have at your disposal bring the Shaykh here.' The astrologer left and when he called on the Shaykh, he showed obvious disrespect: He wrapped his headband around his waist and did other similarly impudent things. In short, when Shaykh Sayf ad-din Bakharzi came to the royal court, he stared so intently at the king that the latter became embarrassed. He immediately descended from his throne, and uttering profuse apologies, began to kiss the hands and feet of the Shaykh. He offered a horse and other presents to the Shaykh. He implored his forgiveness, saying, 'I did not command that you be brought here in this manner.'

"The Shaykh departed the royal court and returned home. The next day the monarch sent that astrologer bound hand and foot to the Shaykh with the message: 'I have given the command for this astrologer to be killed. Now I am sending him to you. In whatever way suits you, kill him.'

"As soon as he set eyes on that astrologer the Shaykh at once freed his hands and feet. He made him put on the cloak that he, the Shaykh, was wearing. 'Today join with me,' he said, 'in remembering God.' That day was Monday. The Shaykh went to the mosque to offer his customary remembrance of God. He took the astrologer with him, and ascending the pulpit, he spoke the following couplet:

To those who do me wrong I would,
If possible, do only good."

After narrating this story, the master observed: "EVERY ACTION THAT COMES FROM MAN—WHETHER GOOD OR BAD—THE CREATOR OF THAT IS GOD ALMIGHTY. Hence whatever is done is done by God. Why then should I be disturbed by someone, no matter what he does?"

In this connection the master recalled an incident that involved Shaykh Abu Saʿid ibn Abiʾl-Khayr—may God sanctify his lofty secret. "Once Shaykh Abu Saʿid was walking along a street. A foolish person approached him from behind and struck him hard on the neck. The Shaykh turned around to see who had hit him. The fool said: 'Why are looking at me? Are you not he who said: "Whatever is done is done by God?" ' 'You are correct,' replied the Shaykh. 'I just wanted to see who was the accursed person whom he had chosen to perform such a task!' "

### V. Assembly 22
### Thursday, 7th of Rabiʿ al-awwal, A.H. 721 (6 April 1321)

I obtained the blessing of kissing his feet. Conversation turned to THE VISION OF GOD. I asked: "The blessing of that vision which has been promised to all believers, will it take place on the Day of Resurrection?" "Yes," replied the master. Then I asked: "After the servant has been granted that blessing, will he see still other blessings?" "It has been reported," replied the master, "that when they will have witnessed that blessing, they will remain in a state of awe for thousands of years." Then he added: "That vision will be such a very, very brief glimpse that afterward one may look for something more."

I recalled the following verse from Shaykh Saʿdi Shirazi—may God have mercy upon him:

Pity that eye never given a glimpse of Your face,
Or that seeing it, still seeks yet another with your grace.

The master—may God remember him with favor—was pleased with this verse, and exclaimed: "How well he has spoken!"

## V. Assembly 23
Monday, 26th of Rabiʿ al-akhir, A.H. 721 (25 May 1321)

I obtained the benefit of kissing his feet. Conversation turned to THE CONSISTENT STRICTNESS AND FEARSOME AUTHORITY OF THE CALIPH ʿUMAR—may God be pleased with him. The master noted: "Once a man came to ʿUmar and said, 'I have been married for six months and today my wife delivered a baby. Pronounce a judgment in this matter.' And the Caliph ʿUmar ordered her to be stoned. In this same assembly the Commander of the Faithful ʿAli—may God be pleased with him—was present. He was pondering what ʿUmar had said. ʿUmar turned to ʿAli and asked, 'What do you say in this matter?' ʿAli replied: 'God Almighty has revealed in the Qur'an, saying "And she bore him and nursed him for thirty months" (Q.46:15). Now since the normal period for nursing an infant is two years, it is not admissible that the period of conception would be only six months?' After that, ʿUmar—may God be pleased with him—rescinded his command, saying, 'What is unacceptable to ʿAli, ʿUmar also disapproves.' "

He then told another story about ʿUmar—may God be pleased with him. "Once a woman came to him and said, 'O Commander of the Faithful, I have committed adultery and conceived a child.' ʿUmar then ordered this woman to be stoned. The Commander of the Faithful ʿAli was also present at this assembly. 'One ought to delay carrying out this order,' he observed. 'Why?' asked ʿUmar. 'Though a sin has been committed,' replied ʿAli, 'it was that woman who committed the sin. That child which is in her womb, what sin did it commit?' After that, the Commander of the Faithful ʿUmar—may God be pleased with him—commanded, 'Spare that woman and keep her under surveillance till the child is delivered.' And then he repeated what he had said before, 'What is unacceptable to ʿAli ʿUmar also disapproves.' "

After that the master told still another story about ʿUMAR'S DEEP CONCERN FOR UPHOLDING ISLAM. "Once a poet recited a poem in praise of the Commander of the Faithful ʿUmar—may God be pleased with him. In that poem, by way of exhortation and advice, he recited a couplet, one line of which was: 'Long life and Islam complete manhood,' that is, together long life and Islam provide all that is essential for one's well-being. When the poet had finished reciting this poem, ʿUmar did not pay him. 'But I offered you a panegyric,' protested the bard, 'why did you not reward me?' 'You mentioned "long life" before Islam,' retorted ʿUmar. 'Had you mentioned Islam first, I would have given you something.' "

From here conversation turned to POETRY. I asked: "Many times I have heard my respected master say: 'It is better to read the Qurʾan than to recite poetry.' Due to the blessing of my master's words, every day I am reading the Qurʾan. It is my hope that from this practice I will prove—God willing—the sincerity of my repentance for those verses that I have recited and am still reciting." The nature of this remark pleased him, and so I continued. I repeated an Arabic dictum, the meaning of which is 'All who fall under the influence of poets will go astray.' "Many times I have heard my respected master repeat the following Tradition: 'Surely for poetry there will be a judgment.' But when poets are people of discernment, why will those who are influenced by them be led astray?' " The master replied: "That judgment of which the Prophet—peace be upon him—spoke applies to the influence of poets whose verse is marked by jest, obscenity, or satire. There were noble companions of the Prophet who also recited poetry. Consider the Commander of the Faithful ʿAli—may God be pleased with him—and others like him." Then on his blessed tongue came two couplets composed by the Commander of the Faithful ʿAli—may God be pleased with him. The meaning of these verses was to the effect that when women come riding on horseback, Dajjal, or the Antichrist, is afraid to come out [and attack them]. The rhyme scheme was on three words: **suruj** (saddles), **khuruj** (come out/attack), and ʿ**uruj** (ascent). The first line of it was:

> When beauties ride on beasts [lit., when women (**furuj**) mount on saddles (**suruj**)].

I asked: "What can be said about the quality of eloquence unique to poetry?" Replied the master: "I have seen it written in a famous book that lying is a sin, but a lie conveyed in verse is not a sin!"

V. Assembly 24

Monday, 17th of Jumada al-ula, A.H. 721 (14 June 1321)

I obtained the blessing of kissing his feet. Conversation turned to ENVY. The master said: "The Prophet—peace be upon him—used to pray, 'O God, make me one who is envied, do not make me one who envies.' " Then the master explained: "Envy is one thing; emulation is another. Envy is to see someone else enjoying a divine favor and to wish that that favor would vanish. Emulation is to see another person enjoying a favor and to wish to obtain a similar favor for one's self. Such is emulation. Envy is forbidden, but emulation is not."

V. Assembly 25

Wednesday, 7th of Ramadan, A.H. 721 (30 September 1321)

I obtained the blessing of kissing his feet. He began to speak of THE SPIRITUAL PROWESS OF SHAYKH QUTB AD-DIN HYDER. [The founder of the Hyderis, Shaykh Qutb ad-din had retired to a cave at the onset of the Mongol invasion of Hindustan.] "After a hundred years," observed the master, "some of his followers made a breach in the entrance to that cave where he had retired. Bowing their heads to the ground, they said: 'We are hopeful that now you may have a word of guidance for us.' To which the saint replied: 'Yes' and fell silent again!"

Conversation turned to SHAYKH QUTB AD-DIN BAKHTIYAR KAKI—may God sanctify his lofty secret. The master said: "Once, on the day of ʿ**id** [the celebration marking the end of Ramadan], Shaykh Qutb ad-din was returning to his residence from the public place of prayer. He came to the area which is now the abode of his blessed grave. Then it was but a deserted place, with no gravestone or tomb. The Shaykh came, stood, and reflected. He reflected for a long time. Dear friends who were accompanying him pleaded: 'Today is the day of celebration (ʿ**id**) and people are expecting the master to return home and eat some food. Why are you tarrying at this place?' The Shaykh replied: 'From this ground I scent the aroma of hearts.' At once he sought the owner of this plot, and purchasing the plot with his own funds, the Shaykh ordered his burial site to be constructed there."

The master—may God remember him with favor—when he came to this point in the discourse, began to shed tears. "That one who said,

'From this ground I scent the aroma of hearts,' look," he exclaimed, "look at how many persons are now resting there in that very place!"

He then told a further story about SHAYKH MAHMUD MU'INA DUZ—may God have mercy upon him. "In the time of Shaykh Mahmud," he recalled, "every slave owner whose slave ran away would come to him and say, 'My slave has run away.' Shaykh Mahmud would then ask for the name of that slave. After reflecting for some time, he would turn to the slave owner, saying, 'You will find him.' And then he would add: 'When you do find him, please tell me.'

"It happened that once a man came and reported to the Shaykh: 'My slave has run away.' The Shaykh asked his name, reflected for awhile, and then announced: 'You will find him, but when you do find him, please tell me.' The man returned home, and after some days he found that slave. But he did not come and tell the Shaykh. A few days later that slave ran away again. The owner, coming to the Shaykh, reported what had happened. Said Shaykh Mahmud: 'When I told you to inform me on finding that slave, it was not because I wanted a report from you; rather, I said that because when you tell me "I have found the slave," a burden is lifted from my heart!' " The master—may God remember him with favor—smiled and added: "Shaykh Mahmud then told the slave owner, 'When you found your slave, even though you had promised: "When I find that slave, I will inform you," you did not tell me. Now that he has run away again, you will not find him.' "

Then he narrated an anecdote about Shaykh al-Islam Farid ad-din—may God sanctify his lofty secret. Once five dervishes came into the presence of the Shaykh. They were harsh in temperament and stood defiantly before the Shaykh. 'Though we have traveled far and wide,' they declared, 'we have yet to find a true dervish.' 'Please be seated,' said Shaykh Farid ad-din—may God sanctify his lofty secret, 'and I will show you a dervish.' They had been standing up and they continued to stand up. 'When you leave,' advised the Shaykh, 'do not take the road through the jungle. Go by another road.' Disregarding the Shaykh's advice, they took the jungle road. Now the Shaykh had sent someone to trail them and to note which road they took. Word came back to him that they had taken the jungle road. On hearing this report, he cried out, 'Oh! Oh!' as if someone had just died. In short, after the defiant dervishes took the jungle road, a violent dust storm blew up. It killed four of them on the spot. The fifth dervish struggled to a well and, after drinking much water, died there."

While narrating this incident, the master—may God remember him with favor—had been sitting on a cot, due to some physical ailment. He apologized to those present. "I have been sitting on a cot," he explained, "due to the slight pain I have in my foot. I hope you do not find fault [that is, I hope you are not offended by what I have done]."

All those present expressed their solicitude for the master, saying, "Long may you live. Our lives are dependent on your life." I recall this couplet which I recited on that occasion:

> You are the world's dear life, and none can hate life.
> Of hating life they stand guilty—all your foes!

The master—may God remember him with favor—then remembered the opening lines of this **qasida:**

> The morning draught from which the nightingale glows,
> Also brought out in joy the blossom of the rose.

The master then told a story about KHWAJA FARID AD-DIN ʿATTAR—may God have mercy upon him. He said: "Shaykh Jalal ad-din Tabrizi—may God reward him well—once met Khwaja Farid ad-din ʿAttar in Nishapur, and later he told Shaykh Baha ad-din Zakariya—may God have mercy upon him—about their meeting. 'I told him that I had seen Khwaja Farid ad-din ʿAttar in Nishapur. The Khwaja asked me to show him a man of God, but I could not point anyone out to him.' Hearing this, Shaykh Baha ad-din asked: 'In such a situation why did you not inform him about Shaykh Shihab ad-din [Suhrawardi, the spiritual guide of both Shaykh Baha ad-din Zakariya and Shaykh Jalal ad-din Tabrizi]?' Replied Shaykh Jalal ad-din: 'So mesmerized was I by Khwaja Farid ad-din's preoccupation with God that I temporarily forgot about the devotion of others!' "

The master—may God remember him with favor—then recalled that he had once seen an old man who told him, "I met Khwaja Farid ad-din ʿAttar in Nishapur when he was in the initial stage of his life as a Sufi; he was overwhelmed with awe." Observed the master: "When attention to God becomes your first concern, such things happen." He then recounted THE CALAMITY WHICH BEFELL KHWAJA FARID AD-DIN ʿATTAR. "He became a martyr," declared the master, "and his martyrdom took place in this way. The infidels arrived in Nishapur and he, together with seventeen of his friends, sat facing toward Mecca, awaiting the infidels' arrival and their own imminent martyrdom. The infidels entered that place, their swords drawn. Khwaja Farid ad-din ʿAttar saw them begin to slaughter his friends and cried out: 'What a violent sword is this! What a brutal blade is that!' But when they turned to slay him, he exclaimed, 'How kind is this sword! How generous, how good it is!' "

The master then related an anecdote about KHWAJA HAKIM SANAI—may God increase his reward. "Shaykh Sayf ad-din Bakharzi—may God illumine his grave—often used to say, 'I became a [true] Muslim due to one **qasida** from the pen of Sanai.' " A dear friend was present. He began to recite one couplet from a **qasida** of Sanai, and it appears that it was a couplet from the same **qasida** of which Shaykh Sayf ad-din had spoken. This was the couplet:

On desire's lofty Sinai playing the lute of your lusts,
That love felt by Moses when told "You'll not see me"—seek not!

And on the blessed lips of the master—may God remember him with favor—came the couplet that comes next:

The thorn on the path trod by vagabonds seeking His court,
On the bride's palm within the bridal canopy—seek not!

I asked: "What is meant by 'bridal canopy'?" "Bridal canopy," explained the master, "alludes to the one who has built the bridal canopy. Because the one who builds is called **ʿammar,** what he has built is called **ʿimari,** that is, structure [or, in this context, bridal canopy]." With reference to these same verses, he recalled that Shaykh Sayf ad-din Bakharzi—may God have mercy upon him—used to say: "Would that someone would take me to that place which contains the dust of Sanai, that I might use it as collyrium for my eyes!"

### V. Assembly 26
### Wednesday, 14th of Ramadan, A.H. 721 (7 October 1321)

I obtained the benefit of kissing his feet. He told a story about QAZI MINHAJ AD-DIN SIRAJ—may God grant him mercy and contentment—AND THE TASTE [FOR GOD] FOUND IN LISTENING TO HIS SERMONS. "Every Monday," recounted the master, "I would go to hear him preach. Beyond description was the comfort to be found in his sermons and recitations, for his intimates and also for others who came to hear him:

> When you begin to speak, everyone else grows dumb.
> When you begin to walk, tears to all eyes do come!

One day," he continued, "as I listened to him, the taste for God overwhelmed me. I lost myself, that is, it was as if I had died or become God knows what. Prior to that time, in listening to **sama**ʿ or in other circumstances, I had never found myself to be like that. This happened, of course, before I had taken the oath of allegiance to my Shaykh."

After that he observed that a dear one had once said to Qazi Minhaj ad-din: "You are not suited for judgeship; you are better suited to be Shaykh al-Islam [i.e., a Sufi master]."

Conversation next turned to SAINTS AND DEPUTIES AND SUPPORTS [three ranks in the hierarchy of Sufi elites]. "I heard something from a Sufi-like person that made a great impression on me," said I. "What was that?" asked the master. I replied: "The man said something to the effect that the world is maintained by the blessing of the pole (**qutb**) [who is one], the supports, who are four, the deputies, who number forty, and the saints, who total four hundred. They exist among the human race in the following fashion: When the pole dies, one of the four supports takes his place, and one of the forty deputies takes the place of the departing support. One of the four hundred saints, in turn, replaces one of the deputies, while one of the common people assumes the place of that saint.

"In my view," I added, "that procedure is not correct. Rather the procedure is that when one of the four hundred saints dies, another does not take his place. Three hundred and ninety-nine saints remain, and when another of their number dies, then only three hundred and ninety-eight remain. It is impossible for someone to succeed one of those four hundred who are the saints because they are bound to their sainthood beyond death."

When the master—may God remember him with favor—had heard my objection, he commented: "No, that is not correct. Sainthood has two categories: sainthood of faith and sainthood of favor. The sainthood of faith is common: Everyone who is a believer can be called a saint of the first category." He then recalled the Qurʾanic verse: " 'God is the protector (**wali**) of those who believe. He makes them to depart from darkness to light' (Q. 2:257). As for the sainthood of favor, it is conferred [only] on one who can perform miracles and has attained a high rank [among God's servants]."

V. Assembly 27
Saturday, 4th of Safar, A.H. 722 (22 February 1322)

I had the honor of kissing his hand. We began to talk about SUFI MASTERS. I asked: "What sort of person was Sidi Ahmad?" Replied the master: "He was a preeminent person among the Arabs, and it is the custom among Arabs that when they attribute preeminence to someone, they call him 'Sidi.' " Then he added: "Sidi Ahmad lived in the period of Shaykh Husyan Mansur Hallaj—may God have mercy on both of them. At the time that they burned Husayn Mansur and cast his ashes into the Tigris River, Sidi Ahmad took some of the water in which ashes were mingled and having blessed it, he then drank it. From that ashen water derived all his subsequent blessings."[96]

V. Assembly 28
Tuesday, 17th of Safar, A.H. 722 (7 March 1322)

I obtained the benefit of kissing his hand. Conversation turned to THE GENEROUS DISPOSITION OF THE DERVISHES AND THEIR BEAUTIFUL CONDUCT. "One evening," he recalled, "a thief entered the home of Shaykh Ahmad Nahrawani—may God grant him mercy and comfort. And this Shaykh Ahmad was a weaver. The thief searched the whole house and found nothing. He was about to leave when Shaykh Ahmad cried out and made him promise that he would wait a minute. Shaykh Ahmad then looked into his own workshop. He took a bundle of yarn that he himself had made, and from it spun seven reams of yarn. After separating these seven reams from the rest of the yarn, he offered them to the thief. 'Take them!' he said. The thief took them and left. The next day that thief, together with his mother and father, returned. Touching their heads to the ground before Shaykh Ahmad, they repented of their thievery."

V. Assembly 29
Sunday, 6th of Rabiʿ al-awwal, A.H. 722 (25 March 1322)

I obtained the good fortune of kissing his feet. That day I brought to see the Shaykh a lad who was a relative of mine. I did so because that lad from time to time experienced mental difficulties. And God knows whether it was due to evil spirits or some other cause. When I brought him before the master—may God remember him with favor—I explained his condition. The master looked at him with his healing glance, and from his blessed lips came the pronouncement: "He will be better."

In this connection he told a story. "There was a youth in Bukhara whom a group of evil spirits (**jinns**) had caused to fall ill. At the time of evening prayer they would snatch him from his home and transport him to their abode, where they would seat him on a tree in their midst. To prevent this occurrence, his mother and father would keep watch over the youth. They even hid him in a cell and put a lock on the door to that cell. Yet every day when evening prayer came, they would find their child sitting on the same tree in the abode of **jinns.** When their distress became unbearable, they took him to see Shaykh Sayf ad-din Bakharzi—may God have mercy upon him. They explained his condition to the saint. Shaykh Sayf ad-din commanded the youth to have his head shaved. Then, giving him a hat, the Shaykh directed: 'If that group visits you again, say, "I have become a disciple of the Shaykh, and I have shaved my head." Also show them the hat [of discipleship] and say, "I have received this hat from the Shaykh himself." ' After his parents took the youth back home, the evil spirits came. The youth told them what the Shaykh had told him to say: 'I was shaved before the Shaykh and he gave me a hat.' They began querying one another: 'Who was the wretch who took this fellow before the Shaykh?' Still mumbling, they left and never returned." The master—may God remember him with favor—when he reached this point in the story, began to cry. Those present also began to cry. What an auspicious time it was! Praise be to God!

After that he told a story about Shaykh Sayf ad-din Bakharzi—may God have mercy upon him. "In the early part of his life, when he was still a young man, he was hostile to the Shaykhs and Sufis. He would rebuke this group, and in the course of rebuking them, he would say many bad things. This was reported to Shaykh Najm ad-din Kubra—may God sanctify his lofty secret. 'Bring me to hear this abuse,' commanded Shaykh Najm ad-din. 'It is not fitting for you to hear such abuse,' protested his retainers. 'He says many bad things about Sufis and Shaykhs. One should not make jests in the presence of the Shaykh.' The more they spoke like this, the more Shaykh Najm ad-din repeated: 'Bring me to hear his abuse.' After much insistence on the part of the Shaykh, they brought him to hear the abuse of Shaykh Sayf ad-din Bakharzi. Shaykh Najm ad-din Kubra entered the assembly and sat down.

Shaykh Sayf ad-din, when he saw Shaykh Najm ad-din, began to say still worse things. However much he spoke unspeakables, Shaykh Najm ad-din nodded his head, slowly saying, 'Praise be to God, what ability has this young man!' When Shaykh Sayf ad-din finally came down from the lecturn, Shaykh Najm ad-din arose and proceeded outside. On arriving at the mosque, he turned his head. 'Is this Sufi not coming?' he asked. That same moment, Shaykh Sayf ad-din, standing in the midst of a crowd, rent his cloak and uttered a loud cry. He came running to where Shaykh Najm ad-din was and fell at his feet. Shaykh Shihab ad-din Suhrawardi—may God have mercy upon him—was also present at this assembly. He, too, came forward and fell at the feet of Shaykh Najm ad-din. Both became his disciples. They say that when Shaykh Najm ad-din returned home from the mosque, Shaykh Sayf ad-din came on foot on his right, Shaykh Shihab ad-din on his left.

"In short, that day both saints accepted discipleship in the presence of Shaykh Najm ad-din Kubra and both had their heads shaved. Then Shaykh Najm ad-din said to Shaykh Sayf ad-din: 'You will have a complete portion in this world, and in the next more than that!' Turning to Shaykh Shihab ad-din, he said: 'You also will have comfort in this world and the next.' "

The master—may God remember him with favor—then added: "When Shaykh Najm ad-din Kubra was coming home from the mosque, Shaykh Sayf ad-din Bakharzi was on his right, Shaykh Shihab ad-din on his left. Similarly, Shaykh Sayf ad-din pulled the boot from the right foot of Shaykh Najm ad-din Kubra, Shaykh Shihab ad-din from his left foot. AND THIS IS A SIGN AMONG SHAYKHS. After this Shaykh Najm ad-din Kubra instructed Shaykh Sayf ad-din: 'Go to Bukhara and settle there.' Shaykh Sayf ad-din protested: 'You know that there are many **ʿulama** there and that they are both jealous of Sufis and angry with them. What will be my fate?' Replied Shaykh Najm ad-din Kubra: 'You go. **We** will take care of the rest.' "[97]

V. Assembly 30
Tuesday, 6th of Rabiʿ al-akhir, A.H. 722 (24 April 1322)

I obtained the benefit of kissing his hand. The master began talking about SHAYKH ABU ISHAQ GAZARUNI.[98] His patronym was Shahriyar, his personal name Abu Ishaq. The master explained his spiritual formation. "He was the son of a weaver. He lived in a small town, but one day while he was spinning some rope, Shaykh ʿAbdallah ibn

Khafif—may God sanctify his lofty secret—passed by and stared at him as though he were trying to detect the signs on his forehead. 'Come!' he said to Abu Ishaq. 'Be my disciple.' Abu Ishaq was stunned. 'What do I know,' he protested, 'about how a disciple should act?' 'Place your hand in my hand,' insisted Shaykh ʿAbdallah, 'and say: "I will be your disciple.'" Abu Ishaq obeyed and taking the Shaykh's hand, he became his disciple. 'What do I do now?' he asked. 'Whatever you eat,' replied Shaykh ʿAbdallah, 'share some of it with others.' Abu Ishaq accepted this directive. Whenever he ate thereafter he would give some of his food to another. One day three dervishes came to the village where he lived. Finding no place to stay, they proceeded on. 'I must be of service to them,' thought Abu Ishaq to himself. At that time he had three loaves of bread. He took them and began running toward the dervishes, for he had realized that it would be a breach of etiquette to have three strangers pass through his town with their needs unmet. He put three loaves of bread before them. These three were men of insight. They took the loaves and ate them. 'This youth has fulfilled his duty,' they each said to one another, 'We must grant him his wish.' One of them said: 'Let us give him this world.' The second said: 'This world may be a source of allurement and distress to him; let us give him the next world.' As they were talking in this vein, the third said: 'Dervishes are manly; let us give him both this world and the next!' "

The master—may God remember him with favor—added: "This Abu Ishaq became a perfected dervish endowed with every spiritual quality, so much so that it has been reported that his tomb contains innumerable benefits and comforts; it is a treasure house overflowing with gold and silver and all sorts of boons!"

Then he narrated an anecdote about SHAYKH AHMAD MAʿSHUQ—may God show him mercy and favor. "He was observing a forty-day fast during winter. One night he left this retreat and came to a deserted river bank. Standing there, he prayed; 'O God, I have come here only that you might tell me who I am.' A voice boomed forth: 'You are he from whom on the Day of Resurrection many will seek intercession to be spared the pain of Hell.' Shaykh Ahmad replied: 'I am not content (with that role).' Again the voice boomed forth: 'You are he due to whose vigilance on the Day of Resurrection many will be granted entrance into Heaven.' To this Ahmad again replied: 'I am still not content. I must know: who am I?' Then the voice boomed forth: 'I have decreed that dervishes and gnostics will be my lovers but you are my beloved (**maʿshuq**).' Then Khwaja Ahmad—may God have mercy upon him—left this place and returned to the city. Everyone whom he met greeted him by saying: 'Peace be unto you, O Shaykh Ahmad Maʿshuq!' " The master—may God remember him with favor—when he came to this point in the story began to weep and sob.

"But he didn't say his prayers," interjected one of those present. "Yes," replied the master, "you are right. When people began to ask him, 'Why don't you pray?' he answered: 'I do pray but I don't recite **Surat al-Fatiha.**' 'What kind of prayer is that, which excludes **Surat al-Fatiha?**' they retorted. And they pressed him insistently on this point. 'Alas,' he admitted, 'I do say **Surat al-Fatiha** but not the verse: "It is You Whom we worship and it is You from Whom we seek help.' " 'Come,' they rejoined, 'recite this verse.' In short, after they repeatedly implored him, he stood to pray and began to recite **Surat al-Fatiha.** When he came to the verse 'It is You Whom we worship, and it is You from Whom we seek help,' out of all his blessed limbs, from every pore of his body, blood began to gush forth. Turning to onlookers, he said, 'See, I am a menstruating woman. It is not right for me to offer prayers!' "

### V. Assembly 31
Tuesday, 11th of the blessed month of Rajab, A.H. 722 (26 July 1322)

I obtained the good fortune of kissing his hand. In these days there was DROUGHT. With reference to this circumstance he told a story. "Once in Delhi there was the onset of a drought. They went to Shaykh Nizam ad-din Abu'l-Muayyad—may God have mercy upon him. All of the city came out to beseech him. Shaykh Nizam ad-din Abu'l-Muayyad mounted the pulpit, and while calling on God, he put his hand up his sleeve and pulled out a cloak. He turned toward heaven and moved his lips [silently]. Drops of rain began to fall. He then began speaking again. The rain stopped. Again Shaykh Nizam ad-din Abu'l-Muayyad pulled that cloak out of his sleeve and turned toward heaven. Rain came pouring down. Afterward, when he returned home, they asked: 'What was that cloak?' It was my mother's skirt,' he replied."

The master then told another story about THE SPIRITUAL PREEMINENCE OF SHAYKH NIZAM AD-DIN ABU'L-MUAYYAD. "He had numerous brothers, various nephews, and other relatives. From time to time he would go to see how his relatives were faring. They all fared well till once, when Shaykh Nizam ad-din Abu'l-Muayyad—may God have mercy upon him—went to visit them, after he had asked how they were, they asked him how he was. 'Stay with me,' replied the

Shaykh, 'that I may sit next to you for awhile lest I leave distraught, bewildered and griefstruck!.' He spoke these words with such pathos that they all began to cry."

V. Assembly 32
Monday, 20th of the blessed month of Shaʿban,
A.H. 722 (3 September 1322)

I received the benefit of kissing his hand. After I had heard from the master the story about Shaykh Ahmad Maʿshuq, I had heard from several others that he was called Muhammad. Finally I asked the master: "Was he called Muhammad or Ahmad?" Replied he: "His name was Ahmad ibn Muhammad Maʿshuq: While his name was Ahmad, his father's was Muhammad."

These are the fragrant scents of the spiritual offerings that I have collected over a period of three years. Combined with the other morals that I have recorded for twelve years, these two volumes cover fifteen years, and if beyond these I catch some more pearls for the soul from that robust oyster, whatever I gather from that ocean of mercy, I will record—God willing.

In the year seven hundred, plus twenty-two more,
There passed in the months of Shaʿban twenty days,
Till the master's instructions in this book were set.
To the world their bounty of good news it conveys.
Since the name of Muhammad is borne by my Shaykh,
As Hassan [ibn Thabit][99] do I, Hasan, him praise.

And praise be to God, the Lord of the universe, that this book, **Morals for the Heart (Fawa'id al-Fu'ad)**, has been completed. And the blessings of God be on the best of humankind, Muhammad, and on all his family and on all his companions.

# NOTES

1. Leo Tolstoy. *Resurrection* (Boston, 1904), p. 123. The obverse is also true, namely, as Tolstoy went on to say, "poetry without mysticism is prose," but we are concerned here only with the first part.

2. John E. Smith, "William James's Account of Mysticism," in Steven T. Katz, ed., *Mysticism and Religious Traditions* (Oxford, 1983), pp. 264–65.

3. Conversation in Fascicle 1, Assembly 14, dated 7 Muharram, A.H. 708 (A.D. June 27 1308).

4. Fascicle 2, Assembly 8. Conversation dated 29 Rajab, A.H. 714.

5. I am indebted for much of the above information to the excellent discussion of historical narrative by Gianna Pomata in her article "Versions of Narrative: Overt and Covert Narrators in Nineteenth Century Historiography," *History Workshop* 27 (Spring 1989): 1–17. Her focus is more methodological than mine, to call into question the requirement of a cleavage between literature and historiography (p. 11), yet her review of the conflict between Thierry and his detractors illumines the difference that characterizes Amir Hasan's narrative labor.

6. Fascicle IV, Assembly 22. Conversation dated 27 Dhu'l-Qa'da, A.H. 715.

7. See my *Notes from A Distant Flute: The Extant Literature of pre-Mughal Indian Sufism* (Tehran: Imperial Iranian Academy of Philosophy, 1978).

8. A modern Indian Muslim scholar, Professor Ziya-ul-Hasan Faruqi of Jamia Millia Islamia, has also attempted a partial English translation of **Fawa'id al-Fu'ad.** In some cases he reproduces the original Persian text of verses and in others, ignoring both meter and rhyme, he provides loose prose equivalents. His footnote apparatus is, however, both careful and informative. See Ziya-ul-Hasan Faruqi, trans., "Fawa'id-ul-Fu'ad of Khwajah Hasan Dehlawi," *Islam and the Modern Age* 11 (1980): 166–91; 12 (1981): 63–73; 13 (1982): 33–44, 126–41, 169–80, 210–28; 14 (1983): 195–213; 15 (1984): 25–36, 167–92; 16 (1985): 231–42.

9. For an extended study of the cross-cultural pitfalls that beset translations such as these, see my article "Can Sufi Texts be Translated? Can They be Translated from IndoPersian to American English?" forthcoming in *Islamic Culture,* Winter 1991.

10. See my earlier article, "The **Lawa'ih** of Qazi Hamid ad-din Na-

gauri," *Indo-Iranica* 28 (1975): 34–53; and *Notes from a Distant Flute*, pp. 60–62.

11. Father Jackson also encountered this verse in the above letter from Maneri. His translation captures the spirit of the original in blank verse without meter:

> Where is the intellect that can attain to Your perfection?
> Where is that spirit which can aspire to Your majesty?
> We want You to raise the beauty-concealing veil,
> But where is the eye that can see Your beauty?

12. This poem and the one that follows epitomize the paean to Hallaj's passion that concludes Part III, Chapter 20, of Daya's masterpiece. See the critical edition by Dr. Muhammad Amin Riyahi (Tehran, 1352), pp. 337 and 339; and Hamid Algar, trans., *The Path of God's Bondsmen from Origin to Return: A Sufi Compendium by Najm al-Din Razi, known as Daya* (Delmar, N.Y.: Caravan Books, 1982), pp. 330 and 332.

13. See Amir Hasan ʿAla Sijzi, **Fawaʾid al-Fuʾad,** ed. Muhammad Latif Malik (Lahore: Malik Siraj al-Din and Sons, 1386/1966), pp. 1–12. I have also attempted to sketch a preliminary profile of the Shaykh's major, often paradoxical traits as part of an inquiry into the nature of Sufi biographical writing in the subcontinent; see Bruce B. Lawrence, "The Chishtiya of Sultanate India: A Case Study of Biographical Complexities in South Asian Islam," in Michael A. Williams, ed., *Charisma and Sacred Biography* (Chico, Calif.: Scholars Press, 1981), pp. 47–67, but especially pp. 57–67.

14. See Najm al-Din Razi, *op. cit.*, p. 1966; and Algar, trans., p. 209, n. 33.

15. The brightest white days occur during the middle of Dhuʾl-Hijja. They may fall on the twelfth and thirteenth (or, according to other authorities, on the thirteenth, fourteenth, and fifteenth days) after the sighting of the new moon.

16. Shaykh Najm ad-din Daya quotes the same Tradition in **Mirsad al-ʿIbad** when discussing **nafs-i lawwama** (the oppressive soul); see Persian text, p. 345, trans. Algar, p. 355, where the Tradition is traced to Ibn Maja.

17. The very first saint mentioned in **Fawaʾid al-Fuʾad,** he is probably identical with Abuʾl-Husyan Nuri, the famed Baghdadi ascetic who died A.D. 907. His notoreity as a lover of God has been noted in several early **tadhkirahs**; it has also been aptly etched by Annemarie Schimmel

in *Mystical Dimensions of Islam* (Chapel Hill, N.C.: UNC Press, 1975), pp. 60–61.

18. On this little known early member of the Chishti order in India, see Bruce B. Lawrence, *Notes from a Distant Flute,* pp. 21–22, 36–38.

19. See also *infra,* Fascicle I, Assembly 24, for Shaykh Nizam ad-din's recollection of how difficult was his own personal encounter with the allure of fame.

20. The **abdal** or deputies are one of the most significant and recurrent categories in Sufi cosmogonic speculation. They are at once "substitutes for the prophets," since prophecy culminated and ended with Muhammad, and at the same time "sustainers of humankind," for it is only due to their existence that the world continues. While Sufi theorists differ as to how the number and hierarchy of deputies are to be calculated, all concur on their pivotal importance.

21. The significance of Shaykh ʿAbd al-Qadir Jilani for institutional Sufism can scarcely be exaggerated. For an overview article, see Bruce B. Lawrence, "ʿAbd al-Qader Jilani," in *Encyclopaedia Iranica* 1/2 (1982): 132–33. On the meaning of the phrase that comes after the saint's name, much could be written. "Sirr" means "secret" in a very special sense, the secret of the saint's special relationship with God, which is known to none other but they two; it is the basis for the distinction elaborated below in **Fawaʾid al-Fuʾad,** between the **wilayat** and **walayat** of each saint; see Fascicle I, Assembly 13. Only secondarily does it come to mean "his grave," i.e., the physical repository of his earthly remains, which acquire their saving/healing power from "his secret."

22. Junayd occupies a position in classical Sufism not dissimilar from that of ʿAbd al-Qadir Jilani in institutional or early medieval Sufism. See Schimmel, *op. cit.,* pp. 57–59.

23. This pithy aphorism is a foretaste of the constant reference to ascetical ideals that are central to the spiritual method of Shaykh Nizam ad-din and most Sufi masters. There is enormous variation, however, in the daily pursuit of these ideals, and ascetical practices are even occasionally held up as a danger, inciting their practitioner to a new level of pride that impedes rather than fosters his journey to the Beauteous but Hidden One.

24. Frequent mention of Malih occurs in **Fawaʾid al-Fuʾad.** Since Amir Hasan was a bachelor, his own family life, apart from time in court or on army maneuvers or at the hospice of Shaykh Nizam ad-din, must have revolved around matters that concerned his servants. Among them

Malih seems to have occupied a place of special privilege, for even as a manumitted slave, he continues to reappear in later assemblies.

25. See Simon Digby, "Qalandars and Related Groups: Elements of Social Deviance in the Religious Life of the Dehli Sultante of the Thirteenth and Fourteenth Centuries," in Yohanan Friedmann, ed. *Islam in Asia*, vol. 1 (South Asia, Jerusalem: Magnes Press, 1984), pp. 60–108, for the most thorough, and fascinating, treatment of **juwaliqs** and other "deviant" groups, including **qalandars** and **hyderis,** all of which find mention in **Fawa'id al-Fu'ad.**

26. This is the first mention of Shaykh Baha ad-din Zakariya in **Fawa'id al-Fu'ad.** There is probably no other contemporary saint with whom Shaykh Farid ad-din had a more complex relationship, yet the persistence of mutual respect between Suhrawardis and Chishtis is evidenced by the fact that Baha ad-din's son and successor, Shaykh Rukn ad-din, performed the funeral prayer for Shaykh Nizam al-Din in 725/1325; see **Siyar al-Awliya,** p. 154.

27. The dyadic construct (**ʿam-khass,** common/elite, general/special) pervades Persian-Arabic literature. It functions as both a literary trope and a social judgment, but here it takes on a specific mystical connotation. The **ʿam** are all those Muslims who stand outside the path of special relationship to God and His Prophet that is uniquely accessed through institutional Sufism and its charismatic mediaries, the **pirs** or masters. The **khass** are the spiritual elite and, therefore, God's elect who become instruments of His grace.

28. Qazi Hamid ad-din Nagauri is among the most celebrated, and elusive, saints of the Delhi Sultanate. See Shaykh ʿAbd al-Haqq Muhaddith Dihlawi, **Akhbar al-Akhyar,** pp. 40–47, and Bruce B. Lawrence, "The **Lawa'ih** of Qadi Hamid ad-din Nagauri," *Indo-Iranica* 20 (1975): 34–53.

29. The emphasis on keeping in continuous use whatever comes to hand is, of course, good not only for mystical ascesis but also for a commercial class whose very existence is predicated on the free circulation of commodities and services. Among Shaykh Nizam ad-din's lay disciples the practical as well as the spiritual benefits of this teaching would have been evident.

30. It is evident that this story has an underlying propaedeutic intent. It symbolizes the search for Truth (the pot), which both the **pir** and his disciple undertake fully, each using both hands—hence the need to have a four-handled pot that they commonly grasp.

31. This is one of many stories from **Fawa'id al-Fu'ad** that is reiter-

ated by Shaykh ʿAbd al-Haqq in **Akhbar al-Akhyar** (pp. 75–76). While its primary moral is the need to be focused on God alone in prayer, it also suggests that too many official scholar-teachers became distracted from God and preoccupied with their own worldly affairs. Like several other of Shaykh Nizam ad-din's directives, it finds its counterpart in Rumi. Quoting the Qurʾanic verse—"Woe to those who pray yet neglect their prayer, who play the hypocrite and deny essentials to the needy" (Q.107:4–7)—Rumi exhorts his listeners to true prayer. "Seek humanity, for that is the goal. The rest is a lot of talk. When talk goes on too long, the point is easily forgotten" (**Fihi ma Fihi,** p. 85).

32. The ambiguity of the Arabic-Persian word **shuhada**ʾ cannot be rendered into English with an equivalent single word. It means, of course, those who profess the faith but it also connotes those who are so committed to their witness of faith that they are willing to sacrifice their lives rather than compromise. Shaykh Nizam ad-din seems to intend the word to have both meanings in the present context.

33. This is the first time after the initial assembly that a recorded assembly takes place on a day other than Friday. In general, after Amir Hasan once breaks the pattern, there seems to be no fixed protocol or other discernible reason that causes one day to be preferred over another in the recording of conversations for **Fawaʾid al-Fuʾad.**

34. One of the major disciples of Shaykh Farid ad-din, he has written a set of aphorisms in Arabic as well as **diwan** of Persian poetry; see *Notes from a Distant Flute,* pp. 24, 38–39.

35. Another major Chishti saint, he was the disciple of Shaykh Nizam ad-din, most renowned for propagating the Chishti tradition in the Deccan. For a major study illumining all aspects of his teaching and subsequent influence, see Carl W. Ernst, "Eternal Garden: Sufism, Politics and History of a South Asian Muslim Shrine" (Albany, N.Y.: SUNY Press, forthcoming).

36. This distinction between elect and ordinary harkens back to the passage earlier in Fascicle I, where Shaykh Nizam ad-din discussed the necessity of an elect being present among common folk; see *supra,* n. 13.

37. Occasionally Amir Hasan seems to pose gratuituous questions, the chief purpose of which is to draw attention to his own participation as recorder in the Shaykh's assembly. Although this may be one such instance, it confirms what is evident throughout **Fawaʾid al-Fuʾad:** Shaykh Nizam ad-din regarded the eleventh-century Khorasanian **pir** as a model for all generations. An insightful summary of his life and significance is set forth in Schimmel, *op. cit.,* pp. 241–44.

38. On the Hyderis, see Digby's article cited *supra* in n. 11.

39. The praise of illiteracy as the foundation of true or intuitive knowledge is frequent in South Asian Sufism. Shaykh Nizam ad-din often tells stories to indicate either the benefit of illiteracy or the delusion of book knowledge, even though he himself had a passion for learning that continued throughout his life, as Professor Nizami has abundantly documented in the Introduction.

40. Despite being a great master, Shaykh Nizam ad-din has to remember, and also to remind others, that he never strove to become what he is. The moral here harks back to the initial assembly of **Fawa'id al-Fu'ad,** even as it anticipates his next recollection, a painful recollection of the sharp rebuke he received from Shaykh Farid ad-din when he tried to demonstrate superior knowledge of texts.

41. The obvious moral of this story is to honor the command of one's **pir,** no matter what it be. At the same time, the narrator (Shaykh Nizam ad-din) admits that Shaykh Farid ad-din, his **pir,** may have made "scholarly" mistakes, even if they did not matter to his disciples. It is a subtle way of drawing attention to the narrator's superior learning without, however, flaunting it.

42. Though the point seems to be Shaykh Nizam ad-din's total obedience to the will of his Shaykh, another point also lurks in this story: Who would have been the principal successor to Shaykh Farid ad-din had it not been Nizam ad-din? One likely candidate was Maulana Badr ad-din. Hence, in citing the latter's acknowledgement of Nizama ad-din's superior devotion to the **pir,** he is assenting also to his selection as the **pir**'s successor.

43. For a closer approximation of the worth of currency in circulation during the Delhi Sultanate, see Simon Digby, "Northern India under the Sultanate: The Currency System," in Tapan Raychaudhuri and Irfan Habib, eds., *The Cambridge Economic History of India* (Cambridge: Cambridge University Press, 1982), pp. 93–102. Digby lists the figures provided by the historian Zia ad-din Barani, Nizami ad-din's contemporary, and also, like Amir Hasan, his lay disciple: 1 silver **tanka** = 48 **jitals** = 192 **dangs** = 480 **dirams** (96). By this reckoning, if one **diram** equalled four cents, then 1 **jital** equalled forty cents, 1 silver **tanka** approximately nineteen dollars.

44. This is an extraordinary passage because it points to a problem that all the great masters of every Sufi order must have faced: What to do with mediocre would-be-disciples? The **pir** "proves" his high spiritual status to the extent that he can discourage such people without being

overwhelmed by their insistence that he reconsider his judgment of them.

45. In **Khair al-Majalis** (pp. 73, 74, and 228), his name is given as Harbabadi.

46. This poem from Sanai appealed not only to Shaykh Nizam ad-din but also to Shaykh Sharaf ad-din b. Yahya Maneri. For a variant translation, see Sharafuddin Maneri, *The Hundred Letters,* trans. Paul Jackson (Ramsey, N.J.: Paulist Press, 1980), p. 180.

47. This is a moral that goes back to the very first assembly of Fascicle I, stressing the relative, and ultimate, unimportance of counting followers to determine the spiritual worth of a saint.

48. For a novel translation of Awhad ad-din Kirmani's quatrains, as also a brief introduction to his life and significance as a Sufi poet, see Peter L. Wilson with Bernd M. Weischer, *Heart's Witness: The Quatrains of Awhadoddin Kermani* (Tehran: Imperial Iranian Academy of Philosophy, 1978).

49. On the significance of Shaykh ʿAli Hujwiri, see Schimmel, *op. cit.*, pp. 88–89, and *passim.*

50. On the importance of Shaykh Sayf ad-din Bakharzi, see **infra,** n. 87.

51. Another major Sufi from the earliest or pre-institutional period of Sufism, Ibrahim b. Adham epitomized **zuhd** or asceticism; see Schimmel, *op. cit.*, pp. 36–37.

52. Just as **Fawaʾid al-Fuʾad** became the first Indo-Persian **malfuzat,** so **Kashf al-Mahjub** in an earlier century (the eleventh) launched the tradition of systematizing Sufi thought and legendizing famous Sufi adepts in the Persian language. For a brief discussion of the style and significance of **Kashf al-Mahjub,** see Annemarie Schimmel, *Islamic Literatures of India* (Wiesbaden: Harrasowitz, 1973), p. 10; and Bruce B. Lawrence, "Sufism," in Keith Crim, ed., *Abingdon Dictionary of Living Religion* (Nashville: Abingdon Press, 1981), p. 729. Though he founded no order, Hujwiri's tomb in Lahore later became, and remains till today, the devotional shrine for a steady stream of visitors.

53. This would have been a descendant of the famous founder of the Chishti **silsilah** in the subcontinent, Muʿin ad-din Sijizi, whose tombcult in Ajmer is now the subject of a full-length monograph; see Peter M. Currie, *The Shrine and Cult of Muʿin ad-din* (New Delhi: Oxford University Press, 1989). While neither Shaykh ʿAbd al-Haqq Muhaddith Dihlawi nor any earlier **tazkira** writer mentions this Khwaja Ahmad, he may have been one of the sons of Muʿin ad-din's best-known son,

Khwaja Fakhr ad-din. According to **Akhbar al-Akhyar** (Delhi 1283/1866), p. 250, Mu'in ad-din had only three sons—Abu Sa'id, Khwaja Fakhr ad-din, and Hazrat Husam ad-din—but of the three only Khwaja Fakhr ad-din had any offspring who have been remembered.

54. This poem is defiantly obscure, unless one realizes the great value that poets in general and Sufis in particular attach to preoccupation with the Beloved; it is a disposition that requires constant vigilance because it exceeds the expected antinomies of human emotion, transcending with equal disdain **both** union and separation. Consider the following two verses in the same vein from **Sawanih** of Shaykh Ahmad Ghazzali:

> I would be disloyal nor could I claim to be in love with you,
> If I ever cried out for your help.
> You may impose union or separation,
> I am untouched by these two; your love is enough for me.
> (See Nasrollah Pourjavady, trans., Ahmad Ghazzali's **Sawanih** [London, 1986] p. 23.)

55. Roughly $9.50. See *supra,* n. 38.

56. The Shaykh uses a pun in Arabic and Persian on the word **qadam.** Its initial meaning is "foot" but its further connotation is "merit," and Hasan has started this entry with an unprecedented invocation on "the following custom." He can only be referring to his own reflexive practice of kissing the master's feet. The first two of the three anecdotes that follow turn subtly on the feet, which is to say the merits, of particular saints. One saint leaves his feet, i.e., soars upward while a second outmaneuvers a yogin till the latter falls at the feet of the Shaykh. I know of no single word, or combination of words, in English that can convey the subtlety of the Persian text at this point, and yet without an elucidation of the elaborate pun invoked the meaning is reduced, if not lost altogether.

57. But, according to ***Siyar al-'Arifin*** (Delhi 1311/1893, p. 121), his name was actually Shaykh Zinda Sijistani.

58. Walwalj is a city in Badakhshan, Central Asia, but we know nothing more about this saint or Amir Hasan's relationship to him.

59. This anecdote, one of the few near doublets in **Fawa'id al-Fu'ad,** bears a striking similarity to the anecdote given in Assembly 8. Only the setting—there a balcony room, here first a graveyard and then a balcony room—differs. The anecdote is undoubtedly repeated because of the profound impact that Baba Farid's final illness had on Nizam ad-din:

Even his own fervent prayer could not deflect or delay the Shaykh's bodily death from a painful illness. Yet the incident also proves a boon to Nizam ad-din, for though his prayer does not affect Baba Farid's illness, his intervention on the latter's behalf evokes a blessing. Moreover, in both versions of this story he is given not only Baba Farid's blessing but also his staff, a graphic token of Nizam ad-din's designation as the Shaykh's principal successor.

60. "No thinker of medieval Islam has attracted the interest of Western scholars more than Ghazzali," observes Schimmel (*Mystical Dimensions of Islam,* p. 97). It would be preposterous to attempt to recapitulate here either Schimmel's own summary of Imam Ghazzali (pp. 91–97) or the numerous other studies of his thought and influence. What is perhaps more curious is the infrequency of his mention by Shaykh Nizam ad-din: While the renowned Shaykh ʿAbd al-Qadir Jilani (see Fascicle 1, Assembly 1) is cited but once, Ghazzali's magnum opus, **Ihya ʿUlum al-Din,** is invoked thrice—here, later in connection with Ibn Sirin, and still later on supererogatory prayer. Yet "lesser" masters of the Path, particularly Indian or Central Asian masters, figure prominently in the pages of **Fawaʾid al-Fuʾad,** principally because of exemplary details from their biographies rather than illustrative citations from their writings.

61. Since 48 **jitals** = one **tanka,** the father of the bride expended more than 2,000 **tankas,** a huge sum of money equivalent to roughly $38,000!

62. There seems to be an inherent contradiction between the message of the first discourse here and the final statement of Assembly 2 above. The latter stresses normative Muslim belief, i.e., that prophets are infallible, while the statement that follows here suggests that prophets too can sin. Has Shaykh Nizam ad-din reversed himself on this crucial teaching? Possibly, but the greater likelihood is that the second statement has to be framed in a personal or psychological context, just as the former derives from a public, confessional stance. Because Prophets **are** infallible, a mark of their infallibility is that they always see themselves as potentially fallible, open to sin as much as are the rest of humankind. It is also noteworthy that when Muhammad reflected on the possibility that he would be negatively evaluated on Judgment Day, the companion prophet whom he imagined would accompany him to Hell was "my brother Jesus." Since followers join leaders in the afterlife, the divine option to send **both** Muhammad and Jesus to Hell would considerably reduce the ranks of those who could be imagined to populate that

celestial realm called Heaven. Precisely the irony of that decision makes it all the more likely that it is included here for rhetorical effect, to emphasize the necessity of maintaining God's independence as well as His omnipotence.

63. On the parallel of this phrase "firm handle" to the well-known Qur'anic phrase **al-ʿurwat al-wuthqa,** see Q.2:257, but more likely, Q.3:103, which not only speaks of "God's rope," but also goes on to say: "You were on the brink of a fiery pit, and He saved you from it!"

64. This reference to Nasir ad-din Mahmud Chiragh-i Dihli is the only such reference in the whole of **Fawa'id al-Fu'ad.** It seems odd that his name, like that of Amir Khusrau, would not have been mentioned more often. The most plausible explanation for their near absence from these pages is indicated by Professor Nizami in the Introduction: Amir Hasan was mainly preoccupied with Shaykh Nizam ad-din's teaching, even though he recorded but a small fraction of what was communicated in the master's assemblies over the fifteen-year period that he frequented the Ghiyaspur **khanqah.**

65. Nightly prayers special to Ramadan, they are to be performed after the evening prayer. They consist of twenty prayer cycles, with a pause (Ar., **tarwiha**) after every four.

66. Numerous Sufis, beginning with Shaykh ʿAli Hujwiri, have identified the **ahl-i suffa,** or **ashab-i suffa,** as precursors of their own ascesis; see **Kashf al-Mahjub,** tr. Nicholson, p. 30.

67. These are ten supererogatory invocations that are to be recited in a prescribed order seven times daily, three or four times after dawn prayer before sunrise and three or four times after evening prayer before nightfall.

68. See n.

69. See Assembly 22 below for the special significance of this term among Chishti masters.

70. This seemingly obscure reference is laden with spiritual significance: Not only the death-date of Sufi masters but the sequence of their deaths in a single generation can be seen to disclose divine portents. The actual historical dates differ from those suggested here, since Shaykh Saʿd ad-din died in either 649/1251 or 650/1252, while Shaykh Sayf ad-din died in 659/1261 (though some sources give 658/1259). The death dates for Shaykh Baha ad-din and Baba Farid are, however, almost exactly three years apart: 7 Safar 661/21 December 1261 and 5 Muharram 664/17 October 1265. In any case, for Shaykh Nizam ad-din this pattern of death dates and not the exact intervals was crucial, so much so

that later he comes back to this point once again in Fascicle V, Assembly 2.

71. This last category is a shorthand reference to the Sufi imperative that one should not enjoy either food or sex. An anecdote depicting its exemplary application is provided above in the tale of the ascetic living with his wife by the river.

72. This is the sole reference in the entire **Fawa'id al-Fu'ad** to the premier poet of the Delhi sultanate, who was also a close companion and lay disciple of Shaykh Nizam ad-din. On the one hand, Amir Khusrau is renowned for having said about **Fawa'id al-Fu'ad** that he would trade all his own writings for this one book, but at the same time the absence of a **malfuzat** from him inspired the production of a spurious **malfuzat** that parallels but does not rival the present work. On both points, see the full discussion by Professor Nizami in the Introduction.

73. See the very beginning of **Fawa'id al-Fu'ad** (Fascicle I, Assembly 1, where this same point is made.

74. **Ayyam-i tashriq** occur immediately at the conclusion of the annual canonical pilgrimage (**hajj**) on the tenth of Dhu'l-Hijjah, and last for three days, that is, until the thirteenth of Dhu'l-Hijja. An auspicious time for all Muslims, it was deemed especially auspicious as the occasion for Amir Hasan's visit to the master.

75. The communal prayer following both canonical Festivals (**ʿid i-kabir** and **ʿid saghir**) takes place in an open-air prayer space (**musalla**), and hence is peculiarly vulnerable to rain, as was the case here.

76. The word **mahfuz** is also used earlier to distinguish the prophets from the saints: While prophets are immune from sin (**macsum**), saints must be protected (**mahfuz**).

77. "Bright days" were the middle days of each lunar month when the new moon was thought to be brightest, while **ʿashura** days were the ninth and tenth days of Muharram, the first month of the new lunar year in the Muslim calendar.

78. See Fascicle II, Assembly 32, on an earlier version of this same directive.

79. For a related anecdote about Shams Dabir, see Fascicle IV, Assembly 10.

80. On both book and author, see Bruce B. Lawrence, "The **Lawa'ih** of Qazi Hamid ad-din Nagauri," *Indo-Iranica* 20 (1975): 34–53.

81. The same anecdote about Abu Hanifa's devotion is narrated in Fascicle IV, Assembly 9.

82. See Fascicle II, Assembly 7 for the longer version of this story.

83. It is at this point that the major textual divergence occurs between Muhammad Latif Malik's collated edition of **Fawa'id al-Fu'ad** and the manuscripts cyclostyled by Newal Kishore (pp. 1721–73) and Bolandshahr (pp. 187–88). The divergence concerns the order of the next three anecdotes, which also comprise the next three paragraphs. They concern, respectively, Shaykh Ahmad Nahrawani (NK: Nahrawali), Whose Disciple was Ahmad Nahrwani? and Dervishes of Badaun. I have followed Malik's order, even though the alternative is equally plausible. It proceeds from the discussion of Khwaja Abu Bakr Muy Tab to a further anecdote about his brother, Shahi Muy Tab, before taking up the anecdote on The Suppression of Miracles. The two intermediate anecdotes, about Khwaja 'Aziz and the Dervish Who Sits in No Scales, appear at the end of this Assembly in the NK edition. Instead of elaborating on reasons for these divergences, one should marvel that there is but this one and not myriad text critical problems in **Fawa'id al-Fu'ad.**

84. This remark is tantamont to a commentary on Q.18:80.

85. The full quatrain has only been preserved by Shaykh 'Abd al-Haqq (**Akhbar al-akhyar,** p. 49).

86. See Fascicle I, Assembly I, on the **abdal.**

87. Though the full form of this quatrain is absent from all copies of **Fawa'id al-Fu'ad,** it is provided by Jamali in **Siyar al-'Arifin** (Dehli, 1311), p. 85. It is too fraught with Baba Farid's pathos not to be quoted here in full.

88. Muhammad Latif Malik (p. 343) prefers the variant reading of Bolandshahr (p. 217), which translates "They have restrained me." Not only does that make little sense, but it does not provide closure to the moral of this assembly, i.e., to stress inner peace or contentment, which is also the moral of the next pericope. The correct reading, followed here, seems to be provided by Newal Kishore (p. 204).

89. For this famous collection of Traditions and its compiler, Marghinani, see the discussion in Fascicle , Assembly , pp.

90. The notion of "seal of the saints" is usually traced back to Hakim al-Tirmidhi, but is most fully developed by Ibn 'Arabi (d. 638/1240), the most illustrious, and also most controversial, Sufi theorist. Though he preceded Nizam ad-din by more than one generation, apart from inferential clues such as the just cited verse, there is no trace of al-Shaykh al-Akbar's influence on either Amir Hasan or Nizam al-din. Ibn 'Arabi is never mentioned by name in **Fawa'id al-Fu'ad,** nor is his equally famous counterpart, the Sufi lyricist, Jalal ad-din Rumi (d.672/1273).

91. This discussion of the two cavities of the heart reflects a distinc-

tion common to Sufis, and is implicit in the choice of **fu'ad** as the second part of the construct forming the title of Hasan's book; see Translator's Introduction, above.

92. Note that in this anecdote the governor of Multan is implicitly praised for his honesty, while in an earlier anecdote concerning Shaykh Farid ad-din the governor of Multan (and Uchch, probably the same individual), was grouped "among the accursed ones." The seeming contradiction is not hard to explain: The governor favored Shaykh Baha ad-din Zakariya instead of the other saint in his province, Shaykh Farid ad-din. Shaykh Nizam ad-din's ambiguous attitude toward Shaykh Baha ad-din Zakariya recurs as a subtextual theme throughout **Fawa'id al-Fu'ad.**

93. See Fascicle IV, Assembly 9, p. 226, for an earlier reference to **musabbi'at-i 'ashr.** It is a lengthy composite prayer to be recited first after the canonical morning prayer (**fajr**) and before sunrise, then again after the canonical evening prayer (**'asr**) and before sunset. The format consists of a mixture of **durud** (paeans to the Prophet Muhammad), Qur'anic recitations, invocations of God's name, and petitionary prayers. Following three **durud,** one is to recite five short Qur'anic **surahs:** (1) **Fatiha,** (2) **Nas,** (3) **Falaq,** (4) **Ikhlas,** and (5) **Kafirun,** followed by (6) **Ayat al-kursi** (the Throne Verse). One is to repeat this sequence seven times, beginning each recitation with the phrase "In the name of God full of Compassion, ever Compassionate." Then one is to say seven times the string of affirmations that translate as: (7) "Glory be to God, and Praise be to God, and there is no god but God, and God is Greatest, and there is no protection nor strength save with God." One concludes this section with the single declaration: "The number is known to God (alone), and the weight is known to God (alone) and the expanse is known to God (alone)." Then follows a paean to the Prophet: (8) "O God, Accept our prayers on behalf of Muhammad Your slave and Your prophet and Your beloved and Your unlettered apostle. Upon him and his family and his companions be blessing and peace." Then two intercessions: (9) "O God, forgive me and my parents who nourished me in my infancy, and forgive all male and female believers and all male and female Muslims, whether they be alive or dead. Surely You are the Nearest Hearer who responds to petitions through Your mercy, O most Merciful of those who show mercy!" And finally: (10) "O God, do to me and to them now and later in spiritual and material affairs, and also with respect to the world beyond, what befits You, and do not do to us, O Lord, what befits us, for you are Forgiving and Forbearing, Generous

and Noble, Sovereign and Just, Full of Pity and Mercy." Numbers 8, 9, and 10 are each to be recited seven times, each recitation being preceded by the phrase "In the name of God the Source of Compassion, ever Compassionate." The whole sequence is followed by invoking two of God's ninety-nine names: O Enforcer (**ya jabbar**), twenty-one times; and O Mighty One (**ya ʿaziz**), forty-two times. The entire prayer concludes with the recitation of the same three **durud** with which it began.

94. This is the subject of the last, and perhaps most controversial, bezel of Ibn al-ʿArabi's **Fusus al-hikam.** See the excellent translation by R. W. Austin, in this same series, pp. 272. It is almost inconceivable that Shaykh Nizam ad-din would have read the **Fusus** and not made some allusion to Ibn al-ʿArabi's very opposite interpretation of the same Tradition. The greater likelihood is that Sufi theory as it emerged among institutional orders in Central and South Asia followed a different metaphysical track—at least initially—than was prevalent in either Anatolia or North Africa, but North Indian saints either contemporaneous with Shaykh Nizam ad-din or in the generation after him were certainly aware of, and engaged by, Ibn ʿArabi's thought; see, for instance, the discussion of Masʿud Bakk, ʿIraqi, and Amir Husayni Sadat in **Notes from a Distant Flute,** pp. 46–49, 64–68.

95. Hamid Algar has provided a superb and definitive English translation of **Mirsad al-ʿIbad** (Delmar, N.Y.: Caravan Books, 1980), which includes a long section (pp. 354–56) extolling the benefits of **samaʿ** without, however, discussing its legality or citing the above verse.

96. This brief anecdote relates to the earlier discussion about Shaykh Walwalji and spittle from the pulpit; see Fascicle II, Assembly 12, p. 146.

97. Throughout **Fawaʾid al-Fuʾad,** Shaykh Sayf ad-din Bakharzi looms as an important precursor and exemplar for Shaykh Nizam ad-din, but in the present anecdote his importance soars to a new level. He is initiated by Shaykh Najm al-Din under extraordinary circumstances and at the same time, his initiation is paired with that of Shaykh Shihab ad-din Suhrawardi. The pairing produces more of a contrast than a complementarity: Though they are co-disciples as well as co-initiates, Shaykh Sayf ad-din is clearly the preferred or favored of the two. Why? He walks on the right, takes off the right boot, etc. The story is striking for several reasons: (1) It is not attested by any of the extant biographical sources on either Shaykh Sayf ad-din or Shaykh Najm al-Din (see Iraj Afshar, "Saif ad-din Bakharzi" in W. B. H. Henning, ed. *A Locust's Leg: Studies in Honor of S. H. Taqizadeh* [London, 1962], pp. 21–27); (2)

Shaykh Najm al-Din is himself reputed to have been initiated into the Suhrawardi **tariqa** by Shaykh Ruzbihan al-Wazzan al-Misri before being sent back to Khwarizm ca. A.D. 1145 (see Hamid Algar, "Kubra, Shaykh Abu'l-Djannab Ahmad ibn 'Umar Najm al-Din," *Encyclopaedia of Islam* [New Edition] V:300–01); (3) Shaykh Najm al-Din and Shaykh Shihab ad-in are not known to have ever met, much less experienced the master-disciple exchange described in **Fawa'id al-Fu'ad.** For a thorough review of all the literature, see Fritz Meier, *Die Fawa'ih al-Gamal wa-fawatih al-galal des Nagm ad-din al-Kubra* (Wiesbaden, 1957), pp. 40–47. Despite great doubt about the historical likelihood that such a meeting ever took place, its delineation would be noteworthy if only because Shaykh Nizam ad-din was convinced that it had occurred. His conviction strengthens the subtextual claim advanced throughout **Fawa'id al-Fu'ad** that the Chishti lineage is superior to its friendly but competitive Suhrawardi rivals. Shaykh Shihab ad-din, the eponynmous founder of the Suhrawardiya, is cast in a subordinate role to Shaykh Sayf ad-din. While the latter is not a Chishti, he serves as a surrogate Chishti master, since both his teachings and his spiritual discipline so closely anticipated that of Shaykh Nizam ad-din. The principal point where the two differ is also worth remembering: While Shaykh Sayf ad-din had virtually no major disciples, Shaykh Nizam ad-din launched the Chishtiya as a pan-Indian order in most of the major regions of the subcontinent. See the Introduction and also K. A. Nizami, **Tarikh-i Masha'ikh-i Chisht** (Delhi, 1953), pp. 171–196.

98. On this saint, the best European language source remains Fritz Meier, ed., **Firdaus al-mursidiya fi asrar as-samadiya,** *Die Vita des Scheich Abu Ishaq al-Kazaruni* (Leipzig, 1948).

99. Among the earliest and foremost Muslim panegyrists, he is a fitting eponymous authority for the recorder of Shaykh Nizam ad-din's discourse in **Fawa'id al-Fu'ad.** His is also the last proper name mentioned (other than that of the Prophet), providing a double closure to the first major Indo-Persian **malfuzat.**

# SELECT BIBLIOGRAPHY

A Select Bibliography for Further Reading in English:

Algar, H., trans. *The Path of God's Bondsmen from Origin to Return: A Sufi Compendium by Najm al-Din Razi, known as Daya.* Delmar, NY, 1982.

Borah, M.I. "The Life and Works of Amir Hasan Dihlavi," *Journal of the Asiatic Society of Bengal* 3/7 (1940):1–59.

Digby, S. "The Sufi Shaikh as a Source of Authority in Medieval India," *Purusartha* 9(1986):57–77.

Ernst, C. *Eternal Garden: Mysticism, History and Politics at a South Asian Sufi Center.* Albany, NY, 1991.

Jackson, P. trans. *Sharafuddin Maneri. The Hundred Letters.* New York, 1980.

———. trans. **Khwan-i Pur Niʿmat** (A Table Laden with Good Things). Delhi: 1986.

Lawrence, B. "The Chishtiya of Sultanate India: A Case Study of Biographical Complexities in South Asian Islam" in Michael A. Williams, ed., *Charisma and Sacred Biography* (Chico, CA, 1982), pp. 47–67.

———. *Notes from a Distant Flute: The Extant Literature of pre-Mughal Indian Sufism.* Tehran, 1978.

Mujeeb, M. *The Indian Muslims.* Montreal, 1967.

Nizami, K.A. *The Life and Times of Shaykh Farid ud-din Ganj-i Shakar.* Aligarh, 1955.

———. *Some Aspects of Religion and Politics in India during the Thirteenth Century.* Aligarh, 1961.

———. "Hind:V—Islam," *Encyclopaedia of Islam* (New Edition), Volume IV: 428–38.

Schimmel, Annemarie. *Mystical Dimensions of Islam.* Chapel Hill, NC, 1975.

# INDEX OF NAMES

# INDEX OF NAMES

# Index of Topics

# INDEX OF TOPICS

## INDEX OF TOPICS

## Other Volumes in this Series

**Julian of Norwich** • SHOWINGS
**Jacob Boehme** • THE WAY TO CHRIST
**Nahman of Bratslav** • THE TALES
**Gregory of Nyssa** • THE LIFE OF MOSES
**Bonaventure** • THE SOUL'S JOURNEY INTO GOD, THE TREE OF LIFE, AND THE LIFE OF ST. FRANCIS
**William Law** • A SERIOUS CALL TO DEVOUT AND HOLY LIFE, AND THE SPIRIT OF LOVE
**Abraham Isaac Kook** • THE LIGHTS OF PENITENCE, LIGHTS OF HOLINESS, THE MORAL PRINCIPLES, ESSAYS, and POEMS
**Ibn 'Ata' Illah** • THE BOOK OF WISDOM and Kwaja Abdullah
**Ansari** • INTIMATE CONVERSATIONS
**Johann Arndt** • TRUE CHRISTIANITY
**Richard of St. Victor** • THE TWELVE PATRIARCHS, THE MYSTICAL ARK, and BOOK THREE OF THE TRINITY
**Origen** • AN EXHORTATION TO MARTYRDOM, PRAYER, AND SELECTED WORKS
**Catherine of Genoa** • PURGATION AND PURGATORY, THE SPIRITUAL DIALOGUE
**Native North American Spirituality of the Eastern Woodlands** • SACRED MYTHS, DREAMS, VISIONS, SPEECHES, HEALING FORMULAS, RITUALS AND CEREMONIALS
**Teresa of Avila** • THE INTERIOR CASTLE
**Apocalyptic Spirituality** • TREATISES AND LETTERS OF LACTANTIUS, ADSO OF MONTIER-EN-DER, JOACHIM OF FIORE, THE FRANCISCAN SPIRITUALS, SAVONAROLA
**Athanasius** • THE LIFE OF ANTONY, A LETTER TO MARCELLINUS
**Catherine of Siena** • THE DIALOGUE
**Sharafuddin Maneri** • THE HUNDRED LETTERS
**Martin Luther** • THEOLOGIA GERMANICA
**Native Mesoamerican Spirituality** • ANCIENT MYTHS, DISCOURSES, STORIES, DOCTRINES, HYMNS, POEMS FROM THE AZTEC, YUCATEC, QUICHE-MAYA AND OTHER SACRED TRADITIONS
**Symeon the New Theologian** • THE DISCOURSES
**Ibn Al'-Aribī** • THE BEZELS OF WISDOM
**Hadewijch** • THE COMPLETE WORKS
**Philo of Alexandria** • THE CONTEMPLATIVE LIFE, THE GIANTS, AND SELECTIONS
**George Herbert** • THE COUNTRY PARSON, THE TEMPLE
**Unknown** • THE CLOUD OF UNKNOWING
**John and Charles Wesley** • SELECTED WRITINGS AND HYMNS
**Meister Eckhart** • THE ESSENTIAL SERMONS, COMMENTARIES, TREATISES AND DEFENSE
**Francisco de Osuna** • THE THIRD SPIRITUAL ALPHABET
**Jacopone da Todi** • THE LAUDS
**Fakhruddin 'Iraqi** • DIVINE FLASHES

Menahem Nahum of Chernobyl • THE LIGHT OF THE EYES
Early Dominicans • SELECTED WRITINGS
John Climacus • THE LADDER OF DIVINE ASCENT
Francis and Clare • THE COMPLETE WORKS
Gregory Palamas • THE TRIADS
Pietists • SELECTED WRITINGS
The Shakers • TWO CENTURIES OF SPIRITUAL REFLECTION
Zohar • THE BOOK OF ENLIGHTENMENT
Luis de León • THE NAMES OF CHRIST
Quaker Spirituality • SELECTED WRITINGS
Emanuel Swedenborg • THE UNIVERSAL HUMAN AND SOUL-BODY INTERACTION
Augustine of Hippo • SELECTED WRITINGS
Safed Spirituality • RULES OF MYSTICAL PIETY, THE BEGINNING OF WISDOM
Maximus Confessor • SELECTED WRITINGS
John Cassian • CONFERENCES
Johannes Tauler • SERMONS
John Ruusbroec • THE SPIRITUAL ESPOUSALS AND OTHER WORKS
Ibn ʿAbbād of Ronda • LETTERS ON THE SŪFĪ PATH
Angelus Silesius • THE CHERUBINIC WANDERER
The Early Kabbalah •
Meister Eckhart • TEACHER AND PREACHER
John of the Cross • SELECTED WRITINGS
Pseudo-Dionysius • THE COMPLETE WORKS
Bernard of Clairvaux • SELECTED WORKS
Devotio Moderna • BASIC WRITINGS
The Pursuit of Wisdom • AND OTHER WORKS BY THE AUTHOR OF THE CLOUD OF UNKNOWING
Richard Rolle • THE ENGLISH WRITINGS
Francis de Sales, Jane de Chantal • LETTERS OF SPIRITUAL DIRECTION
Albert and Thomas • SELECTED WRITINGS
Robert Bellarmine • SPIRITUAL WRITINGS
Nicodemos of the Holy Mountain • A HANDBOOK OF SPIRITUAL COUNSEL
Henry Suso • THE EXEMPLAR, WITH TWO GERMAN SERMONS
Bérulle and the French School • SELECTED WRITINGS
The Talmud • SELECTED WRITINGS
Ephrem the Syrian • HYMNS
Hildegard of Bingen • SCIVIAS
Birgitta of Sweden • LIFE AND SELECTED REVELATIONS
John Donne • SELECTIONS FROM *DIVINE POEMS*, SERMONS, *DEVOTIONS AND PRAYERS*
Jeremy Taylor • SELECTED WORKS
Walter Hilton • *SCALE OF PERFECTION*
Ignatius of Loyola • *SPIRITUAL EXERCISES* AND SELECTED WORKS
Anchoritic Spirituality • *ANCRENE WISSE* AND ASSOCIATED WORKS